OXFORD WORLD'S C

POEMS AND P

CHRISTINA GEORGINA ROSSETTI was born in London on
5 December 1830. Her father, the Italian patriot and poet Gabriele
Rossetti, occupied himself with talking revolutionary politics and
with writing speculative studies of Dante; her well-read mother,
Frances Mary Lavinia Polidori, encouraged her early efforts at writ-
ing verse; her elder brother, the poet and painter Dante Gabriel
Rossetti, helped her select and revise poems for publication. From
the late 1840s, through the 1850s, she wrote the poems that, in 1862,
made up her first major volume, *Goblin Market and Other Poems*; a
further volume, *The Prince's Progress and Other Poems*, followed in
1866. Her writing then took new directions: a book of sophisticated
nursery rhymes, *Sing-Song* (published 1871); and the beginning of a
commitment to writing, as a devout Anglican, a series of devotional
books for the Society for Promoting Christian Knowledge, which
would include her 'reading diary' *Time Flies* (1885) and her com-
mentary on the Apocalypse, *The Face of the Deep* (1892). A third
major volume of poems, *A Pageant and Other Poems*, appeared in
1881, and confirmed her standing as one of the great poets of the age.
She never married, declining two serious proposals—one from a
Roman Catholic painter, the other from a sceptic scholar—for reli-
gious reasons; and illnesses reinforced her reclusive tendencies. In
1892 she developed breast cancer, and she died on 29 December
1894. In 1896, her supportive brother, William Michael Rossetti,
published the poems that she had chosen to leave in manuscript.

SIMON HUMPHRIES was formerly a Fellow and Tutor in English
at Trinity College, Oxford. He is now an independent scholar.

OXFORD WORLD'S CLASSICS

For over 100 years Oxford World's Classics have brought readers closer to the world's great literature. Now with over 700 titles —from the 4,000-year-old myths of Mesopotamia to the twentieth century's greatest novels — the series makes available lesser-known as well as celebrated writing.

The pocket-sized hardbacks of the early years contained introductions by Virginia Woolf, T. S. Eliot, Graham Greene, and other literary figures which enriched the experience of reading. Today the series is recognized for its fine scholarship and reliability in texts that span world literature, drama and poetry, religion, philosophy, and politics. Each edition includes perceptive commentary and essential background information to meet the changing needs of readers.

OXFORD WORLD'S CLASSICS

CHRISTINA ROSSETTI

Poems and Prose

Edited with an Introduction and Notes by
SIMON HUMPHRIES

OXFORD
UNIVERSITY PRESS

OXFORD

UNIVERSITY PRESS

Great Clarendon Street, Oxford OX2 6DP

Oxford University Press is a department of the University of Oxford.
It furthers the University's objective of excellence in research, scholarship,
and education by publishing worldwide in

Oxford New York

Auckland Cape Town Dar es Salaam Hong Kong Karachi
Kuala Lumpur Madrid Melbourne Mexico City Nairobi
New Delhi Shanghai Taipei Toronto

With offices in

Argentina Austria Brazil Chile Czech Republic France Greece
Guatemala Hungary Italy Japan Poland Portugal Singapore
South Korea Switzerland Thailand Turkey Ukraine Vietnam

Oxford is a registered trade mark of Oxford University Press
in the UK and in certain other countries

Published in the United States
by Oxford University Press Inc., New York

Selection, introduction, and editorial material © Simon Humphries 2008

British Library Cataloguing in Publication Data

Data available

Library of Congress Cataloging-in-Publication Data

Data available

Typeset by Cepha Imaging Private Ltd., Bangalore, India
Printed in Great Britain
on acid-free paper by
Clays Ltd., Elcograf S.p.A.

ISBN 978-0-19-280715-1

12

ACKNOWLEDGEMENTS

For permission to consult and to publish manuscripts in their collections, I am greatly indebted to the British Library, the Bodleian Library, the Huntington Library, the University of British Columbia Library, the Princeton University Library, and the Harry Ransom Humanities Research Center at the University of Texas at Austin. I would also like to thank the unfailingly helpful staff of the manuscript departments of these libraries, especially Sue Hodson at the Huntington; George Brandak at the University of British Columbia; Meg Sherry Rich at Princeton; Richard Workman at the Harry Ransom Center; and Greg Colley, Colin Harris, and Judith Priestman at the Bodleian. Mark Samuels Lasner has generously given permission to publish manuscripts in the Mark Samuels Lasner Collection, on loan to the University of Delaware Library. I am also indebted to Declan Kiely at the Pierpont Morgan Library, and to Russ Taylor at the Lee Library of Brigham Young University, for sending me copies of manuscripts in their collections. I would also like to thank the staff of the library of the Oxford Union Society, especially Niels Sampath, for much help.

Like everyone else working in the field of Victorian poetry, I am deeply indebted to R. W. Crump, whose three-volume Louisiana edition of Rossetti's poems, a work of dedicated and meticulous scholarship, is the single most important contribution to Rossetti studies of the past hundred years. I have also benefited from the scholarship and generosity of Tony Harrison, whose Virginia edition of Rossetti's letters is an invaluable resource.

For their help over the years in which I have been studying Christina Rossetti, I am indebted to Kit Andrews, Matthew Bradley, Fabio Camilletti, Anthony Cummins, Jean and Yuna de Lannoy, Stefano Evangelista, Kate Flint, the late Michael Freyne, Lauren Goodlad, Katsuya Hiromoto, Clive Hurst, Felicity James, Lorraine Janzen Kooistra, Jo McDonagh, James McEvoy, Priscilla Martin, Justin Mathews, Lucy Newlyn, Muireann O'Cinneide, Beth Palmer, Christopher Rowland, Kathryn Sutherland, David Sutton, Angela Thirlwell, Sue Usher, and Johannes Zachhuber. My thanks also to the members of the Victoria online conference, especially to Gert Buelens and, Herbert Tucker, for debating the meaning of ll. 314-15 of 'Goblin Market' with me.

At Oxford University Press, I am very grateful to Judith Luna for first suggesting that I edit Rossetti's work and for her encouragement throughout, and also to Rowena Anketell for her meticulous copy-editing. The President and Fellows of Trinity College, Oxford, granted me an invaluable term's research leave in which to begin this edition. The society of Linacre College has sustained me over many years; as has, more recently, that of St Edmund Hall and of Trinity College. I have drawn deeply on what I learnt, long ago, from Gill Carey, Mark Griffith, Joy Jenkyns, Peter McDonald, and Ann Mann. As always, I am enormously grateful to Dinah Birch, Tom Paulin, and Nicholas Shrimpton, who have been there all the way. And, lastly, I cannot begin to say how much I owe to my students at Oxford. Amongst many other things, they kept asking me what I was doing with my time; and this edition is at least part of the answer.

CONTENTS

STORIES

DEVOTIONAL PROSE

LETTERS

INTRODUCTION

Who has seen the wind?
  Neither I nor you:
But when the leaves hang trembling
  The wind is passing thro'.

Who has seen the wind?
  Neither you nor I:
But when the trees bow down their heads
  The wind is passing by.

It is only a nursery rhyme, but even this—from *Sing-Song: A Nursery Rhyme Book* (1872)—suggests the largeness of Christina Rossetti's poetic vision. We can say that it is a puzzle about the visible presence of an invisible power, but there seems to be more to it than that. The leaves are 'trembling', as if in fear; and the trees bow down their heads, as if in a gesture of submission or of reverence. This is surely more than the description of physical effect, more than what is required for the puzzle about seeing the wind; but it is not explained. There is much in Rossetti's poetry that is never explained, and it is this inexplicitness (or secretiveness) that makes her poems so enticing. They leave us wanting to reread them—to try to hear what we did not quite hear, or what they did not quite say.

Yet we do know that Rossetti's view of the world is informed by her Christian beliefs: that the world is under the sway of invisible forces is a foundational assumption of her writing, and it is a theological assumption. Once we understand this, we will perhaps see that those suggestions of fear and of reverence resonate with the latent theological significance of 'wind' which, in the Bible, is both likened to, and is the same Greek word as, the Spirit of God. In the rhyme's theological symbolism, therefore, creation trembles in the presence of, and bows down before, the divine.[1] The rhyme presupposes a view of the world in which the visible becomes a symbol (or, as Rossetti might say, 'type') of the invisible, the material of the spiritual, the natural of the supernatural. Once we recognize this, we begin to understand the largeness of Rossetti's vision of the world, in which 'the two worlds, visible and invisible' appear 'as double against each other': 'wind, water, fire, the sun, a star, a vine, a door, a lamb, will shadow forth mysteries' (pp. 334–5).

---

[1] See notes to ll. 1 and 3 (p. 457).

Or perhaps, instead, when we recognize this symbolism, our response to the rhyme changes? Perhaps, now, it becomes a less open, less enticing, poem—a poem that excludes those who do not possess the theological knowledge to interpret it, and that offers not a puzzle, or a secret, but a religious lesson. If we were to know that the rhyme turns up in hymn books, that might only confirm our worst suspicions.[2] Shades of the Sunday school begin to close upon the poetry.

There is no point in denying that this is a problem—the major problem—that faces readers of Rossetti's work. How do we relate what we may think of as the poetry's 'literary' qualities to its religious content? For some, the poetry achieves an enticing openness in spite of—or even in resistance to—its oppressive load of religious ideas. For others, explication of those religious ideas is the primary task, even if that entails closing down the poetry's open-endedness. But the more we read Rossetti's poetry, the more we may feel that its puzzles and secrets are inseparable from its theological certainties—and also from its theological uncertainties.

A Literary Life

Born in 1830, Christina Georgina Rossetti, by the time of her death at the end of 1894, had been for some decades widely regarded as the greatest 'poetess' of the age, and as one of the finest of all poets. She may not have been wholly surprised by that. For in spite of the defensive self-deprecation that we often find in her letters—and she does like to put herself down—there is, certainly by the 1850s, a solid conviction of her poetic vocation and worth. And even as a child there was aspiration. In 1842, she had begun entering her completed poems into notebooks, as she would continue to do until the mid-1860s. The first of these has, exceptionally, a manuscript title page: 'Poems/by/ C. G. Rossetti'. And also a little preface written by her mother: 'N.B. These verses are truly and literally by my little daughter, who scrupulously rejected all assistance in her rhyming efforts, under the impression that in that case they would not be really her own. The first was written when she was eleven.'[3] By 1847, she was in print—a volume of *Verses*, privately printed by her grandfather, dedicated to her mother.

She was born into a family that encouraged her literary ambitions. In a letter of 1888, she acknowledges her debt to a 'constant association

[2] *Songs of Praise*, enlarged edn. (Oxford, 1931), 466–7.
[3] British Library, Ashley MS. 1362.

with my clever and well read Parents' (p. 400)— Gabriele Rossetti (d. 1854), an Italian patriot and poet and unorthodox (even obsessional) Dante scholar who had left his country in 1821 for political reasons; and Frances Mary Lavinia Polidori (d. 1886), herself of both English and Italian descent. Her mother and her elder sister, the bookish Maria Francesca, became an immediate audience for her work; and, until late 1847, it was Maria Francesca (or, occasionally, Frances) who would copy Christina's poems into her little notebooks.[4] But, for a young woman determined that her poems would be 'really her own', the process of composition was more private. The younger of her brothers, William Michael, recalled that, 'strange as it seems to say so of a sister who, up to the year 1876, was almost constantly in the same house with me . . . I cannot remember ever seeing her in the act of composition . . . She consulted nobody, and solicited no advice'—except in taking the advice of Dante Gabriel, her elder brother, in the preparation of the volumes of poetry she published in the 1860s.[5] William's comment is in line with the compositional practice of the young poet of Christina's tale 'Maude' (c.1850); and we know that Maude Foster has much in common with the young Christina. We see Maude 'slipping out of sight some scrawled paper' when her mother enters the room; her writing-book 'contained original compositions not intended for the public eye' (p. 265); on her deathbed, she asks her cousin to 'destroy what I evidently never intended to be seen' (p. 296). Christina's own scrawled papers—those drafts which must have preceded the copying of completed poems into her notebooks—are lost to us; fortunately, the notebooks which contain those poems she chose not to put before the public eye, and also early texts of many poems that were published in revised versions, do survive.

Her 1888 letter acknowledges Dante Gabriel as '[i]n poetics . . . my acute and most helpful critic' (p. 400), and, more than anyone, it was he who reinforced Christina's confidence in the worth of her poems, and who was instrumental in securing their publication. A poet and painter, Dante Gabriel had, in 1848, been a founder of the Pre-Raphaelite Brotherhood—a group of artists united more by discontent with prevailing conventions of painting than by anything else, but who at least agreed that they would work by studying nature rather

---

[4] Christina herself began copying her poems into notebooks beginning with poems dated 7 Nov. 1847 (noted by William Michael Rossetti inside the back cover of the notebook Bodleian MS. Don. e. 1/3).

[5] *New Poems by Christina Rossetti*, ed. William Michael Rossetti (London, 1896), pp. xii–xiii.

than by studying other artists. Christina, as a woman, was not officially a member—an exclusion that allowed her the affectionate satiric stance of her 'remarkable doggrel on the P.R.B.' which she sent her brother William; but she could hardly not be drawn into the Pre-Raphaelite movement. 'D. G. Rossetti offered two/Good pictures to the public view', goes her 'doggrel', and she herself had modelled for the figure of Mary in both *The Girlhood of Mary Virgin* (1849) and *Ecce Ancilla Domini!* (1850) (p. 385). In 1848 she formed an attachment to one of the P.R.B., the painter James Collinson, only to break off the engagement when he decided to convert from Anglicanism to Roman Catholicism—'a blow from which she did not fully recover for years'.[6] (Her only other attachment would be to the scholar Charles Bagot Cayley in the 1860s, declining his proposal of marriage on the grounds of his lack of religious belief, but remaining a very close friend.) She offered poems to *The Germ*, the P.R.B.'s short-lived literary journal, conceived by Dante Gabriel and edited by William, of which a mere four issues were produced in early 1850. 'Repining', 'A Pause of Thought', 'Song' ('Oh roses for the flush of youth'), 'An End', 'Dream Land', and two further poems not included in this edition, were first published there, appearing as the work of one 'Ellen Alleyn', a pseudonym chosen by Dante Gabriel. From William Michael's later recollections, it is not clear that Christina left to Dante Gabriel the decision on whether or not her own name was to be used, or that she had herself decided against that; but, at any rate, Ellen Alleyn—who sounds as if she belongs to one of the old ballads that both Dante Gabriel and Christina enjoyed and imitated—was his devising.[7]

Christina published little in the 1850s, either because of her own caution, or because her submissions were rejected. We know that she sent some poems to *Blackwood's Magazine* in 1854, with a covering letter claiming that 'poetry is with me, not a mechanism, but an impulse and a reality'; but without success.[8] At the end of the decade, she seems to have become more determined to put her work before the public (or, perhaps, only more successful in doing so). One of her few topical poems appeared in *Once a Week* in 1859: 'In the Round Tower at Jhansi, June 8, 1857', inspired by what seems to have been an untrue

[6] *The Poetical Works of Christina Georgina Rossetti*, ed. William Michael Rossetti (London, 1904), p. lii.

[7] See headnote to 'Repining' (pp. 404–5).

[8] *The Letters of Christina Rossetti*, ed. Antony H. Harrison, 4 vols. (Charlottesville, 1997–2004), I. 98–9.

report of an incident in the Indian Mutiny, strikes a populist note with its commemoration of individual heroism and its fear of the 'swarming' rebels (a lazy borrowing from a newspaper report).[9] And it seems to have been at the end of the 1850s that she began making literary contacts through her membership of the Portfolio Society. Exactly when this society was established is not clear, although its model may have been Dante Gabriel's short-lived 'sketching club to be called *The Folio*', conceived in early 1854, which was supposed to circulate a portfolio in which members would place drawings on which other members would then comment. Barbara Leigh Smith (later Bodichon) was a member, and managed to submit a drawing before the society expired; and she was later a member of the Portfolio.[10] According to Eleanor C. Smyth, who belonged to the Portfolio Society from its beginning—whenever that was—until late in 1861, 'Annie Leigh Smith [Barbara's sister], was the originator of the Portfolio Society and the chooser of its name. A subject—some well-known saying, a phrase, or even a single word, to be illustrated by poem, very brief essay, or oil or water-colour sketch—would be proposed . . . As a rule, the poems were read . . . by one of the other sex, often George MacDonald, whose forte was elocution; and a Portfolio held the sketches, which, after the reading, were turned over and criticized, our votes deciding which picture merited the prize'.[11] It is clear from Smyth's recollections that this was not a feminist society, or exclusively for women—although it included some feminists, as well as some notable women poets (Smyth recalls Jean Ingelow, Isa Craig, and Adelaide Anne Procter; but does not mention Rossetti, whom she would not have met at the meetings). Writing to Barbara in January 1864, the scrupulous Christina—who had been only 'a corresponding member, not an attendant at the meetings, having got into shy and stay-at-home habits'—confesses that 'I used having received notice of the theme, to look up something apposite amongst my old compositions' and is worried as to whether this is allowable and also asks about being admitted again as a member 'on these same lazy terms'—from which it is clear that Christina's association with the society had by then lapsed.[12]

[9] It would subsequently be placed second, after the title poem, in *Goblin Market and Other Poems* (1862), in what looks like a canny move on someone's part.

[10] *The Correspondence of Dante Gabriel Rossetti*, ed. William E. Fredeman et al. (Cambridge, 2002–), I. 321–2, 369.

[11] *Notes and Queries*, 10S: 10 (18 July 1908), 53.

[12] *Letters*, I. 192–3.

It was in the early 1860s, with Dante Gabriel encouraging Alexander Macmillan's interest in her work, that Christina's publishing career took off. In February 1861, 'Up-Hill' appeared in *Macmillan's Magazine*, followed later that year by 'A Birthday' and 'An Apple Gathering'; and then, in the spring of 1862, Macmillan brought out her first published volume, *Goblin Market and Other Poems*, with frontispiece and title-page woodcuts designed by Dante Gabriel (see pp. 103–4). This volume's critical success led to her second volume, *The Prince's Progress and Other Poems* in 1866, again with designs by Dante Gabriel who had himself urged her to develop a sixty-line dirge into what became the volume's title poem—a fairy-tale poem every bit as ambitious in its religious symbolism as the title poem of her previous volume.

The volumes of her verse published by Macmillan would never be more than a modest commercial success—thus her jealous 'green tinge' as the latest edition of fast-selling Jean Ingelow's poems comes off the press (letter to DGR, 23 Dec. 1864; p. 388). Nevertheless, her relationship with 'Mac' proved a lasting one—strong enough to survive Dante Gabriel's ill-judged efforts to persuade her that the terms he offered were too stingy, and to push her towards his own publisher, F. S. Ellis. (*Commonplace, and Other Short Stories* (1870)—which included 'Nick', 'The Lost Titian', and 'A Safe Investment'—was published by Ellis, but was a disappointing commercial failure and excited little critical enthusiasm; plans for Ellis to publish *Sing-Song: A Nursery Rhyme Book* miscarried.) These commercial issues may seem to us difficult to square with Christina's sincere striving for unworldliness, but they were inescapable: the family was not affluent, and the failed efforts of Frances and Christina to establish schools in the early 1850s left them dependent upon William's salary as a clerk in the Inland Revenue Office. Even modest earnings from publications, and from other literary work, were important to Christina: William estimated that 'from 1854 to 1862 she seldom made £10 in a year; from 1862 to 1890 there might be (taking one year with another) an average of perhaps £40 per annum—less rather than more'.[13] Her share of the profits from her volumes of poetry was supplemented by more immediate 'tin' from poems sent to periodicals: in 1861, as an unknown poet first appearing in 'Mac's Mag', 'Up-Hill' earned her a guinea; in 1877, as one of the most distinguished poets of the day, she was paid as much as £10 (with copyright reserved) for 'Mirrors of Life and Death', which appeared in the *Athenaeum*.[14]

[13] *Poetical Works*, p. li.

[14] *Letters*, 1. 143, 146; Accounts Book, Angeli-Dennis Collection, Box 10–1, University of British Columbia.

That Rossetti's series of poetic notebooks stops in the mid-1860s is a sign of her declining poetic productivity. She warns Dante Gabriel that it will be 'a long long while' before any further volume will appear (letter [?April 1865], p. 397); she warns him that no further volume may ever appear—even if 'a few posthumous groans may be found amongst my remains' (letter [?spring 1870], p. 398). Even though she had, by 1870, written most of the rhymes that would make up *Sing-Song: A Nursery Rhyme Book* (1872)—many of them of great sophistication—it is significant that, at this time, her creativity should be released by writing into a seemingly undemanding literary genre. Dante Gabriel's 'unflagging prodment'—whether or not it was designed to unearth a 'latent epic'—could become oppressive (letter [11 March 1865], p. 392).

These warnings were more than a way of dampening the expectations of a brother whose confidence in her poetic powers was inclined to outstrip her own. Christina's health had been precarious from the mid-1840s, and her anticipations of death are not only an aspect of her religious longings (although they are always that). In 1871, she succumbed to Graves' disease, a severe thyroid condition which permanently affected her health and altered her appearance—and reinforced her shy and stay-at-home habits. The 1870s would have been, in any case, difficult years for her. In 1872, the mental instability that would overshadow the last decade of Dante Gabriel's life became disturbingly obvious (in June, he had tried to kill himself). William married in 1874, and Christina's fear of becoming distanced from him probably explains her suspicion of his wife, Lucy Madox Brown; and Christina and Frances eventually leased a house of their own. In 1876, Maria Francesca, by then in an Anglican sisterhood, died of cancer. In 1882, Dante Gabriel died. By the end of 1883, Charles Bagot Cayley, the closest friend Christina ever found outside of her family, was dead.

Christina was still writing poems in these years—Macmillan brought out a collected edition of her poetry in 1875, securing her reputation—but this decade saw a major turn in her writing career towards devotional prose and prose/verse books written for the Society for Promoting Christian Knowledge (SPCK), of which the major works were *Seek and Find: A Double Series of Short Studies of the Benedicite* (1879), *Letter and Spirit: Notes on the Commandments* (1883), *Time Flies: A Reading Diary* (1885), and *The Face of the Deep: A Devotional Commentary on the Apocalypse* (1892). This new direction in her writing suggests that the consciousness of her declining poetic creativity coincided with a decision to speak of her central religious concerns more plainly than she would in her poetry, and to a wider readership than such exacting poetry would ever reach. Yet there was to be a further major volume of poems, *A Pageant and Other Poems* (1881)—a volume which presents itself as a poet's late work (thus the sonnet sequence 'Later Life'), or even as a book of songs sung in a time of barrenness ('The Key-Note'). And Christina, by now, had the confidence to see a volume through to publication without the close collaboration with Dante Gabriel on which she could rely in the 1860s. If some of her later poetry can seem to be retreading her own well-trodden paths, it does still do new things. It is in the 1881 volume that she exploits the possibilities of the sonnet sequence: 'Monna Innominata' stands with 'Goblin Market' and 'The Prince's Progress' among her most ambitious poems. And the roundels included in *Time Flies* are some of her most distinctive works, their formal circularity enacting an anticipated completion. Her very last volume, *Verses*, published in 1893 by the SPCK, collected the poems included in the late devotional books and found a wider readership than any of her previous volumes.

In early 1892, Christina was told that she had breast cancer; in the last months of 1894, she endured not only pain but fear. William recalled that her 'spiritual outlook became gloomy rather than hopeful': 'the terrors of her religion compassed her about, to the overclouding of its radiances'. She did not die in despair, for she trusted in God; but she feared damnation.[15] She died on 29 December 1894.

In 1896, William published most of the poems that Christina had left in manuscript.

Religion and History

The dominant concerns of Rossetti's writing are religious: the hope of eternal life; the fear of judgement; the temptations of the world; the possibility of harmonizing worldly and heavenly love; the imitation of Christ's self-sacrificial suffering; the necessity of divine grace for salvation; the sacraments administered by the Church; the destiny of unbelievers; the uncertainties of biblical interpretation; the understanding of history in the light of biblical prophecy; the watchful longing for the return of Christ. Not every poem she writes has explicit religious reference; but it would be wrong to conclude, on the basis of the division of her 1862 and 1866 volumes into what she refers to as a 'secular'

---

[15] *Some Reminiscences of William Michael Rossetti*, 2 vols. (New York, 1906), 2. 532; *Poetical Works*, p. lix.

section and a section headed 'Devotional Pieces'—Dante Gabriel's
suggestion, later discarded—that religion informed only a part of her
poetic production.[16] Virtually everything she writes is to be under-
stood in a religious context.

A starting point is to locate her in her ecclesiastical context; and, in
what has become the most influential view, she may be seen as 'directly
and fully a product of the Oxford Movement'—part of a poetic tradi-
tion associated with that movement of the 1830s and 1840s for Catholic
revival within the Church of England (a movement also known as
Tractarianism).[17] The influence of the Catholic revival on Rossetti's
work is certainly deep. The church she attended in her formative
years, Christ Church in Albany Street, was in the 1840s perhaps the
most prominent of London churches influenced by the movement.
(That her mother, whose background was Evangelical rather than
High Church, should have been drawn there—'gradually conforming
to the external practices of the High Church section', as William put
it—is not so surprising, for the Evangelical and Oxford movements
were both movements for renewal within the established church.[18])
Tractarian clergy asserted the centrality of the Eucharist to the life of
the worshipper (from its consecration in 1837, Christ Church had
offered the Eucharist every Sunday and on festivals); and, in so far as
Christina's story 'Maude' (c.1850) is autobiographical, it attests this
emphasis. (Even the notorious Eucharistic passage in 'Goblin Market'
(ll. 467–74) will seem less bizarre when we relate that poem to this
ecclesiastical environment.) The opportunities provided by Christ
Church for charity and for lay ministry, under clerical direction, also
inform Rossetti's writing. From the early 1850s, Christ Church had
contacts with homes for the protection and reclamation of 'fallen'
women; and, by 1859, Rossetti herself was helping at the London
Diocesan Penitentiary, Park House, Highgate. Such poems as 'An Apple
Gathering', 'Goblin Market', 'Under the Rose', and 'A Daughter of
Eve', show her engaging—if obliquely—with a general social and
moral problem of which she would have had particular knowledge.
The Christ Church parish was also the origin of the movement for
Anglican sisterhoods, and our reading of poems spoken by women in
religious orders is enriched by the knowledge that the convent life was

[16] DGR suggests this division in his letter to CGR of [c.8 Feb. 1861], *Correspondence*,
2. 349.
[17] G. B. Tennyson, *Victorian Devotional Poetry: The Tractarian Mode* (Cambridge,
Mass., 1981), 198.
[18] *Poetical Works*, p. lv.

not only a subject in poetry or painting informed by nineteenth-century romantic medievalism—though it was indeed that—but was becoming a conceivable life choice within Anglicanism (see 'Three Nuns' in 'Maude', 'The Convent Threshold', 'An "Immurata" Sister'). But Christina did not follow her sister into a sisterhood: she 'went thro' a sort of romantic impression on the subject like many young people', but no more.[19] Lastly, we have seen already that Christina's writing assumes an analogical view of the world—the visible a symbol of the invisible; and the immediate influences on this are undoubtedly Tractarian.

But for all the importance of this ecclesiastical environment, we would be wise to exercise caution when we categorize Rossetti as an Anglo-Catholic writer—as if that description, without qualification, is adequate. Mid-nineteenth-century Anglican identities are often complex, often in flux, and defy tidy categorization. For instance, the prominence of the apocalyptic mode in Rossetti's work—and it is as important to her as it is to Spenser or to Blake—has no particular debt to Tractarianism, but is undoubtedly indebted to the Tractarian minister of Christ Church, William Dodsworth. He was from an Evangelical background and (as his successor rather warily put it) 'was deep in the study of prophesy' before being drawn in by the Tractarian movement and then finally, in 1850, converting to Rome (a not uncommon ecclesiastical trajectory in the period).[20] To approach Rossetti only under the aspect of the Catholic revival can, therefore, obscure those parts of her thought which have no particular debt to Anglo-Catholicism. We will find, for instance, a fundamental assumption of a direct relation with God rather than one mediated by the ecclesiastical institution. One of the most insightful characterizations of her religious identity is that 'She brought under Catholic discipline a strong Protestant individualism'—a judgement that is the more valuable for being somewhat paradoxical; and that 'the personal encounter [with God] that she desired could be aided but not controlled by the ecclesiastical system'.[21] We might try to plot this disciplining of individualism

[19] *Letters*, 3. 196.

[20] Henry W. Burrows, *The Half-Century of Christ Church, St. Pancras, Albany Street* (London, 1887), 10; and see also John O. Waller, 'Christ's Second Coming: Christina Rossetti and the Premillenarianist William Dodsworth', *Bulletin of the New York Public Library*, 73 (1969), 465–82.

[21] Raymond Chapman, *Faith and Revolt: Studies in the Literary Influence of the Oxford Movement* (London, 1970), 197. It is unfortunate that Chapman's acknowledgement of this complexity—even in the context of an essay emphasizing Rossetti's Anglo-Catholicism—has been almost entirely ignored in later criticism.

temporally—perhaps from 'The Dead City' (1847) to the late poem 'An Old-World Thicket' (published 1881) which reprises the earlier poem only to end not with an individual alone in a wood but with the whole Church, symbolized by a flock of sheep, journeying through the wood of this world towards Christ. More often, though, divergent tendencies coexist in Rossetti's writing. For instance, it is often noted that the restraint, even secrecy, of her poetry is informed by the Tractarian doctrine of reserve: sacred truths must be both revealed, and concealed from the uninitiated.[22] Rossetti does indeed inhabit a world of symbols (or 'types') which both reveal and conceal truths, and her own poetry certainly withholds its meanings from those without the knowledge to interpret its symbolisms. Yet, in spite of this, she is detached from the excluding priestly ideology which informs Tractarian statements of the doctrine. Her own writing does not insist on the duty of the initiated to conceal sacred truths from the unworthy. Its viewpoint—that of a laywoman—is very different from that of the major Tractarian theologians. What her writing insists on is man's limited, uncertain, understanding of the sacred truths while in this world.

Her writing also insists on the danger of 'the world': insubstantial, it passes itself off as what it is not, luring man to his death by offering a seductive plenitude. But what do we make of a writer who claims so little investment in this world? It is perhaps this part of her thought that is most often misunderstood: her insistence on detachment and renunciation can be supposed irreconcilable with any form of engagement with the realm of the 'political'. But that is not so: her theological positions constrain such engagement, but they do not preclude it. In fact, her immersion in biblical prophecy drives her denunciations of injustice. This biblical grounding does, however, mean that her understanding of history is generalized: Babylon—embodiment of injustice and wickedness—is any, and every, worldly power. Even the poems on 'The German-French Campaign 1870–1871'—unusual in their explicit topical reference—understand contemporary history by means of biblical prophecy. If we recognize that 'My Dream' is modelled upon the beast visions of biblical apocalyptic, we will be open to the possibility of reading the rise and decline of its kingly crocodile in relation to the Crimean War; but, ultimately, its tyrannical beast

[22] For Mary Arseneau, the doctrine generates what is distinctive in Rossetti's poetry, *Recovering Christina Rossetti: Female Community and Incarnational Poetics* (Basingstoke, 2004), 7, and throughout.

represents every worldly power which will, eventually, be destroyed.[23] It is this perspective that informs such a denunciation of British rule in India as we find in Rossetti's letter of 29 July 1880 to her old friend Amelia Heimann. 'We have just been reading the terrible Indian news', she writes—the 'news' probably being an article in that morning's *Times* which summarized the report of a commission set up to inquire into the causes of Indian famines over the past hundred years, and which ended with the famine of 1876–8 in Southern India in which more than five million died.[24] 'I do think our Indian crown is in great measure the trapping of a splendid misery: & how should it be otherwise, when so much injustice & bloodshed have (I believe) founded & upheld our rule? "All the perfumes of Arabia cannot sweeten this little hand": & the riches & influence of such an empire would be a world well lost, if thus we could learn to do justice & love mercy & walk humbly'.[25] It is a judgement underpinned by the knowledge that all worldly powers will, in time, be lost. Yet the other side of such judgements, empowered by biblical prophecy, is a lack of commitment to reordering the world through political action. There is certainly a dedication to justice and to mercy and to humility—to imitating Christ—while the individual is in this world; but, ultimately, the individual's investment must be in the next world. Rossetti knew from biblical prophecy—Revelation is the biblical text with the deepest presence in her writing—that Babylon is to be destroyed, not reformed.[26]

That Rossetti's engagement with society and politics is shaped by her religious beliefs determines the stance she takes on the status of women. Her refusal to sign up to the cause of women's suffrage on the biblical basis that women are subordinate to men coexists with a conviction that women, by virtue of their very subordination, imitate

[23] See Simon Humphries, 'Christina Rossetti's "My Dream" and Apocalypse', *Notes and Queries*, 55/1 (Mar. 2008), 54–7.

[24] *The Times* (29 July 1880), 4, cols. a–b.

[25] *Letters*, 2. 240. CGR's allusion to Dryden's *All for Love; or, The World Well Lost* invokes an apt imperial context; but the love for which Dryden's Mark Antony lost a world was not that for which CGR would lose it.

[26] William thought Gabriele's revolutionary politics 'may have lingered with her as a kind of antidotal savour against conservatism, but hardly as a practical counterbalance', *Poetical Works*, p. lxx. It would have had to be strong stuff to counter what Christina would hear from the pulpit of Christ Church, Albany Street: Dodsworth saw democracy as 'a direct assault on the prerogative of God', and evidence of the work of the Antichrist, 'the lawless one', *The Signs of the Times: Sermons Preached in Advent, 1848* (London, 1849), 25, 54, 78.

Christ's own position through their obedience and their patience. It is a conviction that informs her two most audacious poems: in 'Goblin Market', Lizzie's suffering, for her sister's sake, is explicitly Christlike; in 'The Prince's Progress', the princess's patience is no less Christlike. And yet, alongside these poems, and drawing on a potent biblical anti-feminism, she can personify the malignant world as a woman ('The World'), and anticipate—on the figurative level—this obscene woman being set on fire ('Foul is she and ill-favoured, set askew', in *The Face of the Deep*) (p. 373). To read Rossetti's work closely is, in places, a very disturbing experience. It is not surprising that those who do not share Rossetti's religious beliefs can find her dependence upon scripture—understood as a divinely inspired, and therefore authoritative, body of texts—somewhat hard to take.

It is sometimes supposed, especially on the evidence of poems which are little more than close weaves of scriptural texts, that religion, grounded in scripture, is disabling for Rossetti as a poet—as if poetry comes out of an escape from, rather than an engagement with, religious ideas. Yet such a view overlooks the extent to which religion, far from being disabling, is intimate with Rossetti's imaginative energy, and is the primary source of her intellectual reach and rigour. For Rossetti's engagement with religious ideas is far from being one of mere restatement of certainties—not least because scripture itself is so often obscure, even contradictory. What, for instance, is the status of the world following the Fall? Was only man corrupted by the transgression in Genesis 3, or was the world itself corrupted? It is an uncertainty deep within Christian theology—the scanty scriptural evidence is contradictory—and one which informs some of Rossetti's most remarkable poetry (see '"A Fair World Tho' a Fallen" ——', '"Consider the Lilies of the Field"', 'The World', 'An Afterthought', 'Shut Out', 'From House to Home', 'Goblin Market', and 'An Old-World Thicket').[27] Or, what happens to the soul in the time between death and resurrection? Once more, scripture provides no clear and consistent direction on this; and, once more, this eschatological question is open to imaginative probing (see 'Dream Land', 'Rest', 'Life Hidden', 'Remember', 'A Dirge' ('She was as sweet as violets in the Spring'), and 'The Ghost's Petition').[28] No Rossetti poem is more familiar than the 'Song' ('When I am dead, my dearest'), but to put it in the context

[27] See Simon Humphries, 'The Uncertainty of "Goblin Market"', *Victorian Poetry*, 45/4 (Winter 2007), 391–413.

[28] See Linda E. Marshall, 'What the Dead Are Doing Underground: Hades and Heaven in the Writings of Christina Rossetti', *Victorian Newsletter*, 72 (Fall 1987), 55–60.

of theological speculation on the continuing consciousness of the
soul in the intermediate state between the world and heaven is to
defamiliarize it:

> And dreaming through the twilight
> That doth not rise nor set,
> Haply I may remember,
> And haply may forget.

The personal uncertainty of the poem's first stanza — will her dearest
remember her? — shrinks before this eschatological uncertainty: what-
ever her feelings for her dearest, could his (or her) remembrance ever
be reciprocated in this dream land? What started as one kind of poem
becomes, thrillingly, something very different. Rossetti's poetic vision
is enlarged, not narrowed, by theology.

Literary Influences

Rossetti's theological perspectives often transmute her immediate
poetic influences. This edition begins with the 1846 poem 'Sappho',
and also includes the 1848 poem 'What Sappho Would Have Said Had
Her Leap Cured Instead of Killing Her'. Such poems show Rossetti
doing what an immature poet would do: imitating the kind of poem
written by her precursors — in this case, the models including Sappho
poems by such successful poets as Felicia Hemans (1793–1835),
whose 'The Last Song of Sappho' is probably a direct influence on the
1846 poem, and Letitia Elizabeth Landon (1802–38) — the 'L.E.L.'
commemorated in Rossetti's poem of that title. For such poets,
Sappho was available, in translations and imitations, as an acceptable
figure of the 'poetess' — an appropriation that relied on understanding
her predominantly homosexual love poetry to have been heterosexual
(as, until late in the century, it usually was understood). This reading
was supported by the legend that Sappho killed herself, out of love for
the boatman Phaon, by leaping into the sea; a legend that made her
creativity inseparable from desertion and early death. As a figure of the
poetess — in Hemans's poem, the strings of her lyre are now broken as
'The heart whose music made them sweet' is broken — she embodied
an often limiting conception of women's poetry as being written
directly from the emotions.[29] It is into this tradition that the young

[29] On the importance of Sappho to Victorian women poets, see Angela Leighton,
Victorian Women Poets: Writing Against the Heart (London, 1992) and Yopie Prins,
Victorian Sappho (Princeton, 1999).

Rossetti writes. Yet the figure of the poetess does not seem to be her primary concern: only the titles of her Sappho poems tell us that the suffering speaker is a poet. And even though her Sappho does what she is supposed to do—lament, longing for death—this is a far more sophisticated use of the poetic models than it might seem. In the context of other early poems spoken by pagan speakers ('From the Antique' ('It's a weary life, it is') and 'From the Antique' ('I wish that I were dying')) we may suspect that Rossetti's primary concern is theological. When Sappho (in 1846) longs for 'the long night that knows no morrow', it is evident that she can have no expectation of an end to 'death's dreamless sleep'; so, too, the speaker of 'From the Antique' ('I wish that I were dying') wishes to die 'Never to rise again', to sleep but 'without morn'. It is an ironic use of pagan speakers who can have no conception of the morrow for which Christians wait, lost in a world before Christ triumphed over death. In their theological exploitation of poetic models, these superficially derivative poems share the intelligence that informs Rossetti's most original and distinctive work.[30]

Rossetti's poetry takes more from *The Pilgrim's Progress* than from any other literary work—a debt which has been obscured by the determination of critics to read her work as entirely a product of Tractarianism. A familiarity with Bunyan's book was not unusual in the nineteenth century, when even households that owned only a few books might be expected to have this one on their shelves; and it was not the possession of any one denomination. And the ambitious title poems of Rossetti's 1862 and 1866 volumes would not have been written without the example of *The Pilgrim's Progress*. It provides, of course—so the ironic allusion in the title tells us—a structural model for 'The Prince's Progress'. It also provides the most important source for the theological structure of 'Goblin Market'. In the Second Part of *The Pilgrim's Progress*, before they have gone far on their pilgrimage, Christiana catches her boys eating fruit from trees that overhang a wall bordering their path. Later, one of the boys, Matthew, becomes ill. The local physician, who knows that the boy has eaten the deadly fruit of Beelzebub's orchard, then cures him with a purge made *ex carne et sanguine Christi* that is to be taken 'in half a quarter of a pint of the tears of repentance'. If it is not taken with repentance, it will 'do no good'. The boy takes it: 'It caused him to purge, it caused him to sleep and rest quietly, it put him into a fine heat and breathing sweat, and did

---

[30] It is not surprising that, late in life, Rossetti should pick out 'Cleon' and 'Karshish' as among Robert Browning's most interesting poems, *Letters*, 4. 235.

quite rid him of his gripes'. When he has recovered, he can talk to the young women of the Palace 'of his distemper and how he was healed'. It is an experience that later makes Matthew wary of eating apples; but, on that later occasion, he is told that apples are not dangerous in themselves:

> Apples were they with which we were beguiled,
> Yet sin, not apples hath our souls defiled.
> Apples forbid, if eat, corrupts the blood:
> To eat such, when commanded, does us good.[31]

We see that Bunyan gives 'Goblin Market' what biblical texts do not: a narrative structure that links poisonous fruit ('the fruit forbidden' (l. 479) that acts as 'poison in the blood' (l. 555)) with a restorative Eucharistic purge ('Eat me, drink me, love me' (l. 471) is the Christlike Lizzie's command).[32]

Rossetti was no promiscuous reader, and the importance of Bunyan to these major poems demonstrates her concentrated exploitation of her somewhat restricted reading (restricted, that is, as it seemed to William Michael).[33] Shakespeare, for instance, cannot be counted a major presence in her work, but he is a notable source of titles: '"Look on This Picture and on This"', '"Cannot Sweeten"', '"One Foot on Sea, and One on Shore"', and probably 'The Bourne'; and also the manuscript titles of 'Autumn' ('Ding Dong Bell') and of the first part of 'Memory' ('A Blank'). We do know from William Michael that the two authors Christina was most drawn to were Plato and Dante. We might not expect a philosopher to be a notable resource for her poetry, although 'A Valentine', written for her mother in 1882, does allude to the distinction in the *Symposium* between two kinds of Love (perhaps surprisingly, but not unintelligibly, given that the higher kind, of which Frances is an embodiment, is exclusively homosexual); but we may see that a poet for whom the world is insubstantial, a shadow of the eternal world, would respond to Plato. We would expect Dante to be a major presence: not only Gabriele Rossetti, but each of his children, engaged with Dante—whether in criticism, translation, or creative works. Yet, while Christina's poetry—especially her later poetry— does take from Dante, it is interesting for its taking less than we

---

[31] John Bunyan, *The Pilgrim's Progress*, ed. Roger Sharrock (Harmondsworth, 1965), 240–1, 279–82, 317–18.

[32] See Simon Humphries, 'Christina Rossetti's "Goblin Market" and Bunyan's Orchard of Beelzebub', *Notes and Queries*, 55/1 (Mar. 2008), 49–51.

[33] *Poetical Works*, pp. lxix–lxx.

might expect. In a letter to William Michael in 1892, she remarks 'You see, all too late I am being sucked into the Dantesque vortex', which suggests she had knowingly kept, for much of her life, a certain distance from any deep study of Dante.[34] It seems that the single-mindedness with which Gabriele pursued his often dubious theories about Dante's work could become an obstacle to his children's study of the poet. It is in a late sonnet sequence 'Monna Innominata' (published 1881) that we find Christina's major engagement with Dante, in the context of an audacious appropriation of the tradition of courtly love poetry. Yet her response to Beatrice is ambivalent—doubtless, in part, because Dante's earthly love of Beatrice in *La Vita Nuova* is less likely to excite a woman poet than a male poet, but perhaps also because the function of the heavenly Beatrice in the *Commedia* could be problematic to those with a Protestant suspicion of intermediaries between the individual and God. And while, as early as 'The Dead City' (1847), there is a discernible awareness of the opening of the *Commedia* (made explicit in the epigraph to 'An Old-World Thicket'), her poetry does not draw heavily upon that work: the *Commedia* is far less generative than *The Pilgrim's Progress* (even the locus of the dark wood is partly mediated by Spenser: see note to 'An Old-World Thicket', ll. 5–10 (p. 471)). Perhaps this is because the conception of Dante's poem is so remote from Rossetti's poetry. Dante, lost in the *selva oscura*, is found and guided by Virgil through hell and purgatory, and then by Beatrice herself through heaven; but the viewpoint of Rossetti's poetry remains from within the wood of the world, through which individuals must make their own way—a world of ultimately uncertain status, which may itself be a guide towards the substantial spiritual world, or which may be a place of deception. A personal guide, dispatched from heaven, may turn up ('Repining'); he may also then run away ('From House to Home').

Revising Hands

Christina never appears overly anxious about influences on her poetry. More often it is Dante Gabriel who is anxious on her behalf. Reading 'From House to Home' during the preparation of her 1862 volume, and worried by the poem's indebtedness to Tennyson, he asked 'could not something be done to make it less like *Palace of Art*'. But Christina did little, perhaps aware that her theological concerns produce a very

---

[34] *Letters*, 4. 289.

different poem from her model. Dante Gabriel's interest in those theological concerns was never, as far as the evidence goes, especially deep. In the late 1840s, he himself had been committed to using Christian symbolism in poetry and painting, and Christina can hardly not have taken a keen interest in his work; but there is little evidence that, by then, he subscribed to the central tenets of Christianity. His interest, unlike hers, was almost entirely aesthetic.

Yet he had significant influence on the selection and revision of poems for inclusion in Christina's major volumes of 1862 and 1866: late in life, she recorded her 'general indebtedness' to his 'suggestive wit and revising hand' in their preparation. (She noted, further, that the title of her poem 'Goblin Market' was Dante Gabriel's suggestion.[35]) And that these volumes were published as the work of one 'Christina Rossetti' may itself have been influenced by Dante Gabriel's decision in designing their illustrated title pages (see p. 103). The volumes she published which were not generally indebted to Dante Gabriel came out under the name 'Christina G. Rossetti'—the name by which she signed herself, and over which she published in periodicals. The name by which we have come to know Christina is not precisely that by which she knew herself.

Unfortunately, it is not always clear whether the initiative for revising a poem was Christina's or her brother's. (The letters from Christina to Dante Gabriel during preparation of the 1866 volume are thus of particular importance in understanding the dynamics of this collaboration.) But we do see Christina taking up Dante Gabriel's suggestion to shorten 'The Ghost's Petition', and the manuscript text's explicitly religious last stanzas are cut off.[36] And we see, in Christina's notebook containing poems from 1853–4, Dante Gabriel's pencilled instruction, on a twelve-stanza poem, 'Take 2 stanzas', with his chosen stanzas then numbered—an excision which produces 'The Bourne', a poem stripped of explicit religious reference, and which ends with a resonant paradox. (The manuscript poem ends by looking beyond the grave to the consolations of heaven.) These examples demonstrate a pattern of revision we find elsewhere, whether or not prompted by Dante Gabriel: stanzas are excised from longer poems, endings are lopped off—especially endings that express religious certitude—to produce more concise and more open-ended poems (see 'May—' ('Sweet Life is dead'), 'Shut Out', 'By the Sea', and 'Who Shall

---

[35] *The Complete Poems of Christina Rossetti*, ed. R. W. Crump, 3 vols. (Baton Rouge, 1979–90), 1. 234.

[36] Information on major revisions of poems will be found in the notes to this edition.

Deliver Me?'). If it looks brutal, it is an assured brutality which is dictated by what might be described as an aesthetic of inexplicitness. In the case of 'Two Choices', her brother's direction to cut the poem's last twelve lines was disregarded by Christina, perhaps as being too brutal: in terms of her original conception of the poem, so unkind a cut would have rendered the poem not only inexplicit, but no longer intelligible.

There were also occasional disagreements over which poems were worthy of publication. Dante Gabriel disliked the explicit reference to social or political issues in a small number of poems—what he took to be the influence of Elizabeth Barrett Browning, and 'utterly foreign to your primary impulses'.[37] Christina's own declared incapacity to 'turn to politics or philanthropy with Mrs Browning' (p. 398) suggests that her own sense of her primary impulses was not so very different; but, characteristically, she was somewhat less anxious about this particular influence, less protective of her distinctiveness. In 'The Lowest Room', Dante Gabriel found 'A real taint, to some extent, of modern vicious style derived from the same source—what might be called a falsetto muscularity'. The comment reflects both a general opposition to poetry that has a social or political design upon the reader, but also a particular belief that such direct engagement is especially unconvincing in a woman poet. Yet this is not quite to say that he opposed political reference in Christina's poetry per se. In the very same letter in which he comments on 'The Lowest Room', he finds 'the two poems on the Franco-Prussian War ['The German-French Campaign 1870–1871'] very noble—particularly the second, which is, I dare say, the best thing said in verse on the subject . . . the first of the two poems seems to me just a little echoish of the Barrett-Browning style': a distinction which aesthetic considerations may explain (perhaps a certain prosiness in the first poem contrasted with the more obviously well-wrought second poem, with its virtuosic rhyming on 'France'?). He also judges 'A Royal Princess' to be tainted with this vicious influence, and yet it is almost certain that it was he who insisted that it be published in the 1866 volume. Christina wanted to omit it; he thought it too good to omit—a judgement which we may take as indicative of his acute appreciation of her work. One obvious difference between 'The Lowest Room' and 'A Royal Princess' is that the former ends in moralism, and the latter in uncertainty.

[37] Letters of Dante Gabriel Rossetti, ed. Oswald Doughty and John Robert Wahl, 4 vols. (Oxford, 1965–7), 3. 1380.

Dante Gabriel was not merely imposing his own aesthetic prefer-
ences on Christina's poetry: he was also responding to qualities that
were already present in her work. When the elderly Christina recalled
that, in her earliest phase of writing, she had 'a distinct aim at concise-
ness' (p. 400) that could produce obscurity, this would also be an apt
description of the collaborative aim that appears to have directed the
revision of her poems in the 1850s and 1860s. The 1848 poem which,
with only its title revised, was published as 'A Pause of Thought' in
the second issue of *The Germ*, already demonstrates this withholding
of meaning in its refusal to specify the object that is sought but never
found: 'that which is not, nor can be', 'a hope', 'the object', 'It', 'an
empty name'—'a name' which is never named (p. 19). The aesthetic
of inexplicitness that appears to have guided the collaborative revision
of Christina's work was, in fact, consistent with that which produced
many poems which were never subjected to radical revision.

We can understand why reticence, even radical uncertainty, should
be essential to the poetry. We have seen that, for Rossetti, to live in the
world is to live with questions that may only ever be resolved when this
world has passed away. Not only may the world be misread—an ever-
present danger—but it may be impossible to know if it has been mis-
read. It is true that deep theological certainties underlie the poetry; but
Rossetti's restless mind is more excited by what is uncertain. This,
therefore, is one answer to the question of how the aesthetic qualities
of the poetry are to be related to its religious content: it is through its
withholding of meaning and of closure that the poetry witnesses to the
condition of living in a world where truth is seen only darkly, when it
is seen at all.

If we require an explanation for Christina's cooperation with (and it
is certainly more than mere acquiescence in) Dante Gabriel's criticism
of her poetry, the most plausible explanation is, therefore, that she
understood that revision could further emphasize what was already a
distinctive aspect of her writing. Critics have occasionally tried to
belittle Christina by portraying her as a woman poet too weak to resist
her bullying brother's interference; but the evidence, as the corres-
pondence over preparation of the 1866 volume makes amply clear, is
that Christina valued his criticism while being prepared to reject it.[38]
She never found the process of being criticized a comfortable one

---

[38] Constance W. Hassett gives an indispensable scholarly account of this collabor-
ation in *Christina Rossetti: The Patience of Style* (Charlottesville, 2005), 85–106. In pre-
paring his own 1870 volume, Dante Gabriel wanted Christina to 'read my things & give
any hints that occur to her', *Correspondence*, 4. 248, 253.

(there were always her 'nerves'); but her willingness to expose her work to a critic who, even though energetically supportive, could be forthright to the point of tactlessness, is a mark of her seriousness as a poet.

Today, Christina Rossetti's poetry seems so obviously one of the great things that Victorian literature has to offer that we may forget how recently, and rapidly, it has regained such a status. Through much of the twentieth century, it received little critical attention. This was partly because of the generally low view taken of Victorian poetry in literary criticism at the time—criticism, in this, influenced by aggressive modernist depreciations of the preceding generation; but there can be little doubt that it was also partly because of an inclination to overlook the work of women poets. In the last decades of the twentieth century, this changed: the feminist project of recovering and promoting women writers, coinciding with a rising valuation of Victorian poetry generally, has brought Christina Rossetti to the centre of our view of Victorian literature.

A CHRONOLOGY OF
CHRISTINA ROSSETTI

1830 Born (5 Dec.) at 38 Charlotte Street, Portland Place, London, the youngest of the four children of Gabriele Rossetti and Frances Mary Lavinia (Polidori).

1847 *Verses: Dedicated to Her Mother* printed privately by grandfather, Gaetano Polidori.

1848–50 Declines a proposal of marriage from the painter James Collinson on the grounds of his Roman Catholicism; accepts his proposal when he returns to the Church of England; breaks the engagement when he reconverts.

1850 The four issues of the Pre-Raphaelite Brotherhood's journal *The Germ* published (Jan.–Apr.), containing seven of her poems.

1851–2 Assists Frances in an unsuccessful day school at 38 Arlington Street, Camden Town, London.

1853–4 With Frances, sets up another unsuccessful day school at Frome, Somerset.

1854 Returns to London with her parents, living with William at 45 Upper Albany Street (166 Albany Street) (Mar.). Gabriele dies (26 Apr.). Application to follow an aunt's example in going to Scutari, under Florence Nightingale's scheme, to nurse the wounded of the Crimean War is declined on the grounds of her age.

1857 'In the Round Tower at Jhansi, June 8, 1857' written in response to a report of an incident during the Indian Mutiny (Sept.).

1859 Helping at the London Diocesan Penitentiary for 'fallen' women, Highgate.

1861 Travels in northern France with William and Frances (June–July).

1862 *Goblin Market and Other Poems* published by Macmillan (Apr.).

1865 A second edition of *Goblin Market and Other Poems* published (Mar.). Travels to northern Italy with William and Frances (May–June).

1866 *The Prince's Progress and Other Poems* published by Macmillan (June). Declines a proposal from Charles Bagot Cayley on the grounds of his lack of religious belief.

1867 Moves, with William, Frances, and Maria Francesca, to 56 Euston Square (5 Endsleigh Gardens) (June).

1870 *Commonplace, and Other Short Stories* published by Ellis (May). Writes the two poems on 'The German-French Campaign 1870–1871' (?autumn/winter 1870–1).

1871 Develops Graves' disease. *Sing-Song* published by Routledge (Nov.; dated 1872).

1874 *Annus Domini*, a book of prayers, published by Parker (Mar.). The children's book *Speaking Likenesses* published by Macmillan (Nov.).

1875 *Goblin Market, the Prince's Progress and Other Poems* published by Macmillan (Nov.).

1876 Moves, with Frances, to 30 Torrington Square (Sept.). Maria Francesca dies (24 Nov.).

1879 *Seek and Find* published by SPCK (Oct.).

1881 *A Pageant and Other Poems* published by Macmillan (July). *Called to be Saints* published by SPCK (Oct.).

1882 Dante Gabriel dies (9 Apr.).

1883 *Letter and Spirit* published by SPCK (May). Charles Bagot Cayley dies (5 Dec.).

1885 *Time Flies* published by SPCK (May).

1886 Frances dies (8 Apr.).

1892 *The Face of the Deep* published by SPCK (Apr.). Diagnosed with breast cancer; mastectomy performed (May).

1893 *Verses*, comprising poems taken from the late devotional books, published by SPCK (Sept.). Second edition of *Sing-Song* published by Macmillan (Dec.).

1894 Dies (29 Dec.). Buried at Highgate Cemetery.

NOTE ON THE TEXT

This edition brings together, in one chronological ordering, poems which Rossetti published and poems which she left in manuscript; but not every poem can be dated exactly. Up to the mid-1860s, Rossetti's regular practice was to copy her poems into notebooks, and to give their date of completion. (That these datings are to be taken as dates of completion, rather than of copying, is suggested by the group of 'Odds and Ends', in Bodleian MS. Don. e. 1/8, which is marked, exceptionally, 'Copied, September 1853'.) These dates do not, of course, tell us when composition of a poem began, and it would be simplistic (and, in some instances, wholly implausible) to take a notebook date as being the day on which a poem was 'written'. Rossetti's later revision of poems that were entered in her notebooks further complicates this chronological ordering. In the case of three poems included in this edition, revision is so radical that it produces what may be considered two distinct poems rather than two versions of the one poem, and both the unpublished and the published texts are therefore presented together at the date of completion of the manuscript poem: 'From the Antique' ('I wish that I were dying') and 'One Sea-Side Grave'; 'A Yawn' and 'By the Sea'; 'En Route' and 'An "Immurata" Sister'. From the mid-1860s, the completion dates of poems are often not known, and all the poems taken from *A Pageant and Other Poems* (1881) are therefore arranged according to their order in that volume—a volume which, with its keynote of being the work of the poet's later life, approaches a thematic and tonal unity which is not attempted in the major volumes of 1862 and 1866.

In editing the manuscript poems, the main uncertainty—if only an occasional one—is over responsibility for deletions and revisions: interventions are made by Dante Gabriel when helping Christina in the selection and revision of poems for publication, and by William Michael when preparing poems for posthumous publication, as well as by Christina herself. William Michael, in the notes to his editions of Christina's poems, does record his major interventions (e.g. his shortening of 'Look on This Picture and on This') but not those that he evidently considered minor (e.g. he has, in their manuscripts, pencilled-in titles for some untitled poems not included in this edition). His silent revisions of poems included in this edition are mostly minor corrective revisions (e.g. in 'A Dirge' ('She was as sweet as violets in the Spring')). In the case of 'Two Choices', however—a poem only before published under William Michael's title 'Listening'—different editorial ascriptions of responsibility for deletions and revisions will produce very different poems.

We know that it was Rossetti's usual practice—in keeping with her usual reluctance to write to order—to submit to the Portfolio Society old compositions that would suit the subjects set for contributions, rather than writing poems in response to the chosen subjects (see Introduction, p. xxi). The letter P is pencilled beside the titles of these poems in the notebooks. The copies of her Portfolio poems at Princeton (C0222, Princeton University Library, with wrapper marked 'Portfolio') may therefore show what had been the subjects set for contributions as well as, or instead of, the poems' former titles: we can conclude that 'Reflection' was a Society subject, and that both 'A Study (A Soul)' and 'A Coast-Nightmare' are accommodations of notebook titles to the Society's set subject. In this edition, where the copy-text of a poem is a Portfolio copy, its heading/title has been retained: if Rossetti would have been unlikely to have published poems under clumsy compound titles, these titles do reflect the circumstances in which the manuscripts were produced.

We know that Rossetti was very careful in proof-reading her published volumes. Her 1866 volume also benefited from Dante Gabriel's no less vigilant proof-reading (see note to 'Songs in a Cornfield', ll. 60–1 (p. 445)). The texts in the English volumes, approved by her, can therefore be ascribed a high level of authority. Even the privately printed *Verses*, published as early as 1847, over which we might expect Rossetti to have had less control than over her mature volumes, is no careless production (if not—as a few authorial corrections in copies show—without error). In this edition, the texts of published poems which were included in volumes (as most were) are taken from the first English volumes in which they appeared. (The texts of published prose works are also taken from their first editions.) Rossetti's main work of revision of poems occurs between notebook manuscript and publication. Subsequent revision of poems published in the volumes of 1862 and 1866 is usually minor—some smoothing out of small awkwardnesses in later editions. There is, however, some indication of a tendency to revise lines that might be taken as too sexually suggestive (see notes to 'Noble Sisters', l. 46 (p. 440); 'The Prince's Progress', l. 340 (p. 450)). The division of each of the 1862 and 1866 volumes into two sections, the second section being headed 'Devotional Pieces', was not continued in the 1875 collected edition. (In the publication notes to the present edition, poems published in the 'Devotional Pieces' sections are marked thus: *1862 (D)*, and *1866 (D)*.)

Obvious minor errors in published texts have been silently corrected; any other emendation has been noted. Otherwise, apart from some standardization in accordance with the publisher's style, the texts presented here are faithful to the stated manuscript and printed copy-texts. The occasional inconsistencies of capitalization and hyphenation in both manuscript and print have been retained, posing little problem to the reader. It may be noted that, in earlier manuscripts, an apostrophe may be used in possessive pronouns (e.g. 'our's'); and that, in both manuscript and print, compounds are not always hyphenated as the modern reader might expect (e.g. 'lily laden' in 'By the Water', l. 2; 'long set' and 'heart sick' in 'Love Lies Bleeding', ll. 7, 12). This edition standardizes thus: double inverted commas become single inverted commas; repeated inverted commas at the beginning of successive lines are removed; those poem titles which are not capitalized in manuscript are capitalized; full stops are removed from titles; ampersands used for the sake of space in revising manuscript poems become 'and' (but, in ('Sleeping at last, the trouble & tumult over'), in which ampersands are used throughout, they are retained).

The degree sign (°) indicates a note at the end of the book. The headnotes to each poem and prose work are not cued.

POEMS AND PROSE

Sappho

I sigh at day-dawn, and I sigh
When the dull day is passing by.
I sigh at evening, and again
I sigh when night brings sleep to men.
Oh! it were better far to die
Than thus for ever mourn and sigh,
And in death's dreamless sleep to be
Unconscious that none weep for me;
Eased from my weight of heaviness,
Forgetful of forgetfulness,   10
Resting from pain and care and sorrow
Through the long night that knows no morrow;
Living unloved, to die unknown,
Unwept, untended and alone.°

The Dead City

Once I rambled in a wood
With a careless hardihood°
Heeding not the tangled way;°
Labyrinths around me lay,
But for them I never stood.

On, still on, I wandered on,
And the sun above me shone;
And the birds around me winging
With their everlasting singing
Made me feel not quite alone.   10

In the branches of the trees
Murmured like the hum of bees
The low sound of happy breezes,
Whose sweet voice that never ceases
Lulls the heart to perfect ease.

Streamlets bubbled all around
On the green and fertile ground,

POEMS

Through the rushes and the grass,
Like a sheet of liquid glass,
With a soft and trickling sound.   20

And I went, I went on faster,
Contemplating no disaster,
And I plucked ripe blackberries,
But the birds with envious eyes,
Came and stole them from their master.°

For the birds here were all tame;
Some with bodies like a flame;
Some that glanced the branches through,
Pure and colourless as dew;
Fearlessly to me they came.   30

Before me no mortal stood
In the mazes of that wood;
Before me the birds had never
Seen a man, but dwelt for ever
In a happy solitude:

Happy solitude, and blest
With beatitude of rest;
Where the woods are ever vernal,
And the life and joy eternal,
Without Death's or Sorrow's test.°   40

Oh most blessed solitude!
Oh most full beatitude!
Where are quiet without strife,
And imperishable life,
Nothing marred, and all things good.

And the bright sun, life begetting,
Never rising, never setting,
Shining warmly overhead,
Nor too pallid, nor too red,
Lulled me to a sweet forgetting—   50

Sweet forgetting of the time;
And I listened for no chime,

Which might warn me to be gone;
But I wandered on, still on,
'Neath the boughs of oak and lime.

Know I not how long I strayed
In the pleasant leafy shade;
But the trees had gradually
Grown more rare, the air more free,
The sun hotter overhead.   60

Soon the birds no more were seen
Glancing through the living green,
And a blight had passed upon
All the trees; and the pale sun
Shone with a strange lurid sheen.

Then a darkness spread around:
I saw nought; I heard no sound:
Solid darkness overhead,
With a trembling cautious tread
Passed I o'er the unseen ground.   70

But at length a pallid light
Broke upon my searching sight;
A pale solitary ray
Like a star at dawn of day
Ere the sun is hot and bright.

Towards its faintly glimmering beam
I went on as in a dream;
A strange dream of hope and fear!
And I saw, as I drew near,
'T was in truth no planet's gleam,   80

But a lamp above a gate
Shone in solitary state,
O'er a desert drear and cold,
O'er a heap of ruins old,
O'er a scene most desolate.

By that gate I entered lone
A fair city of white stone;

And a lovely light to see
Dawned, and spread most gradually
Till the air grew warm and shone.   90

Through the splendid streets I strayed
In that radiance without shade;
Yet I heard no human sound;
All was still and silent round
As a city of the dead.

All the doors were open wide;
Lattices on every side
In the wind swung to and fro—
Wind that whispered very low:
'Go and see the end of pride.'   100

With a fixed determination
Entered I each habitation;
But they all were tenantless.
All was utter loneliness,
All was deathless desolation.

In the noiseless market-place
Was no care-worn busy face;
There were none to buy or sell,
None to listen or to tell,
In this silent emptiness.   110

Through the city on I went
Full of awe and wonderment.
Still the light around me shone,
And I wandered on, still on,
In my great astonishment.

Till at length I reached a place
Where, amid an ample space,
Rose a palace for a king;
Golden was the turreting,
And of solid gold the base.   120

The great porch was ivory,
And the steps were ebony;

Diamond and chrysoprase°
Set the pillars in a blaze,
Capitalled with jewelry.

None was there to bar my way,
And the breezes seemed to say,
'Touch not these, but pass them by
Pressing onwards;' therefore I
Entered in and made no stay.   130

All around was desolate.
I went on; a silent state
Reigned in each deserted room,
And I hastened through the gloom
Till I reached an outer gate.

Soon a shady avenue,
Blossom-perfumed, met my view;
Here and there the sunbeams fell
On pure founts whose sudden swell
Up from marble basons flew.   140

Every tree was fresh and green;
Not a withered leaf was seen
Through the veil of flowers and fruit;
Strong and sapful were the root,
The top boughs, and all between.

Vines were climbing every where,
Full of purple grapes and fair.
And far off I saw the corn
With its heavy head down borne
By the odour-laden air.   150

Who shall strip the bending vine?
Who shall tread the press for wine?
Who shall bring the harvest in
When the pallid ears begin
In the sun to glow and shine?

On I went alone, alone,
Till I saw a tent that shone

With each bright and lustrous hue;
It was trimmed with jewels too,
And with flowers; not one was gone.   160

Then the breezes whispered me:
'Enter in, and look, and see,
How for luxury and pride
A great multitude have died.'
And I entered tremblingly.

Lo, a splendid banquet laid
In the cool and pleasant shade.
Mighty tables, every thing
Of sweet Nature's furnishing
That was rich and rare, displayed;   170

And each strange and luscious cate°
Practised Art makes delicate;
With a thousand fair devices
Full of odours and of spices;
And a warm voluptuous state.

All the vessels were of gold,°
Set with gems of worth untold.
In the midst a fountain rose
Of pure milk, whose rippling flows
In a silver bason rolled.   180

In green emerald baskets were
Sun-red apples, streaked and fair;
Here the nectarine and peach
And ripe plum lay, and on each
The bloom rested every where.

Grapes were hanging overhead,
Purple, pale, and ruby-red;
And in panniers all around
Yellow melons shone, fresh found,
With the dew upon them spread.   190

And the apricot and pear,
And the pulpy fig were there,

Cherries and dark mulberries,
Bunchy currants, strawberries,
And the lemon wan and fair.

And unnumbered others too,
Fruits of every size and hue,
Juicy in their ripe perfection,
Cool beneath the cool reflection
Of the curtains' skyey blue.   200

All the floor was strewn with flowers
Fresh from sunshine and from showers,
Roses, lilies, jessamine;
And the ivy ran between,
Like a thought in happy hours.

And this feast too lacked no guest,
With its warm delicious rest;
With its couches softly sinking,
And its glow not made for thinking,
But for careless joy at best.   210

Many banqueters were there,
Wrinkled age, the young, the fair;
In the splendid revelry
Flushing cheek and kindling eye
Told of gladness without care.

Yet no laughter rang around,
Yet they uttered forth no sound;
With the smile upon his face
Each sat moveless in his place,
Silently, as if spell bound.   220

The low whispering voice was gone,
And I felt awed and alone.
In my great astonishment
To the feasters up I went—
Lo, they all were turned to stone!

Yea they all were statue-cold,
Men and women, young and old;

With the life-like look and smile,
And the flush; and all the while
The hard fingers kept their hold.   230

Here a little child was sitting
With a merry glance, befitting
Happy age and heedless heart;
There a young man sat apart,
With a forward look unweeting.°

Nigh them was a maiden fair,
And the ringlets of her hair
Round her slender fingers twined;
And she blushed as she reclined,°
Knowing that her love was there.   240

Here a dead man sat to sup,
In his hand a drinking cup;
Wine cup of the heavy gold,
Human hand stony and cold,
And no life breath struggling up.

There a mother lay and smiled
Down upon her infant child;
Happy child and happy mother,
Laughing back to one another
With a gladness undefiled.   250

Here an old man slept, worn out
With the revelry and rout;
Here a strong man sat and gazed
On a girl whose eyes upraised
No more wandered round about.

And none broke the stillness—none;
I was the sole living one.
And methought that silently
Many seemed to look on me
With strange steadfast eyes that shone.   260

Full of fear I would have fled;
Full of fear I bent my head,

Shutting out each stony guest.
When I looked again, the feast
And the tent had vanished.

Yes, once more I stood alone
Where the happy sunlight shone,
And a gentle wind was sighing,
And the little birds were flying,
And the dreariness was gone.   270

All these things that I have said
Awed me and made me afraid.
What was I that I should see
So much hidden mystery?°
And I straightway knelt and prayed.°

Spring Quiet

Gone were but the Winter,
   Come were but the Spring,
I would go to a covert°
   Where the birds sing;°

Where in the whitethorn
   Singeth a thrush,
And a robin sings
   In the holly-bush.

Full of fresh scents
   Are the budding boughs   10
Arching high over
   A cool green house:

Full of sweet scents,
   And whispering air
Which sayeth softly:
   'We spread no snare;

'Here dwell in safety,
   Here dwell alone,

With a clear stream
    And a mossy stone.   20

'Here the sun shineth
    Most shadily;
Here is heard an echo
    Of the far sea,
        Though far off it be.'

Repining

She sat alway thro' the long day°
Spinning the weary thread away;°
And ever said in undertone:
'Come, that I be no more alone.'

From early dawn to set of sun
Working, her task was still undone;
And the long thread seemed to increase
Even while she spun and did not cease.
She heard the gentle turtle-dove
Tell to its mate a tale of love;   10
She saw the glancing swallows fly,
Ever a social company;
She knew each bird upon its nest
Had cheering songs to bring it rest;
None lived alone save only she;—
The wheel went round more wearily;
She wept and said in undertone:
'Come, that I be no more alone.'

Day followed day, and still she sighed
For love, and was not satisfied;   20
Until one night, when the moonlight
Turned all the trees to silver white,
She heard, what ne'er she heard before,
A steady hand undo the door.
The nightingale since set of sun
Her throbbing music had not done,
And she had listened silently;

But now the wind had changed, and she
Heard the sweet song no more, but heard
Beside her bed a whispered word: 30
'Damsel, rise up; be not afraid;°
For I am come at last,' it said.

She trembled, tho' the voice was mild;
She trembled like a frightened child;—
Till she looked up, and then she saw
The unknown speaker without awe.
He seemed a fair young man, his eyes°
Beaming with serious charities;°
His cheek was white, but hardly pale;
And a dim glory like a veil 40
Hovered about his head, and shone
Thro' the whole room till night was gone.

So her fear fled; and then she said,
Leaning upon her quiet bed:
'Now thou art come, I prithee stay,
That I may see thee in the day,
And learn to know thy voice, and hear
It evermore calling me near.'

He answered: 'Rise, and follow me.'
But she looked upwards wonderingly: 50
'And whither would'st thou go, friend? stay°
Until the dawning of the day.'
But he said: 'The wind ceaseth, Maid;
Of chill nor damp be thou afraid.'

She bound her hair up from the floor,
And passed in silence from the door.

So they went forth together, he
Helping her forward tenderly.
The hedges bowed beneath his hand;
Forth from the streams came the dry land 60
As they passed over; evermore°
The pallid moonbeams shone before;

And the wind hushed, and nothing stirred;
Not even a solitary bird,
Scared by their footsteps, fluttered by
Where aspen-trees stood steadily.

As they went on, at length a sound
Came trembling on the air around;
The undistinguishable hum
Of life, voices that go and come   70
Of busy men, and the child's sweet
High laugh, and noise of trampling feet.

Then he said: 'Wilt thou go and see?'
And she made answer joyfully;
'The noise of life, of human life,
Of dear communion without strife,
Of converse held 'twixt friend and friend;
Is it not here our path shall end?'
He led her on a little way
Until they reached a hillock: 'Stay.'   80

It was a village in a plain.
High mountains screened it from the rain
And stormy wind; and nigh at hand
A bubbling streamlet flowed, o'er sand
Pebbly and fine, and sent life up
Green succous stalk and flower-cup.°

Gradually, day's harbinger,
A chilly wind began to stir.
It seemed a gentle powerless breeze
That scarcely rustled thro' the trees;   90
And yet it touched the mountain's head
And the paths man might never tread.
But hearken: in the quiet weather
Do all the streams flow down together? —
No, 'tis a sound more terrible
Than tho' a thousand rivers fell.
The everlasting ice and snow
Were loosened then, but not to flow; —
With a loud crash like solid thunder

The avalanche came, burying under 100
The village; turning life and breath
And rest and joy and plans to death.

'Oh! let us fly, for pity fly;
Let us go hence, friend, thou and I.
There must be many regions yet
Where these things make not desolate.'
He looked upon her seriously;
Then said: 'Arise and follow me.'
The path that lay before them was
Nigh covered over with long grass; 110
And many slimy things and slow
Trailed on between the roots below.
The moon looked dimmer than before;
And shadowy cloudlets floating o'er
Its face sometimes quite hid its light,
And filled the skies with deeper night.

At last, as they went on, the noise
Was heard of the sea's mighty voice;
And soon the ocean could be seen
In its long restlessness serene. 120
Upon its breast a vessel rode
That drowsily appeared to nod
As the great billows rose and fell,
And swelled to sink, and sank to swell.°

Meanwhile the strong wind had come forth
From the chill regions of the North,
The mighty wind invisible.
And the low waves began to swell;
And the sky darkened overhead;
And the moon once looked forth, then fled 130
Behind dark clouds; while here and there
The lightning shone out in the air;
And the approaching thunder rolled
With angry pealings manifold.°
How many vows were made, and prayers
That in safe times were cold and scarce.
Still all availed not; and at length

The waves arose in all their strength,
And fought against the ship, and filled
The ship. Then were the clouds unsealed, 140
And the rain hurried forth, and beat
On every side and over it.

Some clung together, and some kept
A long stern silence, and some wept.
Many half-crazed looked on in wonder
As the strong timbers rent asunder;
Friends forgot friends, foes fled to foes;—
And still the water rose and rose.

'Ah woe is me! Whom I have seen
Are now as tho' they had not been. 150
In the earth there is room for birth,
And there are graves enough in earth;
Why should the cold sea, tempest-torn,
Bury those whom it hath not borne?'

He answered not, and they went on.
The glory of the heavens was gone;
The moon gleamed not nor any star;
Cold winds were rustling near and far,
And from the trees the dry leaves fell
With a sad sound unspeakable. 160

The air was cold; till from the South
A gust blew hot, like sudden drouth,
Into their faces; and a light
Glowing and red, shone thro' the night.

A mighty city full of flame
And death and sounds without a name.
Amid the black and blinding smoke,
The people, as one man, awoke.
Oh! happy they who yesterday
On the long journey went away; 170
Whose pallid lips, smiling and chill,
While the flames scorch them smile on still;
Who murmur not; who tremble not
When the bier crackles fiery hot;

Who, dying, said in love's increase:
'Lord, let thy servant part in peace.'°

Those in the town could see and hear
A shaded river flowing near;
The broad deep bed could hardly hold
Its plenteous waters calm and cold.   180
Was flame-wrapped all the city wall,
The city gates were flame-wrapped all.

What was man's strength, what puissance then?
Women were mighty as strong men.
Some knelt in prayer, believing still,
Resigned unto a righteous will,
Bowing beneath the chastening rod,
Lost to the world, but found of God.
Some prayed for friend, for child, for wife;
Some prayed for faith; some prayed for life;   190
While some, proud even in death, hope gone,
Steadfast and still, stood looking on.

'Death—death—oh! let us fly from death;
Where'er we go it followeth;
All these are dead; and we alone
Remain to weep for what is gone.
What is this thing? thus hurriedly
To pass into eternity;
To leave the earth so full of mirth;
To lose the profit of our birth;   200
To die and be no more; to cease,
Having numbness that is not peace.
Let us go hence; and, even if thus
Death everywhere must go with us,
Let us not see the change, but see
Those who have been or still shall be.'

He sighed and they went on together;
Beneath their feet did the grass wither;
Across the heaven high overhead
Dark misty clouds floated and fled;   210
And in their bosom was the thunder,

And angry lightnings flashed out under,
Forked and red and menacing;
Far off the wind was muttering;
It seemed to tell, not understood,
Strange secrets to the listening wood.

Upon its wings it bore the scent
Of blood of a great armament:°
Then saw they how on either side
Fields were down-trodden far and wide.   220
That morning at the break of day
Two nations had gone forth to slay.

As a man soweth so he reaps.
The field was full of bleeding heaps;
Ghastly corpses of men and horses
That met death at a thousand sources;
Cold limbs and putrifying flesh;
Long love-locks clotted to a mesh
That stifled; stiffened mouths beneath
Staring eyes that had looked on death.   230

But these were dead: these felt no more
The anguish of the wounds they bore.
Behold, they shall not sigh again,
Nor justly fear, nor hope in vain.
What if none wept above them?—is
The sleeper less at rest for this?
Is not the young child's slumber sweet
When no man watcheth over it?
These had deep calm; but all around
There was a deadly smothered sound,   240
The choking cry of agony
From wounded men who could not die;
Who watched the black wing of the raven
Rise like a cloud 'twixt them and heaven,
And in the distance flying fast
Beheld the eagle come at last.

She knelt down in her agony:
'O Lord, it is enough,' said she:

'My heart's prayer putteth me to shame;
Let me return to whence I came.   250
Thou who for love's sake didst reprove,
Forgive me for the sake of love.'

A Pause of Thought

I looked for that which is not, nor can be,
    And hope deferred made my heart sick in truth:°
    But years must pass before a hope of youth
        Is resigned utterly.

I watched and waited with a steadfast will:
    And though the object seemed to flee away
    That I so longed for, ever day by day
        I watched and waited still.

Sometimes I said: This thing shall be no more;
    My expectation wearies and shall cease;   10
    I will resign it now and be at peace:
        Yet never gave it o'er.

Sometimes I said: It is an empty name
    I long for; to a name why should I give
    The peace of all the days I have to live?—
        Yet gave it all the same.

Alas, thou foolish one! alike unfit
    For healthy joy and salutary pain:
    Thou knowest the chase useless, and again
        Turnest to follow it.   20

What Sappho Would Have Said Had Her Leap Cured Instead of Killing Her

Love, Love, that having found a heart
    And left it, leav'st it desolate;—
    Love, Love, that art more strong than Hate,

More lasting and more full of art;—
O blessèd Love, return, return,
Brighten the flame that needs must burn.

Among the stately lilies pale,
    Among the roses flushing red,
    I seek a flower meet for my head,
A wreath wherewith to bind my veil: 10
I seek in vain; a shadow-pain
Lies on my heart; and all in vain.

The rose hath too much life in it;
    The lily is too much at rest.
    Surely a blighted rose were best,
Or cankered lily flower more fit;
Or purple violet, withering
While yet the year is in its spring.

I walk down by the river side
    Where the low willows touch the stream;   20
    Beneath the ripple and sun-gleam
The slippery cold fishes glide,
Where flags and reeds and rushes lave
Their roots in the unsullied wave.

Methinks this is a drowsy place:
    Disturb me not; I fain would sleep:
    The very winds and waters keep
Their voices under; and the race°
Of Time seems to stand still, for here
Is night or twilight all the year.   30

A very holy hushedness
    Broods here for ever: like a dove
    That, having built its nest above
A quiet place, feels the excess
Of calm sufficient, and would fain
Not wake, but drowse on without pain.

And slumbering on its mossy nest
    Haply hath dreams of pleasant Spring;

And in its vision prunes its wing°
And takes swift flight, yet is at rest. 40
Yea, is at rest: and still the calm
Is wrapped around it like a charm.

I would have quiet too in truth,
    And here will sojourn for a while.
    Lo; I have wandered many a mile,
Till I am foot-sore in my youth.
I will lie down; and quite forget
The doubts and fears that haunt me yet.

My pillow underneath my head
    Shall be green grass; thick fragrant leaves 50
    My canopy; the spider weaves
Meet curtains for my narrow bed;°
And the dew can but cool my brow
That is so dry and burning now.

Ah, would that it could reach my heart,
    And fill the void that is so dry
    And aches and aches;—but what am I
To shrink from my self-purchased part?
It is in vain, is all in vain;
I must go forth and bear my pain. 60

Must bear my pain, till Love shall turn
    To me in pity and come back.
    His footsteps left a smouldering track
Where he went forth, that still doth burn.
Oh come again, thou pain divine,
Fill me and make me wholly thine.

Song

When I am dead, my dearest,
    Sing no sad songs for me;
Plant thou no roses at my head,
    Nor shady cypress tree:

Be the green grass above me
   With showers and dewdrops wet;°
And if thou wilt, remember,
   And if thou wilt, forget.

I shall not see the shadows,
   I shall not feel the rain;   10
I shall not hear the nightingale
   Sing on, as if in pain:
And dreaming through the twilight
   That doth not rise nor set,
Haply I may remember,
   And haply may forget.°

To Lalla, Reading My Verses Topsy-Turvy

Darling little Cousin,
   With your thoughtful look
Reading topsy-turvy
   From a printed book

English hieroglyphics,
   More mysterious
To you, than Egyptian
   Ones would be to us; —

Leave off for a minute
   Studying, and say   10
What is the impression
   That those marks convey?

Only solemn silence,
   And a wondering smile:
But your eyes are lifted
   Unto mine the while.

In their gaze so steady
   I can surely trace
That a happy spirit
   Lighteth up your face.   20

Tender, happy spirit,
  Innocent and pure;
Teaching more than science,
  And than learning more.

How should I give answer
  To that asking look?
Darling little Cousin
  Go back to your book.

Read on: if you knew it,
  You have cause to boast:—   30
You are much the wisest,
  Though I know the most.

Song

Oh roses for the flush of youth,
  And laurel for the perfect prime;°
But pluck an ivy branch for me°
  Grown old before my time.

Oh violets for the grave of youth,
  And bay for those dead in their prime;
Give me the withered leaves I chose
  Before in the old time.

Have You Forgotten?

Have you forgotten how one Summer night
  We wandered forth together with the moon,
    While warm winds hummed to us a sleepy tune?
Have you forgotten how you praised both light
And darkness; not embarrassed yet not quite
    At ease? and how you said the glare of noon
    Less pleased you than the stars? but very soon
You blushed, and seemed to doubt if you were right.
We wandered far and took no note of time;

Till on the air there came the distant call   10
Of church bells: we turned hastily, and yet
Ere we reached home sounded a second chime.°
  But what; have you indeed forgotten all?
Ah how then is it I cannot forget?

An End

Love, strong as Death, is dead.°
Come, let us make his bed
Among the dying flowers:
A green turf at his head;
And a stone at his feet,
Whereon we may sit
In the quiet evening hours.

He was born in the Spring,
And died before the harvesting:
On the last warm summer day   10
He left us; he would not stay
For Autumn twilight cold and grey.
Sit we by his grave, and sing
He is gone away.

To few chords and sad and low
Sing we so:
Be our eyes fixed on the grass
Shadow-veiled as the years pass,
While we think of all that was
In the long ago.   20

Two Pursuits

A voice said: 'Follow, follow:' and I rose
  And followed far into the dreamy night,
  Turning my back upon the pleasant light.
It led me where the bluest water flows,

And would not let me drink; where the corn grows
   I dared not pause, but went uncheered by sight
   Or touch; until at length in evil plight
It left me, wearied out with many woes.
Some time I sat as one bereft of sense:
   But soon another voice from very far   10
Called: 'Follow, follow:' and I rose again.°
   Now on my night has dawned a blessèd star;
Kind, steady hands my sinking steps sustain,
And will not leave me till I shall go hence.

Dream Land

   Where sunless rivers weep°
   Their waves into the deep,
   She sleeps a charmèd sleep:
      Awake her not.
   Led by a single star,
   She came from very far
   To seek where shadows are
      Her pleasant lot.°

   She left the rosy morn,
   She left the fields of corn,   10
   For twilight cold and lorn°
      And water springs.
   Through sleep, as through a veil,
   She sees the sky look pale,
   And hears the nightingale
      That sadly sings.

   Rest, rest, a perfect rest
   Shed over brow and breast;
   Her face is toward the west,
      The purple land.°   20
   She cannot see the grain
   Ripening on hill and plain;°
   She cannot feel the rain
      Upon her hand.

Rest, rest, for evermore
Upon a mossy shore;
Rest, rest at the heart's core
    Till time shall cease:
Sleep that no pain shall wake,
Night that no morn shall break   30
Till joy shall overtake
    Her perfect peace.

After Death

SONNET

The curtains were half drawn, the floor was swept
    And strewn with rushes, rosemary and may°
    Lay thick upon the bed on which I lay,
Where through the lattice ivy-shadows crept.
He leaned above me, thinking that I slept
    And could not hear him; but I heard him say:
    'Poor child, poor child:' and as he turned away
Came a deep silence, and I knew he wept.
He did not touch the shroud, or raise the fold
    That hid my face, or take my hand in his,   10
        Or ruffle the smooth pillows for my head:
        He did not love me living; but once dead
    He pitied me; and very sweet it is
To know he still is warm though I am cold.

Rest

SONNET

O Earth, lie heavily upon her eyes;°
    Seal her sweet eyes weary of watching, Earth;
    Lie close around her; leave no room for mirth
With its harsh laughter, nor for sound of sighs.
She hath no questions, she hath no replies,
    Hushed in and curtained with a blessèd dearth°
    Of all that irked her from the hour of birth;°

With stillness that is almost Paradise.°
Darkness more clear than noon-day holdeth her,
   Silence more musical than any song;   10
Even her very heart has ceased to stir:
Until the morning of Eternity
Her rest shall not begin nor end, but be;
   And when she wakes she will not think it long.

Life Hidden

Roses and lilies grow above the place
   Where she sleeps the long sleep that doth not dream.
If we could look upon her hidden face
   Nor shadow would be there nor garish gleam
   Of light: her life is lapsing like a stream
That makes no noise but floweth on apace
   Seawards; while many a shade and shady beam
Vary the ripples in their gliding chase.
She doth not see, but knows: she doth not feel,
   And yet is sensible: she hears no sound,   10
Yet counts the flight of time and doth not err.
Peace far and near; peace to ourselves and her:
   Her body is at peace in holy ground,
Her spirit is at peace where Angels kneel.

Remember

SONNET

Remember me when I am gone away,
   Gone far away into the silent land;
   When you can no more hold me by the hand,
Nor I half turn to go yet turning stay.
Remember me when no more day by day
   You tell me of our future that you planned:
   Only remember me; you understand
It will be late to counsel then or pray.°
Yet if you should forget me for a while
   And afterwards remember, do not grieve: 10

For if the darkness and corruption leave
　A vestige of the thoughts that once I had,°
Better by far you should forget and smile
　Than that you should remember and be sad.

('So I grew half delirious and quite sick')

So I grew half delirious and quite sick,
And thro' the darkness saw strange faces grin
Of Monsters at me. One put forth a fin,
And touched me clammily: I could not pick
A quarrel with it: it began to lick
My hand, making meanwhile a piteous din
And shedding human tears: it would begin
To near me, then retreat. I heard the quick
Pulsation of my heart, I marked the fight
Of life and death within me; then sleep threw   10
Her veil around me; but this thing is true:
When I awoke the sun was at his height,
And I wept sadly, knowing that one new
Creature had love for me, and others spite.

A Dirge

She was as sweet as violets in the Spring,
　As fair as any rose in Summer time:
　　But frail are roses in their prime
　And violets in their blossoming.
Even so was she:
　And now she lies,
　　The earth upon her fast closed eyes,
Dead in the darkness silently.°

The sweet Spring violets never bud again,
　The roses bloom and perish in a morn: 10
　　They see no second quickening dawn,°
　Their beauty dies as tho' in vain.
Must she die so

For evermore,
　　Cold as the sand upon the shore,
As passionless for joy and woe?—°

Nay, she is worth much more than flowers that fade
　　And yet shall be made fair with purple fruit;°
　　　Branch of the Living Vine, Whose Root°
　　From all eternity is laid.   20
Another Sun°
　　Than this of our's,
　　　Has withered up indeed her flowers
But ripened her grapes every one.

'A Fair World Tho' a Fallen' ——

You tell me that the world is fair, in spite
　　Of the old fall; and that I should not turn
　　So to the grave, and let my spirit yearn
After the quiet of the long last night.
Have I then shut mine eyes against the light,
　　Grief-deafened lest my spirit should discern?
　　Yet how could I keep silence when I burn?
And who can give me comfort?—hear the right.
Have patience with the weak and sick at heart,
　　Bind up the wounded with a tender touch,°   10
　　　Comfort the sad, tear-blinded as they go:—
For tho' I failed to choose the better part,
　　　Were it a less unutterable woe
If we should come to love this world too much?—

'A Bruised Reed Shall He Not Break'

I will accept thy will to do and be,°
　　Thy hatred and intolerance of sin,°
　　Thy will at least to love, that burns within
　　　And thirsteth after Me:
So will I render fruitful, blessing still,°
　　The germs and small beginnings in thy heart,°

Because thy will cleaves to the better part.—°
  Alas, I cannot will.°

Dost not thou will, poor soul? Yet I receive
  The inner unseen longings of the soul,   10
   I guide them turning towards Me; I control
    And charm hearts till they grieve:
If thou desire, it yet shall come to pass,
  Though thou but wish indeed to choose My love;
  For I have power in earth and heaven above.—
    I cannot wish, alas!

What, neither choose nor wish to choose? and yet
  I still must strive to win thee and constrain:°
  For thee I hung upon the cross in pain,
    How then can I forget?   20
If thou as yet dost neither love, nor hate,°
  Nor choose, nor wish,—resign thyself, be still
  Till I infuse love, hatred, longing, will.—°
    I do not deprecate.°

Moonshine

Fair the sun riseth,
  Bright as bright can be,
Fair the sun shineth
  On a fair fair sea.

'Across the water
  Wilt thou come with me,
Miles and long miles, love,
  Over the salt sea?'—

'If thou wilt hold me
  Truly by the hand,°   10
I will go with thee
  Over sea and sand.

'If thou wilt hold me
  That I shall not fall,

I will go with thee,
   Love, in spite of all.'

Fair the moon riseth
   On her heavenly way
Making the waters
   Fairer than by day.   20

A little vessel
   Rocks upon the sea,
Where stands a maiden
   Fair as fair can be.

Her smile rejoices
   Though her mouth is mute,
She treads the vessel
   With her little foot.

Truly he holds her
   Faithful to his pledge,   30
Guiding the vessel
   From the water's edge.

Fair the moon saileth
   With her pale fair light,
Fair the girl gazeth
   Out into the night.

Saith she: 'Like silver
   Shines thy hair, not gold;' —
Saith she: 'I shiver
   In thy steady hold.   40

'Love,' she saith weeping,
   'Loose thy hold awhile,
My heart is freezing
   In thy freezing smile.'

The moon is hidden
   By a silver cloud,

Fair as a halo
   Or a maiden's shroud.

No more beseeching,
   Ever on they go: 50
The vessel rocketh
   Softly to and fro;

And still he holds her
   That she shall not fall,
Till pale mists whiten
   Dimly over all.

Onward and onward
   Far across the sea;
Onward and onward,
   Pale as pale can be;   60

Onward and onward,
   Ever hand in hand,
From sun and moon light
   For another land.

'To What Purpose is This Waste?'

A windy shell singing upon the shore:°
A lily budding in a desert place;°
Blooming alone
With no companion
To praise its perfect perfume and its grace:
A rose crimson and blushing at the core,
Hedged in with thorns behind it and before:
A fountain in the grass,
Whose shadowy waters pass
Only to nourish birds and furnish food   10
For squirrels of the wood:
An oak deep in the forest's heart, the house
Of black-eyed tiny mouse;
Its strong roots fit for fuel roofing in

The hoarded nuts, acorns and grains of wheat;
Shutting them from the wind and scorching heat,
And sheltering them when the rains begin:
A precious pearl deep buried in the sea
Where none save fishes be:
The fullest merriest note   20
For which the skylark strains his silver throat,
Heard only in the sky
By other birds that fitfully
Chase one another as they fly:
The ripest plum down tumbled to the ground
By southern winds most musical of sound,
But by no thirsty traveller found:
Honey of wild bees in their ordered cells
Stored, not for human mouths to taste:—
I said, smiling superior down: What waste   30
Of good, where no man dwells.

This I said on a pleasant day in June
Before the sun had set, tho' a white moon
Already flaked the quiet blue
Which not a star looked thro'.
But still the air was warm, and drowsily
It blew into my face:
So since that same day I had wandered deep
Into the country, I sought out a place
For rest beneath a tree,   40
And very soon forgot myself in sleep:
Not so mine own words had forgotten me.
Mine eyes were opened to behold°
All hidden things,
And mine ears heard all secret whisperings:
So my proud tongue that had been bold
To carp and to reprove,
Was silenced by the force of utter Love.

All voices of all things inanimate
Join with the song of Angels and the song   50
Of blessed Spirits, chiming with
Their Hallelujahs. One wind wakeneth°
Across the sleeping sea, crisping along

The waves, and brushes thro' the great
Forests and tangled hedges, and calls out
Of rivers a clear sound,
And makes the ripe corn rustle on the ground,
And murmurs in a shell;
Till all their voices swell
Above the clouds in one loud hymn   60
Joining the song of Seraphim,
Or like pure incense circle round about
The walls of Heaven, or like a well-spring rise
In shady Paradise.

A lily blossoming unseen
Holds honey in its silver cup
Whereon a bee may sup,
Till being full she takes the rest
And stores it in her waxen nest:
While the fair blossom lifted up   70
On its one stately stem of green,
Is type of her, the Undefiled,°
Arrayed in white, whose eyes are mild
As a white dove's, whose garment is
Blood-cleansed from all impurities
And earthly taints,
Her robe the righteousness of Saints.

And other eyes than our's
Were made to look on flowers,
Eyes of small birds and insects small: 80
The deep sun-blushing rose
Round which the prickles close
Opens her bosom to them all.
The tiniest living thing
That soars on feathered wing,
Or crawls among the long grass out of sight,
Has just as good a right
To its appointed portion of delight
As any King.°

Why should we grudge a hidden water stream   90
To birds and squirrels while we have enough?

As if a nightingale should cease to sing
Lest we should hear, or finch leafed out of sight°
Warbling its fill in summer light;
As if sweet violets in the spring
Should cease to blow, for fear our path should seem
Less weary or less rough.

So every oak that stands a house
For skilful mouse,
And year by year renews its strength,   100
Shakes acorns from a hundred boughs
Which shall be oaks at length.

Who hath weighed the waters and shall say°
What is hidden in the depths from day?
Pearls and precious stones and golden sands,
Wondrous weeds and blossoms rare,
Kept back from human hands,
But good and fair,
A silent praise as pain is silent prayer.
A hymn, an incense rising toward the skies,   110
As our whole life should rise;
An offering without stint from earth below,
Which Love accepteth so.

Thus is it with a warbling bird,
With fruit bloom-ripe and full of seed,
With honey which the wild bees draw
From flowers, and store for future need
By a perpetual law.
We want the faith that hath not seen
Indeed, but hath believed His truth   120
Who witnessed that His work was good:°
So we pass cold to age from youth.
Alas for us: for we have heard
And known, but have not understood.

O earth, earth, earth, thou yet shalt bow
Who art so fair and lifted up,
Thou yet shalt drain the bitter cup.
Men's eyes that wait upon thee now,

All eyes shall see thee lost and mean,
Exposed and valued at thy worth,   130
While thou shalt stand ashamed and dumb.—
Ah, when the Son of Man shall come,
Shall He find faith upon the earth?—

From the Antique / One Sea-Side Grave

From the Antique

I wish that I were dying,
  Deep-drowsing without pain:
I wish that I were lying
  Below the wind and rain,
  Never to rise again.

Forgetful of the roses,
  Forgetful of the thorn;
So sleeping, as reposes
  A child until the dawn,
  So sleeping without morn.°   10

Cold as the cold Decembers,
  Past as the days that set;
While only one remembers
  And all the rest forget,
  But one remembers yet.

One Sea-Side Grave

Unmindful of the roses,
  Unmindful of the thorn,
A reaper tired reposes
  Among his gathered corn:
  So might I, till the morn!

Cold as the cold Decembers,
  Past as the days that set,

While only one remembers
And all the rest forget,—
But one remembers yet. 10

Whitsun Eve

The white dove cooeth in her downy nest,°
Keeping her young ones warm beneath her breast:
The white moon saileth thro' the cool clear sky,
Screened by a tender mist in passing by:
The white rose buds, with thorns upon its stem,
All the more precious and more dear for them:
The stream shines silver in the tufted grass,
The white clouds scarcely dim it as they pass:
Deep in the valleys lily cups are white,
They send up incense all the holy night: 10
Our souls are white, made clean in Blood once shed:°
White blessed Angels watch around our bed:—
O spotless Lamb of God, still keep us so,
Thou Who wert born for us in time of snow.°

What?

Strengthening as secret manna,°
Fostering as clouds above,
Kind as a hovering dove,
Full as a plenteous river,
Our glory and our banner°
For ever and for ever.

Dear as a dying cadence
Of music in the drowsy night;
Fair as the flowers which maidens
Pluck for an hour's delight, 10
And then forget them quite.

Gay as a cowslip meadow
Fresh opening to the sun
When new day is begun;

Soft as a sunny shadow
When day is almost done.

Glorious as purple twilight,
Pleasant as budding tree,
Untouched as any islet
Shrined in an unknown sea;   20
Sweet as a fragrant rose amid the dew; —
As sweet, as fruitless too.

A bitter dream to wake from,
But oh how pleasant while we dream;
A poisoned fount to take from,
But oh how sweet the stream.

A Pause

They made the chamber sweet with flowers and leaves,
    And the bed sweet with flowers on which I lay;
    While my soul, love-bound, loitered on its way.°
I did not hear the birds about the eaves,
Nor hear the reapers talk among the sheaves:
    Only my soul kept watch from day to day,
    My thirsty soul kept watch for one away: —
Perhaps he loves, I thought, remembers, grieves.
At length there came the step upon the stair,
    Upon the lock the old familiar hand: 10
Then first my spirit seemed to scent the air
    Of Paradise; then first the tardy sand
Of time ran golden; and I felt my hair°
    Put on a glory, and my soul expand.°

Song

Two doves upon the selfsame branch,°
    Two lilies on a single stem,
Two butterflies upon one flower: —
    Oh happy they who look on them.

Who look upon them hand in hand
    Flushed in the rosy summer light;
Who look upon them hand in hand
    And never give a thought to night.

Sleep at Sea

Sound the deep waters:—°
    Who shall sound that deep?—
Too short the plummet,
    And the watchmen sleep.
Some dream of effort
    Up a toilsome steep;
Some dream of pasture grounds
    For harmless sheep.

White shapes flit to and fro
    From mast to mast;   10
They feel the distant tempest
    That nears them fast:
Great rocks are straight ahead,
    Great shoals not past;
They shout to one another
    Upon the blast.

Oh, soft the streams drop music
    Between the hills,
And musical the birds' nests
    Beside those rills: 20
The nests are types of home°
    Love-hidden from ills,
The nests are types of spirits
    Love-music fills.

So dream the sleepers,
    Each man in his place;
The lightning shows the smile
    Upon each face:
The ship is driving, driving,
    It drives apace: 30

And sleepers smile, and spirits
   Bewail their case.

The lightning glares and reddens
   Across the skies;
It seems but sunset
   To those sleeping eyes.
When did the sun go down
   On such a wise?
From such a sunset
   When shall day arise?   40

'Wake,' call the spirits:°
   But to heedless ears:
They have forgotten sorrows
   And hopes and fears;
They have forgotten perils
   And smiles and tears;
Their dream has held them long,
   Long years and years.

'Wake,' call the spirits again:
   But it would take   50
A louder summons
   To bid them awake.
Some dream of pleasure
   For another's sake;
Some dream, forgetful
   Of a lifelong ache.

One by one slowly,
   Ah, how sad and slow!
Wailing and praying
   The spirits rise and go: 60
Clear stainless spirits
   White as white as snow;
Pale spirits, wailing
   For an overthrow.

One by one flitting,
   Like a mournful bird

Whose song is tired at last
    For no mate heard.
The loving voice is silent,
    The useless word;   70
One by one flitting
    Sick with hope deferred.

Driving and driving,
    The ship drives amain:°
While swift from mast to mast
    Shapes flit again,
Flit silent as the silence
    Where men lie slain;
Their shadow cast upon the sails
    Is like a stain.   80

No voice to call the sleepers,
    No hand to raise:
They sleep to death in dreaming
    Of length of days.
Vanity of vanities,
    The Preacher says:
Vanity is the end
    Of all their ways.

'Consider the Lilies of the Field'

Flowers preach to us if we will hear:—
The rose saith in the dewy morn:
I am most fair;
Yet all my loveliness is born
Upon a thorn.
The poppy saith amid the corn:
Let but my scarlet head appear°
And I am held in scorn;
Yet juice of subtle virtue lies°
Within my cup of curious dyes.   10
The lilies say: Behold how we°
Preach without words of purity.
The violets whisper from the shade

Which their own leaves have made:
Men scent our fragrance on the air,
Yet take no heed
Of humble lessons we would read.°

But not alone the fairest flowers:
The merest grass
Along the roadside where we pass,   20
Lichen and moss and sturdy weed,
Tell of His love who sends the dew,
The rain and sunshine too,
To nourish one small seed.

A Study (A Soul)

She stands as pale as Parian statues stand;°
   Like Cleopatra when she turned at bay,
   And felt her strength above the Roman sway,
And felt the aspic writhing in her hand.
Her face is steadfast toward the shadowy land,
   For dim beyond it looms the land of day;
   Her feet are steadfast; all the arduous way
That foot-track hath not wavered on the sand.
She stands there like a beacon thro' the night,
   A pale clear beacon where the storm-drift is;   10
She stands alone, a wonder deathly white;
She stands there patient, nerved with inner might,
   Indomitable in her feebleness,
Her face and will athirst against the light.

The Bourne

Underneath the growing grass,
   Underneath the living flowers,
   Deeper than the sound of showers:
   There we shall not count the hours
By the shadows as they pass.

Youth and health will be but vain,
  Beauty reckoned of no worth:
  There a very little girth
  Can hold round what once the earth
Seemed too narrow to contain.°   10

Paradise

Once in a dream I saw the flowers
  That bud and bloom in Paradise;
  More fair they are than waking eyes
Have seen in all this world of ours.
And faint the perfume-bearing rose,
  And faint the lily on its stem,
And faint the perfect violet
    Compared with them.

I heard the songs of Paradise:
  Each bird sat singing in his place;   10
  A tender song so full of grace
It soared like incense to the skies.
Each bird sat singing to his mate
  Soft cooing notes among the trees:
The nightingale herself were cold
    To such as these.

I saw the fourfold River flow,°
  And deep it was, with golden sand;
  It flowed between a mossy land
With murmured music grave and low.   20
It hath refreshment for all thirst,
  For fainting spirits strength and rest;
Earth holds not such a draught as this
    From east to west.

The Tree of Life stood budding there,
  Abundant with its twelvefold fruits;°
  Eternal sap sustains its roots,
Its shadowing branches fill the air.

Its leaves are healing for the world,
   Its fruit the hungry world can feed,   30
Sweeter than honey to the taste
     And balm indeed.

I saw the gate called Beautiful;°
   And looked, but scarce could look within;
   I saw the golden streets begin,°
And outskirts of the glassy pool.°
Oh harps, oh crowns of plenteous stars,
   Oh green palm branches many-leaved—
Eye hath not seen, nor ear hath heard,
     Nor heart conceived.°   40

I hope to see these things again,
   But not as once in dreams by night;
   To see them with my very sight,
And touch and handle and attain:
To have all Heaven beneath my feet
   For narrow way that once they trod;°
To have my part with all the saints,
     And with my God.

The World

SONNET

By day she wooes me, soft, exceeding fair:
   But all night as the moon so changeth she;
   Loathsome and foul with hideous leprosy
And subtle serpents gliding in her hair.°
By day she wooes me to the outer air,
   Ripe fruits, sweet flowers, and full satiety:°
   But through the night, a beast she grins at me,
A very monster void of love and prayer.
By day she stands a lie: by night she stands
   In all the naked horror of the truth°   10
With pushing horns and clawed and clutching hands.
Is this a friend indeed; that I should sell
   My soul to her, give her my life and youth,
Till my feet, cloven too, take hold on hell?°

Guesses

Was it a chance that made her pause
  One moment at the opened door,
  Pale where she stood so flushed before
As one a spirit overawes: —
Or might it rather be because
She felt the grave was at our feet,
And felt that we should no more meet
  Upon its hither side no more?

Was it a chance that made her turn
  Once toward the window passing by,   10
  One moment with a shrinking eye
Wherein her spirit seemed to yearn: —
Or did her soul then first discern
How long and rough the pathway is
That leads us home from vanities,
  And how it will be good to die?

There was a hill she had to pass;°
  And while I watched her up the hill
  She stooped one moment hurrying still,
But left a rose upon the grass: 20
Was it mere idleness: — or was
Herself with her own self at strife
Till while she chose the better life
  She felt this life has power to kill?

Perhaps she did it carelessly,
  Perhaps it was an idle thought;
  Or else it was the grace unbought,
A pledge to all eternity:
I know not yet how this may be;
But I shall know when face to face   30
In Paradise we find a place
  And love with love that endeth not.

From the Antique

It's a weary life, it is; she said: —°
  Doubly blank in a woman's lot:

I wish and I wish I were a man;
   Or, better than any being, were not:

Were nothing at all in all the world,
   Not a body and not a soul;
Not so much as a grain of dust
   Or drop of water from pole to pole.

Still the world would wag on the same,°
   Still the seasons go and come;   10
Blossoms bloom as in days of old,
   Cherries ripen and wild bees hum.

None would miss me in all the world,
   How much less would care or weep:
I should be nothing; while all the rest
   Would wake and weary and fall asleep.

Two Choices

She listened like a cushat dove°
   That listens to its mate alone;
She listened like a cushat dove
   That loves but only one.

Not fair as men would reckon fair,
   Nor noble as they count the line;
Only as graceful as a bough
   And tendrils of the vine;
Only as noble as sweet Eve
   Your ancestress and mine.   10

And downcast were her dovelike eyes,
   And downcast was her tender cheek,
Her pulses fluttered like a dove
   To hear him speak.

He chose what I had feared to choose—
   (Ah, which was wiser, I or he?)—
He chose a love-warm priceless heart,
   And I a cold bare dignity.

He chose a life like stainless spring
    That buds to summer's perfect glow;   20
I chose a tedious dignity
    As cold as cold as snow:
He chose a garden of delights
    Where still refreshing waters flow;
I chose a barren wilderness
    Whose buds died years ago.

Echo

Come to me in the silence of the night;
    Come in the speaking silence of a dream;
Come with soft rounded cheeks and eyes as bright
    As sunlight on a stream;
      Come back in tears,
O memory, hope, love of finished years.

Oh dream how sweet, too sweet, too bitter sweet,
    Whose wakening should have been in Paradise,
Where souls brimfull of love abide and meet;
    Where thirsting longing eyes   10
      Watch the slow door
That opening, letting in, lets out no more.

Yet come to me in dreams, that I may live
    My very life again though cold in death:
Come back to me in dreams, that I may give
    Pulse for pulse, breath for breath:
      Speak low, lean low,
As long ago, my love, how long ago!

The First Spring Day

I wonder if the sap is stirring yet,
If wintry birds are dreaming of a mate,
If frozen snowdrops feel as yet the sun

And crocus fires are kindling one by one:
    Sing, robin, sing;
I still am sore in doubt concerning Spring.

I wonder if the springtide of this year
Will bring another Spring both lost and dear;
If heart and spirit will find out their Spring,
Or if the world alone will bud and sing: 10
    Sing, hope, to me;
Sweet notes, my hope, soft notes for memory.

The sap will surely quicken soon or late,
The tardiest bird will twitter to a mate;
So Spring must dawn again with warmth and bloom,
Or in this world, or in the world to come:
    Sing, voice of Spring,
Till I too blossom and rejoice and sing.

My Dream

Hear now a curious dream I dreamed last night,
Each word whereof is weighed and sifted truth.°

    I stood beside Euphrates while it swelled
Like overflowing Jordan in its youth:°
It waxed and coloured sensibly to sight;
Till out of myriad pregnant waves there welled
Young crocodiles, a gaunt blunt-featured crew,
Fresh-hatched perhaps and daubed with birthday dew.
The rest if I should tell, I fear my friend
My closest friend would deem the facts untrue;   10
And therefore it were wisely left untold;
Yet if you will, why hear it to the end.

    Each crocodile was girt with massive gold
And polished stones that with their wearers grew:°
But one there was who waxed beyond the rest,
Wore kinglier girdle and a kingly crown,
Whilst crowns and orbs and sceptres starred his breast.
All gleamed compact and green with scale on scale,

But special burnishment adorned his mail
And special terror weighed upon his frown;   20
His punier brethren quaked before his tail,
Broad as a rafter, potent as a flail.
So he grew lord and master of his kin:
But who shall tell the tale of all their woes?
An execrable appetite arose,
He battened on them, crunched, and sucked them in.°
He knew no law, he feared no binding law,°
But ground them with inexorable jaw:
The luscious fat distilled upon his chin,
Exuded from his nostrils and his eyes,   30
While still like hungry death he fed his maw;
Till every minor crocodile being dead
And buried too, himself gorged to the full,
He slept with breath oppressed and unstrung claw.°
Oh marvel passing strange which next I saw:
In sleep he dwindled to the common size,
And all the empire faded from his coat.°
Then from far off a wingèd vessel came,°
Swift as a swallow, subtle as a flame:
I know not what it bore of freight or host,   40
But white it was as an avenging ghost.
It levelled strong Euphrates in its course;
Supreme yet weightless as an idle mote
It seemed to tame the waters without force
Till not a murmur swelled or billow beat:
Lo, as the purple shadow swept the sands,
The prudent crocodile rose on his feet
And shed appropriate tears and wrung his hands.°

    What can it mean? you ask. I answer not
For meaning, but myself must echo, What?   50
And tell it as I saw it on the spot.

Cobwebs

    It is a land with neither night nor day,°
        Nor heat nor cold, nor any wind, nor rain,
        Nor hills nor valleys; but one even plain

Stretches thro' long unbroken miles away:
While thro' the sluggish air a twilight grey
    Broodeth; no moons or seasons wax and wane,
    No ebb and flow is there along the main,
No bud-time no leaf-falling there for aye.
No ripple on the sea, no shifting sand,°
    No beat of wings to stir the stagnant space,   10
No pulse of life thro' all the loveless land
And loveless sea; no trace of days before,
    No guarded home, no toil-won restingplace
No future hope no fear for evermore.

May

I cannot tell you how it was;
But this I know: it came to pass
Upon a bright and breezy day
When May was young; ah, pleasant May!
As yet the poppies were not born
Between the blades of tender corn;
The last eggs had not hatched as yet,
Nor any bird foregone its mate.

    I cannot tell you what it was;
But this I know: it did but pass.   10
It passed away with sunny May,
With all sweet things it passed away,
And left me old, and cold, and grey.

An Afterthought

Oh lost garden Paradise: —
Were the roses redder there
Than they blossom otherwhere?
Was the night's delicious shade
More intensely star inlaid?
Who can tell what memories
Of lost beloved Paradise
Saddened Eve with sleepless eyes? —

Fair first mother lulled to rest
In a choicer garden nest,   10
Curtained with a softer shading
Than thy tenderest child is laid in,
Was the sundawn brighter far
Than our daily sundawns are?
Was that love, first love of all
Warmer, deeper, better worth
Than has warmed poor hearts of earth
Since the utter ruinous fall? —

Ah supremely happy once,
Ah supremely broken hearted   20
When her tender feet departed
From the accustomed paths of peace:
Catching Angel orisons
For the last last time of all,
Shedding tears that would not cease
For the bitter bitter fall.

Yet the accustomed hand for leading,
Yet the accustomed heart for love;°
Sure she kept one part of Eden
Angels could not strip her of.   30
Sure the fiery messenger
Kindling for his outraged Lord,
Willing with the perfect Will,°
Yet rejoiced the flaming sword°
Chastening sore but sparing still
Shut her treasure out with her.

What became of Paradise?
Did the cedars droop at all
(Springtide hastening to the fall)
Missing the beloved hand—   40
Or did their green perfection stand
Unmoved beneath the perfect skies? —°
Paradise was rapt on high,°
It lies before the gate of Heaven: —°
Eve now slumbers there forgiven,
Slumbers Rachel comforted,°

Slumber all the blessed dead
Of days and months and years gone by,
A solemn swelling company.

They wait for us beneath the trees   50
Of Paradise that lap of ease:
They wait for us, till God shall please.

Oh come the day of death, that day
Of rest which cannot pass away:
When the last work is wrought, the last
Pang of pain is felt and past
And the blessed door made fast.°

May—

Sweet Life is dead. —°
                            Not so:
   I meet him day by day,
Where bluest fountains flow
And trees are white as snow
   For it is time of May.
Even now from long ago
   He will not say me nay;°
   He is most fair to see;
And if I wander forth, I know
   He wanders forth with me.°   10

But Life is dead to me;
The worn-out year was failing
West winds took up a wailing
   To watch his funeral:
   Bare poplars shivered tall
And lank vines stretched to see;
   'Twixt him and me a wall
Was frozen of earth like stone
With brambles overgrown;
   Chill darkness wrapped him like a pall   20
And I am left alone.

How can you call him dead?
   He buds out everywhere:

In every hedgerow rank,°
On every mossgrown bank
   I find him here and there.
He crowns my willing head
With may flowers white and red,
He rears my tender heartsease bed;°
   He makes my branch to bud and bear,   30
And blossoms where I tread.°

Shut Out

The door was shut. I looked between
   Its iron bars; and saw it lie,
   My garden, mine, beneath the sky,
Pied with all flowers bedewed and green:

From bough to bough the song-birds crossed,
   From flower to flower the moths and bees;
   With all its nests and stately trees
It had been mine, and it was lost.

A shadowless spirit kept the gate,
   Blank and unchanging like the grave.   10
   I peering through said: 'Let me have
Some buds to cheer my outcast state.'

He answered not. 'Or give me, then,
   But one small twig from shrub or tree;
   And bid my home remember me
Until I come to it again.'

The spirit was silent; but he took
   Mortar and stone to build a wall;
   He left no loophole great or small
Through which my straining eyes might look: 20

So now I sit here quite alone
   Blinded with tears; nor grieve for that,
   For nought is left worth looking at
Since my delightful land is gone.

A violet bed is budding near,
　　Wherein a lark has made her nest:
　　And good they are, but not the best;
And dear they are, but not so dear.°

By the Water

There are rivers lapsing down
　　Lily laden to the sea;
Every lily is a boat
　　For bees, one, two, or three:
I wish there were a fairy boat
　　For you, my friend, and me.

And if there were a fairy boat
　　And if the river bore us
We should not care for all the past
　　Nor all that lies before us,　　　　　　　　　10
Not for the hopes that buoyed us once
　　Nor for the fears that tore us.

We would rock upon the river,
　　Scarcely floating by,
Rocking rocking like the lilies
　　You, my friend, and I:
Rocking like the stately lilies
　　Beneath the statelier sky.

But, ah, where is that river
　　Whose hyacinth banks descend　　　　　　　20
Down to the sweeter lilies
　　Till soft their shadows blend
Into a watery twilight? —
　　And, ah, where is my friend? —

A Chilly Night

I rose at the dead of night
　　And went to the lattice alone
To look for my Mother's ghost
　　Where the ghostly moonlight shone.

My friends had failed one by one,
    Middleaged, young, and old,
Till the ghosts were warmer to me
    Than my friends that had grown cold.

I looked and I saw the ghosts
    Dotting plain and mound: 10
They stood in the blank moonlight
    But no shadow lay on the ground;
They spoke without a voice
    And they leapt without a sound.

I called: 'O my Mother dear,'—
    I sobbed: 'O my Mother kind,
Make a lonely bed for me°
    And shelter it from the wind:

'Tell the others not to come
    To see me night or day;   20
But I need not tell my friends
    To be sure to keep away.'

My Mother raised her eyes,
    They were blank and could not see;
Yet they held me with their stare
    While they seemed to look at me.

She opened her mouth and spoke,
    I could not hear a word
While my flesh crept on my bones
    And every hair was stirred.   30

She knew that I could not hear
    The message that she told
Whether I had long to wait
    Or soon should sleep in the mould:
I saw her toss her shadowless hair
    And wring her hands in the cold.

I strained to catch her words
    And she strained to make me hear,
But never a sound of words
    Fell on my straining ear.   40

From midnight to the cockcrow
　　I kept my watch in pain
While the subtle ghosts grew subtler°
　　In the sad night on the wane.

From midnight to the cockcrow
　　I watched till all were gone,
Some to sleep in the shifting sea
　　And some under turf and stone:
Living had failed and dead had failed
　　And I was indeed alone.　　　　　　50

Amen

It is over. What is over?
　　Nay, how much is over truly!—
Harvest days we toiled to sow for;
　　Now the sheaves are gathered newly,
　　Now the wheat is garnered duly.

It is finished. What is finished?
　　Much is finished known or unknown:
Lives are finished; time diminished;
　　Was the fallow field left unsown?
　　Will these buds be always unblown?　　　10

It suffices. What suffices?
　　All suffices reckoned rightly:
Spring shall bloom where now the ice is,
　　Roses make the bramble sightly,
　　And the quickening sun shine brightly,
　　And the latter wind blow lightly,
And my garden teem with spices.°

A Bed of Forget-Me-Nots

Is love so prone to change and rot
We are fain to rear forget-me-not
By measure in a garden plot?—

I love its growth at large and free
By untrod path and unlopped tree,
Or nodding by the unpruned hedge,
Or on the water's dangerous edge
Where flags and meadowsweet blow rank°
With rushes on the quaking bank.

Love is not taught in learning's school,   10
Love is not parcelled out by rule;
Hath curb or call an answer got?—
So free must be forget-me-not.
Give me the flame no dampness dulls,
The passion of the instinctive pulse,
Love steadfast as a fixèd star,°
Tender as doves with nestlings are,
More large than time, more strong than death:
This all creation travails of—
She groans not for a passing breath—°   20
This is forget-me-not and love.

'Look on This Picture and on This'

I wish we once were wedded,—then I must be true;
You should hold my will in yours to do or to undo:
But now I hate myself Eva when I look at you.°

You have seen her hazel eyes, her warm dark skin,
Dark hair—but oh those hazel eyes a devil is dancing in:—
You my saint lead up to heaven she lures down to sin.

Listen Eva I repent, indeed I do my love:
How should I choose a peacock and leave and grieve a dove?—
If I could turn my back on her and follow you above.

No it's not her beauty bloomed like an autumn peach,   10
Not her pomp of beauty too high for me to reach;
It's her eyes, her witching manner—ah the lore they teach.

You are winning, well I know it, who should know but I?
You constrain me, I must yield or else must hasten by:—
But she, she fascinates me, I can neither fight nor fly.

She's so redundant, stately;—in truth now have you seen°
Ever anywhere such beauty, such a stature, such a mien?
She may be queen of devils but she's every inch a queen.

If you sing to me, I hear her subtler sweeter still
Whispering in each tender cadence strangely sweet to fill   20
All that lacks in music all my soul and sense and will.

If you dance, tho' mine eyes follow where my hand I gave
I only see her presence like a sunny wave
I only feel her presence like a wind too strong to rave.

If we talk: I love you, do you love me again?—
Tho' your lips speak it's her voice I flush to hear so plain
Say: Love you? yes I love you, love can neither change nor wane.

But, you ask, why struggle? I have given you up:
Take again your pledges, snap the cord and break the cup:
Feast you with your temptation for I in heaven will sup.—   30

Can I bear to think upon you strong to break not bend,
Pale with inner intense passion silent to the end,
Bear to leave you, bear to grieve you, O my dove my friend?—

One short pang and you would rise a light in heaven
While we grovelled in the darkness mean and unforgiven
Tho' our cup of love brimmed sevenfold crowns of love were seven.

What shall I choose, what can I choose for you and her and me;
With you the haven of rest, with her the tossing miry sea;
Time's love with her, or choose with you love's all eternity.—

Nay, you answer coldly yet with a quivering voice: 40
That is over, doubt and struggle, we have sealed our choice;
Leave me to my contentment vivid with fresh hopes and joys.

Listening so, I hide mine eyes and fancy years to come:
You cherished in another home with no cares burdensome;
You straitened in a windingsheet pulseless at peace and dumb.

So I fancy—The new love has driven the old away;
She has found a dearer shelter a dearer stronger stay;
Perhaps now she would thank me for the freedom of that day.

Open house and heart barred to me alone the door;
Children bound to meet her, babies crow before;—   50
Blessed wife and blessed mother whom I may see no more.

Or I fancy—In the grave her comely body lies;
She is 'tiring for the Bridegroom till the morning star shall rise,
Then to shine a glory in the nuptials of the skies.

No more yearning tenderness, no more pale regret,
She will not look for me when the marriage guests are set,
She joys with joy eternal as we had never met.

I would that one of us were dead, were gone no more to meet,
Or she and I were dead together stretched here at your feet,
That she and I were strained together in one windingsheet: 60

Hidden away from all the world upon this bitter morn;
Hidden from all the scornful world, from all your keener scorn;
Secure and secret in the dark as blessed babe unborn.

A pitiless fiend is in your eyes to tempt me and to taunt:
If you were dead I verily believe that you would haunt
The home you loved, the man you loved, you said you loved—avaunt.

Why do you face me with those eyes so calm they drive me mad,
Too proud to droop before me and own that you are sad?
Why have you a lofty angel made me mean and cursed and bad?

How have you the heart to face me with that passion in your stare   70
Deathly silent? weep before me, rave at me in your despair—
If you keep patience wings will spring and a halo from your hair.

Yet what matters—yea what matters? your frenzy can but mock:
You do not hold my heart's life key to lock and to unlock,
The door will not unclose to you tho' long you wait and knock.

Have I wronged you? nay not I nor she in deed or will:
You it is alone that mingle the venomous cup and fill;
Why are you so little lovely that I cannot love you still?—

One pulse, one tone, one ringlet of her's outweighs the whole
Of you, your puny graces puny body puny soul: 80
You but a taste of sweetness, she an overrunning bowl.

Did I make you, that you blame me because you are not best?
Not so, be wise, take patience, turn away and be at rest:
Shall I not know her lovelier who is far loveliest? —

See now how proud you are, like us after all, no saint;
Not so upright but that you are bowed with the old bent;
White at white-heat, tainted with the devil's special taint.°

Sit you still and wring the cup drop after loathsome drop:
You have let loose a torrent it is not you can stop;
You have sowed a noisome field-ful, now reap the stinging crop.   90

Did you think to sit in safety, to watch me torn and tost
Struggling like a mad dog, watch her tempting doubly lost?
Howl you, you wretched woman, for your flimsy hopes are crost.

Be still, tho' you may writhe you shall hear the branding truth:
You who thought to sit in judgment on our souls forsooth,
To sit in frigid judgment on our ripe luxuriant youth.

Did I love you? never from the first cold day to this;
You are not sufficient for my aim of life, my bliss;
You are not sufficient, but I found the one that is.

She wine of love that warms me from this life's mortal chill: 100
Drunk with love I drink again, athirst I drink my fill;
Lapped in love I care not doth it make alive or kill.

Then did I never love you? — ah the sting struck home at last;
You are drooping, fainting, dying — the worst of death is past;
A light is on your face from the nearing heaven forecast.

Never? — yes I loved you then; I loved: the word still charms: —
For the first time last time lie here in my heart my arms,
For the first last time as if I shielded you from harms.

I trampled you, poor dove, to death; you clung to me, I spurned;
I taunted you, I tortured you, while you sat still and yearned: —   110
Oh lesson taught in anguish but in double anguish learned.

For after all I loved you, loved you then, I love you yet.
Listen love I love you: see, the seal of truth is set
On my face in tears — you cannot see? then feel them wet.

Pause at heaven's dear gate, look back, one moment back to grieve;
You go home thro' death to life; but I, I still must live:
On the threshold of heaven's love, O love can you forgive?—

Fully freely fondly, with heart truth above an oath,
With eager utter pardon given unasked and nothing loth,
Heaping coals of fire upon our heads forgiving both.°   120

One word more—not one: one look more—too late too late:—
Lapped in love she sleeps who was lashed with scorn and hate;
Nestling in the lap of love the dove has found a mate.

Night has come, the night of rest; day will come, that day:
To her glad dawn of glory kindled from the deathless ray;
To us a searching fire and strict balances to weigh.

The tearless tender eyes are closed, the tender lips are dumb:
I shall not see or hear them more until that day shall come:°
Then they must speak, what will they say—what then will be the sum?—

Shall we stand upon the left and she upon the right—   130
We smirched with endless death and shame, she glorified in white:
Will she sound our accusation in intolerable light?

Or open-armed to us in love—type of another Love—
As she forgave us once below will she forgive above,
Enthroned to all eternity our sister-friend and dove?—

The Lowest Room

Like flowers sequestered from the sun
    And wind of summer, day by day
I dwindled paler, whilst my hair
      Showed the first tinge of grey.

'Oh what is life, that we should live?
    Or what is death, that we must die?
A bursting bubble is our life:
      I also, what am I?'

'What is your grief? now tell me, sweet,
    That I may grieve,' my sister said;   10

And stayed a white embroidering hand
    And raised a golden head:

Her tresses showed a richer mass,
   Her eyes looked softer than my own,
Her figure had a statelier height,
    Her voice a tenderer tone.

'Some must be second and not first;
   All cannot be the first of all:
Is not this, too, but vanity?
    I stumble like to fall.   20

'So yesterday I read the acts
   Of Hector and each clangorous king
With wrathful great Aeacides:—°
    Old Homer leaves a sting.'

The comely face looked up again,
   The deft hand lingered on the thread:
'Sweet, tell me what is Homer's sting,
    Old Homer's sting?' she said.

'He stirs my sluggish pulse like wine,
   He melts me like the wind of spice,   30
Strong as strong Ajax' red right hand,°
    And grand like Juno's eyes.°

'I cannot melt the sons of men,
   I cannot fire and tempest-toss:—
Besides, those days were golden days,
    Whilst these are days of dross.'

She laughed a feminine low laugh,
   Yet did not stay her dexterous hand:
'Now tell me of those days,' she said,
    'When time ran golden sand.'   40

'Then men were men of might and right,
   Sheer might, at least, and weighty swords;
Then men in open blood and fire
    Bore witness to their words,

'Crest-rearing kings with whistling spears;
     But if these shivered in the shock°
They wrenched up hundred-rooted trees,
     Or hurled the effacing rock.°

'Then hand to hand, then foot to foot,
     Stern to the death-grip grappling then,   50
Who ever thought of gunpowder
     Amongst these men of men?

'They knew whose hand struck home the death,
     They knew who broke but would not bend,
Could venerate an equal foe
     And scorn a laggard friend.

'Calm in the utmost stress of doom,
     Devout toward adverse powers above,
They hated with intenser hate
     And loved with fuller love.   60

'Then heavenly beauty could allay
     As heavenly beauty stirred the strife:
By them a slave was worshipped more
     Than is by us a wife.'

She laughed again, my sister laughed;
     Made answer o'er the laboured cloth:
'I rather would be one of us
     Than wife, or slave, or both.'

'Oh better then be slave or wife
     Than fritter now blank life away: 70
Then night had holiness of night,
     And day was sacred day.

'The princess laboured at her loom,
     Mistress and handmaiden alike;
Beneath their needles grew the field
     With warriors armed to strike.

'Or, look again, dim Dian's face°
     Gleamed perfect through the attendant night;

Were such not better than those holes
    Amid that waste of white?   80

'A shame it is, our aimless life;
   I rather from my heart would feed
From silver dish in gilded stall
    With wheat and wine the steed—

'The faithful steed that bore my lord
   In safety through the hostile land,
The faithful steed that arched his neck
    To fondle with my hand.'°

Her needle erred; a moment's pause,
   A moment's patience, all was well.   90
Then she: 'But just suppose the horse,
    Suppose the rider fell?

'Then captive in an alien house,
   Hungering on exile's bitter bread,—
They happy, they who won the lot
    Of sacrifice,' she said.

Speaking she faltered, while her look
   Showed forth her passion like a glass:
With hand suspended, kindling eye,
    Flushed cheek, how fair she was!   100

'Ah well, be those the days of dross;
   This, if you will, the age of gold:
Yet had those days a spark of warmth,
    While these are somewhat cold—

'Are somewhat mean and cold and slow,
   Are stunted from heroic growth:
We gain but little when we prove
    The worthlessness of both.'

'But life is in our hands,' she said:
   'In our own hands for gain or loss: 110
Shall not the Sevenfold Sacred Fire
    Suffice to purge our dross?'°

'Too short a century of dreams,
   One day of work sufficient length:
Why should not you, why should not I
    Attain heroic strength?

'Our life is given us as a blank;
   Ourselves must make it blest or curst:
Who dooms me I shall only be
    The second, not the first?   120

'Learn from old Homer, if you will,
   Such wisdom as his books have said:
In one the acts of Ajax shine,
    In one of Diomed.

'Honoured all heroes whose high deeds
   Through life, through death, enlarge their span:
Only Achilles in his rage
    And sloth is less than man.'

'Achilles only less than man?
   He less than man who, half a god,   130
Discomfited all Greece with rest,
    Cowed Ilion with a nod?°

'He offered vengeance, lifelong grief°
   To one dear ghost, uncounted price:
Beasts, Trojans, adverse gods, himself,
    Heaped up the sacrifice.

'Self-immolated to his friend,
   Shrined in world's wonder, Homer's page,
Is this the man, the less than men
    Of this degenerate age?'   140

'Gross from his acorns, tusky boar
   Does memorable acts like his;
So for her snared offended young
    Bleeds the swart lioness.'

But here she paused; our eyes had met,
   And I was whitening with the jeer;

She rose; 'I went too far,' she said;
    Spoke low; 'Forgive me, dear.

'To me our days seem pleasant days,
    Our home a haven of pure content;   150
Forgive me if I said too much,
    So much more than I meant.

'Homer, though greater than his gods,
    With rough-hewn virtues was sufficed
And rough-hewn men: but what are such
    To us who learn of Christ?'

The much-moved pathos of her voice,
    Her almost tearful eyes, her cheek
Grown pale, confessed the strength of love
    Which only made her speak: 160

For mild she was, of few soft words,
    Most gentle, easy to be led,
Content to listen when I spoke
    And reverence what I said;

I elder sister by six years;
    Not half so glad, or wise, or good:
Her words rebuked my secret self
    And shamed me where I stood.

She never guessed her words reproved
    A silent envy nursed within,   170
A selfish, souring discontent
    Pride-born, the devil's sin.

I smiled, half bitter, half in jest:
    'The wisest man of all the wise
Left for his summary of life
    "Vanity of vanities."°

'Beneath the sun there's nothing new:
    Men flow, men ebb, mankind flows on:
If I am wearied of my life,
    Why so was Solomon.   180

'Vanity of vanities he preached
   Of all he found, of all he sought:
Vanity of vanities, the gist
    Of all the words he taught.

'This in the wisdom of the world,
   In Homer's page, in all, we find:
As the sea is not filled, so yearns
    Man's universal mind.

'This Homer felt, who gave his men
   With glory but a transient state: 190
His very Jove could not reverse
    Irrevocable fate.

'Uncertain all their lot save this—
   Who wins must lose, who lives must die:
All trodden out into the dark
    Alike, all vanity.'

She scarcely answered when I paused
   But rather to herself said: 'One
Is here,' low-voiced and loving, 'Yea,
    Greater than Solomon.'°   200

So both were silent, she and I:
   She laid her work aside, and went
Into the garden-walks, like spring,
    All gracious with content;

A little graver than her wont,
   Because her words had fretted me;
Not warbling quite her merriest tune
    Bird-like from tree to tree.

I chose a book to read and dream:
   Yet half the while with furtive eyes   210
Marked how she made her choice of flowers
    Intuitively wise,

And ranged them with instinctive taste
   Which all my books had failed to teach;

Fresh rose herself, and daintier
    Than blossom of the peach.

By birthright higher than myself,
    Though nestling of the self-same nest:
No fault of hers, no fault of mine,
    But stubborn to digest.   220

I watched her, till my book unmarked
    Slid noiseless to the velvet floor;
Till all the opulent summer-world
    Looked poorer than before.

Just then her busy fingers ceased,
    Her fluttered colour went and came:
I knew whose step was on the walk,
    Whose voice would name her name.

*   *   *

Well, twenty years have passed since then:
    My sister now, a stately wife   230
Still fair, looks back in peace and sees
    The longer half of life—

The longer half of prosperous life,
    With little grief, or fear, or fret:
She, loved and loving long ago,
    Is loved and loving yet.

A husband honourable, brave,
    Is her main wealth in all the world:
And next to him one like herself,
    One daughter golden-curled;   240

Fair image of her own fair youth,
    As beautiful and as serene,
With almost such another love
    As her own love has been.

Yet, though of world-wide charity,
    And in her home most tender dove,

Her treasure and her heart are stored
    In the home-land of love:

She thrives, God's blessed husbandry;°
    Most like a vine which full of fruit   250
Doth cling and lean and climb toward heaven,
    While earth still binds its root.

I sit and watch my sister's face:
    How little altered since the hours
When she, a kind, light-hearted girl,
    Gathered her garden flowers;

Her song just mellowed by regret
    For having teased me with her talk;
Then all-forgetful as she heard
    One step upon the walk.   260

While I? I sat alone and watched;
    My lot in life, to live alone
In mine own world of interests,
    Much felt but little shown.

Not to be first: how hard to learn
    That lifelong lesson of the past;
Line graven on line and stroke on stroke;
    But, thank God, learned at last.

So now in patience I possess
    My soul year after tedious year,°   270
Content to take the lowest place,
    The place assigned me here.

Yet sometimes, when I feel my strength
    Most weak, and life most burdensome,
I lift mine eyes up to the hills
    From whence my help shall come:

Yea, sometimes still I lift my heart
    To the Archangelic trumpet-burst,
When all deep secrets shall be shown,
    And many last be first.°   280

A Triad

SONNET

Three sang of love together: one with lips
   Crimson, with cheeks and bosom in a glow,
Flushed to the yellow hair and finger tips;
    And one there sang who soft and smooth as snow
    Bloomed like a tinted hyacinth at a show;
And one was blue with famine after love,
    Who like a harpstring snapped rang harsh and low
The burden of what those were singing of.
One shamed herself in love; one temperately
    Grew gross in soulless love, a sluggish wife;   10
One famished died for love. Thus two of three
    Took death for love and won him after strife;
One droned in sweetness like a fattened bee:
    All on the threshold, yet all short of life.

Love from the North

I had a love in soft south land,
   Beloved through April far in May;
He waited on my lightest breath,
   And never dared to say me nay.

He saddened if my cheer was sad,
   But gay he grew if I was gay;
We never differed on a hair,
   My yes his yes, my nay his nay.

The wedding hour was come, the aisles
   Were flushed with sun and flowers that day;   10
I pacing balanced in my thoughts:
   'It's quite too late to think of nay.' —

My bridegroom answered in his turn,
   Myself had almost answered 'yea:'
When through the flashing nave I heard
   A struggle and resounding 'nay'.

Bridemaids and bridegroom shrank in fear,
   But I stood high who stood at bay:
'And if I answer yea, fair Sir,
   What man art thou to bar with nay?'   20

He was a strong man from the north,
   Light-locked, with eyes of dangerous gray:
'Put yea by for another time
   In which I will not say thee nay.'

He took me in his strong white arms,
   He bore me on his horse away
O'er crag, morass, and hairbreadth pass,
   But never asked me yea or nay.

He made me fast with book and bell,°
   With links of love he makes me stay;   30
Till now I've neither heart nor power
   Nor will nor wish to say him nay.

In an Artist's Studio

One face looks out from all his canvasses,
   One selfsame figure sits or walks or leans;
   We found her hidden just behind those screens,
That mirror gave back all her loveliness.
A queen in opal or in ruby dress,
   A nameless girl in freshest summer greens,
   A saint, an angel; — every canvass means
The same one meaning, neither more nor less.
He feeds upon her face by day and night,
   And she with true kind eyes looks back on him   10
Fair as the moon and joyful as the light:
   Not wan with waiting, not with sorrow dim;
Not as she is, but was when hope shone bright;
   Not as she is, but as she fills his dream.

A Better Resurrection

   I have no wit, no words, no tears;°
     My heart within me like a stone

Is numbed too much for hopes or fears;
  Look right, look left, I dwell alone;
I lift mine eyes, but dimmed with grief
  No everlasting hills I see;°
My life is in the falling leaf:°
    O Jesus, quicken me.

My life is like a faded leaf,
  My harvest dwindled to a husk;   10
Truly my life is void and brief
  And tedious in the barren dusk;
My life is like a frozen thing,
  No bud nor greenness can I see:
Yet rise it shall—the sap of Spring;
    O Jesus, rise in me.

My life is like a broken bowl,°
  A broken bowl that cannot hold
One drop of water for my soul
  Or cordial in the searching cold;°   20
Cast in the fire the perished thing,
  Melt and remould it, till it be
A royal cup for Him my King:
    O Jesus, drink of me.

'The Heart Knoweth Its Own Bitterness'

When all the over-work of life
  Is finished once, and fast asleep°
We swerve no more beneath the knife
  But taste that silence cool and deep;
Forgetful of the highways rough,
  Forgetful of the thorny scourge,
  Forgetful of the tossing surge,
Then shall we find it is enough?—

How can we say 'enough' on earth;
  'Enough' with such a craving heart: 10
I have not found it since my birth
  But still have bartered part for part.°

I have not held and hugged the whole,
   But paid the old to gain the new;
   Much have I paid, yet much is due,
Till I am beggared sense and soul.

I used to labour, used to strive
   For pleasure with a restless will:
Now if I save my soul alive
   All else what matters, good or ill?   20
I used to dream alone, to plan
   Unspoken hopes and days to come:—
   Of all my past this is the sum:
I will not lean on child of man.

To give, to give, not to receive,
   I long to pour myself, my soul;
Not to keep back or count or leave
   But king with king to give the whole:°
I long for one to stir my deep—
   I have had enough of help and gift—   30
   I long for one to search and sift
Myself, to take myself and keep.

You scratch my surface with your pin,
   You stroke me smooth with hushing breath;—
Nay pierce, nay probe, nay dig within,
   Probe my quick core and sound my depth.°
You call me with a puny call,
   You talk, you smile, you nothing do;
   How should I spend my heart on you,
My heart that so outweighs you all?   40

Your vessels are by much too strait;°
   Were I to pour you could not hold,
Bear with me: I must bear to wait
   A fountain sealed thro' heat and cold.°
Bear with me days or months or years;
   Deep must call deep until the end
   When friend shall no more envy friend
Nor vex his friend at unawares.

Not in this world of hope deferred,
   This world of perishable stuff;—   50

Eye hath not seen, nor ear hath heard,
  Nor heart conceived that full 'enough':°
Here moans the separating sea,
  Here harvests fail, here breaks the heart;
  There God shall join and no man part,°
I full of Christ and Christ of me.

In the Round Tower at Jhansi, June 8, 1857

A hundred, a thousand to one; even so;
  Not a hope in the world remained:
The swarming howling wretches below°
  Gained and gained and gained.

Skene looked at his pale young wife:—
  'Is the time come?'—'The time is come!'—
Young, strong, and so full of life:
  The agony struck them dumb.

Close his arm about her now,
  Close her cheek to his,   10
Close the pistol to her brow—
  God forgive them this!

'Will it hurt much?'—'No, mine own:
  I wish I could bear the pang for both.'
'I wish I could bear the pang alone:
  Courage, dear, I am not loth.'

Kiss and kiss: 'It is not pain
  Thus to kiss and die.
One kiss more.'—'And yet one again.'—
  'Good bye.'—'Good bye.'   20

'Reflection'

Gazing thro' her chamber window
  Sits my soul's dear soul;
Looking northward, looking southward,
  Looking to the goal,
  Looking back without control.—

I have strewn thy path, beloved,
   With plumed meadowsweet,
Iris and pale perfumed lilies,
   Roses most complete:
     Wherefore pause on listless feet? —   10

But she sits and never answers;
   Gazing gazing still
On swift fountain, shadowed valley,
   Cedared sunlit hill:
     Who can guess or read her will?

Who can guess or read the spirit
   Shrined within her eyes,
Part a longing, part a languor,
   Part a mere surprize,
     While slow mists do rise and rise? —   20

Is it love she looks and longs for;
   Is it rest or peace;
Is it slumber self-forgetful
   In its utter ease;
     Is it one or all of these?

So she sits and doth not answer
   With her dreaming eyes,
With her languid look delicious
   Almost Paradise,
     Less than happy, over wise.   30

Answer me, O self-forgetful—
   Or of what beside? —
Is it day dream of a maiden,
   Vision of a bride,
     Is it knowledge, love, or pride?

Cold she sits thro' all my kindling,
   Deaf to all I pray:
I have wasted might and wisdom,
   Wasted night and day:
     Deaf she dreams to all I say.   40

Now if I could guess her secret
    Were it worth the guess? —
Time is lessening, hope is lessening,
    Love grows less and less:
    What care I for *no* or *yes*? —

I will give her stately burial,
    Tho', when she lies dead:
For dear memory of the past time,
    Of her royal head,
    Of the much I strove and said.   50

I will give her stately burial,
    Willow branches bent;
Have her carved in alabaster,
    As she dreamed and leant
    While I wondered what she meant.

A Coast-Nightmare

I have a friend in ghostland — °
    Early found, ah me, how early lost! —
Blood-red seaweeds drip along that coastland
    By the strong sea wrenched and tossed.
In every creek there slopes a dead man's islet,
    And such an one in every bay;
All unripened in the unended twilight: °
    For there comes neither night nor day.

Unripe harvest there hath none to reap it
    From the watery misty place;   10
Unripe vineyard there hath none to keep it
    In unprofitable space.
Living flocks and herds are nowhere found there;
    Only ghosts in flocks and shoals:
Indistinguished hazy ghosts surround there
    Meteors whirling on their poles;
Indistinguished hazy ghosts abound there;
    Troops, yea swarms, of dead men's souls. —

Have they towns to live in? —
    They have towers and towns from sea to sea;   20

Of each town the gates are seven;
   Of one of these each ghost is free.
Civilians, soldiers, seamen,
   Of one town each ghost is free:
They are ghastly men those ghostly freemen:
   Such a sight may you not see.—

How know you that your lover
   Of death's tideless waters stoops to drink?—°
Me by night doth mouldy darkness cover,
   It makes me quake to think: 30
All night long I feel his presence hover
   Thro' the darkness black as ink.

Without a voice he tells me
   The wordless secrets of death's deep:
If I sleep, his trumpet voice compels me
   To stalk forth in my sleep:
If I wake, he hunts me like a nightmare;°
   I feel my hair stand up, my body creep:
Without light I see a blasting sight there,
   See a secret I must keep.   40

Another Spring

If I might see another Spring
   I'd not plant summer flowers and wait:
I'd have my crocuses at once,
My leafless pink mezereons,°
   My chill-veined snowdrops, choicer yet
   My white or azure violet,
Leaf-nested primrose; anything
   To blow at once not late.

If I might see another Spring
   I'd listen to the daylight birds   10
That build their nests and pair and sing,
Nor wait for mateless nightingale;
   I'd listen to the lusty herds,
   The ewes with lambs as white as snow,

I'd find out music in the hail
   And all the winds that blow.

If I might see another Spring—
   Oh stinging comment on my past
That all my past results in 'if'—
   If I might see another Spring   20
I'd laugh to-day, to-day is brief;
I would not wait for anything:
   I'd use to-day that cannot last,
   Be glad to-day and sing.

'For One Sake'

One passed me like a flash of lightning by
   To ring clear bells of heaven beyond the stars.°
   Then said I: Wars and rumours of your wars°
Are dull with din of what and where and why;
My heart is where these troubles draw not nigh:
   Let me alone till heaven shall burst its bars,
   Break up its fountains, roll its flashing cars°
Earthwards with fire to test and purify.°
Let me alone tonight, and one night more
   Of which I shall not count the eventide;   10
Its morrow will not be as days before;
Let me alone to dream, perhaps to weep;
   To dream of her the imperishable bride,
Dream while I wake and dream on while I sleep.

A Birthday

My heart is like a singing bird
   Whose nest is in a watered shoot;
My heart is like an apple tree
   Whose boughs are bent with thickset fruit;
My heart is like a rainbow shell
   That paddles in a halcyon sea;°
My heart is gladder than all these
   Because my love is come to me.

Raise me a dais of silk and down;
   Hang it with vair and purple dyes;°   10
Carve it in doves, and pomegranates,
   And peacocks with a hundred eyes;
Work it in gold and silver grapes,
   In leaves, and silver fleurs-de-lys;
Because the birthday of my life
   Is come, my love is come to me.

An Apple Gathering

I plucked pink blossoms from mine apple tree
   And wore them all that evening in my hair:
Then in due season when I went to see
   I found no apples there.

With dangling basket all along the grass
   As I had come I went the selfsame track:
My neighbours mocked me while they saw me pass
   So empty-handed back.

Lilian and Lilias smiled in trudging by,°
   Their heaped-up basket teazed me like a jeer;   10
Sweet-voiced they sang beneath the sunset sky,
   Their mother's home was near.

Plump Gertrude passed me with her basket full,
   A stronger hand than hers helped it along;
A voice talked with her through the shadows cool
   More sweet to me than song.

Ah Willie, Willie, was my love less worth
   Than apples with their green leaves piled above?
I counted rosiest apples on the earth
   Of far less worth than love.   20

So once it was with me you stooped to talk
   Laughing and listening in this very lane:
To think that by this way we used to walk
   We shall not walk again!

I let my neighbours pass me, ones and twos
    And groups; the latest said the night grew chill,
And hastened: but I loitered, while the dews°
    Fell fast I loitered still.

My Secret

I tell my secret? No indeed, not I:
Perhaps some day, who knows?
But not to-day; it froze, and blows, and snows,
And you're too curious: fie!
You want to hear it? well:
Only, my secret's mine, and I won't tell.

    Or, after all, perhaps there's none:
Suppose there is no secret after all,
But only just my fun.
To-day's a nipping day, a biting day;   10
In which one wants a shawl,
A veil, a cloak, and other wraps:
I cannot ope to every one who taps,
And let the draughts come whistling through my hall;
Come bounding and surrounding me,
Come buffeting, astounding me,
Nipping and clipping through my wraps and all.
I wear my mask for warmth: who ever shows
His nose to Russian snows
To be pecked at by every wind that blows?   20
You would not peck? I thank you for good will,
Believe, but leave that truth untested still.

    Spring's an expansive time: yet I don't trust
March with its peck of dust,
Nor April with its rainbow-crowned brief showers,
Nor even May, whose flowers
One frost may wither through the sunless hours.

    Perhaps some languid summer day,
When drowsy birds sing less and less,
And golden fruit is ripening to excess,   30
If there's not too much sun nor too much cloud,

And the warm wind is neither still nor loud,
Perhaps my secret I may say,
Or you may guess.

Autumn

I dwell alone—I dwell alone, alone,
Whilst full my river flows down to the sea,
   Gilded with flashing boats
    That bring no friend to me:
O love-songs, gurgling from a hundred throats,
   O love-pangs, let me be.

Fair fall the freighted boats which gold and stone
   And spices bear to sea:
Slim, gleaming maidens swell their mellow notes,
   Love-promising, entreating —   10
    Ah! sweet, but fleeting —
  Beneath the shivering, snow-white sails.
  Hush! the wind flags and fails —
Hush! they will lie becalmed in sight of strand —
  Sight of my strand, where I do dwell alone;
Their songs wake singing echoes in my land —
  They cannot hear me moan.

One latest, solitary swallow flies
   Across the sea, rough autumn-tempest tost,
   Poor bird, shall it be lost?   20
Dropped down into this uncongenial sea,
    With no kind eyes
    To watch it while it dies,
     Unguessed, uncared for, free:
     Set free at last,
     The short pang past,
In sleep, in death, in dreamless sleep locked fast.°

Mine avenue is all a growth of oaks,
   Some rent by thunder strokes,
Some rustling leaves and acorns in the breeze;   30
   Fair fall my fertile trees,
That rear their goodly heads, and live at ease.

A spider's web blocks all mine avenue;
   He catches down and foolish painted flies,
     That spider wary and wise.
Each morn it hangs a rainbow strung with dew°
   Betwixt boughs green with sap,
    So fair, few creatures guess it is a trap:
     I will not mar the web,
Though sad I am to see the small lives ebb.   40

It shakes—my trees shake—for a wind is roused
     In cavern where it housed:
     Each white and quivering sail,
     Of boats among the water leaves
Hollows and strains in the full-throated gale:
     Each maiden sings again—
Each languid maiden, whom the calm
Had lulled to sleep with rest and spice and balm.
    Miles down my river to the sea
      They float and wane,   50
    Long miles away from me.

  Perhaps they say: 'She grieves,
    Uplifted, like a beacon, on her tower.'
    Perhaps they say: 'One hour
More, and we dance among the golden sheaves.'
    Perhaps they say: 'One hour
     More, and we stand,
     Face to face, hand in hand;
Make haste, O slack gale, to the looked-for land!'

    My trees are not in flower,   60
    I have no bower,
    And gusty creaks my tower,
And lonesome, very lonesome, is my strand.

Advent

  This Advent moon shines cold and clear,
    These Advent nights are long;
  Our lamps have burned year after year
    And still their flame is strong.

'Watchman, what of the night?' we cry°
    Heart-sick with hope deferred:
'No speaking signs are in the sky,'
    Is still the watchman's word.

The Porter watches at the gate,°
    The servants watch within;   10
The watch is long betimes and late,
    The prize is slow to win.
'Watchman, what of the night?' but still
    His answer sounds the same:
'No daybreak tops the utmost hill,
    Nor pale our lamps of flame.'

One to another hear them speak
    The patient virgins wise:
'Surely He is not far to seek'—
    'All night we watch and rise.'   20
'The days are evil looking back,
    The coming days are dim;
Yet count we not His promise slack,
    But watch and wait for Him.'

One with another, soul with soul,
    They kindle fire from fire:
'Friends watch us who have touched the goal.'
    'They urge us, come up higher.'
'With them shall rest our waysore feet,
    With them is built our home,   30
With Christ.'— 'They sweet, but He most sweet,
    Sweeter than honeycomb.'

There no more parting, no more pain,
    The distant ones brought near,
The lost so long are found again,
    Long lost but longer dear:
Eye hath not seen, ear hath not heard,
    Nor heart conceived that rest,
With them our good things long deferred,
    With Jesus Christ our Best.   40

We weep because the night is long,
   We laugh for day shall rise,
We sing a slow contented song
   And knock at Paradise.
Weeping we hold Him fast, Who wept°
   For us, we hold Him fast;
And will not let Him go except
   He bless us first or last.

Weeping we hold Him fast to-night;
   We will not let Him go   50
Till daybreak smite our wearied sight
   And summer smite the snow:
Then figs shall bud, and dove with dove
   Shall coo the livelong day;
Then He shall say, 'Arise, My love,
   My fair one, come away.'

At Home

When I was dead, my spirit turned
   To seek the much frequented house:
I passed the door, and saw my friends
   Feasting beneath green orange boughs;
From hand to hand they pushed the wine,
   They sucked the pulp of plum and peach;
They sang, they jested, and they laughed,
   For each was loved of each.

I listened to their honest chat:
   Said one: 'To-morrow we shall be   10
Plod plod along the featureless sands
   And coasting miles and miles of sea.'
Said one: 'Before the turn of tide
   We will achieve the eyrie-seat.'
Said one: 'To-morrow shall be like
   To-day, but much more sweet.'°

'To-morrow,' said they, strong with hope,
   And dwelt upon the pleasant way:

'To-morrow,' cried they one and all,
    While no one spoke of yesterday.   20
Their life stood full at blessed noon;
    I, only I, had passed away:
'To-morrow and to-day,' they cried;
    I was of yesterday.

I shivered comfortless, but cast
    No chill across the tablecloth;
I all-forgotten shivered, sad
    To stay and yet to part how loth:
I passed from the familiar room,
    I who from love had passed away,   30
Like the remembrance of a guest
    That tarrieth but a day.°

Up-Hill

Does the road wind up-hill all the way?°
    Yes, to the very end.
Will the day's journey take the whole long day?
    From morn to night, my friend.

But is there for the night a resting-place?°
    A roof for when the slow dark hours begin.
May not the darkness hide it from my face?
    You cannot miss that inn.

Shall I meet other wayfarers at night?
    Those who have gone before.   10
Then must I knock, or call when just in sight?
    They will not keep you standing at that door.

Shall I find comfort, travel-sore and weak?
    Of labour you shall find the sum.°
Will there be beds for me and all who seek?
    Yea, beds for all who come.

The Convent Threshold

There's blood between us, love, my love,
There's father's blood, there's brother's blood;

And blood's a bar I cannot pass:°
I choose the stairs that mount above,
Stair after golden skyward stair,
To city and to sea of glass.°
My lily feet are soiled with mud,
With scarlet mud which tells a tale
Of hope that was, of guilt that was,
Of love that shall not yet avail;   10
Alas, my heart, if I could bare
My heart, this selfsame stain is there:
I seek the sea of glass and fire
To wash the spot, to burn the snare;
Lo, stairs are meant to lift us higher:
Mount with me, mount the kindled stair.

    Your eyes look earthward, mine look up.
I see the far-off city grand,
Beyond the hills a watered land,
Beyond the gulf a gleaming strand   20
Of mansions where the righteous sup;
Who sleep at ease among their trees,
Or wake to sing a cadenced hymn
With Cherubim and Seraphim;
They bore the Cross, they drained the cup,
Racked, roasted, crushed, wrenched limb from limb,
They the offscouring of the world:°
The heaven of starry heavens unfurled,
The sun before their face is dim.

You looking earthward what see you?   30
Milk-white wine-flushed among the vines,
Up and down leaping, to and fro,
Most glad, most full, made strong with wines,
Blooming as peaches pearled with dew,
Their golden windy hair afloat,
Love-music warbling in their throat,
Young men and women come and go.

    You linger, yet the time is short:
Flee for your life, gird up your strength
To flee; the shadows stretched at length   40

Show that day wanes, that night draws nigh;
Flee to the mountain, tarry not.°
Is this a time for smile and sigh,
For songs among the secret trees°
Where sudden blue birds nest and sport?
The time is short and yet you stay:
To-day while it is called to-day
Kneel, wrestle, knock, do violence, pray;°
To-day is short, to-morrow nigh:
Why will you die? why will you die?   50

    You sinned with me a pleasant sin:
Repent with me, for I repent.
Woe's me the lore I must unlearn!
Woe's me that easy way we went,
So rugged when I would return!
How long until my sleep begin,
How long shall stretch these nights and days?
Surely, clean Angels cry, she prays;
She laves her soul with tedious tears:
How long must stretch these years and years?   60

    I turn from you my cheeks and eyes,
My hair which you shall see no more—
Alas for joy that went before,
For joy that dies, for love that dies.
Only my lips still turn to you,
My livid lips that cry, Repent.
Oh weary life, oh weary Lent,°
Oh weary time whose stars are few.

    How should I rest in Paradise,
Or sit on steps of heaven alone?   70
If Saints and Angels spoke of love
Should I not answer from my throne:
Have pity upon me, ye my friends,
For I have heard the sound thereof:
Should I not turn with yearning eyes,
Turn earthwards with a pitiful pang?
Oh save me from a pang in heaven.
By all the gifts we took and gave,

Repent, repent, and be forgiven:
This life is long, but yet it ends;   80
Repent and purge your soul and save:
No gladder song the morning stars
Upon their birthday morning sang
Than Angels sing when one repents.°

   I tell you what I dreamed last night:
A spirit with transfigured face
Fire-footed clomb an infinite space.°
I heard his hundred pinions clang,°
Heaven-bells rejoicing rang and rang,
Heaven-air was thrilled with subtle scents,   90
Worlds spun upon their rushing cars:°
He mounted shrieking: 'Give me light.'
Still light was pour'd on him, more light;
Angels, Archangels he outstripped
Exultant in exceeding might,
And trod the skirts of Cherubim.
Still 'Give me light,' he shrieked; and dipped
His thirsty face, and drank a sea,
Athirst with thirst it could not slake.
I saw him, drunk with knowledge, take   100
From aching brows the aureole crown—
His locks writhed like a cloven snake—
He left his throne to grovel down
And lick the dust of Seraphs' feet:
For what is knowledge duly weighed?
Knowledge is strong, but love is sweet;
Yea all the progress he had made
Was but to learn that all is small
Save love, for love is all in all.

   I tell you what I dreamed last night: 110
It was not dark, it was not light,
Cold dews had drenched my plenteous hair
Through clay; you came to seek me there.
And 'Do you dream of me?' you said.
My heart was dust that used to leap
To you; I answered half asleep:
'My pillow is damp, my sheets are red,
There's a leaden tester to my bed:°

Find you a warmer playfellow,
A warmer pillow for your head,   120
A kinder love to love than mine.'
You wrung your hands; while I like lead
Crushed downwards through the sodden earth:
You smote your hands but not in mirth,
And reeled but were not drunk with wine.°

   For all night long I dreamed of you:
I woke and prayed against my will,
Then slept to dream of you again.
At length I rose and knelt and prayed:
I cannot write the words I said,°   130
My words were slow, my tears were few;
But through the dark my silence spoke
Like thunder. When this morning broke,
My face was pinched, my hair was grey,
And frozen blood was on the sill
Where stifling in my struggle I lay.

   If now you saw me you would say:
Where is the face I used to love?
And I would answer: Gone before;
It tarries veiled in paradise.°   140
When once the morning star shall rise,
When earth with shadow flees away
And we stand safe within the door,
Then you shall lift the veil thereof.
Look up, rise up: for far above
Our palms are grown, our place is set;
There we shall meet as once we met
And love with old familiar love.

Christian and Jew

A DIALOGUE

'Oh happy happy land!
Angels like rushes stand
  About the wells of light.'—°
  'Alas, I have not eyes for this fair sight:°
Hold fast my hand.'—

'As in a soft wind, they
Bend all one blessed way,
    Each bowed in his own glory, star with star.'—°
    'I cannot see so far,
    Here shadows are.'—°   10

'White-winged the cherubim,
Yet whiter seraphim,
    Glow white with intense fire of love.'—
'Mine eyes are dim:
    I look in vain above,
And miss their hymn.'—

'Angels, Archangels cry
One to other ceaselessly
    (I hear them sing)
    One "Holy, Holy, Holy" to their King.'—°   20
'I do not hear them, I.'—

'At one side Paradise
    Is curtained from the rest,
Made green for wearied eyes;
    Much softer than the breast
Of mother-dove clad in a rainbow's dyes.

'All precious souls are there
    Most safe, elect by grace,
    All tears are wiped for ever from their face:
Untired in prayer   30
    They wait and praise
    Hidden for a little space.

'Boughs of the Living Vine°
They spread in summer shine
    Green leaf with leaf:
Sap of the Royal Vine it stirs like wine
    In all both less and chief.

'Sing to the Lord,
    All spirits of all flesh, sing;
For He hath not abhorred   40

Our low estate nor scorned our offering:
　　Shout to our King.'—

'But Zion said:
　　My Lord forgetteth me.
Lo, she hath made her bed
　　In dust; forsaken weepeth she
　　Where alien rivers swell the sea.

'She laid her body as the ground,
　　Her tender body as the ground to those
Who passed; her harpstrings cannot sound   50
In a strange land; discrowned°
　　She sits, and drunk with woes.'—

'O drunken not with wine,°
　　Whose sins and sorrows have fulfilled the sum,—
　　Be not afraid, arise, be no more dumb;
Arise, shine,
　　For thy light is come.'—

'Can these bones live?'—
　　　　　　　　　　　　'God knows:°
The prophet saw such clothed with flesh and skin;   60
　　A wind blew on them and life entered in;
They shook and rose.
　　Hasten the time, O Lord, blot out their sin,
　　Let life begin.'

A Yawn / By the Sea

A Yawn

I grow so weary: is it death
　　This awful woful weariness?
It is a weight to heave my breath,
　　A weight to wake, a weight to sleep;
　　I have no heart to work or weep.

The sunshine teazes and the dark;
　　Only the twilight dulls my grief:

Is this the Ark, the strong safe Ark,
  Or the tempestuous drowning sea
  Whose crested coursers foam for me?   10

Why does the sea moan evermore?
  Shut out from Heaven it makes its moan,
It frets against the boundary shore:
  All earth's full rivers cannot fill
  The sea, that drinking thirsteth still.°

Sheer miracles of loveliness
  Lie hid in its unlooked-on bed:
Salt passionless anemones
  Blow flower-like; just enough alive
  To blow and propagate and thrive.   20

Shells quaint with curve or spot or spike,
  Encrusted live things argus-eyed,°
All fair alike yet all unlike,
  Are born without a pang and die
  Without a pang and so pass by.

I would I lived without a pang:
  Oh happy they who day by day
Quiescent neither sobbed nor sang;
  Unburdened with a what or why
  They live and die and so pass by.   30

By the Sea

Why does the sea moan evermore?
  Shut out from heaven it makes its moan,
It frets against the boundary shore;
  All earth's full rivers cannot fill
  The sea, that drinking thirsteth still.

Sheer miracles of loveliness
  Lie hid in its unlooked-on bed:
Anemones, salt, passionless,
  Blow flower-like; just enough alive
  To blow and multiply and thrive.   10

Shells quaint with curve, or spot, or spike,
   Encrusted live things argus-eyed,
All fair alike, yet all unlike,
   Are born without a pang, and die
   Without a pang, and so pass by.

From House to Home

The first was like a dream through summer heat,
   The second like a tedious numbing swoon,
While the half-frozen pulses lagged to beat
   Beneath a winter moon.

'But,' says my friend, 'what was this thing and where?'
   It was a pleasure-place within my soul;°
An earthly paradise supremely fair
   That lured me from the goal.

The first part was a tissue of hugged lies;
   The second was its ruin fraught with pain: 10
Why raise the fair delusion to the skies
   But to be dashed again?°

My castle stood of white transparent glass°
   Glittering and frail with many a fretted spire,
But when the summer sunset came to pass
   It kindled into fire.°

My pleasaunce was an undulating green,°
   Stately with trees whose shadows slept below,
With glimpses of smooth garden-beds between
   Like flame or sky or snow.   20

Swift squirrels on the pastures took their ease,
   With leaping lambs safe from the unfeared knife;
All singing-birds rejoicing in those trees
   Fulfilled their careless life.

Woodpigeons cooed there, stockdoves nestled there;
   My trees were full of songs and flowers and fruit,

Their branches spread a city to the air
   And mice lodged in their root.

My heath lay farther off, where lizards lived
   In strange metallic mail, just spied and gone;   30
Like darted lightnings here and there perceived
   But no where dwelt upon.

Frogs and fat toads were there to hop or plod
   And propagate in peace, an uncouth crew,
Where velvet-headed rushes rustling nod
   And spill the morning dew.

All caterpillars throve beneath my rule,
   With snails and slugs in corners out of sight;
I never marred the curious sudden stool
   That perfects in a night.   40

Safe in his excavated gallery
   The burrowing mole groped on from year to year;
No harmless hedgehog curled because of me
   His prickly back for fear.

Oft times one like an angel walked with me,°
   With spirit-discerning eyes like flames of fire,
But deep as the unfathomed endless sea
   Fulfilling my desire:

And sometimes like a snowdrift he was fair,
   And sometimes like a sunset glorious red,   50
And sometimes he had wings to scale the air
   With aureole round his head.

We sang our songs together by the way,
   Calls and recalls and echoes of delight;
So communed we together all the day,
   And so in dreams by night.

I have no words to tell what way we walked,
   What unforgotten path now closed and sealed;
I have no words to tell all things we talked,
   All things that he revealed: 60

This only can I tell: that hour by hour
    I waxed more feastful, lifted up and glad;
I felt no thorn-prick when I plucked a flower,
    Felt not my friend was sad.

'To-morrow,' once I said to him with smiles:
    'To-night,' he answered gravely and was dumb,
But pointed out the stones that numbered miles
    And miles and miles to come.

'Not so,' I said: 'to-morrow shall be sweet;
    To-night is not so sweet as coming days.'   70
Then first I saw that he had turned his feet,
    Had turned from me his face:

Running and flying miles and miles he went,
    But once looked back to beckon with his hand
And cry: 'Come home, O love, from banishment:°
    Come to the distant land.'

That night destroyed me like an avalanche;°
    One night turned all my summer back to snow:
Next morning not a bird upon my branch,
    Not a lamb woke below,—   80

No bird, no lamb, no living breathing thing;
    No squirrel scampered on my breezy lawn,
No mouse lodged by his hoard: all joys took wing
    And fled before that dawn.

Azure and sun were starved from heaven above,
    No dew had fallen, but biting frost lay hoar:
O love, I knew that I should meet my love,
    Should find my love no more.

'My love no more,' I muttered stunned with pain:
    I shed no tear, I wrung no passionate hand,   90
Till something whispered: 'You shall meet again,
    Meet in a distant land.'

Then with a cry like famine I arose,
    I lit my candle, searched from room to room,

Searched up and down; a war of winds that froze
   Swept through the blank of gloom.

I searched day after day, night after night;
   Scant change there came to me of night or day:
'No more,' I wailed, 'no more:' and trimmed my light,
   And gnashed but did not pray,   100

Until my heart broke and my spirit broke:
   Upon the frost-bound floor I stumbled, fell,
And moaned: 'It is enough: withhold the stroke.
   Farewell, O love, farewell.'

Then life swooned from me. And I heard the song
   Of spheres and spirits rejoicing over me:
One cried: 'Our sister, she hath suffered long.'—
   One answered: 'Make her see.'—

One cried: 'Oh blessèd she who no more pain,
   Who no more disappointment shall receive.'—   110
One answered: 'Not so: she must live again;
   Strengthen thou her to live.'

So while I lay entranced a curtain seemed
   To shrivel with crackling from before my face;
Across mine eyes a waxing radiance beamed
   And showed a certain place.

I saw a vision of a woman, where
   Night and new morning strive for domination;
Incomparably pale, and almost fair,
   And sad beyond expression.   120

Her eyes were like some fire-enshrining gem,
   Were stately like the stars, and yet were tender;
Her figure charmed me like a windy stem
   Quivering and drooped and slender.

I stood upon the outer barren ground,
   She stood on inner ground that budded flowers;
While circling in their never-slackening round
   Danced by the mystic hours.°

But every flower was lifted on a thorn,
  And every thorn shot upright from its sands   130
To gall her feet; hoarse laughter pealed in scorn
  With cruel clapping hands.

She bled and wept, yet did not shrink; her strength
  Was strung up until daybreak of delight:°
She measured measureless sorrow toward its length,
  And breadth, and depth, and height.

Then marked I how a chain sustained her form,
  A chain of living links not made nor riven:
It stretched sheer up through lightning, wind, and storm,
  And anchored fast in heaven.   140

One cried: 'How long? yet founded on the Rock°
  She shall do battle, suffer, and attain.'—
One answered: 'Faith quakes in the tempest shock:
  Strengthen her soul again.'

I saw a cup sent down and come to her
  Brim full of loathing and of bitterness:
She drank with livid lips that seemed to stir
  The depth, not make it less.

But as she drank I spied a hand distil
  New wine and virgin honey; making it   150
First bitter-sweet, then sweet indeed, until
  She tasted only sweet.

Her lips and cheeks waxed rosy-fresh and young;
  Drinking she sang: 'My soul shall nothing want;'
And drank anew: while soft a song was sung,
  A mystical slow chant.

One cried: 'The wounds are faithful of a friend:
  The wilderness shall blossom as a rose.'—
One answered: 'Rend the veil, declare the end,
  Strengthen her ere she goes.'   160

Then earth and heaven were rolled up like a scroll;°
  Time and space, change and death, had passed away;

Weight, number, measure, each had reached its whole;
   The day had come, that day.

Multitudes—multitudes—stood up in bliss,
   Made equal to the angels, glorious, fair;
With harps, palms, wedding-garments, kiss of peace,
   And crowned and haloed hair.

They sang a song, a new song in the height,°
   Harping with harps to Him Who is Strong and True: 170
They drank new wine, their eyes saw with new light,
   Lo, all things were made new.

Tier beyond tier they rose and rose and rose°
   So high that it was dreadful, flames with flames:
No man could number them, no tongue disclose
   Their secret sacred names.°

As though one pulse stirred all, one rush of blood
   Fed all, one breath swept through them myriad-voiced,
They struck their harps, cast down their crowns, they stood
   And worshipped and rejoiced.   180

Each face looked one way like a moon new-lit,
   Each face looked one way towards its Sun of Love;
Drank love and bathed in love and mirrored it
   And knew no end thereof.

Glory touched glory on each blessèd head,
   Hands locked dear hands never to sunder more:
These were the new-begotten from the dead
   Whom the great birthday bore.

Heart answered heart, soul answered soul at rest,
   Double against each other, filled, sufficed: 190
All loving, loved of all; but loving best
   And best beloved of Christ.

I saw that one who lost her love in pain,
   Who trod on thorns, who drank the loathsome cup;
The lost in night, in day was found again;
   The fallen was lifted up.

They stood together in the blessèd noon,
   They sang together through the length of days;
Each loving face bent Sunwards like a moon
   New-lit with love and praise.°   200

Therefore, O friend, I would not if I might
   Rebuild my house of lies, wherein I joyed
One time to dwell: my soul shall walk in white,
   Cast down but not destroyed.

Therefore in patience I possess my soul;
   Yea, therefore as a flint I set my face,°
To pluck down, to build up again the whole—°
   But in a distant place.

These thorns are sharp, yet I can tread on them;
   This cup is loathsome, yet He makes it sweet: 210
My face is steadfast toward Jerusalem,°
   My heart remembers it.

I lift the hanging hands, the feeble knees—
   I, precious more than seven times molten gold—
Until the day when from His storehouses
   God shall bring new and old;

Beauty for ashes, oil of joy for grief,
   Garment of praise for spirit of heaviness:°
Although to-day I fade as doth a leaf,
   I languish and grow less.   220

Although to-day He prunes my twigs with pain
   Yet doth His blood nourish and warm my root:
To-morrow I shall put forth buds again
   And clothe myself with fruit.

Although to-day I walk in tedious ways,
   To-day His staff is turned into a rod,
Yet will I wait for Him the appointed days
   And stay upon my God.°

Winter Rain

Every valley drinks,
    Every dell and hollow:
Where the kind rain sinks and sinks,
    Green of Spring will follow.

Yet a lapse of weeks
    Buds will burst their edges,
Strip their wool-coats, glue-coats, streaks,
    In the woods and hedges;

Weave a bower of love
    For birds to meet each other,   10
Weave a canopy above
    Nest and egg and mother.

But for fattening rain
    We should have no flowers,
Never a bud or leaf again
    But for soaking showers;

Never a mated bird
    In the rocking tree-tops,
Never indeed a flock or herd
    To graze upon the lea-crops.   20

Lambs so woolly white,
    Sheep the sun-bright leas on,
They could have no grass to bite
    But for rain in season.

We should find no moss
    In the shadiest places,
Find no waving meadow grass
    Pied with broad-eyed daisies:

But miles of barren sand,
    With never a son or daughter,   30
Not a lily on the land,
    Or lily on the water.

L.E.L.

Whose heart was breaking for a little love.

E. B. BROWNING

Downstairs I laugh, I sport and jest with all:
    But in my solitary room above
I turn my face in silence to the wall;°
    My heart is breaking for a little love.
        Though winter frosts are done,
        And birds pair every one,
And leaves peep out, for springtide is begun.

I feel no spring, while spring is wellnigh blown,
    I find no nest, while nests are in the grove:
Woe's me for mine own heart that dwells alone,   10
    My heart that breaketh for a little love.
        While golden in the sun
        Rivulets rise and run,
While lilies bud, for springtide is begun.

All love, are loved, save only I; their hearts
    Beat warm with love and joy, beat full thereof:
They cannot guess, who play the pleasant parts,
    My heart is breaking for a little love.
        While beehives wake and whirr,
        And rabbit thins his fur,   20
In living spring that sets the world astir.

I deck myself with silks and jewelry,
    I plume myself like any mated dove:
They praise my rustling show, and never see
    My heart is breaking for a little love.
        While sprouts green lavender
        With rosemary and myrrh,
For in quick spring the sap is all astir.

Perhaps some saints in glory guess the truth,
    Perhaps some angels read it as they move,   30
And cry one to another full of ruth,
    'Her heart is breaking for a little love.'

Though other things have birth,
And leap and sing for mirth,
When springtime wakes and clothes and feeds the earth.

Yet saith a saint: 'Take patience for thy scathe;'°
Yet saith an angel: 'Wait, for thou shalt prove
True best is last, true life is born of death,
O thou, heart-broken for a little love.
Then love shall fill thy girth,   40
And love make fat thy dearth,
When new spring builds new heaven and clean new earth.'

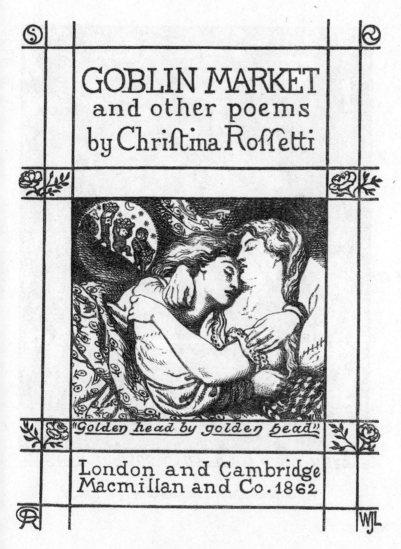

GOBLIN MARKET
and other poems
by Christina Rossetti

"Golden head by golden head"

London and Cambridge
Macmillan and Co. 1862

Title-page of *Goblin Market and Other Poems* (1862).

"Buy from us with @ golden curl"

Frontispiece of *Goblin Market and Other Poems* (1862).

Goblin Market

Morning and evening
Maids heard the goblins cry:
'Come buy our orchard fruits,
Come buy, come buy:
Apples and quinces,
Lemons and oranges,
Plump unpecked cherries,
Melons and raspberries,
Bloom-down-cheeked peaches,
Swart-headed mulberries,   10
Wild free-born cranberries,
Crab-apples, dewberries,
Pine-apples, blackberries,
Apricots, strawberries;—
All ripe together
In summer weather,—
Morns that pass by,
Fair eves that fly;
Come buy, come buy:
Our grapes fresh from the vine,   20
Pomegranates full and fine,
Dates and sharp bullaces,
Rare pears and greengages,
Damsons and bilberries,
Taste them and try:
Currants and gooseberries,
Bright-fire-like barberries,
Figs to fill your mouth,
Citrons from the South,
Sweet to tongue and sound to eye;°   30
Come buy, come buy.'

   Evening by evening
Among the brookside rushes,
Laura bowed her head to hear,
Lizzie veiled her blushes:
Crouching close together
In the cooling weather,
With clasping arms and cautioning lips,

With tingling cheeks and finger tips.
'Lie close,' Laura said,   40
Pricking up her golden head:
'We must not look at goblin men,
We must not buy their fruits:
Who knows upon what soil they fed
Their hungry thirsty roots?'
'Come buy,' call the goblins
Hobbling down the glen.
'Oh,' cried Lizzie, 'Laura, Laura,
You should not peep at goblin men.'
Lizzie covered up her eyes,   50
Covered close lest they should look;
Laura reared her glossy head,
And whispered like the restless brook:
'Look, Lizzie, look, Lizzie,
Down the glen tramp little men.
One hauls a basket,
One bears a plate,
One lugs a golden dish
Of many pounds weight.
How fair the vine must grow   60
Whose grapes are so luscious;
How warm the wind must blow
Through those fruit bushes.'
'No,' said Lizzie: 'No, no, no;
Their offers should not charm us,
Their evil gifts would harm us.'°
She thrust a dimpled finger
In each ear, shut eyes and ran:°
Curious Laura chose to linger
Wondering at each merchant man.   70
One had a cat's face,
One whisked a tail,
One tramped at a rat's pace,
One crawled like a snail,
One like a wombat prowled obtuse and furry,
One like a ratel tumbled hurry skurry.
She heard a voice like voice of doves
Cooing all together:
They sounded kind and full of loves
In the pleasant weather.   80

Laura stretched her gleaming neck
Like a rush-imbedded swan,
Like a lily from the beck,
Like a moonlit poplar branch,
Like a vessel at the launch
When its last restraint is gone.

Backwards up the mossy glen
Turned and trooped the goblin men,
With their shrill repeated cry,
'Come buy, come buy.'   90
When they reached where Laura was
They stood stock still upon the moss,
Leering at each other,
Brother with queer brother;
Signalling each other,
Brother with sly brother.
One set his basket down,
One reared his plate;
One began to weave a crown
Of tendrils, leaves and rough nuts brown   100
(Men sell not such in any town);
One heaved the golden weight
Of dish and fruit to offer her:
'Come buy, come buy,' was still their cry.
Laura stared but did not stir,
Longed but had no money:
The whisk-tailed merchant bade her taste
In tones as smooth as honey,
The cat-faced purr'd,
The rat-paced spoke a word   110
Of welcome, and the snail-paced even was heard;
One parrot-voiced and jolly
Cried 'Pretty Goblin' still for 'Pretty Polly;'—°
One whistled like a bird.

But sweet-tooth Laura spoke in haste:
'Good folk, I have no coin;
To take were to purloin:
I have no copper in my purse,
I have no silver either,
And all my gold is on the furze°   120

That shakes in windy weather
Above the rusty heather.'
'You have much gold upon your head,'
They answered all together:
'Buy from us with a golden curl.'
She clipped a precious golden lock,
She dropped a tear more rare than pearl,
Then sucked their fruit globes fair or red:
Sweeter than honey from the rock,°
Stronger than man-rejoicing wine,   130
Clearer than water flowed that juice;
She never tasted such before,
How should it cloy with length of use?
She sucked and sucked and sucked the more
Fruits which that unknown orchard bore;
She sucked until her lips were sore;
Then flung the emptied rinds away
But gathered up one kernel-stone,
And knew not was it night or day
As she turned home alone.   140

    Lizzie met her at the gate
Full of wise upbraidings:
'Dear, you should not stay so late,
Twilight is not good for maidens;
Should not loiter in the glen
In the haunts of goblin men.
Do you not remember Jeanie,°
How she met them in the moonlight,
Took their gifts both choice and many,
Ate their fruits and wore their flowers   150
Plucked from bowers
Where summer ripens at all hours?
But ever in the noonlight
She pined and pined away;
Sought them by night and day,
Found them no more but dwindled and grew grey;
Then fell with the first snow,
While to this day no grass will grow
Where she lies low:
I planted daisies there a year ago   160
That never blow.

You should not loiter so.'
'Nay, hush,' said Laura:
'Nay, hush, my sister:
I ate and ate my fill,
Yet my mouth waters still;
To-morrow night I will
Buy more:' and kissed her:
'Have done with sorrow;
I'll bring you plums to-morrow   170
Fresh on their mother twigs,
Cherries worth getting;
You cannot think what figs
My teeth have met in,
What melons icy-cold
Piled on a dish of gold
Too huge for me to hold,
What peaches with a velvet nap,
Pellucid grapes without one seed:
Odorous indeed must be the mead   180
Whereon they grow, and pure the wave they drink
With lilies at the brink,
And sugar-sweet their sap.'

   Golden head by golden head,
Like two pigeons in one nest
Folded in each other's wings,
They lay down in their curtained bed:
Like two blossoms on one stem,
Like two flakes of new-fall'n snow,
Like two wands of ivory   190
Tipped with gold for awful kings.
Moon and stars gazed in at them,
Wind sang to them lullaby,
Lumbering owls forbore to fly,
Not a bat flapped to and fro
Round their rest:
Cheek to cheek and breast to breast
Locked together in one nest.

   Early in the morning
When the first cock crowed his warning,   200
Neat like bees, as sweet and busy,

Laura rose with Lizzie:
Fetched in honey, milked the cows,
Aired and set to rights the house,
Kneaded cakes of whitest wheat,
Cakes for dainty mouths to eat,
Next churned butter, whipped up cream,
Fed their poultry, sat and sewed;
Talked as modest maidens should:
Lizzie with an open heart,   210
Laura in an absent dream,
One content, one sick in part;
One warbling for the mere bright day's delight,
One longing for the night.

    At length slow evening came:
They went with pitchers to the reedy brook;
Lizzie most placid in her look,
Laura most like a leaping flame.
They drew the gurgling water from its deep;
Lizzie plucked purple and rich golden flags,   220
Then turning homewards said: 'The sunset flushes
Those furthest loftiest crags;
Come, Laura, not another maiden lags,
No wilful squirrel wags,
The beasts and birds are fast asleep.'
But Laura loitered still among the rushes
And said the bank was steep.

    And said the hour was early still,
The dew not fall'n, the wind not chill:
Listening ever, but not catching   230
The customary cry,
'Come buy, come buy,'
With its iterated jingle
Of sugar-baited words:
Not for all her watching
Once discerning even one goblin
Racing, whisking, tumbling, hobbling;
Let alone the herds
That used to tramp along the glen,
In groups or single,   240
Of brisk fruit-merchant men.

    Till Lizzie urged, 'O Laura, come;
I hear the fruit-call but I dare not look:
You should not loiter longer at this brook:
Come with me home.
The stars rise, the moon bends her arc,
Each glowworm winks her spark,
Let us get home before the night grows dark:
For clouds may gather
Though this is summer weather,   250
Put out the lights and drench us through;
Then if we lost our way what should we do?'

    Laura turned cold as stone
To find her sister heard that cry alone,
That goblin cry,
'Come buy our fruits, come buy.'
Must she then buy no more such dainty fruit?
Must she no more that succous pasture find,°
Gone deaf and blind?
Her tree of life drooped from the root:°   260
She said not one word in her heart's sore ache;
But peering thro' the dimness, nought discerning,
Trudged home, her pitcher dripping all the way;
So crept to bed, and lay
Silent till Lizzie slept;
Then sat up in a passionate yearning,
And gnashed her teeth for baulked desire, and wept
As if her heart would break.

    Day after day, night after night,
Laura kept watch in vain   270
In sullen silence of exceeding pain.
She never caught again the goblin cry:
'Come buy, come buy;'—
She never spied the goblin men
Hawking their fruits along the glen:
But when the noon waxed bright
Her hair grew thin and grey;
She dwindled, as the fair full moon doth turn
To swift decay and burn
Her fire away.   280

One day remembering her kernel-stone
She set it by a wall that faced the south;
Dewed it with tears, hoped for a root,
Watched for a waxing shoot,
But there came none;
It never saw the sun,
It never felt the trickling moisture run:
While with sunk eyes and faded mouth
She dreamed of melons, as a traveller sees
False waves in desert drouth   290
With shade of leaf-crowned trees,
And burns the thirstier in the sandful breeze.

She no more swept the house,
Tended the fowls or cows,
Fetched honey, kneaded cakes of wheat,
Brought water from the brook:
But sat down listless in the chimney-nook
And would not eat.

Tender Lizzie could not bear
To watch her sister's cankerous care   300
Yet not to share.
She night and morning
Caught the goblins' cry:
'Come buy our orchard fruits,
Come buy, come buy:'—
Beside the brook, along the glen,
She heard the tramp of goblin men,
The voice and stir
Poor Laura could not hear;
Longed to buy fruit to comfort her,   310
But feared to pay too dear.
She thought of Jeanie in her grave,
Who should have been a bride;
But who for joys brides hope to have
Fell sick and died°
In her gay prime,
In earliest Winter time,
With the first glazing rime,
With the first snow-fall of crisp Winter time.

Till Laura dwindling   320
Seemed knocking at Death's door:
Then Lizzie weighed no more
Better and worse;
But put a silver penny in her purse,
Kissed Laura, crossed the heath with clumps of furze
At twilight, halted by the brook:
And for the first time in her life
Began to listen and look.

Laughed every goblin
When they spied her peeping: 330
Came towards her hobbling,
Flying, running, leaping,
Puffing and blowing,
Chuckling, clapping, crowing,
Clucking and gobbling,
Mopping and mowing,°
Full of airs and graces,
Pulling wry faces,
Demure grimaces,
Cat-like and rat-like,
Ratel- and wombat-like,   340
Snail-paced in a hurry,
Parrot-voiced and whistler,
Helter skelter, hurry skurry,
Chattering like magpies,
Fluttering like pigeons,
Gliding like fishes,—
Hugged her and kissed her,
Squeezed and caressed her:
Stretched up their dishes,
Panniers, and plates: 350
'Look at our apples
Russet and dun,°
Bob at our cherries,°
Bite at our peaches,
Citrons and dates,
Grapes for the asking,
Pears red with basking
Out in the sun,

Plums on their twigs;   360
Pluck them and suck them,
Pomegranates, figs.'—

  'Good folk,' said Lizzie,
Mindful of Jeanie:
'Give me much and many:'—
Held out her apron,
Tossed them her penny.
'Nay, take a seat with us,
Honour and eat with us,'
They answered grinning: 370
'Our feast is but beginning.
Night yet is early,
Warm and dew-pearly,
Wakeful and starry:
Such fruits as these
No man can carry;
Half their bloom would fly,
Half their dew would dry,
Half their flavour would pass by.
Sit down and feast with us,   380
Be welcome guest with us,
Cheer you and rest with us.'—
'Thank you,' said Lizzie: 'But one waits
At home alone for me:
So without further parleying,
If you will not sell me any
Of your fruits though much and many,
Give me back my silver penny
I tossed you for a fee.'—
They began to scratch their pates,   390
No longer wagging, purring,
But visibly demurring,
Grunting and snarling.
One called her proud,
Cross-grained, uncivil;
Their tones waxed loud,
Their looks were evil.
Lashing their tails
They trod and hustled her,

Elbowed and jostled her,   400
Clawed with their nails,
Barking, mewing, hissing, mocking,
Tore her gown and soiled her stocking,
Twitched her hair out by the roots,
Stamped upon her tender feet,
Held her hands and squeezed their fruits
Against her mouth to make her eat.

   White and golden Lizzie stood,
Like a lily in a flood, —
Like a rock of blue-veined stone   410
Lashed by tides obstreperously, —
Like a beacon left alone
In a hoary roaring sea,
Sending up a golden fire, —
Like a fruit-crowned orange-tree
White with blossoms honey-sweet°
Sore beset by wasp and bee, —
Like a royal virgin town°
Topped with gilded dome and spire
Close beleaguered by a fleet   420
Mad to tug her standard down.

   One may lead a horse to water,
Twenty cannot make him drink.
Though the goblins cuffed and caught her,
Coaxed and fought her,
Bullied and besought her,
Scratched her, pinched her black as ink,
Kicked and knocked her,
Mauled and mocked her,
Lizzie uttered not a word;°   430
Would not open lip from lip
Lest they should cram a mouthful in:
But laughed in heart to feel the drip
Of juice that syrupped all her face,
And lodged in dimples of her chin,
And streaked her neck which quaked like curd.
At last the evil people
Worn out by her resistance

Flung back her penny, kicked their fruit
Along whichever road they took,   440
Not leaving root or stone or shoot;
Some writhed into the ground,
Some dived into the brook
With ring and ripple,
Some scudded on the gale without a sound,
Some vanished in the distance.

   In a smart, ache, tingle,
Lizzie went her way;
Knew not was it night or day;
Sprang up the bank, tore thro' the furze,   450
Threaded copse and dingle,
And heard her penny jingle
Bouncing in her purse,—
Its bounce was music to her ear.
She ran and ran
As if she feared some goblin man
Dogged her with gibe or curse
Or something worse:
But not one goblin skurried after,
Nor was she pricked by fear;   460
The kind heart made her windy-paced
That urged her home quite out of breath with haste
And inward laughter.

   She cried 'Laura,' up the garden,
'Did you miss me?°
Come and kiss me.
Never mind my bruises,
Hug me, kiss me, suck my juices
Squeezed from goblin fruits for you,
Goblin pulp and goblin dew.   470
Eat me, drink me, love me;
Laura, make much of me:
For your sake I have braved the glen
And had to do with goblin merchant men.'°

   Laura started from her chair,
Flung her arms up in the air,

Clutched her hair:
'Lizzie, Lizzie, have you tasted
For my sake the fruit forbidden?
Must your light like mine be hidden,   480
Your young life like mine be wasted,
Undone in mine undoing
And ruined in my ruin,
Thirsty, cankered, goblin-ridden?'—
She clung about her sister,
Kissed and kissed and kissed her:
Tears once again
Refreshed her shrunken eyes,
Dropping like rain
After long sultry drouth;   490
Shaking with aguish fear, and pain,°
She kissed and kissed her with a hungry mouth.

   Her lips began to scorch,
That juice was wormwood to her tongue,°
She loathed the feast:°
Writhing as one possessed she leaped and sung,
Rent all her robe, and wrung
Her hands in lamentable haste,°
And beat her breast.
Her locks streamed like the torch   500
Borne by a racer at full speed,
Or like the mane of horses in their flight,
Or like an eagle when she stems the light°
Straight toward the sun,
Or like a caged thing freed,
Or like a flying flag when armies run.

   Swift fire spread through her veins, knocked at her heart,
Met the fire smouldering there
And overbore its lesser flame;°
She gorged on bitterness without a name: 510
Ah! fool, to choose such part
Of soul-consuming care!
Sense failed in the mortal strife:
Like the watch-tower of a town
Which an earthquake shatters down,

Like a lightning-stricken mast,
Like a wind-uprooted tree
Spun about,
Like a foam-topped waterspout
Cast down headlong in the sea,   520
She fell at last;
Pleasure past and anguish past,
Is it death or is it life?

   Life out of death.
That night long Lizzie watched by her,
Counted her pulse's flagging stir,
Felt for her breath,
Held water to her lips, and cooled her face
With tears and fanning leaves:
But when the first birds chirped about their eaves,   530
And early reapers plodded to the place
Of golden sheaves,
And dew-wet grass
Bowed in the morning winds so brisk to pass,
And new buds with new day
Opened of cup-like lilies on the stream,
Laura awoke as from a dream,
Laughed in the innocent old way,
Hugged Lizzie but not twice or thrice;
Her gleaming locks showed not one thread of grey,   540
Her breath was sweet as May
And light danced in her eyes.

   Days, weeks, months, years,
Afterwards, when both were wives
With children of their own;
Their mother-hearts beset with fears,
Their lives bound up in tender lives;
Laura would call the little ones
And tell them of her early prime,
Those pleasant days long gone   550
Of not-returning time:
Would talk about the haunted glen,
The wicked, quaint fruit-merchant men,
Their fruits like honey to the throat

But poison in the blood;
(Men sell not such in any town:)
Would tell them how her sister stood
In deadly peril to do her good,
And win the fiery antidote:
Then joining hands to little hands   560
Would bid them cling together,
'For there is no friend like a sister
In calm or stormy weather;
To cheer one on the tedious way,
To fetch one if one goes astray,
To lift one if one totters down,
To strengthen whilst one stands.'

Spring

Frost-locked all the winter,
Seeds, and roots, and stones of fruits,
What shall make their sap ascend
That they may put forth shoots?
Tips of tender green,
Leaf, or blade, or sheath;
Telling of the hidden life
That breaks forth underneath,
Life nursed in its grave by Death.

Blows the thaw-wind pleasantly,   10
Drips the soaking rain,
By fits looks down the waking sun:
Young grass springs on the plain;
Young leaves clothe early hedgerow trees;
Seeds, and roots, and stones of fruits,
Swollen with sap put forth their shoots;
Curled-headed ferns sprout in the lane;
Birds sing and pair again.

There is no time like Spring,
When life's alive in everything,   20
Before new nestlings sing,

Before cleft swallows speed their journey back°
Along the trackless track—
God guides their wing,
He spreads their table that they nothing lack—,
Before the daisy grows a common flower,
Before the sun has power
To scorch the world up in his noontide hour.

There is no time like Spring,
Like Spring that passes by;   30
There is no life like Spring-life born to die,—
Piercing the sod,
Clothing the uncouth clod,
Hatched in the nest,
Fledged on the windy bough,
Strong on the wing:
There is no time like Spring that passes by,
Now newly born, and now
Hastening to die.

Sister Maude

Who told my mother of my shame,
    Who told my father of my dear?
Oh who but Maude, my sister Maude,
    Who lurked to spy and peer.

Cold he lies, as cold as stone,
    With his clotted curls about his face:
The comeliest corpse in all the world
    And worthy of a queen's embrace.

You might have spared his soul, sister,
    Have spared my soul, your own soul too: 10
Though I had not been born at all,
    He'd never have looked at you.

My father may sleep in Paradise,
    My mother at Heaven-gate:
But sister Maude shall get no sleep
    Either early or late.

My father may wear a golden gown,
   My mother a crown may win;
If my dear and I knocked at Heaven-gate
   Perhaps they'd let us in: 20
But sister Maude, oh sister Maude,
   Bide *you* with death and sin.

Noble Sisters

'Now did you mark a falcon,
   Sister dear, sister dear,
Flying toward my window
   In the morning cool and clear?
With jingling bells about her neck,
   But what beneath her wing?
It may have been a ribbon,
   Or it may have been a ring.'—
     'I marked a falcon swooping
      At the break of day: 10
      And for your love, my sister dove,
      I 'frayed the thief away.'—°

'Or did you spy a ruddy hound,
   Sister fair and tall,
Went snuffing round my garden bound,
   Or crouched by my bower wall?
With a silken leash about his neck;
   But in his mouth may be
A chain of gold and silver links,
   Or a letter writ to me.'—   20
     'I heard a hound, highborn sister,
      Stood baying at the moon:
      I rose and drove him from your wall
      Lest you should wake too soon.'—

'Or did you meet a pretty page
   Sat swinging on the gate;
Sat whistling whistling like a bird,
   Or may be slept too late:
With eaglets broidered on his cap,
   And eaglets on his glove?   30

If you had turned his pockets out,
   You had found some pledge of love.'—
     'I met him at this daybreak,
      Scarce the east was red:
     Lest the creaking gate should anger you,
      I packed him home to bed.'—

'Oh patience, sister. Did you see
   A young man tall and strong,
Swift-footed to uphold the right
   And to uproot the wrong,   40
Come home across the desolate sea
   To woo me for his wife?
And in his heart my heart is locked,
   And in his life my life.'—
     'I met a nameless man, sister,
      Hard by your chamber door:°
     I said: Her husband loves her much,
      And yet she loves him more.'—

'Fie, sister, fie, a wicked lie,
   A lie, a wicked lie,   50
I have none other love but him,
   Nor will have till I die.
And you have turned him from our door,
   And stabbed him with a lie:
I will go seek him thro' the world
   In sorrow till I die.'—
     'Go seek in sorrow, sister,
      And find in sorrow too:
     If thus you shame our father's name
      My curse go forth with you.'—   60

'No Thank You, John'

I never said I loved you, John:
   Why will you teaze me day by day,
And wax a weariness to think upon
   With always 'do' and 'pray?'

You know I never loved you, John;
   No fault of mine made me your toast:

Why will you haunt me with a face as wan
    As shows an hour-old ghost?

I dare say Meg or Moll would take
    Pity upon you, if you'd ask: 10
And pray don't remain single for my sake
    Who can't perform that task.

I have no heart?—Perhaps I have not;
    But then you're mad to take offence
That I don't give you what I have not got:
    Use your own common sense.

Let bygones be bygones:
    Don't call me false, who owed not to be true:
I'd rather answer 'No' to fifty Johns
    Than answer 'Yes' to you.   20

Let's mar our pleasant days no more,
    Song-birds of passage, days of youth:
Catch at to-day, forget the days before;
    I'll wink at your untruth.

Let us strike hands as hearty friends;
    No more, no less; and friendship's good:
Only don't keep in view ulterior ends,
    And points not understood

In open treaty. Rise above
    Quibbles and shuffling off and on: 30
Here's friendship for you if you like; but love,—
    No thank you, John.

Mirage

The hope I dreamed of was a dream,
    Was but a dream; and now I wake
Exceeding comfortless, and worn, and old,
    For a dream's sake.

I hang my harp upon a tree,
    A weeping willow in a lake;°

I hang my silenced harp there, wrung and snapt
    For a dream's sake.

Lie still, lie still, my breaking heart;
    My silent heart, lie still and break: 10
Life, and the world, and mine own self, are changed
    For a dream's sake.

Old and New Year Ditties

3

Passing away, saith the World, passing away:
Chances, beauty and youth sapped day by day:
Thy life never continueth in one stay.°
Is the eye waxen dim, is the dark hair changing to grey
That hath won neither laurel nor bay?
I shall clothe myself in Spring and bud in May:°
Thou, root-stricken, shalt not rebuild thy decay
On my bosom for aye.
Then I answered: Yea.

Passing away, saith my Soul, passing away: 10
With its burden of fear and hope, of labour and play;
Hearken what the past doth witness and say:
Rust in thy gold, a moth is in thine array,°
A canker is in thy bud, thy leaf must decay.
At midnight, at cockcrow, at morning, one certain day
Lo, the Bridegroom shall come and shall not delay:
Watch thou and pray.
Then I answered: Yea.

Passing away, saith my God, passing away:
Winter passeth after the long delay: 20
New grapes on the vine, new figs on the tender spray,
Turtle calleth turtle in Heaven's May.°
Though I tarry wait for Me, trust Me, watch and pray.
Arise, come away, night is past and lo it is day,
My love, My sister, My spouse, thou shalt hear Me say.
Then I answered: Yea.

Promises like Piecrust

Promise me no promises,
   So will I not promise you;
Keep we both our liberties,
   Never false and never true:
Let us hold the die uncast,
   Free to come as free to go;
For I cannot know your past,
   And of mine what can you know?

You, so warm, may once have been
   Warmer towards another one;   10
I, so cold, may once have seen
   Sunlight, once have felt the sun:
Who shall show us if it was
   Thus indeed in time of old?
Fades the image from the glass°
   And the fortune is not told.

If you promised, you might grieve
   For lost liberty again;
If I promised, I believe
   I should fret to break the chain: 20
Let us be the friends we were,
   Nothing more but nothing less;
Many thrive on frugal fare
   Who would perish of excess.

A Royal Princess

I, a princess, king-descended, decked with jewels, gilded, drest,
Would rather be a peasant with her baby at her breast,
For all I shine so like the sun, and am purple like the west.

Two and two my guards behind, two and two before,
Two and two on either hand, they guard me evermore;
Me, poor dove that must not coo—eagle that must not soar.

All my fountains cast up perfumes, all my gardens grow
Scented woods and foreign spices, with all flowers in blow
That are costly, out of season as the seasons go.

All my walls are lost in mirrors, whereupon I trace   10
Self to right hand, self to left hand, self in every place,
Self-same solitary figure, self-same seeking face.

Then I have an ivory chair high to sit upon,
Almost like my father's chair, which is an ivory throne;
There I sit uplift and upright, there I sit alone.

Alone by day, alone by night, alone days without end;
My father and my mother give me treasures, search and spend—
O my father! O my mother! have you ne'er a friend?

As I am a lofty princess, so my father is
A lofty king, accomplished in all kingly subtilties,   20
Holding in his strong right hand world-kingdoms' balances.

He has quarrelled with his neighbours, he has scourged his foes;
Vassal counts and princes follow where his pennon goes,
Long-descended valiant lords whom the vulture knows.

On whose track the vulture swoops, when they ride in state
To break the strength of armies and topple down the great:
Each of these my courteous servant, none of these my mate.

My father counting up his strength sets down with equal pen°
So many head of cattle, head of horses, head of men;
These for slaughter, these for breeding, with the how and when.   30

Some to work on roads, canals; some to man his ships;
Some to smart in mines beneath sharp overseers' whips;
Some to trap fur-beasts in lands where utmost winter nips.

Once it came into my heart and whelmed me like a flood,
That these too are men and women, human flesh and blood;
Men with hearts and men with souls, though trodden down like mud.°

Our feasting was not glad that night, our music was not gay;
On my mother's graceful head I marked a thread of grey,
My father frowning at the fare seemed every dish to weigh.

I sat beside them sole princess in my exalted place, 40
My ladies and my gentlemen stood by me on the dais:
A mirror showed me I look old and haggard in the face;

It showed me that my ladies all are fair to gaze upon,
Plump, plenteous-haired, to every one love's secret lore is known,
They laugh by day, they sleep by night; ah me, what is a throne?

The singing men and women sang that night as usual,
The dancers danced in pairs and sets, but music had a fall,
A melancholy windy fall as at a funeral.°

Amid the toss of torches to my chamber back we swept;
My ladies loosed my golden chain; meantime I could have wept 50
To think of some in galling chains whether they waked or slept.

I took my bath of scented milk, delicately waited on,
They burned sweet things for my delight, cedar and cinnamon,
They lit my shaded silver lamp and left me there alone.

A day went by, a week went by. One day I heard it said:
'Men are clamouring, women, children, clamouring to be fed;
Men like famished dogs are howling in the streets for bread.'

So two whispered by my door, not thinking I could hear,
Vulgar naked truth, ungarnished for a royal ear;
Fit for cooping in the background, not to stalk so near. 60

But I strained my utmost sense to catch this truth, and mark:
'There are families out grazing like cattle in the park.'
'A pair of peasants must be saved even if we build an ark.'

A merry jest, a merry laugh, each strolled upon his way;
One was my page, a lad I reared and bore with day by day;
One was my youngest maid as sweet and white as cream in May.

Other footsteps followed softly with a weightier tramp;
Voices said: 'Picked soldiers have been summoned from the camp
To quell these base-born ruffians who make free to howl and stamp.'

'Howl and stamp?' one answered: 'They made free to hurl a stone 70
At the minister's state coach, well aimed and stoutly thrown.'
'There's work then for the soldiers, for this rank crop must be mown.'

'One I saw, a poor old fool with ashes on his head,
Whimpering because a girl had snatched his crust of bread:
Then he dropped; when some one raised him, it turned out he was dead.'

'After us the deluge,' was retorted with a laugh:°
'If bread's the staff of life, they must walk without a staff.'
'While I've a loaf they're welcome to my blessing and the chaff.'

These passed. The king: stand up. Said my father with a smile:
'Daughter mine, your mother comes to sit with you awhile,   80
She's sad to-day, and who but you her sadness can beguile?'

He too left me. Shall I touch my harp now while I wait,—
(I hear them doubling guard below before our palace gate—)
Or shall I work the last gold stitch into my veil of state;

Or shall my woman stand and read some unimpassioned scene,
There's music of a lulling sort in words that pause between;
Or shall she merely fan me while I wait here for the queen?

Again I caught my father's voice in sharp word of command:
'Charge!' a clash of steel: 'Charge again, the rebels stand.
Smite and spare not, hand to hand; smite and spare not, hand to
    hand.'   90

There swelled a tumult at the gate, high voices waxing higher;
A flash of red reflected light lit the cathedral spire;
I heard a cry for faggots, then I heard a yell for fire.

'Sit and roast there with your meat, sit and bake there with your
    bread,
You who sat to see us starve,' one shrieking woman said:
'Sit on your throne and roast with your crown upon your head.'

Nay, this thing will I do, while my mother tarrieth,
I will take my fine spun gold, but not to sew therewith,
I will take my gold and gems, and rainbow fan and wreath;

With a ransom in my lap, a king's ransom in my hand,   100
I will go down to this people, will stand face to face, will stand
Where they curse king, queen, and princess of this cursed land.

They shall take all to buy them bread, take all I have to give;
I, if I perish, perish; they to-day shall eat and live;°
I, if I perish, perish; that's the goal I half conceive:°

Once to speak before the world, rend bare my heart and show
The lesson I have learned which is death, is life, to know.
I, if I perish, perish; in the name of God I go.

In Progress

Ten years ago it seemed impossible
    That she should ever grow so calm as this,
    With self-remembrance in her warmest kiss
And dim dried eyes like an exhausted well.
Slow-speaking when she has some fact to tell,
    Silent with long-unbroken silences,
    Centred in self yet not unpleased to please,
Gravely monotonous like a passing bell.
Mindful of drudging daily common things,
    Patient at pastime, patient at her work,   10
Wearied perhaps but strenuous certainly.
Sometimes I fancy we may one day see
    Her head shoot forth seven stars from where they lurk
And her eyes lightnings and her shoulders wings.

Good Friday

Am I a stone and not a sheep
    That I can stand, O Christ, beneath Thy Cross,°
    To number drop by drop Thy Blood's slow loss,
And yet not weep?

Not so those women loved
    Who with exceeding grief lamented Thee;
    Not so fallen Peter weeping bitterly;
Not so the thief was moved;

Not so the Sun and Moon
    Which hid their faces in a starless sky,   10
A horror of great darkness at broad noon—
    I, only I.

Yet give not o'er,
    But seek Thy sheep, true Shepherd of the flock;
Greater than Moses, turn and look once more
    And smite a rock.°

A Dream

SONNET

Once in a dream (for once I dreamed of you)
    We stood together in an open field;
    Above our heads two swift-winged pigeons wheeled,°
Sporting at ease and courting full in view.
When loftier still a broadening darkness flew,
    Down-swooping, and a ravenous hawk revealed;
    Too weak to fight, too fond to fly, they yield;
So farewell life and love and pleasures new.
Then as their plumes fell fluttering to the ground,
    Their snow-white plumage flecked with crimson drops,   10
        I wept, and thought I turned towards you to weep:
    But you were gone; while rustling hedgerow tops
Bent in a wind which bore to me a sound
    Of far-off piteous bleat of lambs and sheep.

The Queen of Hearts

How comes it, Flora, that, whenever we
Play cards together, you invariably,
    However the pack parts,
    Still hold the Queen of Hearts?

I've scanned you with a scrutinizing gaze,
Resolved to fathom these your secret ways:
    But, sift them as I will,
    Your ways are secret still.

I cut and shuffle; shuffle, cut, again;
But all my cutting, shuffling, proves in vain: 10
    Vain hope, vain forethought too;
    That Queen still falls to you.

I dropped her once, prepense; but, ere the deal°
Was dealt, your instinct seemed her loss to feel:

'There should be one card more,'
You said, and searched the floor.

I cheated once; I made a private notch
In Heart-Queen's back, and kept a lynx-eyed watch;
    Yet such another back
    Deceived me in the pack: 20

The Queen of Clubs assumed by arts unknown
An imitative dint that seemed my own;
    This notch, not of my doing,
    Misled me to my ruin.

It baffles me to puzzle out the clue,
Which must be skill, or craft, or luck in you:
    Unless, indeed, it be
    Natural affinity.

A Bird's-Eye View

    'Croak, croak, croak,'
    Thus the Raven spoke,
    Perched on his crooked tree
    As hoarse as hoarse could be.
    Shun him and fear him,
    Lest the Bridegroom hear him;
    Scout him and rout him
    With his ominous eye about him.°

    Yet, 'Croak, croak, croak,'
    Still tolled from the oak;   10
    From that fatal black bird,
    Whether heard or unheard:
    'O ship upon the high seas,
    Freighted with lives and spices,
    Sink, O ship,' croaked the Raven:
    'Let the Bride mount to heaven.'

    In a far foreign land
    Upon the wave-edged sand,
    Some friends gaze wistfully

Across the glittering sea.
'If we could clasp our sister,'
Three say, 'now we have missed her!'
'If we could kiss our daughter!'
Two sigh across the water.

Oh, the ship sails fast
With silken flags at the mast,
And the home-wind blows soft;
But a Raven sits aloft,
Chuckling and choking,
Croaking, croaking, croaking:—   30
Let the beacon-fire blaze higher;
Bridegroom, watch; the Bride draws nigher.

On a sloped sandy beach,
Which the spring-tide billows reach,
Stand a watchful throng
Who have hoped and waited long:
'Fie on this ship, that tarries
With the priceless freight it carries.
The time seems long and longer:
O languid wind, wax stronger;'—   40

Whilst the Raven perched at ease
Still croaks and does not cease,
One monotonous note
Tolled from his iron throat:
'No father, no mother,
But I have a sable brother:
He sees where ocean flows to,
And he knows what he knows too.'

A day and a night
They kept watch worn and white;   50
A night and a day
For the swift ship on its way:
For the Bride and her maidens
—Clear chimes the bridal cadence—
For the tall ship that never
Hove in sight for ever.

On either shore, some
Stand in grief loud or dumb
As the dreadful dread
Grows certain though unsaid.   60
For laughter there is weeping,
And waking instead of sleeping,
And a desperate sorrow
Morrow after morrow.

Oh, who knows the truth,
How she perished in her youth,
And like a queen went down
Pale in her royal crown:
How she went up to glory
From the sea-foam chill and hoary,   70
From the sea-depth black and riven
To the calm that is in Heaven?

They went down, all the crew,
The silks and spices too,
The great ones and the small,
One and all, one and all.
Was it through stress of weather,
Quicksands, rocks, or all together?
Only the Raven knows this,
And he will not disclose this. —   80

After a day and year
The bridal bells chime clear;
After a year and a day
The Bridegroom is brave and gay:
Love is sound, faith is rotten;
The old Bride is forgotten: —
Two ominous Ravens only
Remember, black and lonely.

A Dumb Friend

I planted a young tree when I was young;
    But now the tree is grown and I am old:
    There wintry robin shelters from the cold
        And tunes his silver tongue.

A green and living tree I planted it,
  A glossy-foliaged tree of evergreen:
  All thro' the noontide heat it spread a screen
    Whereunder I might sit.

But now I only watch it where it towers:
  I, sitting at my window, watch it tossed   10
  By rattling gale, or silvered by the frost;
    Or, when sweet summer flowers,

Wagging its round green head with stately grace
  In tender winds that kiss it and go by:
  It shows a green full age; and what show I?
    A faded wrinkled face.

So often have I watched it, till mine eyes
  Have filled with tears and I have ceased to see,
  That now it seems a very friend to me
    In all my secrets wise.   20

A faithful pleasant friend, who year by year
  Grew with my growth and strengthened with my strength,
  But whose green lifetime shows a longer length:
    When I shall not sit here

It still will bud in spring, and shed rare leaves°
  In autumn, and in summer heat give shade,
  And warmth in winter; when my bed is made
    In shade the cypress weaves.

Maiden-Song

  Long ago and long ago,
    And long ago still,
  There dwelt three merry maidens
    Upon a distant hill.
  One was tall Meggan,
    And one was dainty May,
  But one was fair Margaret,
    More fair than I can say,
  Long ago and long ago.

When Meggan plucked the thorny rose, 10
  And when May pulled the briar,
Half the birds would swoop to see,
  Half the beasts draw nigher;
Half the fishes of the streams
  Would dart up to admire:
But when Margaret plucked a flag-flower,
  Or poppy hot aflame,
All the beasts and all the birds
  And all the fishes came
To her hand more soft than snow. 20

Strawberry leaves and May-dew°
  In brisk morning air,
Strawberry leaves and May-dew
  Make maidens fair.
'I go for strawberry leaves,'
  Meggan said one day:
'Fair Margaret can bide at home,
  But you come with me, May;
Up the hill and down the hill,
  Along the winding way 30
You and I are used to go.'

So these two fair sisters
  Went with innocent will
Up the hill and down again,
  And round the homestead hill:
While the fairest sat at home,
  Margaret like a queen,
Like a blush-rose, like the moon
  In her heavenly sheen,
Fragrant-breathed as milky cow 40
  Or field of blossoming bean,
Graceful as an ivy bough
  Born to cling and lean;
Thus she sat to sing and sew.

When she raised her lustrous eyes
  A beast peeped at the door;
When she downward cast her eyes
  A fish gasped on the floor;°

When she turned away her eyes
   A bird perched on the sill,   50
Warbling out its heart of love,
   Warbling warbling still,
With pathetic pleadings low.

Light-foot May with Meggan
   Sought the choicest spot,
Clothed with thyme-alternate grass:
   Then, while day waxed hot,
Sat at ease to play and rest,
   A gracious rest and play;
The loveliest maidens near or far,   60
   When Margaret was away,
Who sat at home to sing and sew.

Sun-glow flushed their comely cheeks,
   Wind-play tossed their hair,
Creeping things among the grass
   Stroked them here and there;
Meggan piped a merry note,
   A fitful wayward lay,
While shrill as bird on topmost twig
   Piped merry May;   70
Honey-smooth the double flow.

Sped a herdsman from the vale,
   Mounting like a flame,
All on fire to hear and see
   With floating locks he came.
Looked neither north nor south,
   Neither east nor west,
But sat him down at Meggan's feet
   As love-bird on his nest,
And wooed her with a silent awe,   80
   With trouble not expressed;
She sang the tears into his eyes,
   The heart out of his breast:
So he loved her, listening so.

She sang the heart out of his breast,
   The words out of his tongue;

Hand and foot and pulse he paused
    Till her song was sung.
Then he spoke up from his place
    Simple words and true: 90
'Scanty goods have I to give,
    Scanty skill to woo;
But I have a will to work,
    And a heart for you:
Bid me stay or bid me go.'

Then Meggan mused within herself:
    'Better be first with him,
Than dwell where fairer Margaret sits,
    Who shines my brightness dim,
For ever second where she sits,   100
    However fair I be:
I will be lady of his love,
    And he shall worship me;
I will be lady of his herds
    And stoop to his degree,
At home where kids and fatlings grow.'

Sped a shepherd from the height
    Headlong down to look,
(White lambs followed, lured by love
    Of their shepherd's crook):   110
He turned neither east nor west,
    Neither north nor south,
But knelt right down to May, for love
    Of her sweet-singing mouth;
Forgot his flocks, his panting flocks
    In parching hill-side drouth;
Forgot himself for weal or woe.

Trilled her song and swelled her song
    With maiden coy caprice
In a labyrinth of throbs,   120
    Pauses, cadences;
Clear-noted as a dropping brook,
    Soft-noted like the bees,
Wild-noted as the shivering wind
    Forlorn through forest trees:

Love-noted like the wood-pigeon
   Who hides herself for love,
Yet cannot keep her secret safe,
   But cooes and cooes thereof:
Thus the notes rang loud or low.   130

He hung breathless on her breath;
   Speechless, who listened well;
Could not speak or think or wish
   Till silence broke the spell.
Then he spoke, and spread his hands
   Pointing here and there:
'See my sheep and see the lambs,
   Twin lambs which they bare.
All myself I offer you,
   All my flocks and care,   140
Your sweet song hath moved me so.'

In her fluttered heart young May
   Mused a dubious while:
'If he loves me as he says' —
   Her lips curved with a smile:
'Where Margaret shines like the sun,
   I shine but like a moon;
If sister Meggan makes her choice
   I can make mine as soon;
At cockcrow we were sister-maids,   150
   We may be brides at noon.'
Said Meggan, 'Yes;' May said not 'No.'

Fair Margaret stayed alone at home,
   Awhile she sang her song,
Awhile sat silent, then she thought:
   'My sisters loiter long.'
That sultry noon had waned away,
   Shadows had waxen great:
'Surely,' she thought within herself,
   'My sisters loiter late.'   160
She rose, and peered out at the door,
   With patient heart to wait,
And heard a distant nightingale
   Complaining of its mate;

Then down the garden slope she walked,
  Down to the garden gate,
Leaned on the rail and waited so.

The slope was lightened by her eyes
  Like summer lightning fair,
Like rising of the haloed moon   170
  Lightened her glimmering hair,
While her face lightened like the sun
  Whose dawn is rosy white.
Thus crowned with maiden majesty
  She peered into the night,
Looked up the hill and down the hill,
  To left hand and to right,
Flashing like fire-flies to and fro.

Waiting thus in weariness
  She marked the nightingale   180
Telling, if any one would heed,
  Its old complaining tale.
Then lifted she her voice and sang,
  Answering the bird:
Then lifted she her voice and sang,
  Such notes were never heard
From any bird when Spring's in blow.

The king of all that country
  Coursing far, coursing near,
Curbed his amber-bitted steed,   190
  Coursed amain to hear;
All his princes in his train,
  Squire, and knight, and peer,
With his crown upon his head,
  His sceptre in his hand,
Down he fell at Margaret's knees
  Lord king of all that land,
To her highness bending low.

Every beast and bird and fish
  Came mustering to the sound,   200
Every man and every maid
  From miles of country round:

Meggan on her herdsman's arm,
  With her shepherd May,
Flocks and herds trooped at their heels
  Along the hill-side way;
No foot too feeble for the ascent,
  Not any head too grey;
Some were swift and none were slow.

So Margaret sang her sisters home   210
  In their marriage mirth;
Sang free birds out of the sky,
  Beasts along the earth,
Sang up fishes of the deep—
  All breathing things that move
Sang from far and sang from near
  To her lovely love;
Sang together friend and foe;

Sang a golden-bearded king
  Straightway to her feet,   220
Sang him silent where he knelt
  In eager anguish sweet.
But when the clear voice died away,
  When longest echoes died,
He stood up like a royal man
  And claimed her for his bride.
So three maids were wooed and won
  In a brief May-tide,
Long ago and long ago.

The Lowest Place

Give me the lowest place: not that I dare
  Ask for that lowest place, but Thou hast died
That I might live and share
  Thy glory by Thy side.

Give me the lowest place: or if for me
  That lowest place too high, make one more low
Where I may sit and see
  My God and love Thee so.

Somewhere or Other

Somewhere or other there must surely be
    The face not seen, the voice not heard,
The heart that not yet—never yet—ah me!
    Made answer to my word.

Somewhere or other, may be near or far;
    Past land and sea, clean out of sight;
Beyond the wandering moon, beyond the star
    That tracks her night by night.

Somewhere or other, may be far or near;
    With just a wall, a hedge, between;   10
With just the last leaves of the dying year
    Fallen on a turf grown green.

What Would I Give?

What would I give for a heart of flesh to warm me through,
Instead of this heart of stone ice-cold whatever I do;°
Hard and cold and small, of all hearts the worst of all.

What would I give for words, if only words would come;
But now in its misery my spirit has fallen dumb:
Oh, merry friends, go your way, I have never a word to say.

What would I give for tears, not smiles but scalding tears,
To wash the black mark clean, and to thaw the frost of years,
To wash the stain ingrain and to make me clean again.°

Who Shall Deliver Me?

God strengthen me to bear myself;
    That heaviest weight of all to bear,
    Inalienable weight of care.

All others are outside myself;
    I lock my door and bar them out,
    The turmoil, tedium, gad-about.

I lock my door upon myself,
And bar them out; but who shall wall
Self from myself, most loathed of all?

If I could once lay down myself,   10
And start self-purged upon the race°
That all must run! Death runs apace.

If I could set aside myself,
And start with lightened heart upon
The road by all men overgone!

God harden me against myself,
This coward with pathetic voice
Who craves for ease, and rest, and joys:

Myself, arch-traitor to myself;
My hollowest friend, my deadliest foe,   20
My clog whatever road I go.°

Yet One there is can curb myself,
Can roll the strangling load from me,
Break off the yoke and set me free.°

The Ghost's Petition

'There's a footstep coming: look out, and see.' —
    'The leaves are falling, the wind is calling;
No one cometh across the lea.' —

'There's a footstep coming: O sister, look.' —
    'The ripple flashes, the white foam dashes;
No one cometh across the brook.' —

'But he promised that he would come:
    To-night, to-morrow, in joy or sorrow,
He must keep his word, and must come home.

'For he promised that he would come: 10
    His word was given; from earth or heaven,
He must keep his word, and must come home.

'Go to sleep, my sweet sister Jane;
    You can slumber, who need not number
Hour after hour, in doubt and pain.

'I shall sit here awhile, and watch;
    Listening, hoping, for one hand groping
In deep shadow to find the latch.'

After the dark, and before the light,
    One lay sleeping; and one sat weeping,
Who had watched and wept the weary night.

After the night, and before the day,
    One lay sleeping; and one sat weeping—
Watching, weeping for one away.

There came a footstep climbing the stair;
    Some one standing out on the landing
Shook the door like a puff of air—

Shook the door, and in he passed.
    Did he enter? In the room centre
Stood her husband: the door shut fast.

'O Robin, but you are cold—
    Chilled with the night-dew: so lily-white you
Look like a stray lamb from our fold.

'O Robin, but you are late:
    Come and sit near me—sit here and cheer me.'—
(Blue the flame burnt in the grate.)

'Lay not down your head on my breast:
    I cannot hold you, kind wife, nor fold you
In the shelter that you love best.

'Feel not after my clasping hand:
    I am but a shadow, come from the meadow
Where many lie, but no tree can stand.

'We are trees which have shed their leaves:
    Our heads lie low there, but no tears flow there;
Only I grieve for my wife who grieves.

'I could rest if you would not moan
   Hour after hour; I have no power
To shut my ears where I lie alone.

'I could rest if you would not cry;
   But there's no sleeping while you sit weeping—   50
Watching, weeping so bitterly.'—

'Woe's me! woe's me! for this I have heard.
   Oh, night of sorrow!—oh, black to-morrow!
Is it thus that you keep your word?

'O you who used so to shelter me
   Warm from the least wind—why, now the east wind
Is warmer than you, whom I quake to see.

'O my husband of flesh and blood,
   For whom my mother I left, and brother,
And all I had, accounting it good,   60

'What do you do there, underground,
   In the dark hollow? I'm fain to follow.
What do you do there?—what have you found?'—

'What I do there I must not tell:
   But I have plenty: kind wife, content ye:
It is well with us—it is well.

'Tender hand hath made our nest;
   Our fear is ended, our hope is blended
With present pleasure, and we have rest.'—

'Oh, but Robin, I'm fain to come,   70
   If your present days are so pleasant;
For my days are so wearisome.

'Yet I'll dry my tears for your sake:
   Why should I tease you, who cannot please you
Any more with the pains I take?'°

Twice

I took my heart in my hand
   (O my love, O my love),
I said: Let me fall or stand,
   Let me live or die,
But this once hear me speak—
   (O my love, O my love)—
Yet a woman's words are weak;
   You should speak, not I.

You took my heart in your hand
   With a friendly smile,   10
With a critical eye you scanned,
   Then set it down,
And said: It is still unripe,
   Better wait awhile;
Wait while the skylarks pipe,
   Till the corn grows brown.

As you set it down it broke—
   Broke, but I did not wince;
I smiled at the speech you spoke,
   At your judgment that I heard: 20
But I have not often smiled
   Since then, nor questioned since,
Nor cared for corn-flowers wild,
   Nor sung with the singing bird.

I take my heart in my hand,
   O my God, O my God,
My broken heart in my hand:
   Thou hast seen, judge Thou.
My hope was written on sand,
   O my God, O my God;   30
Now let Thy judgment stand—
   Yea, judge me now.

This contemned of a man,
   This marred one heedless day,
This heart take Thou to scan
   Both within and without:

Refine with fire its gold,°
   Purge Thou its dross away—
Yea, hold it in Thy hold,
   Whence none can pluck it out.   40

I take my heart in my hand—
   I shall not die, but live—
Before Thy face I stand;
   I, for Thou callest such:
All that I have I bring,
   All that I am I give,
Smile Thou and I shall sing,
   But shall not question much.

Under Willows

Under willows among the graves
   One was walking, ah welladay!°
Where each willow her green boughs waves
   Come April prime, come May.
Under willows among the graves
   She met her lost love, ah welladay!
Where in Autumn each wild wind raves
   And whirls sere leaves away.

He looked at her with a smile,
   She looked at him with a sigh,   10
Both paused to look awhile;
   Then he passed by,
Passed by and whistled a tune;
   She stood silent and still:
It was the sunniest day in June,
   Yet one felt a chill.

Under willows among the graves
   I know a certain black black pool
Scarce wrinkled when Autumn raves;
   Under the turf is cool;   20
Under the water it must be cold;
   Winter comes cold when Summer's past;
Though she live to be old, so old,
   She shall die at last.

Bird or Beast?

Did any bird come flying
   After Adam and Eve,
When the door was shut against them
   And they sat down to grieve?

I think not Eve's peacock
   Splendid to see,
And I think not Adam's eagle;
   But a dove may be.

Did any beast come pushing
   Through the thorny hedge 10
Into the thorny thistly world
   Out from Eden's edge?

I think not a lion
   Though his strength is such;
But an innocent loving lamb
   May have done as much.

If the dove preached from her bough
   And the lamb from his sod,
The lamb and the dove
   Were preachers sent from God. 20

A Sketch

The blindest buzzard that I know
   Does not wear wings to spread and stir,
   Nor does my special mole wear fur
And grub among the roots below;
   He sports a tail indeed, but then
   It's to a coat; he's man with men;
     His quill is cut to a pen.

In other points our friend's a mole,
   A buzzard, beyond scope of speech:
   He sees not what's within his reach, 10
Misreads the part, ignores the whole.
   Misreads the part so reads in vain,

Ignores the whole tho' patent plain,
　　Misreads both parts again.

My blindest buzzard that I know,
　　My special mole, when will you see?
　　Oh no, you must not look at me,
There's nothing hid for me to show.
　　I might show facts as plain as day;
　　But since your eyes are blind, you'd say: 20
　　　'Where? What?' and turn away.

Songs in a Cornfield

A song in a cornfield
　　Where corn begins to fall,
Where reapers are reaping,
　　Reaping one, reaping all.
Sing pretty Lettice,
　　Sing Rachel, sing May;
Only Marian cannot sing
　　While her sweetheart's away.

Where is he gone to
　　And why does he stay?   10
He came across the green sea
　　But for a day,
Across the deep green sea
　　To help with the hay.
His hair was curly yellow
　　And his eyes were grey,
He laughed a merry laugh
　　And said a sweet say.
Where is he gone to
　　That he comes not home?   20
To-day or to-morrow
　　He surely will come.
Let him haste to joy
　　Lest he lag for sorrow,
For one weeps to-day
　　Who'll not weep to-morrow:

To-day she must weep
   For gnawing sorrow,
To-night she may sleep
   And not wake to-morrow.   30

May sang with Rachel
   In the waxing warm weather,
Lettice sang with them,
   They sang all together: —

'Take the wheat in your arm
   Whilst day is broad above,
Take the wheat to your bosom,
   But not a false false love.
   Out in the fields
      Summer heat gloweth,   40
   Out in the fields
      Summer wind bloweth,
   Out in the fields
      Summer friend showeth,
   Out in the fields
      Summer wheat groweth:
But in the winter
   When summer heat is dead
And summer wind has veered
   And summer friend has fled,   50
Only summer wheat remaineth,
   White cakes and bread.
Take the wheat, clasp the wheat
   That's food for maid and dove;
Take the wheat to your bosom,
   But not a false false love.'

A silence of full noontide heat
   Grew on them at their toil:
The farmer's dog woke up from sleep,
   The green snake hid her coil   60
Where grass stood thickest: bird and beast°
   Sought shadows as they could,
The reaping men and women paused
   And sat down where they stood;

They ate and drank and were refreshed,
 For rest from toil is good.

While the reapers took their ease,
 Their sickles lying by,
Rachel sang a second strain,
 And singing seemed to sigh: —   70

   'There goes the swallow —
   Could we but follow!
    Hasty swallow stay,
    Point us out the way;
Look back swallow, turn back swallow, stop swallow.

   'There went the swallow —
   Too late to follow:
    Lost our note of way,
    Lost our chance to-day;
Good bye swallow, sunny swallow, wise swallow.   80

   'After the swallow
   All sweet things follow:
    All things go their way,
    Only we must stay,
Must not follow; good bye swallow, good swallow.'°

Then listless Marian raised her head
 Among the nodding sheaves;
Her voice was sweeter than that voice;
 She sang like one who grieves:
Her voice was sweeter than its wont   90
 Among the nodding sheaves;
All wondered while they heard her sing
 Like one who hopes and grieves: —

  'Deeper than the hail can smite,
  Deeper than the frost can bite,
  Deep asleep through day and night,
   Our delight.

  'Now thy sleep no pang can break,
  No to-morrow bid thee wake,

Not our sobs who sit and ache   100
   For thy sake.

'Is it dark or light below?
Oh, but is it cold like snow?
Dost thou feel the green things grow
   Fast or slow?

'Is it warm or cold beneath,
Oh, but is it cold like death?
Cold like death, without a breath,
   Cold like death?'

If he comes to-day   110
   He will find her weeping;
If he comes to-morrow
   He will find her sleeping;
If he comes the next day
   He'll not find her at all,
He may tear his curling hair,
   Beat his breast and call.°

Despised and Rejected

My sun has set, I dwell
In darkness as a dead man out of sight;
And none remains, not one, that I should tell
To him mine evil plight
This bitter night.
I will make fast my door
That hollow friends may trouble me no more.

'Friend, open to Me.'—Who is this that calls?°
Nay, I am deaf as are my walls:
Cease crying, for I will not hear   10
Thy cry of hope or fear.
Others were dear,
Others forsook me: what art thou indeed
That I should heed
Thy lamentable need?
Hungry should feed,
Or stranger lodge thee here?

'Friend, My Feet bleed.
Open thy door to Me and comfort Me.'
I will not open, trouble me no more.   20
Go on thy way footsore,
I will not rise and open unto thee.

'Then is it nothing to thee? Open, see°
Who stands to plead with thee.
Open, lest I should pass thee by, and thou
One day entreat My Face
And howl for grace,
And I be deaf as thou art now.
Open to Me.'

Then I cried out upon him: Cease,   30
Leave me in peace:
Fear not that I should crave
Aught thou mayst have.
Leave me in peace, yea trouble me no more,
Lest I arise and chase thee from my door.
What, shall I not be let
Alone, that thou dost vex me yet?

But all night long that voice spake urgently:
'Open to Me.'
Still harping in mine ears: 40
'Rise, let Me in.'
Pleading with tears:
'Open to Me that I may come to thee.'
While the dew dropped, while the dark hours were cold:
'My Feet bleed, see My Face,
See My Hands bleed that bring thee grace,
My Heart doth bleed for thee,
Open to Me.'

So till the break of day:
Then died away   50
That voice, in silence as of sorrow;
Then footsteps echoing like a sigh
Passed me by,
Lingering footsteps slow to pass.

On the morrow
I saw upon the grass
Each footprint marked in blood, and on my door
The mark of blood for evermore.°

Jessie Cameron

'Jessie, Jessie Cameron,
   Hear me but this once,' quoth he.
'Good luck go with you, neighbour's son,
   But I'm no mate for you,' quoth she.
Day was verging toward the night
   There beside the moaning sea,
Dimness overtook the light
   There where the breakers be.
'O Jessie, Jessie Cameron,
   I have loved you long and true.'—   10
'Good luck go with you, neighbour's son,
   But I'm no mate for you.'

She was a careless, fearless girl,
   And made her answer plain,
Outspoken she to earl or churl,
   Kindhearted in the main,
But somewhat heedless with her tongue
   And apt at causing pain;
A mirthful maiden she and young,
   Most fair for bliss or bane.   20
'Oh, long ago I told you so,
   I tell you so to-day:
Go you your way, and let me go
   Just my own free way.'

The sea swept in with moan and foam
   Quickening the stretch of sand;
They stood almost in sight of home;
   He strove to take her hand.
'Oh, can't you take your answer then,
   And won't you understand?   30
For me you're not the man of men,

I've other plans are planned.
You're good for Madge, or good for Cis,
　　Or good for Kate, may be:
But what's to me the good of this
　　While you're not good for me?'

They stood together on the beach,
　　They two alone,
And louder waxed his urgent speech,
　　His patience almost gone:　　　　　　　　40
'Oh, say but one kind word to me,
　　Jessie, Jessie Cameron.'—
'I'd be too proud to beg,' quoth she,
　　And pride was in her tone.
And pride was in her lifted head,
　　And in her angry eye,
And in her foot, which might have fled,
　　But would not fly.

Some say that he had gipsy blood,
　　That in his heart was guile:　　　　　　　50
Yet he had gone through fire and flood
　　Only to win her smile.
Some say his grandam was a witch,
　　A black witch from beyond the Nile,
Who kept an image in a niche
　　And talked with it the while.
And by her hut far down the lane
　　Some say they would not pass at night,
Lest they should hear an unked strain°
　　Or see an unked sight.　　　　　　　　60

Alas, for Jessie Cameron!—
　　The sea crept moaning, moaning nigher:
She should have hastened to begone,—
　　The sea swept higher, breaking by her:
She should have hastened to her home
　　While yet the west was flushed with fire,
But now her feet are in the foam,
　　The sea-foam sweeping higher.
O mother, linger at your door,

And light your lamp to make it plain,   70
But Jessie she comes home no more,
   No more again.

They stood together on the strand,
   They only each by each;
Home, her home, was close at hand,
   Utterly out of reach.
Her mother in the chimney nook
   Heard a startled sea-gull screech,
But never turned her head to look
   Towards the darkening beach: 80
Neighbours here and neighbours there
   Heard one scream, as if a bird
Shrilly screaming cleft the air:—
   That was all they heard.

Jessie she comes home no more,
   Comes home never;
Her lover's step sounds at his door
   No more for ever.
And boats may search upon the sea
   And search along the river,   90
But none know where the bodies be:
   Sea-winds that shiver,
Sea-birds that breast the blast,
   Sea-waves swelling,
Keep the secret first and last
   Of their dwelling.

Whether the tide so hemmed them round
   With its pitiless flow,
That when they would have gone they found
   No way to go;   100
Whether she scorned him to the last
   With words flung to and fro,
Or clung to him when hope was past,
   None will ever know:
Whether he helped or hindered her,
   Threw up his life or lost it well,
The troubled sea for all its stir
   Finds no voice to tell.

Only watchers by the dying
   Have thought they heard one pray   110
Wordless, urgent; and replying
   One seem to say him nay:
And watchers by the dead have heard
   A windy swell from miles away,
With sobs and screams, but not a word
   Distinct for them to say:
And watchers out at sea have caught
   Glimpse of a pale gleam here or there,
Come and gone as quick as thought,
   Which might be hand or hair.   120

Weary in Well-Doing

I would have gone; God bade me stay:
   I would have worked; God bade me rest.
He broke my will from day to day,
   He read my yearnings unexpressed
     And said them nay.

Now I would stay; God bids me go:
   Now I would rest; God bids me work.
He breaks my heart tossed to and fro,
   My soul is wrung with doubts that lurk
     And vex it so.   10

I go, Lord, where Thou sendest me;
   Day after day I plod and moil:°
But, Christ my God, when will it be
   That I may let alone my toil
     And rest with Thee?

Paradise: in a Symbol

Golden-winged, silver-winged,
   Winged with flashing flame,
Such a flight of birds I saw,
   Birds without a name:

Singing songs in their own tongue
   (Song of songs) they came.

One to another calling,
   Each answering each,
One to another calling
   In their proper speech: 10
High above my head they wheeled,
   Far out of reach.

On wings of flame they went and came
   With a cadenced clang,°
Their silver wings tinkled,
   Their golden wings rang,
The wind it whistled through their wings
   Where in Heaven they sang.

They flashed and they darted
   Awhile before mine eyes,   20
Mounting, mounting, mounting still
   In haste to scale the skies—
Birds without a nest on earth,
   Birds of Paradise.

Where the moon riseth not,
   Nor sun seeks the west,°
There to sing their glory
   Which they sing at rest,
There to sing their love-song
   When they sing their best: 30

Not in any garden
   That mortal foot hath trod,
Not in any flowering tree
   That springs from earthly sod,
But in the garden where they dwell,
   The Paradise of God.

Grown and Flown

I loved my love from green of Spring
   Until sere Autumn's fall;

But now that leaves are withering
  How should one love at all?
  One heart's too small
For hunger, cold, love, everything.

I loved my love on sunny days
  Until late Summer's wane;
But now that frost begins to glaze
  How should one love again?
  Nay, love and pain
Walk wide apart in diverse ways.

I loved my love—alas to see
  That this should be, alas!
I thought that this could scarcely be,
  Yet has it come to pass:
  Sweet sweet love was,
Now bitter bitter grown to me.

Eve

'While I sit at the door
Sick to gaze within°
Mine eye weepeth sore
For sorrow and sin:
As a tree my sin stands
To darken all lands;
Death is the fruit it bore.

'How have Eden bowers grown
Without Adam to bend them!
How have Eden flowers blown
Squandering their sweet breath
Without me to tend them!
The Tree of Life was ours,
Tree twelvefold-fruited,°
Most lofty tree that flowers,
Most deeply rooted:
I chose the tree of death.

'Hadst thou but said me nay,
Adam, my brother,
I might have pined away;
I, but none other:
God might have let thee stay
Safe in our garden,
By putting me away
Beyond all pardon.

'I, Eve, sad mother
Of all who must live,
I, not another,
Plucked bitterest fruit to give
My friend, husband, lover —
O wanton eyes run over;
Who but I should grieve? —
Cain hath slain his brother:°
Of all who must die mother,
Miserable Eve!'

Thus she sat weeping,
Thus Eve our mother,
Where one lay sleeping
Slain by his brother.
Greatest and least
Each piteous beast
To hear her voice
Forgot his joys
And set aside his feast.

The mouse paused in his walk
And dropped his wheaten stalk;
Grave cattle wagged their heads
In rumination;
The eagle gave a cry
From his cloud station;
Larks on thyme beds
Forbore to mount or sing;
Bees drooped upon the wing;
The raven perched on high
Forgot his ration;

The conies in their rock,
A feeble nation,
Quaked sympathetical;
The mocking-bird left off to mock;
Huge camels knelt as if   60
In deprecation;°
The kind hart's tears were falling;
Chattered the wistful stork;
Dove-voices with a dying fall
Cooed desolation
Answering grief by grief.

Only the serpent in the dust
Wriggling and crawling
Grinned an evil grin and thrust
His tongue out with its fork.   70

The Prince's Progress

Till all sweet gums and juices flow,
Till the blossom of blossoms blow,
The long hours go and come and go,
    The bride she sleepeth, waketh, sleepeth,
Waiting for one whose coming is slow: —
        Hark! the bride weepeth.

'How long shall I wait, come heat come rime?' —
'Till the strong Prince comes, who must come in time'
(Her women say), 'there's a mountain to climb,
    A river to ford. Sleep, dream and sleep: 10
Sleep' (they say): 'we've muffled the chime,
        Better dream than weep.'

In his world-end palace the strong Prince sat,°
Taking his ease on cushion and mat,
Close at hand lay his staff and his hat.
    'When wilt thou start? the bride waits, O youth.' —
'Now the moon's at full; I tarried for that,
        Now I start in truth.

'But tell me first, true voice of my doom,
Of my veiled bride in her maiden bloom;   20
Keeps she watch through glare and through gloom,
    Watch for me asleep and awake?'—
'Spell-bound she watches in one white room,
        And is patient for thy sake.°

'By her head lilies and rosebuds grow;
The lilies droop, will the rosebuds blow?
The silver slim lilies hang the head low;
    Their stream is scanty, their sunshine rare;
Let the sun blaze out, and let the stream flow,
        They will blossom and wax fair.   30

'Red and white poppies grow at her feet,
The blood-red wait for sweet summer heat,
Wrapped in bud-coats hairy and neat;
    But the white buds swell, one day they will burst,
Will open their death-cups drowsy and sweet—
        Which will open the first?'

Then a hundred sad voices lifted a wail,
And a hundred glad voices piped on the gale:
'Time is short, life is short,' they took up the tale:
    'Life is sweet, love is sweet, use to-day while you may;   40
Love is sweet, and to-morrow may fail;°
        Love is sweet, use to-day.'

While the song swept by, beseeching and meek,
Up rose the Prince with a flush on his cheek,
Up he rose to stir and to seek,
    Going forth in the joy of his strength;
Strong of limb if of purpose weak,
        Starting at length.

Forth he set in the breezy morn,
Crossing green fields of nodding corn,   50
As goodly a Prince as ever was born;
    Carolling with the carolling lark;—
Sure his bride will be won and worn,
        Ere fall of the dark.

So light his step, so merry his smile,
A milkmaid loitered beside a stile,
Set down her pail and rested awhile,
   A wave-haired milkmaid, rosy and white;
The Prince, who had journeyed at least a mile,
      Grew athirst at the sight.   60

'Will you give me a morning draught?' —
'You're kindly welcome,' she said, and laughed.
He lifted the pail, new milk he quaffed;
   Then wiping his curly black beard like silk:
'Whitest cow that ever was calved
      Surely gave you this milk.'

Was it milk now, or was it cream?
Was she a maid, or an evil dream?
Her eyes began to glitter and gleam;
   He would have gone, but he stayed instead;   70
Green they gleamed as he looked in them:
      'Give me my fee,' she said. —

'I will give you a jewel of gold.' —
'Not so; gold is heavy and cold.' —
'I will give you a velvet fold
   Of foreign work your beauty to deck.' —
'Better I like my kerchief rolled
      Light and white round my neck.' —

'Nay,' cried he, 'but fix your own fee.' —
She laughed, 'You may give the full moon to me;   80
Or else sit under this apple-tree
   Here for one idle day by my side;
After that I'll let you go free,
      And the world is wide.'

Loth to stay, but to leave her slack,
He half turned away, then he quite turned back:
For courtesy's sake he could not lack
   To redeem his own royal pledge;
Ahead too the windy heaven lowered black
      With a fire-cloven edge.°   90

So he stretched his length in the apple-tree shade,
Lay and laughed and talked to the maid,
Who twisted her hair in a cunning braid
   And writhed it shining in serpent-coils,
And held him a day and a night fast laid
     In her subtle toils.°

At the death of night and the birth of day,
When the owl left off his sober play
And the bat hung himself out of the way,
   Woke the song of mavis and merle,°   100
And heaven put off its hodden grey,°
     For mother-o'-pearl.

Peeped up daisies here and there,
Here, there, and everywhere;
Rose a hopeful lark in the air,
   Spreading out towards the sun his breast;
While the moon set solemn and fair
     Away in the West.

'Up, up, up,' called the watchman lark,
In his clear réveillée: 'Hearken, oh hark!   110
Press to the high goal, fly to the mark.
   Up, O sluggard, new morn is born;
If still asleep when the night falls dark,
     Thou must wait a second morn.'

'Up, up, up,' sad glad voices swelled:
'So the tree falls and lies as it's felled.
Be thy bands loosed, O sleeper, long held
   In sweet sleep whose end is not sweet.
Be the slackness girt and the softness quelled
     And the slowness fleet.'   120

Off he set. The grass grew rare,
A blight lurked in the darkening air,°
The very moss grew hueless and spare,
   The last daisy stood all astunt;
Behind his back the soil lay bare,
     But barer in front.

A land of chasm and rent, a land
Of rugged blackness on either hand:
If water trickled its track was tanned
    With an edge of rust to the chink;   130
If one stamped on stone or on sand
      It returned a clink.

A lifeless land, a loveless land,
Without lair or nest on either hand:
Only scorpions jerked in the sand,
    Black as black iron, or dusty pale;
From point to point sheer rock was manned
      By scorpions in mail.

A land of neither life nor death,
Where no man buildeth or fashioneth,   140
Where none draws living or dying breath;
    No man cometh or goeth there,
No man doeth, seeketh, saith,
      In the stagnant air.

Some old volcanic upset must
Have rent the crust and blackened the crust;
Wrenched and ribbed it beneath its dust
    Above earth's molten centre at seethe,
Heaved and heaped it by huge upthrust
      Of fire beneath.   150

Untrodden before, untrodden since:
Tedious land for a social Prince;
Halting, he scanned the outs and ins,°
    Endless, labyrinthine, grim,
Of the solitude that made him wince,
      Laying wait for him.

By bulging rock and gaping cleft,
Even of half mere daylight reft,
Rueful he peered to right and left,
    Muttering in his altered mood: 160
'The fate is hard that weaves my weft,°
      Though my lot be good.'

Dim the changes of day to night,
Of night scarce dark to day not bright.
Still his road wound towards the right,
   Still he went, and still he went,
Till one night he espied a light,
      In his discontent.

Out it flashed from a yawn-mouthed cave,°
Like a red-hot eye from a grave.   170
No man stood there of whom to crave
   Rest for wayfarer plodding by:
Though the tenant were churl or knave
      The Prince might try.

In he passed and tarried not,
Groping his way from spot to spot,
Towards where the cavern flare glowed hot:—
   An old, old mortal, cramped and double,
Was peering into a seething-pot,°
      In a world of trouble.   180

The veriest atomy he looked,°
With grimy fingers clutching and crooked,
Tight skin, a nose all bony and hooked,
   And a shaking, sharp, suspicious way;
His blinking eyes had scarcely brooked
      The light of day.

Stared the Prince, for the sight was new;
Stared, but asked without more ado:
'May a weary traveller lodge with you,
   Old father, here in your lair?   190
In your country the inns seem few,
      And scanty the fare.'

The head turned not to hear him speak;
The old voice whistled as through a leak
(Out it came in a quavering squeak):
   'Work for wage is a bargain fit:
If there's aught of mine that you seek
      You must work for it.

'Buried alive from light and air
This year is the hundredth year,   200
I feed my fire with a sleepless care,
   Watching my potion wane or wax:
Elixir of Life is simmering there,
     And but one thing lacks.

'If you're fain to lodge here with me,
Take that pair of bellows you see—
Too heavy for my old hands they be—
   Take the bellows and puff and puff:
When the steam curls rosy and free
     The broth's boiled enough.   210

'Then take your choice of all I have;
I will give you life if you crave.
Already I'm mildewed for the grave,
   So first myself I must drink my fill:
But all the rest may be yours, to save
     Whomever you will.'

'Done,' quoth the Prince, and the bargain stood.
First he piled on resinous wood,
Next plied the bellows in hopeful mood;
   Thinking, 'My love and I will live.   220
If I tarry, why life is good,
     And she may forgive.'

The pot began to bubble and boil;
The old man cast in essence and oil,
He stirred all up with a triple coil
   Of gold and silver and iron wire,
Dredged in a pinch of virgin soil,
     And fed the fire.

But still the steam curled watery white;
Night turned to day and day to night;   230
One thing lacked, by his feeble sight
   Unseen, unguessed by his feeble mind:
Life might miss him, but Death the blight
     Was sure to find.

So when the hundredth year was full
The thread was cut and finished the school.
Death snapped the old worn-out tool,
   Snapped him short while he stood and stirred
(Though stiff he stood as a stiff-necked mule)°
     With never a word.   240

Thus at length the old crab was nipped.°
The dead hand slipped, the dead finger dipped
In the broth as the dead man slipped, —
   That same instant, a rosy red
Flushed the steam, and quivered and clipped°
     Round the dead old head.

The last ingredient was supplied
(Unless the dead man mistook or lied).
Up started the Prince, he cast aside
   The bellows plied through the tedious trial,   250
Made sure that his host had died,
     And filled a phial.

'One night's rest,' thought the Prince: 'This done,
Forth I start with the rising sun:
With the morrow I rise and run,
   Come what will of wind or of weather.
This draught of Life when my Bride is won
     We'll drink together.'

Thus the dead man stayed in his grave,
Self-chosen, the dead man in his cave;   260
There he stayed, were he fool or knave,
   Or honest seeker who had not found:
While the Prince outside was prompt to crave
     Sleep on the ground.

'If she watches, go bid her sleep;
Bid her sleep, for the road is steep:
He can sleep who holdeth her cheap,
   Sleep and wake and sleep again.
Let him sow, one day he shall reap,
     Let him sow the grain.   270

'When there blows a sweet garden rose,
Let it bloom and wither if no man knows:
But if one knows when the sweet thing blows,
    Knows, and lets it open and drop,
If but a nettle his garden grows
        He hath earned the crop.'

Through his sleep the summons rang,
Into his ears it sobbed and it sang.
Slow he woke with a drowsy pang,
    Shook himself without much debate,   280
Turned where he saw green branches hang,
        Started though late.

For the black land was travelled o'er,
He should see the grim land no more.
A flowering country stretched before
    His face when the lovely day came back:
He hugged the phial of Life he bore,
        And resumed his track.

By willow courses he took his path,
Spied what a nest the kingfisher hath,   290
Marked the fields green to aftermath,°
    Marked where the red-brown field-mouse ran,
Loitered awhile for a deep-stream bath,
        Yawned for a fellow-man.

Up on the hills not a soul in view,
In the vale not many nor few;
Leaves, still leaves, and nothing new.
    It's oh for a second maiden, at least,
To bear the flagon, and taste it too,
        And flavour the feast.   300

Lagging he moved, and apt to swerve;
Lazy of limb, but quick of nerve.
At length the water-bed took a curve,
    The deep river swept its bankside bare;
Waters streamed from the hill-reserve—
        Waters here, waters there.

High above, and deep below,
Bursting, bubbling, swelling the flow,
Like hill-torrents after the snow,—
    Bubbling, gurgling, in whirling strife,   310
Swaying, sweeping, to and fro,—
        He must swim for his life.°

Which way?—which way?—his eyes grew dim
With the dizzying whirl—which way to swim?
The thunderous downshoot deafened him;
    Half he choked in the lashing spray:
Life is sweet, and the grave is grim—
        Which way?—which way?

A flash of light, a shout from the strand:
'This way—this way; here lies the land!'   320
His phial clutched in one drowning hand;
    He catches—misses—catches a rope;
His feet slip on the slipping sand:
        Is there life?—is there hope?

Just saved, without pulse or breath,—
Scarcely saved from the gulp of death;
Laid where a willow shadoweth—
    Laid where a swelling turf is smooth.
(O Bride! but the Bridegroom lingereth
        For all thy sweet youth.)   330

Kind hands do and undo,
Kind voices whisper and coo:
'I will chafe his hands'—'And I'—'And you
    Raise his head, put his hair aside.'
(If many laugh, one well may rue:
        Sleep on, thou Bride.)

So the Prince was tended with care:
One wrung foul ooze from his clustered hair;
Two chafed his hands, and did not spare;
    But one held his drooping head breast-high,°   340
Till his eyes oped, and at unaware
        They met eye to eye.

Oh, a moon face in a shadowy place,
And a light touch and a winsome grace,
And a thrilling tender voice that says:
    'Safe from waters that seek the sea—
Cold waters by rugged ways—
        Safe with me.'

While overhead bird whistles to bird,
And round about plays a gamesome herd: 350
'Safe with us'—some take up the word—
    'Safe with us, dear lord and friend:
All the sweeter if long deferred
        Is rest in the end.'

Had he stayed to weigh and to scan,
He had been more or less than a man:
He did what a young man can,
    Spoke of toil and an arduous way—
Toil to-morrow, while golden ran
        The sands of to-day.   360

Slip past, slip fast,
Uncounted hours from first to last,
Many hours till the last is past,
    Many hours dwindling to one—
One hour whose die is cast,
        One last hour gone.

Come, gone—gone for ever—
Gone as an unreturning river—
Gone as to death the merriest liver—
    Gone as the year at the dying fall—   370
To-morrow, to-day, yesterday, never—
        Gone once for all.

Came at length the starting-day,
With last words, and last, last words to say,
With bodiless cries from far away—
    Chiding wailing voices that rang
Like a trumpet-call to the tug and fray;
        And thus they sang:

'Is there life?—the lamp burns low;
Is there hope?—the coming is slow: 380
The promise promised so long ago,
   The long promise, has not been kept.
Does she live?—does she die?—she slumbers so
    Who so oft has wept.

'Does she live?—does she die?—she languisheth
As a lily drooping to death,
As a drought-worn bird with failing breath,
   As a lovely vine without a stay,
As a tree whereof the owner saith,
    "Hew it down to-day."'   390

Stung by that word the Prince was fain
To start on his tedious road again.
He crossed the stream where a ford was plain,
   He clomb the opposite bank though steep,
And swore to himself to strain and attain
    Ere he tasted sleep.

Huge before him a mountain frowned
With foot of rock on the valley ground,
And head with snows incessant crowned,
   And a cloud mantle about its strength,   400
And a path which the wild goat hath not found
    In its breadth and length.

But he was strong to do and dare:
If a host had withstood him there,
He had braved a host with little care
   In his lusty youth and his pride,
Tough to grapple though weak to snare.
    He comes, O Bride.

Up he went where the goat scarce clings,
Up where the eagle folds her wings,   410
Past the green line of living things,
   Where the sun cannot warm the cold,—
Up he went as a flame enrings
    Where there seems no hold.

Up a fissure barren and black,
Till the eagles tired upon his track,
And the clouds were left behind his back,
   Up till the utmost peak was past.
Then he gasped for breath and his strength fell slack;
     He paused at last.   420

Before his face a valley spread
Where fatness laughed, wine, oil, and bread,°
Where all fruit-trees their sweetness shed,
   Where all birds made love to their kind,
Where jewels twinkled, and gold lay red
     And not hard to find.

Midway down the mountain side
(On its green slope the path was wide)
Stood a house for a royal bride,
   Built all of changing opal stone,   430
The royal palace, till now descried
     In his dreams alone.

Less bold than in days of yore,
Doubting now though never before,
Doubting he goes and lags the more:
   Is the time late? does the day grow dim?
Rose, will she open the crimson core
     Of her heart to him?°

Take heart of grace! the potion of Life
May go far to woo him a wife: 440
If she frown, yet a lover's strife
   Lightly raised can be laid again:
A hasty word is never the knife
     To cut love in twain.

Far away stretched the royal land,
Fed by dew, by a spice-wind fanned:
Light labour more, and his foot would stand
   On the threshold, all labour done;
Easy pleasure laid at his hand,
     And the dear Bride won.   450

His slackening steps pause at the gate—
Does she wake or sleep?—the time is late—
Does she sleep now, or watch and wait?
  She has watched, she has waited long,
Watching athwart the golden grate
    With a patient song.

Fling the golden portals wide,
The Bridegroom comes to his promised Bride;
Draw the gold-stiff curtains aside,
  Let them look on each other's face,   460
She in her meekness, he in his pride—
    Day wears apace.

Day is over, the day that wore.
What is this that comes through the door,
The face covered, the feet before?
  This that coming takes his breath;
This Bride not seen, to be seen no more
    Save of Bridegroom Death?

Veiled figures carrying her
Sweep by yet make no stir;   470
There is a smell of spice and myrrh,
  A bride-chant burdened with one name;
The bride-song rises steadier
    Than the torches' flame:

'Too late for love, too late for joy,
  Too late, too late!
You loitered on the road too long,
  You trifled at the gate:
The enchanted dove upon her branch
    Died without a mate;   480
The enchanted princess in her tower
  Slept, died, behind the grate;
Her heart was starving all this while
    You made it wait.

'Ten years ago, five years ago,
  One year ago,

Even then you had arrived in time,
   Though somewhat slow;
Then you had known her living face
   Which now you cannot know: 490
The frozen fountain would have leaped,
   The buds gone on to blow,
The warm south wind would have awaked
      To melt the snow.

'Is she fair now as she lies?
   Once she was fair;
Meet queen for any kingly king,
   With gold-dust on her hair.
Now these are poppies in her locks,
   White poppies she must wear;   500
Must wear a veil to shroud her face
   And the want graven there:
Or is the hunger fed at length,
      Cast off the care?

'We never saw her with a smile
   Or with a frown;
Her bed seemed never soft to her,
   Though tossed of down;
She little heeded what she wore,
   Kirtle, or wreath, or gown;°   510
We think her white brows often ached
   Beneath her crown,
Till silvery hairs showed in her locks
   That used to be so brown.

'We never heard her speak in haste:
   Her tones were sweet,
And modulated just so much
   As it was meet:
Her heart sat silent through the noise
   And concourse of the street.   520
There was no hurry in her hands,
   No hurry in her feet;
There was no bliss drew nigh to her,
   That she might run to greet.

'You should have wept her yesterday,
   Wasting upon her bed:
But wherefore should you weep to-day
   That she is dead?
Lo, we who love weep not to-day,
   But crown her royal head.   530
Let be these poppies that we strew,
   Your roses are too red:
Let be these poppies, not for you
   Cut down and spread.'

Memory

I

I nursed it in my bosom while it lived,
   I hid it in my heart when it was dead;
In joy I sat alone, even so I grieved
   Alone and nothing said.

I shut the door to face the naked truth,
   I stood alone—I faced the truth alone,
Stripped bare of self-regard or forms or ruth°
   Till first and last were shown.

I took the perfect balances and weighed;
   No shaking of my hand disturbed the poise;   10
Weighed, found it wanting: not a word I said,
   But silent made my choice.

None know the choice I made; I make it still.
   None know the choice I made and broke my heart,
Breaking mine idol: I have braced my will°
   Once, chosen for once my part.°

I broke it at a blow, I laid it cold,
   Crushed in my deep heart where it used to live.
My heart dies inch by inch; the time grows old,
   Grows old in which I grieve.   20

II

I have a room whereinto no one enters
   Save I myself alone:
   There sits a blessed memory on a throne,
There my life centres.

While winter comes and goes—oh tedious comer!—
   And while its nip-wind blows;
   While bloom the bloodless lily and warm rose°
Of lavish summer.

If any should force entrance he might see there
   One buried yet not dead,   30
   Before whose face I no more bow my head
Or bend my knee there;

But often in my worn life's autumn weather
   I watch there with clear eyes,
   And think how it will be in Paradise
When we're together.

Amor Mundi

'Oh, where are you going with your love-locks flowing°
   On the west wind blowing along this valley track?'
'The downhill path is easy, come with me an it please ye,°
   We shall escape the uphill by never turning back.'

So they two went together in glowing August weather,
   The honey-breathing heather lay to their left and right;
And dear she was to doat on, her swift feet seemed to float on
   The air like soft twin pigeons too sportive to alight.

'Oh, what is that in heaven where grey cloud-flakes are seven,
   Where blackest clouds hang riven just at the rainy skirt?'   10
'Oh, that's a meteor sent us, a message dumb, portentous,
   An undeciphered solemn signal of help or hurt.'°

'Oh, what is that glides quickly where velvet flowers grow thickly,
   Their scent comes rich and sickly?' 'A scaled and hooded worm.'
'Oh, what's that in the hollow, so pale I quake to follow?'
   'Oh, that's a thin dead body which waits the eternal term.'

'Turn again, O my sweetest,—turn again, false and fleetest:
  This beaten way thou beatest, I fear is hell's own track.'
'Nay, too steep for hill mounting; nay, too late for cost counting:
  This downhill path is easy, but there's no turning back.'   20

From Sunset to Star Rise

Go from me, summer friends, and tarry not:
  I am no summer friend, but wintry cold,
  A silly sheep benighted from the fold,°
A sluggard with a thorn-choked garden plot.
Take counsel, sever from my lot your lot,
  Dwell in your pleasant places, hoard your gold;
  Lest you with me should shiver on the wold,°
Athirst and hungering on a barren spot.
For I have hedged me with a thorny hedge,°
  I live alone, I look to die alone: 10
Yet sometimes when a wind sighs through the sedge°
  Ghosts of my buried years and friends come back,
My heart goes sighing after swallows flown
  On sometime summer's unreturning track.°

Under the Rose

The iniquity of the fathers upon the children.

Oh the rose of keenest thorn!
One hidden summer morn
Under the rose I was born.

I do not guess his name
Who wrought my Mother's shame,
And gave me life forlorn,
But my Mother, Mother, Mother,
I know her from all other.
My Mother pale and mild,
Fair as ever was seen,   10
She was but scarce sixteen,
Little more than a child,
When I was born
To work her scorn.
With secret bitter throes,

In a passion of secret woes,
She bore me under the rose.

One who my Mother nursed
Took me from the first: —
'O nurse, let me look upon   20
This babe that costs so dear;
To-morrow she will be gone:
Other mothers may keep
Their babes awake and asleep,
But I must not keep her here.' —
Whether I know or guess,
I know this not the less.

So I was sent away
That none might spy the truth:
And my childhood waxed to youth   30
And I left off childish play.
I never cared to play
With the village boys and girls;
And I think they thought me proud,
I found so little to say
And kept so from the crowd:
But I had the longest curls
And I had the largest eyes
And my teeth were small like pearls;
The girls might flout and scout me,°   40
But the boys would hang about me
In sheepish mooning wise.°

Our one-street village stood
A long mile from the town,
A mile of windy down
And bleak one-sided wood,°
With not a single house.
Our town itself was small,
With just the common shops,
And throve in its small way.   50
Our neighbouring gentry reared
The good old-fashioned crops,
And made old-fashioned boasts°

Of what John Bull would do
If Frenchman Frog appeared,
And drank old-fashioned toasts,
And made old-fashioned bows
To my Lady at the Hall.

My Lady at the Hall
Is grander than they all: 60
Hers is the oldest name
In all the neighbourhood;
But the race must die with her
Though she's a lofty dame,
For she's unmarried still.
Poor people say she's good
And has an open hand
As any in the land,
And she's the comforter
Of many sick and sad;   70
My nurse once said to me
That everything she had
Came of my Lady's bounty:
'Though she's greatest in the county
She's humble to the poor,
No beggar seeks her door
But finds help presently.
I pray both night and day
For her, and you must pray:
But she'll never feel distress   80
If needy folk can bless.'

I was a little maid
When here we came to live
From somewhere by the sea.
Men spoke a foreign tongue
There where we used to be
When I was merry and young,
Too young to feel afraid;
The fisher-folk would give
A kind strange word to me,   90
There by the foreign sea:
I don't know where it was,
But I remember still

Our cottage on a hill,
And fields of flowering grass
On that fair foreign shore.

I liked my old home best,
But this was pleasant too:
So here we made our nest
And here I grew.   100
And now and then my Lady
In riding past our door
Would nod to Nurse and speak,
Or stoop and pat my cheek;
And I was always ready
To hold the field-gate wide
For my Lady to go through;
My Lady in her veil
So seldom put aside,
My Lady grave and pale.   110

I often sat to wonder
Who might my parents be,
For I knew of something under
My simple-seeming state.
Nurse never talked to me
Of mother or of father,
But watched me early and late
With kind suspicious cares:
Or not suspicious, rather
Anxious, as if she knew   120
Some secret I might gather
And smart for unawares.
Thus I grew.

But Nurse waxed old and grey,
Bent and weak with years.
There came a certain day
That she lay upon her bed
Shaking her palsied head,
With words she gasped to say
Which had to stay unsaid.   130
Then with a jerking hand
Held out so piteously

She gave a ring to me
Of gold wrought curiously,
A ring which she had worn
Since the day that I was born,
She once had said to me:
I slipped it on my finger;
Her eyes were keen to linger
On my hand that slipped it on;   140
Then she sighed one rattling sigh
And stared on with sightless eye:—
The one who loved me was gone.

How long I stayed alone
With the corpse, I never knew,
For I fainted dead as stone:
When I came to life once more
I was down upon the floor,
With neighbours making ado
To bring me back to life.   150
I heard the sexton's wife
Say: 'Up, my lad, and run
To tell it at the Hall;
She was my Lady's nurse,
And done can't be undone.
I'll watch by this poor lamb.
I guess my Lady's purse
Is always open to such:
I'd run up on my crutch
A cripple as I am,'   160
(For cramps had vexed her much)
'Rather than this dear heart
Lack one to take her part.'

For days day after day
On my weary bed I lay
Wishing the time would pass;
Oh, so wishing that I was
Likely to pass away:
For the one friend whom I knew
Was dead, I knew no other,   170
Neither father nor mother;
And I, what should I do?

One day the sexton's wife
Said: 'Rouse yourself, my dear:
My Lady has driven down
From the Hall into the town,
And we think she's coming here.
Cheer up, for life is life.'

But I would not look or speak,
Would not cheer up at all.   180
My tears were like to fall,
So I turned round to the wall
And hid my hollow cheek
Making as if I slept,
As silent as a stone,
And no one knew I wept.
What was my Lady to me,
The grand lady from the Hall?
She might come, or stay away,
I was sick at heart that day: 190
The whole world seemed to be
Nothing, just nothing to me,
For aught that I could see.

Yet I listened where I lay:
A bustle came below,
A clear voice said: 'I know;
I will see her first alone,
It may be less of a shock
If she's so weak to-day:' —
A light hand turned the lock,   200
A light step crossed the floor,
One sat beside my bed:
But never a word she said.

For me, my shyness grew
Each moment more and more:
So I said never a word
And neither looked nor stirred;
I think she must have heard
My heart go pit-a-pat:
Thus I lay, my Lady sat,   210

More than a mortal hour—°
(I counted one and two
By the house-clock while I lay):
I seemed to have no power
To think of a thing to say,
Or do what I ought to do,
Or rouse myself to a choice.

At last she said: 'Margaret,
Won't you even look at me?'
A something in her voice   220
Forced my tears to fall at last,
Forced sobs from me thick and fast;
Something not of the past,
Yet stirring memory;
A something new, and yet
Not new, too sweet to last,
Which I never can forget.

I turned and stared at her:
Her cheek showed hollow-pale;
Her hair like mine was fair,   230
A wonderful fall of hair
That screened her like a veil;
But her height was statelier,
Her eyes had depth more deep;
I think they must have had
Always a something sad,
Unless they were asleep.

While I stared, my Lady took
My hand in her spare hand
Jewelled and soft and grand,   240
And looked with a long long look
Of hunger in my face;
As if she tried to trace
Features she ought to know,
And half hoped, half feared, to find.
Whatever was in her mind
She heaved a sigh at last,
And began to talk to me.

'Your nurse was my dear nurse,
And her nursling's dear,' said she: 250
'I never knew that she was worse
Till her poor life was past'
(Here my Lady's tears dropped fast):
'I might have been with her,
But she had no comforter.
She might have told me much
Which now I shall never know,
Never never shall know.'
She sat by me sobbing so,
And seemed so woe-begone,   260
That I laid one hand upon
Hers with a timid touch,
Scarce thinking what I did,
Not knowing what to say:
That moment her face was hid
In the pillow close by mine,
Her arm was flung over me,
She hugged me, sobbing so
As if her heart would break,
And kissed me where I lay.   270

After this she often came
To bring me fruit or wine,
Or sometimes hothouse flowers.
And at nights I lay awake
Often and often thinking
What to do for her sake.
Wet or dry it was the same:
She would come in at all hours,
Set me eating and drinking
And say I must grow strong;   280
At last the day seemed long
And home seemed scarcely home
If she did not come.

Well, I grew strong again:
In time of primroses,
I went to pluck them in the lane;
In time of nestling birds,

I heard them chirping round the house;
And all the herds
Were out at grass when I grew strong,   290
And days were waxen long,
And there was work for bees
Among the May-bush boughs,
And I had shot up tall,
And life felt after all
Pleasant, and not so long
When I grew strong.

I was going to the Hall
To be my Lady's maid:
'Her little friend,' she said to me,   300
'Almost her child,'
She said and smiled
Sighing painfully;
Blushing, with a second flush
As if she blushed to blush.

Friend, servant, child: just this
My standing at the Hall;
The other servants call me 'Miss,'
My Lady calls me 'Margaret,'
With her clear voice musical.   310
She never chides when I forget
This or that; she never chides.
Except when people come to stay,
(And that's not often) at the Hall,
I sit with her all day
And ride out when she rides.
She sings to me and makes me sing;
Sometimes I read to her,
Sometimes we merely sit and talk.
She noticed once my ring   320
And made me tell its history:
That evening in our garden walk
She said she should infer
The ring had been my father's first,
Then my mother's, given for me
To the nurse who nursed

My mother in her misery,
That so quite certainly
Some one might know me, who . . .
Then she was silent, and I too.   330

I hate when people come:
The women speak and stare
And mean to be so civil.
This one will stroke my hair,
That one will pat my cheek
And praise my Lady's kindness,
Expecting me to speak;
I like the proud ones best
Who sit as struck with blindness,
As if I wasn't there.   340
But if any gentleman
Is staying at the Hall
(Though few come prying here),
My Lady seems to fear
Some downright dreadful evil,
And makes me keep my room
As closely as she can:
So I hate when people come,
It is so troublesome.
In spite of all her care,   350
Sometimes to keep alive
I sometimes do contrive
To get out in the grounds
For a whiff of wholesome air,
Under the rose you know:
It's charming to break bounds,
Stolen waters are sweet,°
And what's the good of feet
If for days they mustn't go?
Give me a longer tether,   360
Or I may break from it.

Now I have eyes and ears
And just some little wit:
'Almost my lady's child;'
I recollect she smiled,

Sighed and blushed together;
Then her story of the ring
Sounds not improbable,
She told it me so well
It seemed the actual thing:—   370
Oh, keep your counsel close,
But I guess under the rose,
In long past summer weather
When the world was blossoming,
And the rose upon its thorn:
I guess not who he was
Flawed honour like a glass
And made my life forlorn,
But my Mother, Mother, Mother,
Oh, I know her from all other.   380

My Lady, you might trust
Your daughter with your fame.
Trust me, I would not shame
Our honourable name,
For I have noble blood
Though I was bred in dust
And brought up in the mud.
I will not press my claim,
Just leave me where you will:
But you might trust your daughter,   390
For blood is thicker than water
And you're my mother still.

So my Lady holds her own
With condescending grace,
And fills her lofty place
With an untroubled face
As a queen may fill a throne.
While I could hint a tale—
(But then I am her child)—
Would make her quail;   400
Would set her in the dust,
Lorn with no comforter,
Her glorious hair defiled
And ashes on her cheek:

The decent world would thrust
Its finger out at her,
Not much displeased I think
To make a nine days' stir;
The decent world would sink
Its voice to speak of her.   410

Now this is what I mean
To do, no more, no less:
Never to speak, or show
Bare sign of what I know.
Let the blot pass unseen;
Yea, let her never guess
I hold the tangled clue
She huddles out of view.
Friend, servant, almost child,
So be it and nothing more   420
On this side of the grave.
Mother, in Paradise,
You'll see with clearer eyes;
Perhaps in this world even
When you are like to die
And face to face with Heaven
You'll drop for once the lie:
But you must drop the mask, not I.

My Lady promises
Two hundred pounds with me   430
Whenever I may wed
A man she can approve:
And since besides her bounty
I'm fairest in the county
(For so I've heard it said,
Though I don't vouch for this),
Her promised pounds may move
Some honest man to see
My virtues and my beauties;
Perhaps the rising grazier,   440
Or temperance publican,
May claim my wifely duties.
Meanwhile I wait their leisure
And grace-bestowing pleasure,

I wait the happy man;
But if I hold my head
And pitch my expectations
Just higher than their level,
They must fall back on patience:
I may not mean to wed,   450
Yet I'll be civil.

Now sometimes in a dream
My heart goes out of me
To build and scheme,
Till I sob after things that seem
So pleasant in a dream:
A home such as I see
My blessed neighbours live in
With father and with mother,
All proud of one another,   460
Named by one common name
From baby in the bud
To full-blown workman father;
It's little short of Heaven.
I'd give my gentle blood
To wash my special shame
And drown my private grudge;
I'd toil and moil much rather
The dingiest cottage drudge
Whose mother need not blush,   470
Than live here like a lady
And see my Mother flush
And hear her voice unsteady
Sometimes, yet never dare
Ask to share her care.

Of course the servants sneer
Behind my back at me;
Of course the village girls,
Who envy me my curls
And gowns and idleness,   480
Take comfort in a jeer;
Of course the ladies guess
Just so much of my history
As points the emphatic stress

With which they laud my Lady;
The gentlemen who catch
A casual glimpse of me
And turn again to see,
Their valets on the watch
To speak a word with me,   490
All know and sting me wild;
Till I am almost ready
To wish that I were dead,
No faces more to see,
No more words to be said,
My Mother safe at last
Disburdened of her child,
And the past past.

'All equal before God' —
Our Rector has it so,   500
And sundry sleepers nod:
It may be so; I know
All are not equal here,
And when the sleepers wake
They make a difference.
'All equal in the grave' —
That shows an obvious sense:
Yet something which I crave
Not death itself brings near;
How should death half atone   510
For all my past; or make
The name I bear my own?

I love my dear old Nurse
Who loved me without gains;
I love my mistress even,
Friend, Mother, what you will:
But I could almost curse
My Father for his pains;
And sometimes at my prayer
Kneeling in sight of Heaven   520
I almost curse him still:
Why did he set his snare
To catch at unaware

My Mother's foolish youth;
Load me with shame that's hers,
And her with something worse,
A lifelong lie for truth?

I think my mind is fixed
On one point and made up:
To accept my lot unmixed;   530
Never to drug the cup
But drink it by myself.
I'll not be wooed for pelf;°
I'll not blot out my shame
With any man's good name;
But nameless as I stand,
My hand is my own hand,
And nameless as I came
I go to the dark land.

'All equal in the grave'—   540
I bide my time till then:
'All equal before God'—
To-day I feel His rod,
To-morrow He may save:
                Amen.

En Route / An 'Immurata' Sister

En Route

Life flows down to death; we cannot bind
   That current that it should not flee:
Life flows down to death, as rivers find
   The inevitable sea.

———

Wherefore art thou strange, and not my mother?
   Thou hast stolen my heart and broken it:
Would that I might call thy sons 'My brother',
   Call thy daughters 'Sister sweet';
Lying in thy lap not in another,
   Dying at thy feet.   10

Farewell land of love, Italy,
　　Sister-land of Paradise:
With mine own feet I have trodden thee,
　　Have seen with mine own eyes;
I remember, thou forgettest me,
　　I remember thee.

Blessed be the land that warms my heart,
　　And the kindly clime that cheers,
And the cordial faces clear from art,°
　　And the tongue sweet in mine ears:　　　　　20
Take my heart, its truest tenderest part,
　　Dear land, take my tears.

———————

Men work and think, but women feel:
　　And so (for I'm a woman, I)
　　And so I should be glad to die
And cease from impotence of zeal,
And cease from hope, and cease from dread,
　　And cease from yearnings without gain,
　　And cease from all this world of pain,
And be at peace among the dead.　　　　　　30

Why should I seek and never find
　　That something which I have not had?
　　Fair and unutterably sad
The world hath sought time out of mind.
Our words have been already said,
　　Our deeds have been already done:
　　There's nothing new beneath the sun
But there is peace among the dead.°

An 'Immurata' Sister

Life flows down to death; we cannot bind
　　That current that it should not flee:
Life flows down to death, as rivers find
　　The inevitable sea.

Men work and think, but women feel;
  And so (for I'm a woman, I)
  And so I should be glad to die
And cease from impotence of zeal,
And cease from hope, and cease from dread,
  And cease from yearnings without gain,
  And cease from all this world of pain,
And be at peace among the dead.

Hearts that die, by death renew their youth,
  Lightened of this life that doubts and dies;
Silent and contented, while the Truth
  Unveiled makes them wise.

Why should I seek and never find
  That something which I have not had?
  Fair and unutterably sad
The world hath sought time out of mind;
The world hath sought and I have sought,—
  Ah, empty world and empty I!
  For we have spent our strength for nought,
And soon it will be time to die.

Sparks fly upward toward their fount of fire,°
  Kindling, flashing, hovering:—
Kindle, flash, my soul; mount higher and higher,
  Thou whole burnt-offering!

Enrica, 1865

She came among us from the South
  And made the North her home awhile;
  Our dimness brightened in her smile,
Our tongue grew sweeter in her mouth.

We chilled beside her liberal glow,
  She dwarfed us by her ampler scale,
  Her full-blown blossom made us pale,
She summer-like and we like snow.

We Englishwomen, trim, correct,
   All minted in the self-same mould,   10
   Warm-hearted but of semblance cold,
All-courteous out of self-respect.

She woman in her natural graçe,
   Less trammelled she by lore of school,
   Courteous by nature not by rule,
Warm-hearted and of cordial face.

So for awhile she made her home
   Among us in the rigid North,
   She who from Italy came forth
And scaled the Alps and crossed the foam.   20

But if she found us like our sea,
   Of aspect colourless and chill,
   Rock-girt; like it she found us still
Deep at our deepest, strong and free.

A Daughter of Eve

A fool I was to sleep at noon,°
   And wake when night is chilly
Beneath the comfortless cold moon;
A fool to pluck my rose too soon,
   A fool to snap my lily.°

My garden-plot I have not kept;°
   Faded and all-forsaken,
I weep as I have never wept:
Oh it was summer when I slept,
   It's winter now I waken.   10

Talk what you please of future Spring
   And sun-warmed sweet to-morrow:—
Stripped bare of hope and everything,
No more to laugh, no more to sing,
   I sit alone with sorrow.

A Dirge

Why were you born when the snow was falling?
You should have come to the cuckoo's calling,
Or when grapes are green in the cluster,
Or, at least, when lithe swallows muster
  For their far off flying
  From summer dying.

Why did you die when the lambs were cropping?
You should have died at the apples' dropping,
When the grasshopper comes to trouble,
And the wheat-fields are sodden stubble,   10
  And all winds go sighing
  For sweet things dying.

In a Certain Place

I found Love in a certain place
Asleep and cold—or cold and dead?—
All ivory-white upon his bed
All ivory-white his face.
His hands were folded
On his quiet breast,
To his figure laid at rest
Chilly bed was moulded.

His hair hung lax about his brow,
I had not seen his face before;   10
Or if I saw it once, it wore
Another aspect now.
No trace of last night's sorrow,
No shadow of tomorrow;
All at peace (thus all sorrows cease),
All at peace.

I wondered: Were his eyes
Soft or falcon-clear?
I wondered: As he lies

Does he feel me near?   20
In silence my heart spoke
And wondered: If he woke
And found me sitting nigh him
And felt me sitting by him,
If life flushed to his cheek,
He living man with men,
Then if I heard him speak
Oh should I know him then?°

'Cannot Sweeten'

If that's water you wash your hands in
    Why is it black as ink is black?—
Because my hands are foul with my folly:
    Oh the lost time that comes not back!—

If that's water you bathe your feet in
    Why is it red as wine is red?—
Because my feet sought blood in their goings;
    Red red is the track they tread.—

Slew you mother or slew you father
    That your foulness passeth not by?—   10
Not father and oh not mother:
    I slew my love with an evil eye.—

Slew you sister or slew you brother
    That in peace you have not a part?—
Not brother and oh not sister:
    I slew my love with a hardened heart.

He loved me because he loved me,
    Not for grace or beauty I had;
He loved me because he loved me;
    For his loving me I was glad.   20

Yet I loved him not for his loving
    While I played with his love and truth,
Not loving him for his loving,
    Wasting his joy, wasting his youth.

I ate his life as a banquet,
    I drank his life as new wine,°
I fattened upon his leanness,
    Mine to flourish and his to pine.

So his life fled as running water,
    So it perished as water spilt:
If black my hands and my feet as scarlet,   30
    Blacker redder my heart of guilt.

Cold as a stone, as hard, as heavy;
    All my sighs ease it no whit,
All my tears make it no cleaner
    Dropping dropping dropping on it.

Autumn Violets

Keep love for youth, and violets for the spring:
    Or if these bloom when worn-out autumn grieves,
    Let them lie hid in double shade of leaves,
Their own, and others dropped down withering;
For violets suit when home birds build and sing,
    Not when the outbound bird a passage cleaves;
    Not with dry stubble of mown harvest sheaves,
But when the green world buds to blossoming.
Keep violets for the spring, and love for youth,
    Love that should dwell with beauty, mirth, and hope: 10
        Or if a later sadder love be born,
    Let this not look for grace beyond its scope,
But give itself, nor plead for answering truth—
        A grateful Ruth tho' gleaning scanty corn.°

'They Desire a Better Country'

I

I would not if I could undo my past,
    Tho' for its sake my future is a blank;
    My past for which I have myself to thank,
For all its faults and follies first and last.

I would not cast anew the lot once cast,
  Or launch a second ship for one that sank,
  Or drug with sweets the bitterness I drank,
Or break by feasting my perpetual fast.
I would not if I could: for much more dear
  Is one remembrance than a hundred joys,   10
    More than a thousand hopes in jubilee;
  Dearer the music of one tearful voice
    That unforgotten calls and calls to me,
'Follow me here, rise up, and follow here.'°

II

What seekest thou, far in the unknown land?
  In hope I follow joy gone on before;
  In hope and fear persistent more and more,
As the dry desert lengthens out its sand.
Whilst day and night I carry in my hand
  The golden key to ope the golden door°   20
  Of golden home; yet mine eye weepeth sore,
For long the journey is that makes no stand.
And who is this that veiled doth walk with thee?
  Lo, this is Love that walketh at my right;
    One exile holds us both, and we are bound
  To selfsame home-joys in the land of light.
Weeping thou walkest with him; weepeth he?—
    Some sobbing weep, some weep and make no sound.°

III

A dimness of a glory glimmers here
  Thro' veils and distance from the space remote,   30
  A faintest far vibration of a note
Reaches to us and seems to bring us near;
Causing our face to glow with braver cheer,
  Making the serried mist to stand afloat,°
  Subduing languor with an antidote,
And strengthening love almost to cast out fear:
Till for one moment golden city walls
  Rise looming on us, golden walls of home,
Light of our eyes until the darkness falls;
  Then thro' the outer darkness burdensome   40

I hear again the tender voice that calls,
  'Follow me hither, follow, rise, and come.'

From SING-SONG: A NURSERY RHYME BOOK

Love me,—I love you,
  Love me, my baby;
Sing it high, sing it low,
  Sing it as may be.

Mother's arms under you,
  Her eyes above you;
Sing it high, sing it low,
  Love me,—I love you.

* * *

My baby has a father and a mother,
  Rich little baby!
Fatherless, motherless, I know another
  Forlorn as may be:
  Poor little baby!

* * *

'Kookoorookoo! kookoorookoo!'
  Crows the cock before the morn;
'Kikirikee! kikirikee!'
  Roses in the east are born.

'Kookoorookoo! kookoorookoo!'
  Early birds begin their singing;
'Kikirikee! kikirikee!'
  The day, the day, the day is springing.

* * *

Dead in the cold, a song-singing thrush,
Dead at the foot of a snowberry bush,—

Weave him a coffin of rush,
Dig him a grave where the soft mosses grow,
Raise him a tombstone of snow.

* * *

Crying, my little one, footsore and weary?
    Fall asleep, pretty one, warm on my shoulder:
I must tramp on through the winter night dreary,
    While the snow falls on me colder and colder.

You are my one, and I have not another;
    Sleep soft, my darling, my trouble and treasure;
Sleep warm and soft in the arms of your mother,
    Dreaming of pretty things, dreaming of pleasure.

* * *

Heartsease in my garden bed,°
    With sweetwilliam white and red,
Honeysuckle on my wall: —
    Heartsease blossoms in my heart
When sweet William comes to call,
    But it withers when we part,
And the honey-trumpets fall.

* * *

If I were a Queen,
    What would I do?
I'd make you King,
    And I'd wait on you.

If I were a King,
    What would I do?
I'd make you Queen,
    For I'd marry you.

* * *

The days are clear,
    Day after day,

When April's here,
    That leads to May,
And June
Must follow soon:
    Stay, June, stay! —
If only we could stop the moon
And June!

* * *

Twist me a crown of wind-flowers;°
    That I may fly away
To hear the singers at their song,
    And players at their play.

Put on your crown of wind-flowers:
    But whither would you go?
Beyond the surging of the sea
    And the storms that blow.

Alas! your crown of wind-flowers
    Can never make you fly: 10
I twist them in a crown to-day,
    And to-night they die.

* * *

How many seconds in a minute?
Sixty, and no more in it.

How many minutes in an hour?
Sixty for sun and shower.

How many hours in a day?
Twenty-four for work and play.

How many days in a week?
Seven both to hear and speak.

How many weeks in a month?
Four, as the swift moon runn'th.   10

How many months in a year?
Twelve the almanack makes clear.

How many years in an age?
One hundred says the sage.

How many ages in time?
No one knows the rhyme.

             *   *   *

What is pink? a rose is pink
By the fountain's brink.
What is red? a poppy's red
In its barley bed.
What is blue? the sky is blue
Where the clouds float thro'.
What is white? a swan is white
Sailing in the light.
What is yellow? pears are yellow,
Rich and ripe and mellow.   10
What is green? the grass is green,
With small flowers between.
What is violet? clouds are violet
In the summer twilight.
What is orange? why, an orange,
Just an orange!

             *   *   *

I planted a hand
   And there came up a palm,
I planted a heart
   And there came up balm.°

Then I planted a wish,
   But there sprang a thorn,
While heaven frowned with thunder
   And earth sighed forlorn.

             *   *   *

Under the ivy bush
  One sits sighing,
And under the willow tree
  One sits crying:—

Under the ivy bush
  Cease from your sighing,
But under the willow tree
  Lie down a-dying.

     *   *   *

Margaret has a milking-pail,
  And she rises early;
Thomas has a threshing-flail,
  And he's up betimes:°
Sometimes crossing through the grass
  Where the dew lies pearly,
They say 'Good morrow' as they pass
  By the leafy limes.

     *   *   *

In the meadow—what in the meadow?
Bluebells, buttercups, meadowsweet,
And fairy rings for the children's feet
  In the meadow.

In the garden—what in the garden?
Jacob's-ladder and Solomon's-seal,
And Love-lies-bleeding with none to heal
  In the garden.°

     *   *   *

A frisky lamb
And a frisky child
Playing their pranks
  In a cowslip meadow:
The sky all blue
And the air all mild

And the fields all sun
    And the lanes half shadow.

*   *   *

The wind has such a rainy sound
    Moaning through the town,
The sea has such a windy sound,—
    Will the ships go down?

The apples in the orchard
    Tumble from their tree.—
Oh, will the ships go down, go down,
    In the windy sea?

*   *   *

Minnie bakes oaten cakes,
    Minnie brews ale,
All because her Johnny's coming
        Home from sea.
And she glows like a rose,
    Who was so pale,
And 'Are you sure the church clock goes?'
    Says she.

*   *   *

'Ferry me across the water,
    Do, boatman, do.'
'If you've a penny in your purse
    I'll ferry you.'

'I have a penny in my purse,
    And my eyes are blue;
So ferry me across the water,
    Do, boatman, do.'

'Step into my ferry-boat,
    Be they black or blue,
And for the penny in your purse
    I'll ferry you.'

10

*   *   *

Who has seen the wind?°
   Neither I nor you:
But when the leaves hang trembling°
   The wind is passing thro'.

Who has seen the wind?
   Neither you nor I:
But when the trees bow down their heads
   The wind is passing by.

*   *   *

An emerald is as green as grass;
   A ruby red as blood;
A sapphire shines as blue as heaven;
   A flint lies in the mud.

A diamond is a brilliant stone,
   To catch the world's desire;
An opal holds a fiery spark;
   But a flint holds fire.

*   *   *

I caught a little ladybird
   That flies far away;
I caught a little lady wife°
   That is both staid and gay.°

Come back, my scarlet ladybird,
   Back from far away;
I weary of my dolly wife,°
   My wife that cannot play.

She's such a senseless wooden thing
   She stares the livelong day;   10
Her wig of gold is stiff and cold°
   And cannot change to grey.

*   *   *

Wee wee husband,
   Give me some money,
I have no comfits,
   And I have no honey.

Wee wee wifie,
   I have no money,
Milk, nor meat, nor bread to eat,
   Comfits, nor honey.

*   *   *

'I dreamt I caught a little owl
   And the bird was blue—'

'But you may hunt for ever
And not find such an one.'

'I dreamt I set a sunflower,
   And red as blood it grew—'

'But such a sunflower never
Bloomed beneath the sun.'

*   *   *

Is the moon tired? she looks so pale
Within her misty veil:
She scales the sky from east to west,
And takes no rest.

Before the coming of the night
The moon shows papery white;
Before the dawning of the day
She fades away.

*   *   *

Crimson curtains round my mother's bed,
   Silken soft as may be;
Cool white curtains round about my bed,
   For I am but a baby.

———————

By Way of Remembrance

Remember, if I claim too much of you,
   I claim it of my brother and my friend:
   Have patience with me till the hidden end,
Bitter or sweet, in mercy shut from view.
Pay me my due; though I to pay your due
   Am all too poor and past what will can mend:
   Thus of your bounty you must give and lend
Still unrepaid by aught I look to do.
Still unrepaid by aught of mine on earth:
   But overpaid, please God, when recompense   10
Beyond the mystic Jordan and new birth°
   Is dealt to virtue as to innocence;
When Angels singing praises in their mirth
   Have borne you in their arms and fetched you hence.

Will you be there? my yearning heart has cried:
   Ah me, my love, my love, shall I be there,
   To sit down in your glory and to share
Your gladness, glowing as a virgin bride?
Or will another dearer, fairer-eyed,
   Sit nigher to you in your jubilee;   20
   And mindful one of other will you be
Borne higher and higher on joy's ebbless tide?
— Yea, if I love I will not grudge you this:
   I too shall float upon that heavenly sea
     And sing my joyful praises without ache;
   Your overflow of joy shall gladden me,
     My whole heart shall sing praises for your sake
And find its own fulfilment in your bliss.

In resurrection is it awfuller
   That rising of the All or of the Each: 30
   Of all kins of all nations of all speech,
Or one by one of him and him and her?
When dust reanimate begins to stir
   Here, there, beyond, beyond, reach beyond reach;
   While every wave disgorges on its beach
 Alive or dead-in-life some seafarer.

In resurrection, on the day of days,
    That day of mourning throughout all the earth,
        In resurrection may we meet again:
            No more with stricken hearts to part in twain;   40
        As once in sorrow one, now one in mirth,
One in our resurrection songs of praise.

I love you and you know it—this at least,
    This comfort is mine own in all my pain:
    You know it and can never doubt again,
And love's mere self is a continual feast.
Not oath of mine nor blessing-word of priest
    Could make my love more certain or more plain.—
    Life as a rolling moon doth wax and wane
O weary moon, still rounding, still decreased!   50
Life wanes: and when love folds his wings above
    Tired joy, and less we feel his conscious pulse,
        Let us go fall asleep, dear Friend, in peace;—
        A little while, and age and sorrow cease;
    A little while, and love reborn annuls
Loss and decay and death—and all is love.

The German–French Campaign 1870–1871

These two pieces, written during the suspense of a great nation's
agony, aim at expressing human sympathy, not political bias.

I

'THY BROTHER'S BLOOD CRIETH'

All her corn-fields rippled in the sunshine,
    All her lovely vines, sweets-laden, bowed;
Yet some weeks to harvest and to vintage:
    When, as one man's hand, a cloud°
Rose and spread, and, blackening, burst asunder
    In rain and fire and thunder.

Is there nought to reap in the day of harvest?
    Hath the vine in her day no fruit to yield?
Yea, men tread the press, but not for sweetness,
    And they reap a red crop from the field.°   10

Build barns, ye reapers, garner all aright,
    Though your souls be called to-night.

A cry of tears goes up from blackened homesteads,
    A cry of blood goes up from reeking earth:
Tears and blood have a cry that pierces Heaven
    Through all its Hallelujah swells of mirth;
God hears their cry, and though He tarry, yet
    He doth not forget.

Mournful Mother, prone in dust weeping°
    Who shall comfort thee for those who are not?   20
As thou didst, men do to thee; and heap the measure,
    And heat the furnace sevenfold hot:
As thou once, now these to thee—who pitieth thee
    From sea to sea?

O thou King, terrible in strength, and building°
    Thy strong future on thy past!
Though he drink the last, the King of Sheshach,°
    Yet he shall drink at the last.
Art thou greater than great Babylon,
    Which lies overthrown?   30

Take heed, ye unwise among the people;
    O ye fools, when will ye understand?—
He that planted the ear shall He not hear,
    Nor He smite who formed the hand?°
'Vengeance is Mine, is Mine,' thus saith the Lord:—°
    O Man, put up thy sword.

2
'TO-DAY FOR ME'

    She sitteth still who used to dance,
She weepeth sore and more and more:—
Let us sit with thee weeping sore,
    O fair France.   40

    She trembleth as the days advance
Who used to be so light of heart:—

We in thy trembling bear a part,
　　Sister France.

Her eyes shine tearful as they glance:
'Who shall give back my slaughtered sons?
'Bind up,' she saith, 'my wounded ones.' —
　　Alas, France!

She struggles in a deathly trance,
As in a dream her pulses stir,   50
She hears the nations calling her,
　　'France, France, France.'

Thou people of the lifted lance,
Forbear her tears, forbear her blood:
Roll back, roll back, thy whelming flood,°
　　Back from France.

Eye not her loveliness askance,°
Forge not for her a galling chain;
Leave her at peace to bloom again,
　　Vine-clad France.   60

A time there is for change and chance,
A time for passing of the cup:
And One abides can yet bind up
　　Broken France.

A time there is for change and chance:
Who next shall drink the trembling cup,
Wring out its dregs and suck them up
　　After France?

A Christmas Carol

In the bleak mid-winter
　　Frosty wind made moan,
Earth stood hard as iron,
　　Water like a stone;

Snow had fallen, snow on snow,
    Snow on snow,
In the bleak mid-winter
    Long ago.

Our God, Heaven cannot hold Him,
    Nor earth sustain;   10
Heaven and earth shall flee away
    When He comes to reign:
In the bleak mid-winter
    A stable-place sufficed
The Lord God Almighty
    Jesus Christ.

Enough for Him whom cherubim
    Worship night and day,
A breastful of milk
    And a mangerful of hay;   20
Enough for Him whom angels
    Fall down before,
The ox and ass and camel
    Which adore.

Angels and archangels
    May have gathered there,
Cherubim and seraphim
    Throng'd the air,
But only His mother
    In her maiden bliss   30
Worshipped the Beloved
    With a kiss.

What can I give Him,
    Poor as I am?
If I were a shepherd
    I would bring a lamb,
If I were a wise man
    I would do my part,—
Yet what I can I give Him,
    Give my heart.   40

Venus's Looking-Glass

I marked where lovely Venus and her court
   With song and dance and merry laugh went by;
   Weightless, their wingless feet seemed made to fly,
Bound from the ground and in mid air to sport.
Left far behind I heard the dolphins snort,
   Tracking their goddess with a wistful eye,
   Around whose head white doves rose, wheeling high
Or low, and cooed after their tender sort.
All this I saw in Spring. Through Summer heat
   I saw the lovely Queen of Love no more.   10
      But when flushed Autumn through the woodlands went
I spied sweet Venus walk amid the wheat:
   Whom seeing, every harvester gave o'er
      His toil, and laughed and hoped and was content.

Love Lies Bleeding

Love that is dead and buried, yesterday
   Out of his grave rose up before my face;
   No recognition in his look, no trace
Of memory in his eyes dust-dimmed and grey.
While I, remembering, found no word to say,
   But felt my quickened heart leap in its place;
   Caught afterglow thrown back from long set days,°
Caught echoes of all music passed away.
Was this indeed to meet?—I mind me yet°
   In youth we met when hope and love were quick,°   10
      We parted with hope dead, but love alive:
   I mind me how we parted then heart sick,
      Remembering, loving, hopeless, weak to strive:—
Was this to meet? Not so, we have not met.

A Bride Song

Through the vales to my love!
   To the happy small nest of home

Green from basement to roof;
   Where the honey-bees come
To the window-sill flowers,
   And dive from above,
Safe from the spider that weaves
   Her warp and her woof
In some outermost leaves.

Through the vales to my love!   10
   In sweet April hours
   All rainbows and showers,
While dove answers dove, —
   In beautiful May,
When the orchards are tender
   And frothing with flowers, —
   In opulent June,
When the wheat stands up slender
   By sweet-smelling hay,
And half the sun's splendour   20
   Descends to the moon.

Through the vales to my love!
   Where the turf is so soft to the feet
   And the thyme makes it sweet,
And the stately foxglove
   Hangs silent its exquisite bells;
   And where water wells
The greenness grows greener,
   And bulrushes stand
Round a lily to screen her.   30

Nevertheless, if this land,
   Like a garden to smell and to sight,
Were turned to a desert of sand;
   Stripped bare of delight,
   All its best gone to worst,
For my feet no repose,
   No water to comfort my thirst,
And heaven like a furnace above, —
   The desert would be
   As gushing of waters to me,   40

The wilderness be as a rose,°
   If it led me to thee,
   O my love.

A Rose Plant in Jericho

At morn I plucked a rose and gave it Thee,
   A rose of joy and happy love and peace,
     A rose with scarce a thorn:
     But in the chillness of a second morn
   My rose bush drooped, and all its gay increase°
Was but one thorn that wounded me.

I plucked the thorn and offered it to Thee;
   And for my thorn Thou gavest love and peace,
     Not joy this mortal morn:
     If Thou hast given much treasure for a thorn,   10
   Wilt Thou not give me for my rose increase
Of gladness, and all sweets to me?°

My thorny rose, my love and pain, to Thee
   I offer; and I set my heart in peace,
     And rest upon my thorn:°
     For verily I think to-morrow morn
   Shall bring me Paradise, my gift's increase,
Yea, give Thy very Self to me.

[*Dedicatory Sonnet of* A Pageant and Other Poems *(1881)*]

Sonnets are full of love, and this my tome
   Has many sonnets: so here now shall be
   One sonnet more, a love sonnet, from me
To her whose heart is my heart's quiet home,
   To my first Love, my Mother, on whose knee
I learnt love-lore that is not troublesome;
   Whose service is my special dignity,°
And she my loadstar while I go and come.°

And so because you love me, and because
  I love you, Mother, I have woven a wreath   10
    Of rhymes wherewith to crown your honoured name:
    In you not fourscore years can dim the flame
Of love, whose blessed glow transcends the laws
  Of time and change and mortal life and death.

The Key-Note

    Where are the songs I used to know,°
      Where are the notes I used to sing?
    I have forgotten everything
    I used to know so long ago;
    Summer has followed after Spring;
      Now Autumn is so shrunk and sere,
    I scarcely think a sadder thing
      Can be the Winter of my year.

    Yet Robin sings through Winter's rest,
      When bushes put their berries on;   10
      While they their ruddy jewels don,
    He sings out of a ruddy breast;
    The hips and haws and ruddy breast
      Make one spot warm where snowflakes lie,
    They break and cheer the unlovely rest
      Of Winter's pause—and why not I?

Pastime

A boat amid the ripples, drifting, rocking,
  Two idle people, without pause or aim;
While in the ominous west there gathers darkness
    Flushed with flame.

A haycock in a hayfield backing, lapping,°
  Two drowsy people pillowed round about;
While in the ominous west across the darkness
    Flame leaps out.

Better a wrecked life than a life so aimless,
   Better a wrecked life than a life so soft;   10
The ominous west glooms thundering, with its fire
      Lit aloft.

'Italia, Io Ti Saluto!'

To come back from the sweet South, to the North
   Where I was born, bred, look to die;
Come back to do my day's work in its day,
      Play out my play—
   Amen, amen, say I.

To see no more the country half my own,
   Nor hear the half familiar speech,
Amen, I say; I turn to that bleak North
      Whence I came forth—
   The South lies out of reach.   10

But when our swallows fly back to the South,
   To the sweet South, to the sweet South,
The tears may come again into my eyes
      On the old wise,°
   And the sweet name to my mouth.

Mirrors of Life and Death

The mystery of Life, the mystery
Of Death, I see
Darkly as in a glass;°
Their shadows pass,
And talk with me.°

As the flush of a Morning Sky,°
As a Morning Sky colourless—
Each yields its measure of light
To a wet world or a dry;
Each fares through day to night   10
With equal pace,

And then each one
Is done.

As the Sun with glory and grace
In his face,
Benignantly hot,°
Graciously radiant and keen,
Ready to rise and to run,—
Not without spot,
Not even the Sun.°   20

As the Moon
On the wax, on the wane,
With night for her noon;
Vanishing soon,
To appear again.

As Roses that droop
Half warm, half chill, in the languid May,
And breathe out a scent
Sweet and faint;
Till the wind gives one swoop   30
To scatter their beauty away.

As Lilies a multitude,
One dipping, one rising, one sinking,
On rippling waters, clear blue
And pure for their drinking;
One new dead, and one opened anew,
And all good.

As a cankered pale Flower,
With death for a dower,
Each hour of its life half dead;   40
With death for a crown
Weighing down
Its head.

As an Eagle, half strength and half grace,
Most potent to face

Unwinking the splendour of light;°
Harrying the East and the West,
Soaring aloft from our sight;
Yet one day or one night dropped to rest,
On the low common earth   50
Of his birth.

As a Dove,
Not alone,
In a world of her own
Full of fluttering soft noises
And tender sweet voices
Of love.

As a Mouse
Keeping house
In the fork of a tree,   60
With nuts in a crevice,
And an acorn or two;
What cares he
For blossoming boughs,
Or the song-singing bevies
Of birds in their glee,
Scarlet, or golden, or blue?

As a Mole grubbing underground;
When it comes to the light
It grubs its way back again,   70
Feeling no bias of fur°
To hamper it in its stir,
Scant of pleasure and pain,
Sinking itself out of sight
Without sound.

As Waters that drop and drop,
Weariness without end,
That drop and never stop,
Wear that nothing can mend,
Till one day they drop—   80

Stop—
And there's an end,
And matters mend.

As Trees, beneath whose skin
We mark not the sap begin
To swell and rise,
Till the whole bursts out in green:
We mark the falling leaves
When the wide world grieves
And sighs.   90

As a Forest on fire,
Where maddened creatures desire
Wet mud or wings
Beyond all those things
Which could assuage desire
On this side the flaming fire.

As Wind with a sob and sigh
To which there comes no reply
But a rustle and shiver
From rushes of the river;   100
As Wind with a desolate moan,
Moaning on alone.

As a Desert all sand,
Blank, neither water nor land
For solace, or dwelling, or culture,°
Where the storms and the wild creatures howl;
Given over to lion and vulture,
To ostrich, and jackal, and owl:
Yet somewhere an oasis lies;
There waters arise   110
To nourish one seedling of balm,
Perhaps, or one palm.

As the Sea,
Murmuring, shifting, swaying;
One time sunnily playing,
One time wrecking and slaying;

In whichever mood it be,
Worst or best,
Never at rest.

As still Waters and deep,°   120
As shallow Waters that brawl,
As rapid Waters that leap
To their fall.

As Music, as Colour, as Shape,
Keys of rapture and pain
Turning in vain
In a lock which turns not again,
While breaths and moments escape.

As Spring, all bloom and desire;
As Summer, all gift and fire;   130
As Autumn, a dying glow;
As Winter, with nought to show:

Winter which lays its dead all out of sight,
All clothed in white,
All waiting for the long-awaited light.

A Ballad of Boding

There are sleeping dreams and waking dreams;
What seems is not always as it seems.

I looked out of my window in the sweet new morning,
And there I saw three barges of manifold adorning°
Went sailing toward the East:
The first had sails like fire,
The next like glittering wire,
But sackcloth were the sails of the least;°
And all the crews made music, and two had spread a feast.°

The first choir breathed in flutes,   10
And fingered soft guitars;
The second won from lutes
Harmonious chords and jars,°
With drums for stormy bars:

But the third was all of harpers and scarlet trumpeters;
Notes of triumph, then
An alarm again,
As for onset, as for victory, rallies, stirs,°
Peace at last and glory to the vanquishers.

The first barge showed for figurehead a Love with wings;   20
The second showed for figurehead a Worm with stings;°
The third, a Lily tangled to a Rose which clings.
The first bore for freight gold and spice and down;
The second bore a sword, a sceptre, and a crown;
The third, a heap of earth gone to dust and brown.
Winged Love meseemed like Folly in the face;
Stinged Worm meseemed loathly in his place;
Lily and Rose were flowers of grace.

Merry went the revel of the fire-sailed crew,
Singing, feasting, dancing to and fro: 30
Pleasures ever changing, ever graceful, ever new;
Sighs, but scarce of woe;
All the sighing
Wooed such sweet replying;
All the sighing, sweet and low,
Used to come and go
For more pleasure, merely so.
Yet at intervals some one grew tired
Of everything desired,
And sank, I knew not whither, in sorry plight,   40
Out of sight.

The second crew seemed ever
Wider-visioned, graver,
More distinct of purpose, more sustained of will;
With heads erect and proud,
And voices sometimes loud;
With endless tacking, counter-tacking,
All things grasping, all things lacking,
It would seem;
Ever shifting helm, or sail, or shroud,   50
Drifting on as in a dream.
Hoarding to their utmost bent,
Feasting to their fill,

Yet gnawed by discontent,
Envy, hatred, malice, on their road they went.
Their freight was not a treasure,
Their music not a pleasure;
The sword flashed, cleaving through their bands,
Sceptre and crown changed hands.

The third crew as they went   60
Seemed mostly different;
They toiled in rowing, for to them the wind was contrary,
As all the world might see.
They laboured at the oar,
While on their heads they bore
The fiery stress of sunshine more and more.
They laboured at the oar hand-sore,
Till rain went splashing,
And spray went dashing,
Down on them, and up on them, more and more.   70
Their sails were patched and rent,
Their masts were bent,
In peril of their lives they worked and went.
For them no feast was spread,
No soft luxurious bed
Scented and white,
No crown or sceptre hung in sight;
In weariness and painfulness,
In thirst and sore distress,
They rowed and steered from left to right   80
With all their might.
Their trumpeters and harpers round about
Incessantly played out,
And sometimes they made answer with a shout;
But oftener they groaned or wept,
And seldom paused to eat, and seldom slept.
I wept for pity watching them, but more
I wept heart-sore
Once and again to see
Some weary man plunge overboard, and swim   90
To Love or Worm ship floating buoyantly:
And there all welcomed him.

The ships steered each apart and seemed to scorn each other,
Yet all the crews were interchangeable;
Now one man, now another,
—Like bloodless spectres some, some flushed by health,—
Changed openly, or changed by stealth,
Scaling a slippery side, and scaled it well.
The most left Love ship, hauling wealth
Up Worm ship's side;   100
While some few hollow-eyed
Left either for the sack-sailed boat;
But this, though not remote,
Was worst to mount, and whoso left it once
Scarce ever came again,
But seemed to loathe his erst companions,°
And wish and work them bane.

Then I knew (I know not how) there lurked quicksands
        full of dread,
Rocks and reefs and whirlpools in the water bed,
Whence a waterspout   110
Instantaneously leaped out,
Roaring as it reared its head.
Soon I spied a something dim,°
Many-handed, grim,
That went flitting to and fro the first and second ship;
It puffed their sails full out
With puffs of smoky breath
From a smouldering lip,
And cleared the waterspout
Which reeled roaring round about   120
Threatening death.
With a horny hand it steered,
And a horn appeared
On its sneering head upreared
Haughty and high
Against the blackening lowering sky.
With a hoof it swayed the waves;
They opened here and there,
Till I spied deep ocean graves
Full of skeletons   130
That were men and women once

Foul or fair;
Full of things that creep
And fester in the deep
And never breathe the clean life-nurturing air.

The third bark held aloof
From the Monster with the hoof,
Despite his urgent beck,°
And fraught with guile
Abominable his smile;   140
Till I saw him take a flying leap on to that deck.
Then full of awe,
With these same eyes I saw
His head incredible retract its horn
Rounding like babe's new born,
While silvery phosphorescence played
About his dis-horned head.
The sneer smoothed from his lip,
He beamed blandly on the ship;
All winds sank to a moan,   150
All waves to a monotone
(For all these seemed his realm),
While he laid a strong caressing hand upon the helm.

Then a cry well nigh of despair
Shrieked to heaven, a clamour of desperate prayer.
The harpers harped no more,
While the trumpeters sounded sore,
An alarm to wake the dead from their bed:
To the rescue, to the rescue, now or never,
To the rescue, O ye living, O ye dead,   160
Or no more help or hope for ever!—
The planks strained as though they must part asunder,
The masts bent as though they must dip under,
And the winds and the waves at length
Girt up their strength,
And the depths were laid bare,
And heaven flashed fire and volleyed thunder
Through the rain-choked air,
And sea and sky seemed to kiss
In the horror and the hiss   170
Of the whole world shuddering everywhere.

Lo! a Flyer swooping down
With wings to span the globe,
And splendour for his robe
And splendour for his crown.
He lighted on the helm with a foot of fire,
And spun the Monster overboard:
And that monstrous thing abhorred,
Gnashing with balked desire,
Wriggled like a worm infirm   180
Up the Worm
Of the loathly figurehead.
There he crouched and gnashed;
And his head re-horned, and gashed
From the other's grapple, dripped bloody red.

I saw that thing accurst
Wreak his worst
On the first and second crew:
Some with baited hook
He angled for and took,   190
Some dragged overboard in a net he threw,
Some he did to death
With hoof or horn or blasting breath.

I heard a voice of wailing
Where the ships went sailing,
A sorrowful voice prevailing
Above the sound of the sea,
Above the singers' voices,
And musical merry noises;
All songs had turned to sighing,   200
The light was failing,
The day was dying—
Ah me,
That such a sorrow should be!

There was sorrow on the sea and sorrow on the land
When Love ship went down by the bottomless quicksand
To its grave in the bitter wave.
There was sorrow on the sea and sorrow on the land
When Worm ship went to pieces on the rock-bound strand,
And the bitter wave was its grave.   210

But land and sea waxed hoary
In whiteness of a glory
Never told in story
Nor seen by mortal eye,
When the third ship crossed the bar
Where whirls and breakers are,
And steered into the splendours of the sky;
That third bark and that least
Which had never seemed to feast,
Yet kept high festival above sun and moon and star.   220

Yet a Little While

I dreamed and did not seek: to-day I seek
        Who can no longer dream;
But now am all behindhand, waxen weak,
    And dazed amid so many things that gleam
        Yet are not what they seem.

I dreamed and did not work: to-day I work
        Kept wide awake by care
And loss, and perils dimly guessed to lurk;
    I work and reap not, while my life goes bare
        And void in wintry air.   10

I hope indeed; but hope itself is fear
        Viewed on the sunny side;
I hope, and disregard the world that's here,
    The prizes drawn, the sweet things that betide;
        I hope, and I abide.

He and She

        'Should one of us remember,
            And one of us forget,
        I wish I knew what each will do—
            But who can tell as yet?'

'Should one of us remember,
And one of us forget,
I promise you what I will do—
And I'm content to wait for you,
And not be sure as yet.'

Monna Innominata

A SONNET OF SONNETS

Beatrice,° immortalized by 'altissimo poeta . . . cotanto amante';° Laura,° cele-brated by a great though an inferior bard,—have alike paid the exceptional penalty of exceptional honour, and have come down to us resplendent with charms, but (at least, to my apprehension) scant of attractiveness.

These heroines of world-wide fame were preceded by a bevy of unnamed ladies 'donne innominate' sung by a school of less conspicuous poets; and in that land and that period° which gave simultaneous birth to Catholics, to Albi-genses,° and to Troubadours,° one can imagine many a lady as sharing her lover's poetic aptitude, while the barrier between them° might be one held sacred by both, yet not such as to render mutual love incompatible with mutual honour.

Had such a lady spoken for herself, the portrait left us might have appeared more tender, if less dignified, than any drawn even by a devoted friend. Or had the Great Poetess of our own day and nation only been unhappy instead of happy,° her circumstances would have invited her to bequeath to us, in lieu of the 'Portuguese Sonnets,' an inimitable 'donna innominata' drawn not from fancy° but from feeling, and worthy to occupy a niche beside Beatrice and Laura.

I

Lo dì che han detto a' dolci amici addio.

DANTE

Amor, con quanto sforzo oggi mi vinci!

PETRARCA°

Come back to me, who wait and watch for you:—
    Or come not yet, for it is over then,
    And long it is before you come again,
So far between my pleasures are and few.
While, when you come not, what I do I do
    Thinking 'Now when he comes,' my sweetest 'when:'
    For one man is my world of all the men

This wide world holds; O love, my world is you.
Howbeit, to meet you grows almost a pang
  Because the pang of parting comes so soon;   10
  My hope hangs waning, waxing, like a moon
    Between the heavenly days on which we meet:
Ah me, but where are now the songs I sang
    When life was sweet because you called them sweet?

2

Era già l'ora che volge il desio.

DANTE

Ricorro al tempo ch' io vi vidi prima.

PETRARCA°

I wish I could remember that first day,°
  First hour, first moment of your meeting me,
  If bright or dim the season, it might be
Summer or Winter for aught I can say;
So unrecorded did it slip away,
  So blind was I to see and to foresee,
  So dull to mark the budding of my tree
That would not blossom yet for many a May.
If only I could recollect it, such
  A day of days! I let it come and go   10
  As traceless as a thaw of bygone snow;
It seemed to mean so little, meant so much;
If only now I could recall that touch,
  First touch of hand in hand—Did one but know!

3

O ombre vane, fuor che ne l'aspetto!

DANTE

Immaginata guida la conduce.

PETRARCA°

I dream of you to wake: would that I might
  Dream of you and not wake but slumber on;
  Nor find with dreams the dear companion gone,
As Summer ended Summer birds take flight.
In happy dreams I hold you full in sight,

I blush again who waking look so wan;
  Brighter than sunniest day that ever shone,
In happy dreams your smile makes day of night.
Thus only in a dream we are at one,
  Thus only in a dream we give and take   10
    The faith that maketh rich who take or give;
If thus to sleep is sweeter than to wake,
    To die were surely sweeter than to live,
Though there be nothing new beneath the sun.°

4

Poca favilla gran fiamma seconda.

DANTE

Ogni altra cosa, ogni pensier va fore,
E sol ivi con voi rimansi amore.

PETRARCA°

I loved you first: but afterwards your love
  Outsoaring mine, sang such a loftier song
As drowned the friendly cooings of my dove.
  Which owes the other most? my love was long,
  And yours one moment seemed to wax more strong;
I loved and guessed at you, you construed me
And loved me for what might or might not be—
  Nay, weights and measures do us both a wrong.
For verily love knows not 'mine' or 'thine;'
  With separate 'I' and 'thou' free love has done,   10
    For one is both and both are one in love:
Rich love knows nought of 'thine that is not mine;'
    Both have the strength and both the length thereof,
Both of us, of the love which makes us one.

5

Amor che a nulla amato amar perdona.

DANTE

Amor m'addusse in sì gioiosa spene.

PETRARCA°

O my heart's heart, and you who are to me
  More than myself myself, God be with you,

Keep you in strong obedience leal and true°
To Him whose noble service setteth free,°
Give you all good we see or can foresee,
    Make your joys many and your sorrows few,
    Bless you in what you bear and what you do,
Yea, perfect you as He would have you be.
So much for you; but what for me, dear friend?
    To love you without stint and all I can
To-day, to-morrow, world without an end;
      To love you much and yet to love you more,
      As Jordan at his flood sweeps either shore;
Since woman is the helpmeet made for man.°

6

      Or puoi la quantitate
Comprender de l'amor che a te mi scalda.

                DANTE

Non vo' che da tal nodo amor mi scioglia.

                PETRARCA°

Trust me, I have not earned your dear rebuke,
    I love, as you would have me, God the most;°
    Would lose not Him, but you, must one be lost,
Nor with Lot's wife cast back a faithless look°
Unready to forego what I forsook;
    This say I, having counted up the cost,
    This, though I be the feeblest of God's host,
The sorriest sheep Christ shepherds with His crook.
Yet while I love my God the most, I deem
    That I can never love you overmuch;
      I love Him more, so let me love you too;
    Yea, as I apprehend it, love is such
I cannot love you if I love not Him,
    I cannot love Him if I love not you.

7

Qui primavera sempre ed ogni frutto.
DANTE

Ragionando con meco ed io con lui.
PETRARCA°

'Love me, for I love you'—and answer me,
'Love me, for I love you'—so shall we stand
As happy equals in the flowering land
Of love, that knows not a dividing sea.
Love builds the house on rock and not on sand,
Love laughs what while the winds rave desperately;
And who hath found love's citadel unmanned?
And who hath held in bonds love's liberty?
My heart's a coward though my words are brave—
We meet so seldom, yet we surely part
So often; there's a problem for your art!°
Still I find comfort in his Book, who saith,°
Though jealousy be cruel as the grave,
And death be strong, yet love is strong as death.

8

Come dicesse a Dio: D'altro non calme.
DANTE

Spero trovar pietà non che perdono.
PETRARCA°

'I, if I perish, perish'—Esther spake:°
And bride of life or death she made her fair
In all the lustre of her perfumed hair
And smiles that kindle longing but to slake.
She put on pomp of loveliness, to take
Her husband through his eyes at unaware;
She spread abroad her beauty for a snare,
Harmless as doves and subtle as a snake.°
She trapped him with one mesh of silken hair,
She vanquished him by wisdom of her wit,
And built her people's house that it should stand:—
If I might take my life so in my hand,
And for my love to Love put up my prayer,
And for love's sake by Love be granted it!

9

O dignitosa coscienza e netta!
DANTE

Spirto più acceso di virtuti ardenti.
PETRARCA°

Thinking of you, and all that was, and all
   That might have been and now can never be,
   I feel your honoured excellence, and see
Myself unworthy of the happier call:
For woe is me who walk so apt to fall,
   So apt to shrink afraid, so apt to flee,
   Apt to lie down and die (ah, woe is me!)
Faithless and hopeless turning to the wall.°
And yet not hopeless quite nor faithless quite,
Because not loveless; love may toil all night,   10
   But take at morning; wrestle till the break°
     Of day, but then wield power with God and man:—°
     So take I heart of grace as best I can,
   Ready to spend and be spent for your sake.°

10

Con miglior corso e con migliore stella.
DANTE

La vita fugge e non s'arresta un' ora.
PETRARCA°

Time flies, hope flags, life plies a wearied wing;
   Death following hard on life gains ground apace;
   Faith runs with each and rears an eager face,
Outruns the rest, makes light of everything,
Spurns earth, and still finds breath to pray and sing;
   While love ahead of all uplifts his praise,
   Still asks for grace and still gives thanks for grace,
Content with all day brings and night will bring.
Life wanes; and when love folds his wings above
   Tired hope, and less we feel his conscious pulse,   10
     Let us go fall asleep, dear friend, in peace:
     A little while, and age and sorrow cease;
    A little while, and life reborn annuls
Loss and decay and death, and all is love.

11

Vien dietro a me e lascia dir le genti.
                              DANTE

Contando i casi della vita nostra.
                              PETRARCA°

Many in aftertimes will say of you
  'He loved her'—while of me what will they say?
  Not that I loved you more than just in play,
For fashion's sake as idle women do.
Even let them prate; who know not what we knew
  Of love and parting in exceeding pain,
  Of parting hopeless here to meet again,
Hopeless on earth, and heaven is out of view.
But by my heart of love laid bare to you,
  My love that you can make not void nor vain,   10
Love that foregoes you but to claim anew
    Beyond this passage of the gate of death,
  I charge you at the Judgment make it plain
  My love of you was life and not a breath.

12

Amor, che ne la mente mi ragiona.
                              DANTE

Amor vien nel bel viso di costei.
                              PETRARCA°

If there be any one can take my place
  And make you happy whom I grieve to grieve,
  Think not that I can grudge it, but believe
I do commend you to that nobler grace,
That readier wit than mine, that sweeter face;
  Yea, since your riches make me rich, conceive
  I too am crowned, while bridal crowns I weave,
And thread the bridal dance with jocund pace.
For if I did not love you, it might be
  That I should grudge you some one dear delight;   10
    But since the heart is yours that was mine own,
  Your pleasure is my pleasure, right my right,
Your honourable freedom makes me free,
    And you companioned I am not alone.

13

E drizzeremo glí occhi al Primo Amore.

DANTE

Ma trovo peso non da le mie braccia.

PETRARCA°

If I could trust mine own self with your fate,
   Shall I not rather trust it in God's hand?
   Without Whose Will one lily doth not stand,
Nor sparrow fall at his appointed date;°
   Who numbereth the innumerable sand,
Who weighs the wind and water with a weight,°
To Whom the world is neither small nor great,
   Whose knowledge foreknew every plan we planned.
Searching my heart for all that touches you,
   I find there only love and love's goodwill   10
Helpless to help and impotent to do,
     Of understanding dull, of sight most dim;
     And therefore I commend you back to Him
Whose love your love's capacity can fill.

14

E la Sua Volontade è nostra pace.

DANTE

Sol con questi pensier, con altre chiome.

PETRARCA°

Youth gone, and beauty gone if ever there
   Dwelt beauty in so poor a face as this;
   Youth gone and beauty, what remains of bliss?
I will not bind fresh roses in my hair,
To shame a cheek at best but little fair, —
   Leave youth his roses, who can bear a thorn, —
I will not seek for blossoms anywhere,
   Except such common flowers as blow with corn.
Youth gone and beauty gone, what doth remain?
   The longing of a heart pent up forlorn,   10
     A silent heart whose silence loves and longs;
     The silence of a heart which sang its songs

While youth and beauty made a summer morn,
Silence of love that cannot sing again.

'Luscious and Sorrowful'

Beautiful, tender, wasting away for sorrow;
Thus to-day; and how shall it be with thee to-morrow?
　Beautiful, tender—what else?
　　A hope tells.

Beautiful, tender, keeping the jubilee
In the land of home together, past death and sea;°
　No more change or death, no more
　　Salt sea-shore.

'Hollow-Sounding and Mysterious'

　　　　There's no replying
　　　　To the Wind's sighing,
　　　　Telling, foretelling,
　　　　Dying, undying,
　　　　Dwindling and swelling,
　　　　Complaining, droning,
　　　　Whistling and moaning,
　　　　Ever beginning,
　　　　Ending, repeating,
　　　　Hinting and dinning,   10
　　　　Lagging and fleeting—
　　　　We've no replying
　　　　Living or dying
　　　　To the Wind's sighing.

　　　　What are you telling,
　　　　Variable Wind-tone?
　　　　What would be teaching,
　　　　O sinking, swelling,
　　　　Desolate Wind-moan?
　　　　Ever for ever   20
　　　　Teaching and preaching,
　　　　Never, ah never

Making us wiser—
The earliest riser
Catches no meaning,
The last who hearkens
Garners no gleaning
Of wisdom's treasure,
While the world darkens:—
Living or dying,   30
In pain, in pleasure,
We've no replying
To wordless flying
Wind's sighing.

Touching 'Never'

Because you never yet have loved me, dear,
   Think you you never can nor ever will?
   Surely while life remains hope lingers still,
Hope the last blossom of life's dying year.
Because the season and mine age grow sere,
   Shall never Spring bring forth her daffodil,
   Shall never sweeter Summer feast her fill
Of roses with the nightingales they hear?
If you had loved me, I not loving you,
   If you had urged me with the tender plea   10
Of what our unknown years to come might do
(Eternal years, if Time should count too few),
   I would have owned the point you pressed on me,
Was possible, or probable, or true.

A Life's Parallels

Never on this side of the grave again,
   On this side of the river,
On this side of the garner of the grain,°
      Never,—

Ever while time flows on and on and on,
   That narrow noiseless river,
Ever while corn bows heavy-headed, wan,
      Ever,—

Never despairing, often fainting, rueing,
　　But looking back, ah never!　　　10
Faint yet pursuing, faint yet still pursuing°
　　Ever.

Golden Silences

There is silence that saith, 'Ah me!'
　　There is silence that nothing saith;
　　　One the silence of life forlorn,
　　One the silence of death;
One is, and the other shall be.

One we know and have known for long,
　　One we know not, but we shall know,
　　　All we who have ever been born;
　　Even so, be it so,—
There is silence, despite a song.　　　10

Sowing day is a silent day,
　　Resting night is a silent night;
　　　But whoso reaps the ripened corn
　　Shall shout in his delight,
While silences vanish away.

In the Willow Shade

I sat beneath a willow tree,
　　Where water falls and calls;
While fancies upon fancies solaced me,
　　Some true, and some were false.

Who set their heart upon a hope
　　That never comes to pass,
Droop in the end like fading heliotrope°
　　The sun's wan looking-glass.

Who set their will upon a whim
　　Clung to through good and ill,　　　10
Are wrecked alike whether they sink or swim,
　　Or hit or miss their will.

All things are vain that wax and wane,
   For which we waste our breath;
Love only doth not wane and is not vain,
   Love only outlives death.

A singing lark rose toward the sky,
   Circling he sang amain;°
He sang, a speck scarce visible sky-high,
   And then he sank again.   20

A second like a sunlit spark
   Flashed singing up his track;
But never overtook that foremost lark,
   And songless fluttered back.

A hovering melody of birds
   Haunted the air above;
They clearly sang contentment without words,
   And youth and joy and love.

O silvery weeping willow tree
   With all leaves shivering,   30
Have you no purpose but to shadow me
   Beside this rippled spring?

On this first fleeting day of Spring,
   For Winter is gone by,
And every bird on every quivering wing
   Floats in a sunny sky;

On this first Summer-like soft day,
   While sunshine steeps the air,
And every cloud has gat itself away,
   And birds sing everywhere.   40

Have you no purpose in the world
   But thus to shadow me
With all your tender drooping twigs unfurled,
   O weeping willow tree?

With all your tremulous leaves outspread
   Betwixt me and the sun,
While here I loiter on a mossy bed
   With half my work undone;

My work undone, that should be done
  At once with all my might;
For after the long day and lingering sun
  Comes the unworking night.

This day is lapsing on its way,
  Is lapsing out of sight;
And after all the chances of the day
  Comes the resourceless night.

The weeping willow shook its head
  And stretched its shadow long;
The west grew crimson, the sun smouldered red,°
  The birds forbore a song.

Slow wind sighed through the willow leaves,
  The ripple made a moan,
The world drooped murmuring like a thing that grieves;°
  And then I felt alone.

I rose to go, and felt the chill,
  And shivered as I went;
Yet shivering wondered, and I wonder still,
  What more that willow meant;

That silvery weeping willow tree
  With all leaves shivering,
Which spent one long day overshadowing me
  Beside a spring in Spring.

'One Foot on Sea, and One on Shore'

  'Oh tell me once and tell me twice
    And tell me thrice to make it plain,
  When we who part this weary day,
    When we who part shall meet again.'

'When windflowers blossom on the sea
   And fishes skim along the plain,
Then we who part this weary day,
   Then you and I shall meet again.'

'Yet tell me once before we part,
   Why need we part who part in pain?   10
If flowers must blossom on the sea,
   Why, we shall never meet again.

'My cheeks are paler than a rose,
   My tears are salter than the main,
My heart is like a lump of ice
   If we must never meet again.'

'Oh weep or laugh, but let me be,
   And live or die, for all's in vain;
For life's in vain since we must part,
   And parting must not meet again   20

'Till windflowers blossom on the sea
   And fishes skim along the plain;
Pale rose of roses let me be,
   Your breaking heart breaks mine again.'

An October Garden

In my Autumn garden I was fain°
   To mourn among my scattered roses;
   Alas for that last rosebud which uncloses
To Autumn's languid sun and rain
When all the world is on the wane!
   Which has not felt the sweet constraint of June,°
   Nor heard the nightingale in tune.

Broad-faced asters by my garden walk,
   You are but coarse compared with roses:
   More choice, more dear that rosebud which uncloses   10
Faint-scented, pinched, upon its stalk,
That least and last which cold winds balk;

A rose it is though least and last of all,
A rose to me though at the fall.

'Summer is Ended'

To think that this meaningless thing was ever a rose,
  Scentless, colourless, *this!*
 Will it ever be thus (who knows?)
  Thus with our bliss,
 If we wait till the close?

Though we care not to wait for the end, there comes the end
  Sooner, later, at last,
 Which nothing can mar, nothing mend:
  An end locked fast,
 Bent we cannot re-bend.   10

Passing and Glassing

  All things that pass
  Are woman's looking-glass;
They show her how her bloom must fade,
And she herself be laid
With withered roses in the shade;
 With withered roses and the fallen peach,
 Unlovely, out of reach
  Of summer joy that was.

  All things that pass
  Are woman's tiring-glass;°   10
The faded lavender is sweet,
Sweet the dead violet
Culled and laid by and cared for yet;
 The dried-up violets and dried lavender
 Still sweet, may comfort her,
  Nor need she cry Alas!°

  All things that pass
  Are wisdom's looking-glass;

Being full of hope and fear, and still
Brimful of good or ill,   20
  According to our work and will;
    For there is nothing new beneath the sun;
    Our doings have been done,
        And that which shall be was.

The Thread of Life

1

The irresponsive silence of the land,
    The irresponsive sounding of the sea,
    Speak both one message of one sense to me:—
Aloof, aloof, we stand aloof, so stand
Thou too aloof bound with the flawless band
    Of inner solitude; we bind not thee;
    But who from thy self-chain shall set thee free?
What heart shall touch thy heart? what hand thy hand?—
And I am sometimes proud and sometimes meek,
    And sometimes I remember days of old   10
When fellowship seemed not so far to seek
    And all the world and I seemed much less cold,
    And at the rainbow's foot lay surely gold,
And hope felt strong and life itself not weak.

2

Thus am I mine own prison. Everything
    Around me free and sunny and at ease:
    Or if in shadow, in a shade of trees
Which the sun kisses, where the gay birds sing
And where all winds make various murmuring;
    Where bees are found, with honey for the bees;
    Where sounds are music, and where silences
Are music of an unlike fashioning.
Then gaze I at the merrymaking crew,
    And smile a moment and a moment sigh   10
Thinking: Why can I not rejoice with you?
    But soon I put the foolish fancy by:

I am not what I have nor what I do;
   But what I was I am, I am even I.°

3

Therefore myself is that one only thing
   I hold to use or waste, to keep or give;
   My sole possession every day I live,
And still mine own despite Time's winnowing.
Ever mine own, while moons and seasons bring
   From crudeness ripeness mellow and sanative;°
   Ever mine own, till Death shall ply his sieve;°
And still mine own, when saints break grave and sing.
And this myself as king unto my King°
   I give, to Him Who gave Himself for me;   10
Who gives Himself to me, and bids me sing
   A sweet new song of His redeemed set free;°
He bids me sing: O death, where is thy sting?
   And sing: O grave, where is thy victory?°

An Old-World Thicket

   ... Una selva oscura.

DANTE

Awake or sleeping (for I know not which)
   I was or was not mazed within a wood°
   Where every mother-bird brought up her brood
     Safe in some leafy niche
   Of oak or ash, of cypress or of beech,

Of silvery aspen trembling delicately,
   Of plane or warmer-tinted sycomore,
   Of elm that dies in secret from the core,
     Of ivy weak and free,
   Of pines, of all green lofty things that be.°   10

Such birds they seemed as challenged each desire;
   Like spots of azure heaven upon the wing,
   Like downy emeralds that alight and sing,

Like actual coals on fire,
Like anything they seemed, and everything.

Such mirth they made, such warblings and such chat
    With tongue of music in a well-tuned beak,
    They seemed to speak more wisdom than we speak,
        To make our music flat
    And all our subtlest reasonings wild or weak.   20

Their meat was nought but flowers like butterflies,
    With berries coral-coloured or like gold;
    Their drink was only dew, which blossoms hold
        Deep where the honey lies;
Their wings and tails were lit by sparkling eyes.

The shade wherein they revelled was a shade
    That danced and twinkled to the unseen sun;
    Branches and leaves cast shadows one by one,
        And all their shadows swayed
In breaths of air that rustled and that played.   30

A sound of waters neither rose nor sank,
    And spread a sense of freshness through the air;
    It seemed not here or there, but everywhere,
        As if the whole earth drank,
Root fathom deep and strawberry on its bank.

But I who saw such things as I have said,
    Was overdone with utter weariness;
    And walked in care, as one whom fears oppress
        Because above his head
Death hangs, or damage, or the dearth of bread.   40

Each sore defeat of my defeated life
    Faced and outfaced me in that bitter hour;
    And turned to yearning palsy all my power,
        And all my peace to strife,
Self stabbing self with keen lack-pity knife.

Sweetness of beauty moved me to despair,
    Stung me to anger by its mere content,
    Made me all lonely on that way I went,

Piled care upon my care,
Brimmed full my cup, and stripped me empty and bare: 50

For all that was but showed what all was not,
   But gave clear proof of what might never be;
   Making more destitute my poverty,
     And yet more blank my lot,
   And me much sadder by its jubilee.°

Therefore I sat me down: for wherefore walk?
   And closed mine eyes: for wherefore see or hear?
   Alas, I had no shutter to mine ear,
     And could not shun the talk
   Of all rejoicing creatures far or near.   60

Without my will I hearkened and I heard
   (Asleep or waking, for I know not which),
   Till note by note the music changed its pitch;
     Bird ceased to answer bird,
And every wind sighed softly if it stirred.

The drip of widening waters seemed to weep,
   All fountains sobbed and gurgled as they sprang,
Somewhere a cataract cried out in its leap
     Sheer down a headlong steep;
   High over all cloud-thunders gave a clang.   70

Such universal sound of lamentation
   I heard and felt, fain not to feel or hear;°
   Nought else there seemed but anguish far and near;
     Nought else but all creation
   Moaning and groaning wrung by pain or fear,°

Shuddering in the misery of its doom:
   My heart then rose a rebel against light,
   Scouring all earth and heaven and depth and height,
     Ingathering wrath and gloom,
   Ingathering wrath to wrath and night to night.   80

Ah me, the bitterness of such revolt,
   All impotent, all hateful, and all hate,
That kicks and breaks itself against the bolt

    Of an imprisoning fate,
    And vainly shakes, and cannot shake the gate.

Agony to agony, deep called to deep,
    Out of the deep I called of my desire;°
    My strength was weakness and my heart was fire;
      Mine eyes that would not weep
Or sleep, scaled height and depth, and could not sleep;   90

The eyes, I mean, of my rebellious soul,
    For still my bodily eyes were closed and dark:
    A random thing I seemed without a mark,
      Racing without a goal,
    Adrift upon life's sea without an ark.

More leaden than the actual self of lead
    Outer and inner darkness weighed on me.
    The tide of anger ebbed. Then fierce and free
      Surged full above my head
    The moaning tide of helpless misery.   100

Why should I breathe, whose breath was but a sigh?
    Why should I live, who drew such painful breath?
Oh weary work, the unanswerable why!—
      Yet I, why should I die,
    Who had no hope in life, no hope in death?

Grasses and mosses and the fallen leaf
    Make peaceful bed for an indefinite term;
    But underneath the grass there gnaws a worm—
      Haply, there gnaws a grief—
Both, haply always; not, as now, so brief.   110

The pleasure I remember, it is past;
    The pain I feel, is passing passing by;
    Thus all the world is passing, and thus I:
      All things that cannot last
    Have grown familiar, and are born to die.

And being familiar, have so long been borne
    That habit trains us not to break but bend:
Mourning grows natural to us who mourn

In foresight of an end,
But that which ends not who shall brave or mend?   120

Surely the ripe fruits tremble on their bough,
They cling and linger trembling till they drop:
I, trembling, cling to dying life; for how
Face the perpetual Now?
Birthless and deathless, void of start or stop,

Void of repentance, void of hope and fear,
Of possibility, alternative,
Of all that ever made us bear to live
From night to morning here,
Of promise even which has no gift to give.   130

The wood, and every creature of the wood,
Seemed mourning with me in an undertone;
Soft scattered chirpings and a windy moan,
Trees rustling where they stood
And shivered, showed compassion for my mood.

Rage to despair; and now despair had turned
Back to self-pity and mere weariness,
With yearnings like a smouldering fire that burned,
And might grow more or less,
And might die out or wax to white excess.   140

Without, within me, music seemed to be;
Something not music, yet most musical,
Silence and sound in heavenly harmony;
At length a pattering fall
Of feet, a bell, and bleatings, broke through all.

Then I looked up. The wood lay in a glow
From golden sunset and from ruddy sky;
The sun had stooped to earth though once so high;
Had stooped to earth, in slow
Warm dying loveliness brought near and low.°   150

Each water drop made answer to the light,
Lit up a spark and showed the sun his face;
Soft purple shadows paved the grassy space

    And crept from height to height,
      From height to loftier height crept up apace.

While opposite the sun a gazing moon
    Put on his glory for her coronet,
Kindling her luminous coldness to its noon,
      As his great splendour set;
    One only star made up her train as yet.   160

Each twig was tipped with gold, each leaf was edged
    And veined with gold from the gold-flooded west;
Each mother-bird, and mate-bird, and unfledged
      Nestling, and curious nest,
    Displayed a gilded moss or beak or breast.

And filing peacefully between the trees,
    Having the moon behind them, and the sun
Full in their meek mild faces, walked at ease
      A homeward flock, at peace°
    With one another and with every one.   170

A patriarchal ram with tinkling bell
    Led all his kin; sometimes one browsing sheep
    Hung back a moment, or one lamb would leap
      And frolic in a dell;
Yet still they kept together, journeying well,

And bleating, one or other, many or few,
    Journeying together toward the sunlit west;
    Mild face by face, and woolly breast by breast,
      Patient, sun-brightened too,
    Still journeying toward the sunset and their rest.   180

Later Life: a Double Sonnet of Sonnets

I

Before the mountains were brought forth, before
    Earth and the world were made, then God was God:°
And God will still be God, when flames shall roar
    Round earth and heaven dissolving at His nod:

And this God is our God, even while His rod
Of righteous wrath falls on us smiting sore:
And this God is our God for evermore
  Through life, through death, while clod returns to clod.
For though He slay us we will trust in Him;°
  We will flock home to Him by divers ways:
  Yea, though He slay us we will vaunt His praise,
Serving and loving with the Cherubim,
Watching and loving with the Seraphim,
  Our very selves His praise through endless days.

2

Rend hearts and rend not garments for our sins;°
  Gird sackcloth not on body but on soul;
  Grovel in dust with faces toward the goal
Nor won, nor neared: he only laughs who wins.
Not neared the goal, the race too late begins;
  All left undone, we have yet to do the whole;
  The sun is hurrying west and toward the pole
Where darkness waits for earth with all her kins.
Let us to-day while it is called to-day
  Set out, if utmost speed may yet avail—
  The shadows lengthen and the light grows pale:
    For who through darkness and the shadow of death,
Darkness that may be felt, shall find a way,
    Blind-eyed, deaf-eared, and choked with failing breath?

3

Thou Who didst make and knowest whereof we are made,
  Oh bear in mind our dust and nothingness,
  Our wordless tearless dumbness of distress:
Bear Thou in mind the burden Thou hast laid
Upon us, and our feebleness unstayed°
  Except Thou stay us: for the long long race
  Which stretches far and far before our face
Thou knowest,—remember Thou whereof we are made.
If making makes us Thine then Thine we are,
  And if redemption we are twice Thine own:
If once Thou didst come down from heaven afar
    To seek us and to find us, how not save?

Comfort us, save us, leave us not alone,
   Thou Who didst die our death and fill our grave.

4

So tired am I, so weary of to-day,
   So unrefreshed from foregone weariness,
   So overburdened by foreseen distress,
So lagging and so stumbling on my way,
I scarce can rouse myself to watch or pray,
   To hope, or aim, or toil for more or less,—
   Ah, always less and less, even while I press
Forward and toil and aim as best I may.
Half-starved of soul and heartsick utterly,
   Yet lift I up my heart and soul and eyes   10
   (Which fail in looking upward) toward the prize:
Me, Lord, Thou seest though I see not Thee;
   Me now, as once the Thief in Paradise,
Even me, O Lord my Lord, remember me.°

5

Lord, Thou Thyself art Love and only Thou;
   Yet I who am not love would fain love Thee;
   But Thou alone being Love canst furnish me
With that same love my heart is craving now.
Allow my plea! for if Thou disallow,
   No second fountain can I find but Thee;
   No second hope or help is left to me,
No second anything, but only Thou.
O Love accept, according my request;
   O Love exhaust, fulfilling my desire: 10
   Uphold me with the strength that cannot tire,
Nerve me to labour till Thou bid me rest,
   Kindle my fire from Thine unkindled fire,
And charm the willing heart from out my breast.

6

We lack, yet cannot fix upon the lack:
   Not this, nor that; yet somewhat, certainly.
   We see the things we do not yearn to see

Around us: and what see we glancing back?
Lost hopes that leave our hearts upon the rack,
   Hopes that were never ours yet seemed to be,
   For which we steered on life's salt stormy sea
Braving the sunstroke and the frozen pack.°
If thus to look behind is all in vain,
   And all in vain to look to left or right,   10
Why face we not our future once again,
Launching with hardier hearts across the main,
   Straining dim eyes to catch the invisible sight,
And strong to bear ourselves in patient pain?

7

To love and to remember; that is good:
   To love and to forget; that is not well:
   To lapse from love to hatred; that is hell
And death and torment, rightly understood.
Soul dazed by love and sorrow, cheer thy mood;
   More blest art thou than mortal tongue can tell:
   Ring not thy funeral but thy marriage bell,
And salt with hope thy life's insipid food.
Love is the goal, love is the way we wend,
   Love is our parallel unending line   10
      Whose only perfect Parallel is Christ,
Beginning not begun, End without end:
      For He Who hath the Heart of God sufficed,
Can satisfy all hearts,—yea, thine and mine.

8

We feel and see with different hearts and eyes: —
   Ah Christ, if all our hearts could meet in Thee
   How well it were for them and well for me,
Our hearts Thy dear accepted sacrifice.
Thou, only Life of hearts and Light of eyes,
   Our life, our light, if once we turn to Thee,
   So be it, O Lord, to them and so to me;
Be all alike Thine own dear sacrifice.
Thou Who by death hast ransomed us from death,
   Thyself God's sole well-pleasing Sacrifice,   10
      Thine only sacred Self I plead with Thee:

Make Thou it well for them and well for me
That Thou hast given us souls and wills and breath,
  And hearts to love Thee, and to see Thee eyes.

9

Star Sirius and the Pole Star dwell afar
  Beyond the drawings each of other's strength:
  One blazes through the brief bright summer's length
Lavishing life-heat from a flaming car;
  While one unchangeable upon a throne
  Broods o'er the frozen heart of earth alone,
Content to reign the bright particular star
  Of some who wander or of some who groan.
They own no drawings each of other's strength,
  Nor vibrate in a visible sympathy,   10
    Nor veer along their courses each toward each:
  Yet are their orbits pitched in harmony
Of one dear heaven, across whose depth and length
    Mayhap they talk together without speech.

10

Tread softly! all the earth is holy ground.
  It may be, could we look with seeing eyes,
  This spot we stand on is a Paradise
Where dead have come to life and lost been found,
Where Faith has triumphed, Martyrdom been crowned,
  Where fools have foiled the wisdom of the wise;
  From this same spot the dust of saints may rise,
And the King's prisoners come to light unbound.
O earth, earth, earth, hear thou thy Maker's Word:
  'Thy dead thou shalt give up, nor hide thy slain'—°   10
  Some who went weeping forth shall come again
    Rejoicing from the east or from the west,
As doves fly to their windows, love's own bird°
    Contented and desirous to the nest.[1]

[1] 'Quali colombe dal disio chiamate
    Con l'ali aperte e ferme al dolce nido
    Volan per l'aer dal voler portate.' DANTE

11

Lifelong our stumbles, lifelong our regret,
   Lifelong our efforts failing and renewed,
   While lifelong is our witness, 'God is good:'
Who bore with us till now, bears with us yet,
Who still remembers and will not forget,
   Who gives us light and warmth and daily food;
   And gracious promises half understood,
And glories half unveiled, whereon to set
Our heart of hearts and eyes of our desire;
   Uplifting us to longing and to love,   10
Luring us upward from this world of mire,
   Urging us to press on and mount above
   Ourselves and all we have had experience of,
Mounting to Him in love's perpetual fire.

12

A dream there is wherein we are fain to scream,
   While struggling with ourselves we cannot speak:
   And much of all our waking life, as weak
And misconceived, eludes us like the dream.
For half life's seemings are not what they seem,
   And vain the laughs we laugh, the shrieks we shriek;
   Yea, all is vain that mars the settled meek
Contented quiet of our daily theme.
When I was young I deemed that sweets are sweet:
   But now I deem some searching bitters are   10
   Sweeter than sweets, and more refreshing far,
      And to be relished more, and more desired,
And more to be pursued on eager feet,
      On feet untired, and still on feet though tired.

13

Shame is a shadow cast by sin: yet shame
   Itself may be a glory and a grace,
   Refashioning the sin-disfashioned face;
A nobler bruit than hollow-sounded fame,°
A new-lit lustre on a tarnished name,
   One virtue pent within an evil place,
   Strength for the fight, and swiftness for the race,

A stinging salve, a life-requickening flame.
A salve so searching we may scarcely live,
  A flame so fierce it seems that we must die,   10
    An actual cautery thrust into the heart:
    Nevertheless, men die not of such smart;
And shame gives back what nothing else can give,
  Man to himself,—then sets him up on high.

14

When Adam and when Eve left Paradise
  Did they love on and cling together still,
  Forgiving one another all that ill
The twain had wrought on such a different wise?
She propped upon his strength, and he in guise
  Of lover though of lord, girt to fulfil
  Their term of life and die when God should will;
Lie down and sleep, and having slept arise.
Boast not against us, O our enemy!
  To-day we fall, but we shall rise again;   10
We grope to-day, to-morrow we shall see:
    What is to-day that we should fear to-day?
    A morrow cometh which shall sweep away
  Thee and thy realm of change and death and pain.

15

Let woman fear to teach and bear to learn,°
  Remembering the first woman's first mistake.
  Eve had for pupil the inquiring snake,
Whose doubts she answered on a great concern;
But he the tables so contrived to turn,
  It next was his to give and her's to take;
  Till man deemed poison sweet for her sweet sake,
And fired a train by which the world must burn.°
Did Adam love his Eve from first to last?
  I think so; as we love who works us ill,   10
  And wounds us to the quick, yet loves us still.
Love pardons the unpardonable past:
Love in a dominant embrace holds fast
  His frailer self, and saves without her will.

16

Our teachers teach that one and one make two:
   Later, Love rules that one and one make one:
   Abstruse the problems! neither need we shun,
But skilfully to each should yield its due.
The narrower total seems to suit the few,
   The wider total suits the common run;
   Each obvious in its sphere like moon or sun;
Both provable by me, and both by you.
Befogged and witless, in a wordy maze
   A groping stroll perhaps may do us good;   10
   If cloyed we are with much we have understood,
If tired of half our dusty world and ways,
   If sick of fasting, and if sick of food; —
And how about these long still-lengthening days?

17

Something this foggy day, a something which
   Is neither of this fog nor of to-day,
   Has set me dreaming of the winds that play
Past certain cliffs, along one certain beach,°
   And turn the topmost edge of waves to spray:
   Ah pleasant pebbly strand so far away,
So out of reach while quite within my reach,
   As out of reach as India or Cathay!
I am sick of where I am and where I am not,
   I am sick of foresight and of memory,   10
   I am sick of all I have and all I see,
      I am sick of self, and there is nothing new;
Oh weary impatient patience of my lot! —
      Thus with myself: how fares it, Friends, with you?

18

So late in Autumn half the world's asleep,
   And half the wakeful world looks pinched and pale;
   For dampness now, not freshness, rides the gale;
And cold and colourless comes ashore the deep
With tides that bluster or with tides that creep;
   Now veiled uncouthness wears an uncouth veil
   Of fog, not sultry haze; and blight and bale°

Have done their worst, and leaves rot on the heap.
So late in Autumn one forgets the Spring,
    Forgets the Summer with its opulence,   10
The callow birds that long have found a wing,
    The swallows that more lately gat them hence:°
Will anything like Spring, will anything
    Like Summer, rouse one day the slumbering sense?

                                    19

Here now is Winter. Winter, after all,
    Is not so drear as was my boding dream
    While Autumn gleamed its latest watery gleam
On sapless leafage too inert to fall.
Still leaves and berries clothe my garden wall
    Where ivy thrives on scantiest sunny beam;
    Still here a bud and there a blossom seem
Hopeful, and robin still is musical.
Leaves, flowers and fruit and one delightful song
    Remain; these days are short, but now the nights   10
    Intense and long, hang out their utmost lights;
Such starry nights are long, yet not too long;
Frost nips the weak, while strengthening still the strong
    Against that day when Spring sets all to rights.

                                    20

A hundred thousand birds salute the day: —
    One solitary bird salutes the night:°
Its mellow grieving wiles our grief away,
    And tunes our weary watches to delight;
It seems to sing the thoughts we cannot say,
    To know and sing them, and to set them right;
Until we feel once more that May is May,
    And hope some buds may bloom without a blight.
This solitary bird outweighs, outvies,
    The hundred thousand merry-making birds   10
Whose innocent warblings yet might make us wise
Would we but follow when they bid us rise,
    Would we but set their notes of praise to words
And launch our hearts up with them to the skies.

21

A host of things I take on trust: I take
    The nightingales on trust, for few and far
    Between those actual summer moments are
When I have heard what melody they make.
So chanced it once at Como on the Lake:
    But all things, then, waxed musical; each star
    Sang on its course, each breeze sang on its car,°
All harmonies sang to senses wide awake.
All things in tune, myself not out of tune,
    Those nightingales were nightingales indeed: 10
    Yet truly an owl had satisfied my need,
And wrought a rapture underneath that moon,
    Or simple sparrow chirping from a reed;
For June that night glowed like a doubled June.

22

The mountains in their overwhelming might
    Moved me to sadness when I saw them first,
And afterwards they moved me to delight;
    Struck harmonies from silent chords which burst
    Out into song, a song by memory nursed;
For ever unrenewed by touch or sight
Sleeps the keen magic of each day or night,
    In pleasure and in wonder then immersed.
All Switzerland behind us on the ascent,
    All Italy before us we plunged down   10
        St. Gothard, garden of forget-me-not:°
    Yet why should such a flower choose such a spot?
Could we forget that way which once we went
    Though not one flower had bloomed to weave its crown?

23

Beyond the seas we know, stretch seas unknown
    Blue and bright-coloured for our dim and green;
    Beyond the lands we see, stretch lands unseen
With many-tinted tangle overgrown;
And icebound seas there are like seas of stone,
    Serenely stormless as death lies serene;

And lifeless tracts of sand, which intervene
Betwixt the lands where living flowers are blown.
This dead and living world befits our case
    Who live and die: we live in wearied hope,   10
We die in hope not dead; we run a race
To-day, and find no present halting-place;
    All things we see lie far within our scope,
And still we peer beyond with craving face.

24

The wise do send their hearts before them to
    Dear blessed Heaven, despite the veil between;
    The foolish nurse their hearts within the screen
Of this familiar world, where all we do
Or have is old, for there is nothing new:
    Yet elder far that world we have not seen;
    God's Presence antedates what else hath been:
Many the foolish seem, the wise seem few.
Oh foolishest fond folly of a heart
    Divided, neither here nor there at rest!   10
        That hankers after Heaven, but clings to earth;
        That neither here nor there knows thorough mirth,
Half-choosing, wholly missing, the good part:—
    Oh fool among the foolish, in thy quest.

25

When we consider what this life we lead
    Is not, and is: how full of toil and pain,
    How blank of rest and of substantial gain,
Beset by hunger earth can never feed,
And propping half our hearts upon a reed;
    We cease to mourn lost treasures, mourned in vain,
    Lost treasures we are fain and yet not fain
To fetch back for a solace of our need.
For who that feel this burden and this strain,
    This wide vacuity of hope and heart,   10
Would bring their cherished well-beloved again:
    To bleed with them and wince beneath the smart,
To have with stinted bliss such lavish bane,
    To hold in lieu of all so poor a part?

26

This Life is full of numbness and of balk,°
  Of haltingness and baffled short-coming,
  Of promise unfulfilled, of everything
That is puffed vanity and empty talk:
Its very bud hangs cankered on the stalk,
  Its very song-bird trails a broken wing,
  Its very Spring is not indeed like Spring,
But sighs like Autumn round an aimless walk.
This Life we live is dead for all its breath;
  Death's self it is, set off on pilgrimage,   10
  Travelling with tottering steps the first short stage:
    The second stage is one mere desert dust
    Where Death sits veiled amid creation's rust: —
Unveil thy face, O Death who art not Death.

27

I have dreamed of Death:—what will it be to die
  Not in a dream, but in the literal truth
  With all Death's adjuncts ghastly and uncouth,
The pang that is the last and the last sigh?
Too dulled, it may be, for a last good-bye,
  Too comfortless for any one to soothe,
  A helpless charmless spectacle of ruth
Through long last hours, so long while yet they fly.
So long to those who hopeless in their fear
  Watch the slow breath and look for what they dread: 10
While I supine with ears that cease to hear,
    With eyes that glaze, with heart pulse running down
  (Alas! no saint rejoicing on her bed),
    May miss the goal at last, may miss a crown.

28

In life our absent friend is far away:
  But death may bring our friend exceeding near,
  Show him familiar faces long so dear
And lead him back in reach of words we say.
He only cannot utter yea or nay
  In any voice accustomed to our ear;
  He only cannot make his face appear

And turn the sun back on our shadowed day.
The dead may be around us, dear and dead;
  The unforgotten dearest dead may be   10
    Watching us with unslumbering eyes and heart;
Brimful of words which cannot yet be said,
    Brimful of knowledge they may not impart,
    Brimful of love for you and love for me.

'Behold the Man!'

Shall Christ hang on the Cross, and we not look?
  Heaven, earth and hell stood gazing at the first,
  While Christ for long-cursed man was counted cursed;
Christ, God and Man, Whom God the Father strook
And shamed and sifted and one while forsook:—°
  Cry shame upon our bodies we have nursed
  In sweets, our souls in pride, our spirits immersed
In wilfulness, our steps run all acrook.
Cry shame upon us! for He bore our shame
  In agony, and we look on at ease   10
With neither hearts on flame nor cheeks on flame:
  What hast thou, what have I, to do with peace?
Not to send peace but send a sword He came,°
  And fire and fasts and tearful night-watches.°

Resurgam

From depth to height, from height to loftier height,
  The climber sets his foot and sets his face,
  Tracks lingering sunbeams to their halting-place,
And counts the last pulsations of the light.
Strenuous thro' day and unsurprised by night
  He runs a race with Time and wins the race,
  Emptied and stripped of all save only Grace,
Will, Love, a threefold panoply of might.°
Darkness descends for light he toiled to seek:
  He stumbles on the darkened mountain-head,   10
    Left breathless in the unbreathable thin air,

Made freeman of the living and the dead:—
He wots not he has topped the topmost peak,°
　　But the returning sun will find him there.

A Valentine

1882

My blessed Mother dozing in her chair
　　On Christmas Day seemed an embodied Love,
A comfortable Love with soft brown hair
　　Softened and silvered to a tint of dove,°
A better sort of Venus with an air°
　　Angelical from thoughts that dwell above,
A wiser Pallas in whose body fair°
　　Enshrined a blessed soul looks out thereof.
Winter brought Holly then; now Spring has brought
　　Paler and frailer Snowdrops shivering;   10
And I have brought a simple humble thought
　　— I her devoted duteous Valentine—,
A lifelong thought which thrills this song I sing,
　　A lifelong love to this dear Saint of mine.

Birchington Churchyard

A lowly hill which overlooks a flat,
　　Half sea, half country side;
　　A flat-shored sea of low-voiced creeping tide
Over a chalky weedy mat.

A hill of hillocks, flowery and kept green
　　Round Crosses raised for hope,
　　With many-tinted sunsets where the slope
Faces the lingering western sheen.

A lowly hope, a height that is but low,
　　While Time sets solemnly,   10
　　While the tide rises of Eternity,
Silent and neither swift nor slow.

'A Helpmeet for Him'

Woman was made for man's delight;
   Charm, O woman, be not afraid!
His shadow by day, his moon by night,°
   Woman was made.

Her strength with weakness is overlaid;
   Meek compliances veil her might;
Him she stays, by whom she is stayed.°

World-wide champion of truth and right,
   Hope in gloom and in danger aid,
Tender and faithful, ruddy and white,°   10
   Woman was made.

An Echo from Willowwood

O ye, all ye that walk in Willowwood
D. G. ROSSETTI

Two gazed into a pool, he gazed and she,
   Not hand in hand, yet heart in heart, I think,
   Pale and reluctant on the water's brink,
As on the brink of parting which must be.
Each eyed the other's aspect, she and he,
   Each felt one hungering heart leap up and sink,
   Each tasted bitterness which both must drink,
There on the brink of life's dividing sea.
Lilies upon the surface, deep below
   Two wistful faces craving each for each,   10
     Resolute and reluctant without speech:—
A sudden ripple made the faces flow°
   One moment joined, to vanish out of reach:
     So those hearts joined, and ah! were parted so.

('Thy fainting spouse, yet still Thy spouse')

Thy fainting spouse, yet still Thy spouse;
   Thy trembling dove, yet still Thy dove;°

Thine own by mutual vows,
    By mutual love.

Recall Thy vows, if not her vows;
    Recall Thy Love, if not her love:
For weak she is, Thy spouse,
    And tired, Thy dove.

'Son, Remember'

I laid beside thy gate, am Lazarus;
    See me or see me not I still am there,
    Hungry and thirsty, sore and sick and bare,
Dog-comforted and crumbs-solicitous:
While thou in all thy ways art sumptuous,
    Daintily clothed, with dainties for thy fare:
    Thus a world's wonder thou art quit of care,
And be I seen or not seen I am thus.
One day a worm for thee, a worm for me:
    With my worm angel songs and trumpet burst   10
        And plenitude an end of all desire:
But what for thee, alas! but what for thee?
    Fire and an unextinguishable thirst,
        Thirst in an unextinguishable fire.

('Sleeping at last, the trouble & tumult over')

Sleeping at last, the trouble & tumult over,
Sleeping at last, the struggle & horror past,
Cold & white out of sight of friend & of lover
Sleeping at last.

No more a tired heart downcast or overcast,
No more pangs that wring or shifting fears that hover,
Sleeping at last in a dreamless sleep locked fast.

Fast asleep. Singing birds in their leafy cover
Cannot wake her, nor shake her the gusty blast.   10
Under the purple thyme & the purple clover
Sleeping at last.

STORIES

Maude

Prose and Verse

PART 1st

I

'A penny for your thoughts,' said Mrs Foster one bright July morning as she entered the sitting room with a bunch of roses in her hand, and an open letter: 'A penny for your thoughts,' said she addressing her daughter, who, surrounded by a chaos of stationery, was slipping out of sight some scrawled paper. This observation remaining unanswered, the Mother, only too much accustomed to inattention, continued: 'Here is a note from your Aunt Letty; she wants us to go and pass a few days with them. You know Tuesday is Mary's birthday, so they mean to have some young people, and cannot dispense with your company.'

'Do you think of going?' said Maude at last, having locked her writing-book.

'Yes dear: even a short stay in the country may do you good, you have looked so pale lately. Don't you feel quite well? tell me.'

'Oh yes; there is not much the matter, only I am tired and have a headache. Indeed there is nothing at all the matter; besides, the country may work wonders.'

Half satisfied, half uneasy, Mrs Foster asked a few more questions, to have them all answered in the same style: vain questions, put to one who without telling lies was determined not to tell the truth.

When once more alone Maude resumed the occupations which her Mother's entrance had interrupted. Her writing-book was neither Common-Place Book, Album, Scrap-Book nor Diary; it was a compound of all these; and contained original compositions not intended for the public eye, pet extracts, extraordinary little sketches and occasional tracts of journal. This choice collection she now proceeded to enrich with the following sonnet:—°

> Yes, I too could face death and never shrink:
> But it is harder to bear hated life;

To strive with hands and knees weary of strife;
　　To drag the heavy chain whose every link
　　Galls to the bone; to stand upon the brink
Of the deep grave, nor drowse, though it be rife
With sleep; to hold with steady hand the knife
　　Nor strike home: this is courage as I think.
Surely to suffer is more than to do:
　　To do is quickly done; to suffer is   10
　　Longer and fuller of heart-sicknesses:
　　Each day's experience testifies of this:
Good deeds are many, but good lives are few;
　　Thousands taste the full cup; who drains the lees? —

having done which she yawned, leaned back in her chair, and wondered
how she should fill up the time till dinner.

Maude Foster was just fifteen. Small though not positively short,
she might easily be overlooked but would not easily be forgotten. Her
figure was slight and well-made, but appeared almost high-shouldered
through a habitual shrugging stoop. Her features were regular and
pleasing: as a child she had been very pretty; and might have continued
so but for a fixed paleness, and an expression, not exactly of pain, but
languid and preoccupied to a painful degree. Yet even now if at any
time she became thoroughly aroused and interested, her sleepy eyes
would light up with wonderful brilliancy, her cheeks glow with warm
colour, her manner become animated, and drawing herself up to
her full height she would look more beautiful than ever she did as a
child. So Mrs Foster said, and so unhappily Maude knew. She also
knew that people thought her clever, and that her little copies of
verses were handed about and admired. Touching these same verses,
it was the amazement of every one what could make her poetry so
broken-hearted as was mostly the case. Some pronounced that she
wrote very foolishly about things she could not possibly understand;
some wondered if she really had any secret source of uneasiness; while
some simply set her down as affected. Perhaps there was a degree of
truth in all these opinions. But I have said enough: the following
pages will enable my readers to form their own estimate of Maude's
character. Meanwhile let me transport them to another sitting
room; but this time it will be in the country with a delightful garden
look-out.

Mary Clifton was arranging her Mother's special nosegay when that
lady entered.

'Here my dear, I will finish doing the flowers. It is time for you to go to meet your Aunt and Cousin; indeed, if you do not make haste, you will be too late.'

'Thank you, Mamma; the flowers are nearly done;' and Mary ran out of the room.

Before long she and her sister were hurrying beneath a burning sun towards the Railway Station. Through having delayed their start to the very last moment, neither had found time to lay hands on a parasol; but this was little heeded by two healthy girls, full of life and spirits, and longing moreover to spy out their friends. Mary wanted one day of fifteen; Agnes was almost a year older: both were well-grown and well-made, with fair hair, blue eyes and fresh complexions. So far they were alike: what differences existed in other respects remains to be seen.

'How do you do, Aunt? How do you do, Maude?' cried Mary making a sudden dart forward as she discovered our friends, who having left the Station had already made some progress along the dusty road. Then relinquishing her Aunt to Agnes, she seized upon her cousin, and was soon deep in the description of all the pleasures planned for the auspicious morrow.

'We are to do what we like in the morning: I mean, nothing particular is arranged; so I shall initiate you into all the mysteries of the place; all the cats, dogs, rabbits, pigeons, &c; above all I must introduce you to a pig, a special protégé of mine: — that is, if you are inclined, for you look wretchedly pale; aren't you well, dear?'

'Oh yes, quite well, and you must show me everything. But what are we to do afterwards?'

'Oh! afterwards we are to be intensely grand. All our young friends are coming and we are to play at round games, (you were always clever at round games,°) and I expect to have great fun. Besides, I have stipulated for unlimited strawberries and cream; also sundry tarts are in course of preparation. By the way, I count on your introducing some new game among us benighted rustics; you who come from dissipated London.'

'I fear I know nothing new, but will do my best. At any rate I can preside at your toilet and assist in making you irresistible.'

Mary coloured and laughed; then thought no more of the pretty speech, which sounded as if carefully prepared by her polite cousin. The two made a strong contrast: one was occupied by a thousand shifting thoughts of herself, her friends, her plans, what she must do, and what she would do; the other, whatever might employ her tongue, and

to a certain extent her mind, had always an under-current of thought
intent upon herself.

Arrived at the house, greetings were duly and cordially performed;
also an introduction to a new and very fat baby, who received Maude's
advances with a howl of intense dismay. The first day of a visit is often
no very lively affair: so perhaps all parties heard the clock announce
bed-time without much regret.

II

The young people were assembled in Mary's room, deep in the mysteries
of the toilet.

'Here is your wreath, Maude; you must wear it for my sake, and
forgive a surreptitious sprig of bay which I have introduced;' said
Agnes, adjusting the last white rose, and looking affectionately at her
sister and cousin.

Maude was arranging Mary's long fair hair with goodnatured anxiety
to display it to the utmost advantage.

'One more spray of fuchsia; I was always sure fuchsia would make
a beautiful head-dress. There; now you are perfection: only look; look
Agnes.—Oh, I beg your pardon; thank you; my wreath is very nice,
only I have not earned the bay.' Still she did not remove it; and when
placed on her dark hair it well became the really intellectual character
of her face. Her dress was entirely white; simple, fresh and elegant.
Neither she nor Agnes would wear ornaments; but left them to Mary,
in whose honour the entertainment was given, and who in all other
respects was arrayed like her sister.

In the drawingroom Mary proceeded to set in order the presents
received that morning:—a handsomely bound Bible from her Father,
and a small Prayer-book with Cross and clasp from her Mother;
a bracelet of Maude's hair from her Aunt; a cornelian heart from
Agnes, and a pocket bonbonnière from her Cousin, besides pretty
trifles from her little Brothers. In the midst of arrangements and
re-arrangements the servant entered with a large bunch of lilies from
the village school-children and the announcement that Mr and Mrs
Savage were just arrived with their six daughters.

Gradually the guests assembled; young and old, pretty and plain; all
alike seemingly bent on enjoying themselves: some with gifts, and all
with cordial greetings for Mary; for she was a general favourite. There
was slim Rosanna Hunt, her scarf arranged with artful negligence to
hide a slight protrusion of one shoulder; and sweet Magdalen Ellis,

habited as usual in quiet colours.° Then came Jane and Alice Deverell, twins so much alike that few besides their parents knew them apart with any certainty; and their fair brother Alexis who, had he been a girl, would have increased the confusion. There was little Ellen Potter with a round rosy face like an apple, looking as natural and goodhumoured as if, instead of a grand French Governess, she had had her own parents with her like most of the other children; and then came three rather haughty-looking Miss Stantons; and pale Hannah Lindley the orphan; and Harriet Eyre, a thought too showy in her dress.

Mary, all life and spirits, hastened to introduce the new-comers to Maude; who, perfectly unembarrassed, bowed and uttered little speeches with the manner of a practised woman of the world; while the genuine, unobtrusive courtesy of Agnes did more towards making their guests comfortable than the eager goodnature of her sister, or the correct breeding of her cousin.

At length the preliminaries were all accomplished, every one having found a seat, or being otherwise satisfactorily disposed of. The elders of the party were grouped here and there, talking and looking on: the very small children were accommodated in an adjoining apartment with a gigantic Noah's Ark: and the rest of the young people being at liberty to amuse themselves as fancy might prompt, a general appeal was made to Miss Foster for some game, novel, entertaining and ingenious; or, as some of the more diffident hinted, easy.

'I really know nothing new;' said Maude: 'you must have played at Proverbs, What's my thought like, How do you like it, and Magic music°:—or stay, there is one thing we can try:—Bouts rimés.'°

'What?' asked Mary.

'Bouts rimés: it is very easy. Some one gives rhymes, Mamma can do that, and then every one fills them up as they think fit. A sonnet is the best form to select; but, if you wish, we could try eight, or even four lines.'

'But I am certain I could not make a couplet;' said Mary laughing. 'Of course you would get on capitally, and Agnes might manage very well, and Magdalen can do anything; but it is quite beyond me: do pray think of something more suited to my capacity.'

'Indeed I have nothing else to propose. This is very much better than mere common games; but if you will not try it, that ends the matter:' and Maude leaned back in her chair.

'I hope—' began Mary: but Agnes interposed:

'Suppose some of us attempt Bouts rimés; and you meanwhile can settle what we shall do afterwards. Who is ready to test her poetic powers?—What, no one?—Oh, Magdalen, pray join Maude and me.'

This proposal met with universal approbation, and the three girls retreated to a side table; Mary, who supplied the rhymes, exacting a promise that only one sonnet should be composed. Before the next game was fixed upon, the three following productions were submitted for judgement to the discerning public. The first was by Agnes:°

> Would that I were a turnip white,
> Or raven black,
> Or miserable hack
>   Dragging a cab from left to right;
>   Or would I were the showman of a sight,
> Or weary donkey with a laden back,
> Or racer in a sack,
>   Or freezing traveller on an Alpine height;
> Or would I were straw catching as I drown,
>   (A wretched landsman I who cannot swim,)   10
>   Or watching a lone vessel sink,
>   Rather than writing: I would change my pink
> Gauze for a hideous yellow satin gown
>   With deep-cut scolloped edges and a rim.

'Indeed I had no idea of the sacrifice you were making;' observed Maude: 'you did it with such heroic equanimity. Might I however venture to hint that my sympathy with your sorrows would have been greater, had they been expressed in metre?'

'There's gratitude for you,' cried Agnes gaily: 'What have you to expect, Magdalen?' and she went on to read her friend's sonnet:

> 'I fancy the good fairies dressed in white,
> Glancing like moon-beams through the shadows black;
> Without much work to do for king or hack.°
>   Training perhaps some twisted branch aright;
>   Or sweeping faded Autumn leaves from sight
> To foster embryo life; or binding back
> Stray tendrils; or in ample bean-pod sack
>   Bringing wild honey from the rocky height;
> Or fishing for a fly lest it should drown;
>   Or teaching water-lily heads to swim,   10
>   Fearful that sudden rain might make them sink;
>   Or dyeing the pale rose a warmer pink;
> Or wrapping lilies in their leafy gown,
>   Yet letting the white peep beyond the rim. —

Well, Maude?'

'Well, Agnes; Miss Ellis is too kind to feel gratified at hearing that
her verses make me tremble for my own: but such as they are, listen:

> Some ladies dress in muslin full and white,°
> Some gentlemen in cloth succinct and black;
> Some patronise a dog-cart, some a hack,°
>   Some think a painted clarence only right.°
>   Youth is not always such a pleasing sight,
> Witness a man with tassels on his back;
> Or woman in a great-coat like a sack
>   Towering above her sex with horrid height.
> If all the world were water fit to drown
>   There are some whom you would not teach to swim,   10
>   Rather enjoying if you saw them sink;
>   Certain old ladies dressed in girlish pink,
> With roses and geraniums on their gown:—
>   Go to the Bason, poke them o'er the rim.'—

'What a very odd sonnet:' said Mary after a slight pause: 'but surely
men don't wear tassels.'

Her cousin smiled: 'You must allow for poetical licence; and I have
literally seen a man in Regent Street wearing a sort of hooded cloak
with one tassel. Of course every one will understand the Bason to mean
the one in St. James' Park.'

'With these explanations your sonnet is comprehensible,' said
Mary: and Magdalen added with unaffected pleasure: 'And without
them it was by far the best of the three.'

Maude now exerted herself to amuse the party; and soon proved
that ability was not lacking. Game after game was proposed and played
at; and her fund seemed inexhaustible, for nothing was thought too
nonsensical or too noisy for the occasion. Her goodhumour and anima-
tion were infectious: Miss Stanton incurred forfeits with the blandest
smile; Hannah Lindley blushed and dimpled as she had not done for
many months; Rosanna never perceived the derangement of her scarf;
little Ellen exulted in freedom from school-room trammels; the twins
guessed each other's thoughts with marvellous facility; Magdalen
laughed aloud; and even Harriet Eyre's dress looked scarcely too gay
for such an entertainment. Well was it for Mrs Clifton that the straw-
berries, cream and tarts had been supplied with no niggard hand: and
very meagre was the remnant left when the party broke up at a late
hour.

III

Agnes and Mary were discussing the pleasures of the preceding evening as they sat over the unusually late breakfast, when Maude joined them. Salutations being exchanged and refreshments supplied to the last comer, the conversation was renewed.

'Who did you think was the prettiest girl in the room last night? our charming selves of course excepted,' asked Mary: 'Agnes and I cannot agree on this point.'

'Yes,' said her sister, 'we quite agree as to mere prettiness; only I maintain that Magdalen is infinitely more attractive than half the handsome people one sees. There is so much sense in her face, and such sweetness. Besides, her eyes are really beautiful.'

'Miss Ellis has a characteristic countenance, but she appeared to me very far from the belle of the evening. Rosanna Hunt has much more regular features.'

'Surely you don't think Rosanna prettier than Jane and Alice,' interrupted Mary: 'I suppose I never look at those two without fresh pleasure.'

'They have good fair complexions, eyes and hair certainly;' and Maude glanced rather pointedly at her unconscious cousin: 'but to me they have a wax-dollish air which is quite unpleasant. I think one of the handsomest faces in the room was Miss Stanton's.'

'But she has such a disagreeable expression,' rejoined Mary hastily: then colouring she half turned towards her sister, who looked grave, but did not speak.

A pause ensued; and then Agnes said, 'I remember how prejudiced I felt against Miss Stanton when first she came to live here, for her appearance and manners are certainly unattractive: and how ashamed of myself I was when we heard that last year, through all the bitterly cold weather, she rose at six, though she never has a fire in her room, that she might have time before breakfast to make clothes for some of the poorest people in the village. And in the Spring, when the scarlet fever was about, her mother would not let her go near the sick children for fear of contagion; so she saved up all her pocket money to buy wine and soup and such things for them as they recovered.'

'I dare say she is very good;' said Maude: 'but that does not make her pleasing. Besides, the whole family have that disagreeable expression, and I suppose they are not all paragons. But you have both finished breakfast, and make me ashamed by your diligence. What is that beautiful piece of work?'

The sisters looked delighted: 'I am so glad you like it, dear Maude. Mary and I are embroidering a cover for the lectern in our Church; but we feared you might think the ground dull.'

'Not at all; I prefer those quiet shades. Why, how well you do it: is it not very difficult?—Let me see if I understand the devices. There is the Cross and the Crown of Thorns; and those must be the keys of S. Peter, with, of course, the sword of S. Paul. Do the flowers mean anything?'

'I am the Rose of Sharon and the Lily of the Valleys,' answered Agnes pointing: 'That is balm of Gilead, at least it is what we call so; there are myrrh and hyssop, and that is a palm-branch. The border is to be vine-leaves and grapes; with fig-leaves at the corners, thanks to Mary's suggestions. Would you like to help us? there is plenty of room at the frame.'

'No, I should not do it well enough, and have no time to learn, as we go home tomorrow. How I envy you;' she continued in a low voice as if speaking rather to herself than to her hearers: 'you who live in the country, and are exactly what you appear, and never wish for what you do not possess. I am sick of display and poetry and acting.'

'You do not act,' replied Agnes warmly: 'I never knew a more sincere person. One difference between us is that you are less healthy and far more clever than I am. And this reminds me: Miss Savage begged me to ask you for some verses to put in her Album. Would you be so very obliging? any that you have by you would do.'

'She can have the sonnet I wrote last night.'

Agnes hesitated: 'I could not well offer her that, because—'

'Why? she does not tower. Oh! I suppose she has some reprehensible old lady in her family, and so might feel hurt at my Lynch-law. I will find you something else then before I go.'

And that evening, when Agnes went to her cousin's room to help her in packing, Maude consigned to her a neat copy of the following lines:—

> She sat and sang alway°
> By the green margin of a stream,
> Watching the fishes leap and play
>   Beneath the glad sun-beam.
>
> I sat and wept alway
> Beneath the moon's most shadowy beam,
> Watching the blossoms of the may
>   Weep leaves into the stream.°

I wept for memory;
She sang for hope that is so fair;— 10
My tears were swallowed by the sea;
Her songs died on the air.

PART 2nd

I

Rather more than a year had elapsed since Maude parted from her cousins; and now she was expecting their arrival in London every minute: for Mrs Clifton, unable to leave her young family, had gratefully availed herself of Mrs Foster's offer to receive Agnes and Mary during the early Winter months, that they might take music and dancing lessons with their cousin.

At length the rumbling of an approaching cab was heard; then a loud knock and ring. Maude started up: but instead of running out to meet her guests, began poking vigorously at the fire, which soon sent a warm, cheerful light through the apartment; enabling her, when they entered, to discern that Agnes had a more womanly air than at their last meeting, that Mary had outgrown her sister, and that both were remarkably good-looking.

'First let me show you your room, and then we can settle comfortably to tea; we are not to wait for Mamma. She thought you would not mind sleeping together, as our house is so small; and I have done my best to arrange things to your taste, for I know of old you have only one taste between you. Look, my room is next yours, so we can help each other very cosily: only pray don't think of unpacking now; there will be plenty of time this evening, and you must be famished: come.'

But Agnes lingered still, eager to thank her cousin for the good-natured forethought which had robbed her own apartment of flower-vases and inkstand for the accommodation of her guests. The calls of Mary's appetite were however imperious; and very soon the sisters were snugly settled on a sofa by the fire, while Maude in a neighbouring armchair made tea.

'How long it seems since my birthday party;' said Mary, as soon as the eatables had in some measure restored her social powers: 'Why, Maude, you are grown quite a woman; but you look more delicate than ever, and very thin: do you still write verses?' Then without waiting for a reply: 'Those which you gave Miss Savage for her Album were very much admired; and Magdalen Ellis wished at the time for an autograph copy, only she had not courage to trouble you. But perhaps you are not aware that poor Magdalen has done with Albums and such like, at least for the present: she has entered on her noviciate in the Sisterhood of Mercy established near our house.'

'Why poor?' said Maude: 'I think she is very happy.'

'Surely you would not like such a life;' rejoined her cousin: 'They have not proper clothes on their beds, and never go out without a thick veil, which must half blind them. All day long they are at prayers, or teaching children, or attending the sick, or making poor things, or something. Is that to your taste?'

Maude half sighed; and then answered: 'You cannot imagine me either fit or inclined for such a life; still I can perceive that those are very happy who are. When I was preparing for Confirmation Mr Paulson offered me a district;° but I did not like the trouble, and Mamma thought me too unwell for regularity. I have regretted it since though: yet I don't fancy I ever could have talked to the poor people or done the slightest good. — Yes, I continue to write now and then as the humour seizes me; and if Miss Ellis' —

'Sister Magdalen,' whispered Agnes.

'— If Sister Magdalen will accept it, I will try and find her something admissable even within Convent walls. But let us change the subject. On Thursday we are engaged to tea at Mrs Strawdy's. There will be no sort of party, so we need not dress or take any trouble.'

'Will my Aunt go with us?' asked Agnes.

'No. Poor Mamma has been ailing for some time and is by no means strong; so as Mrs Strawdy is an old schoolfellow of her's and a most estimable person, she thinks herself justified in consigning you to my guardianship. On Saturday we must go shopping, as Aunt Letty says you are to get your Winter things in London; and I can get mine at the same time. On Sunday—or does either of you dislike Cathedral services?'

Agnes declared they were her delight; and Mary, who had never attended any, expressed great pleasure at the prospect of hearing what her sister preferred to all secular music.

'Very well,' continued Maude: 'we will go to S. Andrew's then, and you shall be introduced to a perfect service; or at any rate to perhaps the nearest English approach to vocal perfection.° But you know you are to be quite at home here; so we have not arranged any particular plans of amusement, but mean to treat you like ourselves. And now it is high time for you to retire. Here Agnes,' handing to her cousin a folded paper, the result of a rummage in her desk: 'Will you enclose this to Sister Magdalen, and assure her that my verses are honoured

even in my own eyes by her acceptance. You can read them if you like,
and Mary too, of course; only please not in my presence.'

They were as follows:

> Sweet sweet sound of distant waters falling°
>   On a parched and thirsty plain;°
> Sweet sweet song of soaring skylark, calling
>   On the sun to shine again;
> Perfume of the rose, only the fresher
>   For past fertilizing rain;
> Pearls amid the sea, a hidden treasure
>   For some daring hand to gain;—
>   Better, dearer than all these
>   Is the earth beneath the trees: 10
>   Of a much more priceless worth
>   Is the old, brown, common earth.
>
> Little snow-white lamb piteously bleating
>   For thy mother far away;
> Saddest, sweetest nightingale retreating
>   With thy sorrow from the day;
> Weary fawn whom night has overtaken,
>   From the herd gone quite astray;
> Dove whose nest was rifled and forsaken
>   In the budding month of May;—   20
>   Roost upon the leafy trees;
>   Lie on earth and take your ease:
>   Death is better far than birth,
>   You shall turn again to earth.
>
> Listen to the never pausing murmur
>   Of the waves that fret the shore;
> See the ancient pine that stands the firmer
>   For the storm-shock that it bore;
> And the moon her silver chalice filling
>   With light from the great sun's store;   30
> And the stars which deck our temple's ceiling
>   As the flowers deck its floor;
>   Look and hearken while you may,
>   For these things shall pass away:
>   All these things shall fail and cease;
>   Let us wait the end in peace.

Let us wait the end in peace; for truly
   That shall cease which was before:
Let us see our lamps are lighted, duly°
   Fed with oil, nor wanting more: 40
Let us pray while yet the Lord will hear us,
   For the time is almost o'er;
Yea, the end of all is very near us;
   Yea, the Judge is at the door.
Let us pray now while we may;
   It will be too late to pray
When the quick and dead shall all
   Rise at the last trumpet call.

II

When Thursday arrived Agnes and Mary were indisposed with colds; so Mrs Foster insisted on her daughter's making their excuses to Mrs Strawdy. In a dismal frame of mind Maude, assisted by her sympathizing cousins, performed her slight preliminary toilet.

'You have no notion of the utter dreariness of this kind of invitation: I counted on your helping me through the evening, and now you fail me. Thank you, Mary; I shall not waste eau de Cologne on my handkerchief. Goodnight both: mind you go to bed early and get up quite well tomorrow. Goodnight.'

The weather was foggy and raw as Maude stepped into the street; and proved anything but soothing to a temper already fretted; so by the time that she had arrived at her destination, removed her walking things, saluted her hostess and apologized for her cousins, her countenance had assumed an expression neither pleased nor pleasing.

'Let me present my nieces to you, my dear,' said Mrs Strawdy taking her young friend by the hand and leading her towards the fire: 'This is Miss Mowbray, or, as you must call her, Annie; that is Caroline, and that Sophy. They have heard so much of you that any farther introduction is needless;' here Maude bowed rather stiffly: 'But as we are early people you will excuse our commencing with tea, after which we shall have leisure for amusement.'

There was something so genuinely kind and simple in Mrs Strawdy's manner, that even Maude felt mollified, and resolved on doing her best not only towards suppressing all appearance of yawns, but also towards bearing her part in the conversation.

'My cousins will regret their indisposition more than ever, when they learn of how much pleasure it has deprived them;' said she, civilly addressing Miss Mowbray.

A polite bend, smile and murmur formed the sole response: and once more a subject had to be started.

'Have you been very gay lately? I begin to acquire the reputation of an invalid, and so my privacy is respected.'

Annie coloured and looked excessively embarrassed; at last she answered in a low hesitating voice: 'We go out extremely little, partly because we never dance.'

'Nor I either; it really is too fatiguing: yet a ball-room is no bad place for a mere spectator. Perhaps, though, you prefer the Theatre?'

'We never go to the play;' rejoined Miss Mowbray looking more and more uncomfortable.

Maude ran on: 'Oh, I beg your pardon, you do not approve of such entertainments. I never go, but only for want of some one to take me.' Then addressing Mrs Strawdy: 'I think you know my Aunt Mrs Clifton?'

'I visited her years ago with your Mamma,' was the answer: 'when you were quite a little child. I hope she continues in good health. Pray remember me to her and to Mr Clifton when you write.'

'With pleasure. She has a large family now, eight children.'

'That is indeed a large family;' rejoined Mrs Strawdy, intent meanwhile on dissecting a cake with mathematical precision: 'You must try a piece, it is Sophy's own manufacture.'

Despairing of success in this quarter, Maude now directed her attention to Caroline, whose voice she had not heard once in the course of the evening.

'I hope you will favour us with some music after tea; in fact, I can take no denial. You look too blooming to plead a cold, and I feel certain you will not refuse to indulge my love for sweet sounds: of your ability to do so I have heard elsewhere.'

'I shall be most happy; only you must favour us in return.'

'I will do my best,' answered Maude somewhat encouraged: 'but my own performances are very poor. Are you fond of German songs? they form my chief resource.'

'Yes, I like them much.'

Baffled in this quarter also, Miss Foster wanted courage to attack Sophy, whose countenance promised more cake than conversation. The meal seemed endless: she fidgetted under the table with her fingers; pushed about a stool on the noiselessly soft carpet until it came in contact with some one's foot; and at last fairly deprived Caroline of her third cup of coffee, by opening the piano and claiming the fulfilment of her promise.

The young lady complied with obliging readiness. She sang some simple airs, mostly religious, not indeed with much expression, but in a voice clear and warbling as a bird's. Maude felt consoled for all the contrarieties of the day; and was bargaining for one more song before taking Caroline's place at the instrument, when the door opened to admit Mrs and Miss Savage; who having only just reached town, and hearing from Mrs Foster that her daughter was at the house of a mutual friend, resolved on begging the hospitality of Mrs Strawdy, and renewing their acquaintance.

Poor Maude's misfortunes now came thick and fast. Seated between Miss Savage and Sophia Mowbray, she was attacked on either hand with questions concerning her verses. In the first place, did she continue to write? Yes. A flood of exstatic compliments followed this admission: she was so young, so much admired, and, poor thing, looked so delicate. It was quite affecting to think of her lying awake at night meditating° those sweet verses—('I sleep like a top,' Maude put in drily,)—which so delighted her friends, and would so charm the public, if only Miss Foster could be induced to publish. At last the bystanders were called upon to intercede for a recitation.

Maude coloured with displeasure; a hasty answer was rising to her lips, when the absurdity of her position flashed across her mind so forcibly that, almost unable to check a laugh in the midst of her annoyance, she put her handkerchief to her mouth. Miss Savage, impressed with a notion that her request was about to be complied with, raised her hand, imploring silence; and settled herself in a listening attitude.

'You will excuse me;' Maude at last said very coldly: 'I could not think of monopolizing every one's attention. Indeed you are extremely good, but you must excuse me.' And here Mrs Savage interposed desiring her daughter not to tease Miss Foster; and Mrs Strawdy seconded her friend's arguments, by a hint that supper would make its appearance in a few minutes.

Finally the maid announced that Miss Foster was fetched: and Maude shortening her adieus and turning a deaf ear to Annie's suggestion that their acquaintance should not terminate with the first meeting, returned home dissatisfied with her circumstances, her friends and herself.

III

It was Christmas Eve. All day long Maude and her cousins were hard at work putting up holly and mistletoe in wreaths, festoons, or bunches, wherever the arrangement of the rooms admitted of such embellishment. The picture-frames were hidden behind foliage and bright berries; the bird-cages were stuck as full of green as though it had been Summer. A fine sprig of holly was set apart as a centre-bit for the pudding of next day: scratched hands and injured gowns were disregarded: hour after hour the noisy bustle raged: until Mrs Foster, hunted from place to place by her young relatives, heard, with inward satisfaction, that the decorations were completed.

After tea Mary set the backgammon board in array and challenged her Aunt to their customary evening game: Maude complaining of a headache, and promising either to wrap herself in a warm shawl or to go to bed, went to her room: and Agnes, listening to the rattle of the dice, at last came to the conclusion that her presence was not needed down stairs, and resolved to visit the upper regions. Thinking that her cousin was lying down tired and might have fallen asleep, she forbore knocking; but opened the door softly and peeped in.

Maude was seated at a table, surrounded by the old chaos of station-ery; before her lay the locking manuscript-book, into which she had just copied something. That day she had appeared more than usually animated: and now supporting her forehead upon her hand, her eyes cast down till the long lashes nearly rested upon her cheeks, she looked pale, languid, almost in pain. She did not move, but let her visitor come close to her without speaking: Agnes thought she was crying.

'Dear Maude, you have overtired yourself. Indeed, for all our sakes, you should be more careful:' here Agnes passed her arm affectionately round her friend's neck: 'I hoped to find you fast asleep, and instead of this you have been writing in the cold. Still, I did not come to lecture; and am even ready to show my forgiving disposition by reading your new poem: may I?'

Maude glanced quickly up at her cousin's kind face; then answered: 'Yes, if you like;' and Agnes read as follows:

> Vanity of vanities, the Preacher saith,°
> All things are vanity. The eye and ear
> Cannot be filled with what they see and hear:
>   Like early dew, or like the sudden breath
>   Of wind, or like the grass that withereth
> Is man, tossed to and fro by hope and fear:

So little joy hath he, so little cheer,
    Till all things end in the long dust of death.
Today is still the same as yesterday,
    Tomorrow also even as one of them;   10
  And there is nothing new under the sun.
  Until the ancient race of time be run,
    The old thorns shall grow out of the old stem,
And morning shall be cold and twilight grey. —

This sonnet was followed by another, written like a postscript:

I listen to the holy antheming°
That riseth in thy walls continually,
What while the organ pealeth solemnly
    And white-robed men and boys stand up to sing.
  I ask my heart with a sad questioning:
'What lov'st thou here?' and my heart answers me:
'Within the shadows of this sanctuary
    To watch and pray is a most blessed thing.'
To watch and pray, false heart? it is not so:
    Vanity enters with thee, and thy love   10
Soars not to Heaven, but grovelleth below.
  Vanity keepeth guard, lest good should reach
    Thy hardness; not the echoes from above
Can rule thy stubborn feelings or can teach. —

'Was this composed after going to S. Andrew's?'

'No; I wrote it just now, but I was thinking of S. Andrew's. It is horrible to feel such a hypocrite as I do.'

'Oh! Maude, I only wish I were as sensible of my faults as you are of yours. But a hypocrite you are not: don't you see that every line of these sonnets attests your sincerity?'

'You will stay to Communion tomorrow?' asked Maude after a short silence, and without replying to her cousin's speech; even these few words seemed to cost her an effort.

'Of course I shall; why, it is Christmas Day: — at least I trust to do so. Mary and I have been thinking how nice it will be for us all to receive together: so I want you to promise that you will pray for us at the Altar, as I shall for you. Will you?'

'I shall not receive tomorrow,' answered Maude; then hurrying on as if to prevent the other from remonstrating: 'No: at least I will not profane Holy Things; I will not add this to all the rest. I have gone over and over again, thinking I should come right in time, and I do not come right: I will go no more.'

Agnes turned quite pale: 'Stop,' she said interrupting her cousin: 'Stop; you cannot mean,—you do not know what you are saying. You will go no more? Only think, if the struggle is so hard now, what it will be when you reject all help.'

'I do not struggle.'

'You are ill tonight,' rejoined Agnes very gently: 'you are tired and over-excited. Take my advice, dear; say your prayers and get to bed. But do not be very long; if there is anything you miss and will tell me of, I will say it in your stead. Don't think me unfeeling: I was once on the very point of acting as you propose. I was perfectly wretched: harassed and discouraged on all sides. But then it struck me—you won't be angry?—that it was so ungrateful to follow my own fancies, instead of at least endeavouring to do God's Will: and so foolish too; for if our safety is not in obedience, where is it?'

Maude shook her head: 'Your case is different. Whatever your faults may be, (not that I perceive any,) you are trying to correct them; your own conscience tells you that. But I am not trying. No one will say that I cannot avoid putting myself forward and displaying my verses. Agnes, you must admit so much.'

Deep-rooted indeed was that vanity which made Maude take pleasure, on such an occasion, in proving° the force of arguments directed against herself. Still Agnes would not yield; but resolutely did battle for the truth.

'If hitherto it has been so, let it be so no more. It is not too late: besides, think for one moment what will be the end of this. We must all die: what if you keep to your resolution, and do as you have said, and receive the Blessed Sacrament no more?'°—Her eyes filled with tears.

Maude's answer came in a subdued tone: 'I do not mean never to Communicate again. You remember Mr Paulson told us last Sunday that sickness and suffering are sent for our correction. I suffer very much. Perhaps a time will come when these will have done their work on me also; when I shall be purified indeed and weaned from the world. Who knows? the lost have been found, the dead quickened.' She paused as if in thought; then continued: 'You partake of the Blessed Sacrament in peace, Agnes, for you are good; and Mary, for she is harmless: but your conduct cannot serve to direct mine, because I am neither the one nor the other. Some day I may be fit again to approach the Holy Altar, but till then I will at least refrain from dishonouring it.'

Agnes felt almost indignant: 'Maude, how can you talk so? this is not reverence. You cannot mean that for the present you will indulge vanity and display; that you will court admiration and applause; that you will take your fill of pleasure until sickness, or it may be death, strips you of temptation and sin together. Forgive me; I am sure you never meant this: yet what else does a deliberate resolution to put off doing right come to?—and if you are determined at once to do your best, why deprive yourself of the appointed means of grace? Dear Maude, think better of it;' and Agnes knelt beside her cousin, and laid her head against her bosom.

But still Maude, with a sort of desperate wilfulness, kept saying: 'It is of no use; I cannot go tomorrow; it is of no use.' She hid her face, leaning upon the table and weeping bitterly; while Agnes, almost discouraged, quitted the room.

Maude, once more alone, sat for some time just as her cousin left her. Gradually the thick, low sobs became more rare; she was beginning to feel sleepy. At last she roused herself with an effort and commenced undressing; then it struck her that her prayers had still to be said. The idea of beginning them frightened her, yet she could not settle to sleep without saying something. Strange prayers they must have been, offered with a divided heart and a reproachful conscience. Still they were said at length; and Maude lay down harassed, wretched, remorseful, everything but penitent. She was nearly asleep, nearly unconscious of her troubles, when the first stroke of midnight sounded. Immediately a party of Christmas waits° and carollers burst forth with their glad music. The first part was sung in full chorus:

> 'Thank God, thank God, we do believe;°
> Thank God that this is Christmas Eve.
> Even as we kneel upon this day,
> Even so the ancient legends say,
> Nearly two thousand years ago
> The stalled ox knelt, and even so
> The ass knelt full of praise, which they
> Could not express, while we can pray.
> Thank God, thank God, for Christ was born
> Ages ago, as on this morn.   10
> In the snow-season undefiled
> God came to earth a Little Child:
> He put His ancient Glory by
> To live for us and then to die.'—

—Then half the voices sang the following stanza:

> 'How shall we thank God? how shall we
> Thank Him and praise Him worthily?
> What will He have Who loved us thus?
> What presents will He take from us?—
> Will He take gold? or precious heap
> Of gems? or shall we rather steep   20
> The air with incense? or bring myrrh?—
> What man will be our messenger
> To go to Him and ask His Will?
> Which having learned, we will fulfil
> Though He choose all we most prefer:
> What man will be our messenger?'—

—This was answered by the other half:

> 'Thank God, thank God, the Man is found,
> Sure-footed, knowing well the ground.°
> He knows the road, for this the way
> He travelled once, as on this day.   30
> He is our Messenger; beside,
> He is our Door and Path and Guide;
> He also is our Offering;
> He is the Gift That we must bring.'—

—Finally all the singers joined in the conclusion:

> 'Let us kneel down with one accord
> And render thanks unto the Lord:
> For unto us a Child is born
> Upon this happy Christmas morn;
> For unto us a Son is given,°
> Firstborn of God and Heir of Heaven.'—   40

As the echoes died away, Maude fell asleep.

PART 3rd

I

Agnes Clifton to Maude Foster.

12th June 18—.

My dear Maude,

Mamma has written to my Aunt that Mary's marriage is fixed for
the 4th of next month: but as I fear we cannot expect you both so many

days before the time, I also write, hoping that you at least will come without delay. At any rate I shall be at the Station tomorrow afternoon with a chaise for your luggage; so pray take pity on my desolate condition, and avail yourself of the three o'clock train. As we are both bridesmaids elect, I thought it would be very nice for us to be dressed alike, so have procured double quantity of everything; thus you will perceive no pretence remains for your lingering in smoky London.

You will be amused when you see Mary: I have already lost my companion. Mr Herbert calls at least once a day, but sometimes oftener; so all day long Mary is on the alert. She takes much more interest in the roses over the porch than was formerly the case; the creepers outside the windows require continual training, not to say hourly care: I tell her the constitution of the garden must have become seriously weakened lately. One morning I caught her before the glass, trying the effect of seringa° (the English orange-blossom, you know,) in her hair. She looked such a darling. I hinted how flattered Mr Herbert would feel when I told him; which provoked her to offer a few remarks on old maids. Was it not a shame?

Last Thursday Magdalen Ellis was finally received into the Sisterhood of Mercy. I wished much to be present, but could not, as the whole affair was conducted quite privately; only her parents were admitted of the world.° However, I made interest for a lock of her beautiful hair, which I prize highly. It makes me sad to look at it: yet I know she has chosen well; and will, if she perseveres, receive hereafter an abundant recompense for all she has foregone here. Sometimes I think whether such a life can be suited to me; but then I could not bear to leave Mamma: indeed that is just what Magdalen felt so much. I met her yesterday walking with some poor children. Her veil was down, nearly hiding her face; still I fancy she looked thoughtful, but very calm and happy. She says she always prays for me, and asked my prayers; so I begged her to remember you and Mary. Then she enquired how you are; desiring her kindest love to you, and assuring me she makes no doubt your name will be known at some future period: but checking herself almost immediately, she added that she could fancy you very different, as pale Sister Maude. This surprised me; I can fancy nothing of the sort. At last she mentioned the verses you gave her months ago, which she knows by heart and values extremely:—then, having nearly reached my home, we parted.

What a document I have composed; I who have not one minute to spare from Mary's trousseau. Will you give my love to my Aunt; and request her from me to permit your immediately coming to

Your affectionate cousin,

Agnes M. Clifton. —

P.S. Mary would doubtless send a message were she in the room;
I conjecture her to be lurking about somewhere on the watch. Goodbye:
or rather, Come. —

Maude handed the letter to her Mother: 'Can you spare me,
Mamma? I should like to go, but not if it is to inconvenience you.'

'Certainly you shall go, my dear. It is a real pleasure to hear you
express interest on some point, and you cannot be with any one
I approve of more than Agnes. But you must make haste with the packing
now: I will come and help you in a few minutes.'

Still Maude lingered: 'Did you see about Magdalen? I wonder what
made her think of me as a Sister. It is very nice of her; but then she is
so good she never can conceive what I am like. Mamma, should you
mind my being a Nun?'

'Yes, my dear; it would make me miserable. But for the present take
my advice and hurry a little, or the train will leave without you.'

Thus urged, Maude proceeded to bundle various miscellaneous goods
into a trunk; the only article on the safety of which she bestowed much
thought, being the present destined for Mary; a sofa-pillow worked in
glowing shades of wool and silk. This she wrapped carefully in a cloth,
and laid at the bottom: then over it all else was heaped without much
ceremony. Many were the delays occasioned by things mislaid, which
must be looked for; ill-secured, which must be re-arranged; or remem-
bered too late, which yet could not be dispensed with, and so must be
crammed in somewhere. At length, however, the tardy preparations were
completed; and Maude, enveloped in two shawls, though it was the
height of Summer, stepped into a cab; promising strict conformity to her
Mother's injunction that both windows should be kept closed.

Half an hour had not elapsed when another cab drove up to the
door; and out of it Maude was lifted perfectly insensible. She had been
overturned; and, though no limb was broken, had neither stirred nor
spoken since the accident.

II

Maude Foster to Agnes Clifton

2nd July 18—.

My dear Agnes,

You have heard of my mishap? it keeps me not bedridden, but
sofa ridden. My side is dreadfully hurt; I looked at it this morning for

the first time, but hope never again to see so shocking a sight. The pain now and then is extreme, though not always so; sometimes, in fact, I am unconscious of any injury.

Will you convey my best love and wishes to Mary, and tell her how much I regret being away from her at such a time; especially as Mamma will not hear of leaving me. A day or two ago I tried to compose an Epithalamium° for our fair fiancée; which effort resulted in my present enclosure: not much to the purpose, we must admit. You may read it when no better employment offers. The first Nun no one can suspect of being myself, partly because my hair is far from yellow and I do not wear curls; partly because I never did anything half so good as profess.° The second might be Mary, had she mistaken her vocation. The third is Magdalen, of course. But whatever you miss, pray read the mottoes. Put together they form a most exquisite little song which the Nuns sing in Italy. One can fancy Sister Magdalen repeating it with her whole heart.

The Surgeon comes twice a day to dress my wounds; still, all the burden of nursing falls on poor Mamma. How I wish you were here to help us both: we should find plenty to say.

But perhaps ere many months are passed I shall be up and about, when we may go together on a visit to Mary; a most delightful possibility. By the way, how I should love a baby of her's, and what a pretty little creature it ought to be. Do you think Mr Herbert handsome? hitherto I have only heard a partial opinion.

Uh, my side! it gives an awful twinge now and then. You need not read my letter; but I must write it, for I am unable to do anything else. Did the pillow reach safely? It gave me so much pleasure to work it for Mary, who, I hope, likes it. At all events, if not to her taste, she may console herself with the reflection that it is unique; for the pattern was my own designing.

Here comes dinner; goodbye. When will anything so welcome as your kind face gladded the eyes of

    Your affectionate
        Maude Foster? —

P.S. I have turned tippler lately on port wine three times a day. 'To keep you up,' says my Doctor: while I obstinately refuse to be kept up, but insist on becoming weaker and weaker. Mind you write me a full history of your grand doings on a certain occasion: not omitting a detailed account of the lovely bride, her appearance, deportment and toilet. Goodbye once more: when shall I see you all again? —

Three Nuns

I°

Sospira questo core
  E non so dir perchè.°

Shadow, shadow on the wall
  Spread thy shelter over me;
Wrap me with a heavy pall,
  With the dark that none may see.°
Fold thyself around me; come:
Shut out all the troublesome
Noise of life; I would be dumb.

Shadow thou hast reached my feet,
  Rise and cover up my head;
Be my stainless winding sheet,   10
  Buried before I am dead.
Lay thy cool upon my breast:
Once I thought that joy was best,
Now I only care for rest.

By the grating of my cell
  Sings a solitary bird;°
Sweeter than the vesper bell,
  Sweetest song was ever heard.[1]
Sing upon thy living tree:
Happy echoes answer thee,   20
Happy songster, sing to me.

When my yellow hair was curled
  Though men saw and called me fair,
I was weary in the world
  Full of vanity and care.
Gold was left behind, curls shorn
When I came here; that same morn
Made a bride no gems adorn.

Here wrapped in my spotless veil,
  Curtained from intruding eyes,
I whom prayers and fasts turn pale   30
  Wait the flush of Paradise.
But the vigil is so long

---

[1] 'Sweetest eyes were ever seen.' E. B. Browning.°

My heart sickens:—sing thy song,
Blithe bird that canst do no wrong.

Sing on, making me forget
   Present sorrow and past sin.
Sing a little longer yet:
   Soon the matins will begin;
And I must turn back again   40
To that aching worse than pain
I must bear and not complain.

Sing, that in thy song I may
   Dream myself once more a child
In the green woods far away
   Plucking clematis and wild
Hyacinths, till pleasure grew
Tired, yet so was pleasure too,
Resting with no work to do.

In the thickest of the wood,   50
   I remember, long ago
How a stately oak-tree stood,
   With a sluggish pool below
Almost shadowed out of sight.
On the waters dark as night,
Water-lilies lay like light.

There, while yet a child, I thought
   I could live as in a dream,
Secret, neither found nor sought:
   Till the lilies on the stream,   60
Pure as virgin purity,
Would seem scarce too pure for me:—
Ah, but that can never be.

2°

   Sospirerà d'amore,
     Ma non lo dice a me.

I loved him, yes, where was the sin?
   I loved him with my heart and soul.
   But I pressed forward to no goal,
There was no prize I strove to win.

Show me my sin that I may see:—
Throw the first stone, thou Pharisee.

I loved him, but I never sought
   That he should know that I was fair.
   I prayed for him; was my sin prayer?
I sacrificed, he never bought.   10
He nothing gave, he nothing took;
We never bartered look for look.

My voice rose in the sacred choir,
   The choir of Nuns; do you condemn
   Even if, when kneeling among them,
Faith, zeal and love kindled a fire
And I prayed for his happiness
Who knew not? was my error this?

I only prayed that in the end
   His trust and hope may not be vain.   20
   I prayed not we may meet again:
I would not let our names ascend,
No, not to Heaven, in the same breath;
Nor will I join the two in death.

Oh sweet is death; for I am weak
   And weary, and it giveth rest.
   The Crucifix lies on my breast,
And all night long it seems to speak
Of rest; I hear it through my sleep,
And the great comfort makes me weep.   30

Oh sweet is death that bindeth up
   The broken and the bleeding heart.
   The draught chilled, but a cordial part°
Lurked at the bottom of the cup;
And for my patience will my Lord
Give an exceeding great reward.

Yea, the reward is almost won,
   A crown of glory and a palm.
   Soon I shall sing the unknown psalm;°
Soon gaze on light, not on the sun;°   40
And soon, with surer faith, shall pray
For him, and cease not night nor day.

My life is breaking like a cloud;
   God judgeth not as man doth judge.—
   Nay, bear with me; you need not grudge
This peace; the vows that I have vowed
Have all been kept: Eternal Strength
Holds me, though mine own fails at length.

Bury me in the Convent ground
   Among the flowers that are so sweet;   50
   And lay a green turf at my feet,
Where thick trees cast a gloom around.
At my head let a Cross be, white
Through the long blackness of the night.

Now kneel and pray beside my bed
   That I may sleep being free from pain:
   And pray that I may wake again
After His Likeness, Who hath said°
(Faithful is He Who promiseth,)
We shall be satisfied Therewith.°   60

3°

   Rispondimi, cor mio,
     Perchè sospiri tu?
   Risponde: Voglio Iddio,
     Sospiro per Gesù.

My heart is as a freeborn bird
   Caged in my cruel breast,
That flutters, flutters evermore,
   Nor sings, nor is at rest.
But beats against the prison bars,
   As knowing its own nest
Far off beyond the clouded West.

My soul is as a hidden fount°
   Shut in by clammy clay,°
That struggles with an upward moan;   10
   Striving to force its way
Up through the turf, over the grass,
   Up, up into the day,
Where twilight no more turneth grey.

Oh for the grapes of the True Vine
   Growing in Paradise,
Whose tendrils join the Tree of Life
   To that which maketh wise.
Growing beside the Living Well
   Whose sweetest waters rise   20
Where tears are wiped from tearful eyes.

Oh for the waters of that Well
   Round which the Angels stand.
Oh for the Shadow of the Rock
   On my heart's weary land.°
Oh for the Voice to guide me when
   I turn to either hand,
Guiding me till I reach Heaven's strand.

Thou World from which I am come out,
   Keep all thy gems and gold;   30
Keep thy delights and precious things,
   Thou that art waxing old.
My heart shall beat with a new life,
   When thine is dead and cold:
When thou dost fear I shall be bold.

When Earth shall pass away with all
   Her pride and pomp of sin,
The City builded without hands°
   Shall safely shut me in.
All the rest is but vanity   40
   Which others strive to win:
Where their hopes end my joys begin.

I will not look upon a rose
   Though it is fair to see:
The flowers planted in Paradise
   Are budding now for me.
Red roses like love visible
   Are blowing on their tree,
Or white like virgin purity.

I will not look unto the sun   50
   Which setteth night by night:
In the untrodden courts of Heaven

My crown shall be more bright.
Lo, in the New Jerusalem
   Founded and built aright
My very feet shall tread on light.

With foolish riches of this World
   I have bought treasure, where
Nought perisheth: for this white veil
   I gave my golden hair;   60
I gave the beauty of my face
   For vigils, fasts and prayer;
I gave all for this Cross I bear.

My heart trembled when first I took
   The vows which must be kept;
At first it was a weariness
   To watch when once I slept.
The path was rough and sharp with thorns;
   My feet bled as I stepped;
The Cross was heavy and I wept.   70

While still the names rang in mine ears
   Of daughter, sister, wife;
The outside world still looked so fair
   To my weak eyes, and rife
With beauty; my heart almost failed;
   Then in the desperate strife
I prayed, as one who prays for life,

Until I grew to love what once
   Had been so burdensome.
So now when I am faint, because   80
   Hope deferred seems to numb
My heart, I yet can plead; and say
Although my lips are dumb:
'The Spirit and the Bride say, Come.'—°

III

Three weeks had passed away. A burning sun seemed baking the very
dust in the streets, and sucking the last remnant of moisture from the
straw spread in front° of Mrs Foster's house, when the sound of a low
muffled ring was heard in the sick-room; and Maude, now entirely

confined to her bed, raising herself on one arm, looked eagerly towards
the door; which opened to admit a servant with the welcome announce-
ment that Agnes had arrived.

After tea Mrs Foster, almost worn out with fatigue, went to bed;
leaving her daughter under the care of their guest. The first greetings
between the cousins had passed sadly enough. Agnes perceived at a
glance that Maude was, as her last letter hinted, in a most alarming
state: while the sick girl, well aware of her condition, received her
friend with an emotion which showed she felt it might be for the last
time. But soon her spirits rallied.

'I shall enjoy our evening together so much, Agnes;' said she, speak-
ing now quite cheerfully: 'You must tell me all the news. Have you
heard from Mary since your last despatch to me?'

'Mamma received a letter this morning before I set off; and she sent
it hoping to amuse you. Shall I read it aloud?'

'No, let me have it myself.' Her eye travelled rapidly down the
well-filled pages, comprehending at a glance all the tale of happiness.
Mr and Mrs Herbert were at Scarborough; they would thence proceed
to the Lakes; and thence, most probably, homewards, though a pro-
longed tour was mentioned as just possible. But both plans seemed
alike pleasing to Mary; for she was full of her husband, and both were
equally connected with him.

Maude smiled as paragraph after paragraph enlarged on the same
topic. At last she said: 'Agnes, if you could not be yourself, but must
become one of us three: I don't mean as to goodness, of course, but
merely as regards circumstances,— would you change with Sister
Magdalen, with Mary, or with me?'

'Not with Mary, certainly. Neither should I have courage to change
with you; I never should bear pain so well: nor yet with Sister Magdalen,
for I want her fervour of devotion. So at present I fear you must even
put up with me as I am. Will that do?'

There was a pause. A fresh wind had sprung up and the sun was
setting.

At length Maude resumed: 'Do you recollect last Christmas Eve
when I was so wretched, what shocking things I said? How I rejoice
that my next Communion was not indeed delayed till sickness had
stripped me of temptation and sin together.'

'Did I say that? It was very harsh.'

'Not harsh: it was just and right as far as it went, only something
more was required.° But I never told you what altered me. The truth
is, for a time I avoided as much as possible frequenting our parish

Church, for fear of remarks. Mamma, knowing how I love S. Andrew's,
let me go there very often by myself, because the walk is too long for
her. I wanted resolution to do right; yet believe me I was very miserable:
how I could say my prayers at that period is a mystery. So matters
went on; till one day as I was returning from a shop, I met Mr Paulson.
He enquired immediately whether I had been staying in the country?
Of course I answered, No. Had I been ill? again, No. Then gradually
the whole story came out. I never shall forget the shame of my admis-
sions; each word seemed forced from me, yet at last all was told. I will
not repeat all we said then, and on a subsequent occasion when he saw
me at Church: the end was that I partook of the Holy Communion on
Easter Sunday. That was indeed a Feast. I felt as if I never could do
wrong again, and yet—. Well, after my next impatient fit, I wrote
this;' here she took a paper from the table: 'Do you care to see it? I will
rest a little, for talking is almost too much for me.'

> I watched a rosebud very long°
>   Brought on by dew and sun and shower,
>   Waiting to see the perfect flower:
> Then, when I thought it should be strong,
>   It opened at the matin hour
>   And fell at evensong.
>
> I watched a nest from day to day,
>   A green nest, full of pleasant shade,
>   Wherein three little eggs were laid:
> But when they should have hatched in May,   10
>   The two old birds had grown afraid,
>   Or tired, and flew away.
>
> Then in my wrath I broke the bough
>   That I had tended with such care,
>   Hoping its scent should fill the air:
> I crushed the eggs, not heeding how
>   Their ancient promise had been fair:—
>   I would have vengeance now.
>
> But the dead branch spoke from the sod,
>   And the eggs answered me again: 20
>   Because we failed dost thou complain?
> Is thy wrath just? And what if God,
>   Who waiteth for thy fruits in vain,
>   Should also take the rod?—

'You can keep it if you like;' continued Maude, when her cousin had finished reading: 'Only don't let any one else know why it was written. And, Agnes, it would only pain Mamma to look over everything if I die; will you examine the verses, and destroy what I evidently never intended to be seen. They might all be thrown away together, only Mamma is so fond of them.—What will she do?'—and the poor girl hid her face in the pillows.

'But is there no hope, then?'

'Not the slightest, if you mean of recovery; and she does not know it. Don't go away when all's over, but do what you can to comfort her. I have been her misery from my birth, till now there is no time to do better. But you must leave me, please; for I feel completely exhausted. Or stay one moment: I saw Mr Paulson again this morning, and he promised to come tomorrow to administer the Blessed Sacrament to me; so I count on you and Mamma receiving with me, for the last time perhaps: will you?'

'Yes, dear Maude. But you are so young, don't give up hope. And now would you like me to remain here during the night? I can establish myself quite comfortably on your sofa.'

'Thank you, but it could only make me restless. Goodnight, my own dear Agnes.'

'Goodnight, dear Maude. I trust to rise early tomorrow, that I may be with you all the sooner.' So they parted.

That morrow never dawned for Maude Foster.

—

Agnes proceeded to perform the task imposed upon her, with scrupulous anxiety to carry out her friend's wishes. The locked book she never opened: but had it placed in Maude's coffin, with all its records of folly, sin, vanity; and, she humbly trusted, of true penitence also. She next collected the scraps of paper found in her cousin's desk and portfolio, or lying loose upon the table; and proceeded to examine them. Many of these were mere fragments, many half-effaced pencil scrawls, some written on torn backs of letters, and some full of incomprehensible abbreviations. Agnes was astonished at the variety of Maude's compositions. Piece after piece she committed to the flames, fearful lest any should be preserved which were not intended for general perusal: but it cost her a pang to do so; and to see how small a number remained for Mrs Foster. Of three only she took copies for herself. The first was dated ten days after Maude's accident:

> Sleep, let me sleep, for I am sick of care;°
> Sleep, let me sleep, for my pain wearies me.

Shut out the light; thicken the heavy air
With drowsy incense; let a distant stream
　　Of music lull me, languid as a dream,
Soft as the whisper of a Summer sea.

　　Pluck me no rose that groweth on a thorn,
Nor myrtle white and cold as snow in June,
　　Fit for a virgin on her marriage morn:
But bring me poppies brimmed with sleepy death,　　10
And ivy choking what it garlandeth,
And primroses that open to the moon.

　　Listen, the music swells into a song,
A simple song I loved in days of yore;
　　The echoes take it up and up along
The hills, and the wind blows it back again. —
Peace, peace, there is a memory in that strain
Of happy days that shall return no more.

　　Oh peace, your music wakeneth old thought,
But not old hope that made my life so sweet,　　20
　　Only the longing that must end in nought.
Have patience with me, friends, a little while:
For soon where you shall dance and sing and smile,
My quickened dust may blossom at your feet.

　　Sweet thought that I may yet live and grow green,
That leaves may yet spring from the withered root,
　　And buds and flowers and berries half unseen;
Then if you haply muse upon the past,
　　Say this: Poor child, she hath her wish at last;
Barren through life, but in death bearing fruit. —　　30

The second, though written on the same paper, was evidently
composed at a subsequent period:

　　　　　　Fade, tender lily,°
　　　　　　　　Fade, O crimson rose,
　　　　　　Fade every flower,
　　　　　　　　Sweetest flower that blows.

　　　　　　Go, chilly Autumn,
　　　　　　　　Come O Winter cold;
　　　　　　Let the green stalks die away
　　　　　　　　Into common mould.

> Birth follows hard on death,
>   Life on withering.   10
> Hasten, we shall come the sooner
>   Back to pleasant Spring. —

The last was a sonnet, dated the morning before her death:

> What is it Jesus saith unto the soul? — °
> 'Take up the Cross, and come, and follow Me.'
> This word He saith to all; no man may be
>   Without the Cross, wishing to win the goal.
>   Then take it bravely up, setting thy whole
> Body to bear; it will not weigh on thee
> Beyond thy utmost strength: take it; for He
>   Knoweth when thou art weak, and will control
> The powers of darkness that thou need'st not fear.
>   He will be with thee, helping, strengthening,°   10
>   Until it is enough: for lo, the day
> Cometh when He shall call thee: thou shalt hear
>   His Voice That says: 'Winter is past, and Spring
> Is come; arise, My Love, and come away.' — °

Agnes cut one long tress from Maude's head; and on her return home laid it in the same paper with the lock of Magdalen's hair. These she treasured greatly: and, gazing on them, would long and pray for the hastening of that eternal morning, which shall reunite in God those who in Him, or for His Sake, have parted here.

Amen for us all.

—The End. —

Nick

There dwelt in a small village, not a thousand miles from Fairyland, a poor man, who had no family to labour for or friend to assist. When I call him poor, you must not suppose he was a homeless wanderer, trusting to charity for a night's lodging; on the contrary, his stone house, with its green verandah and flower-garden, was the prettiest and snuggest in all the place, the doctor's only excepted. Neither was his store of provisions running low: his farm supplied him with milk, eggs, mutton, butter, poultry, and cheese in abundance; his fields with hops and barley for beer, and wheat for bread; his orchard with fruit and cider; and his kitchen-garden with vegetables and wholesome herbs. He had, moreover, health, an appetite to enjoy all these good things, and strength to walk about his possessions. No, I call him poor because, with all these, he was discontented and envious. It was in vain that his apples were the largest for miles around, if his neighbour's vines were the most productive by a single bunch; it was in vain that his lambs were fat and thriving, if some one else's sheep bore twins: so, instead of enjoying his own prosperity, and being glad when his neighbours prospered too, he would sit grumbling and bemoaning himself as if every other man's riches were his poverty. And thus it was that one day our friend Nick leaned over Giles Hodge's gate, counting his cherries.

'Yes,' he muttered, 'I wish I were sparrows to eat them up, or a blight to kill your fine trees altogether.'

The words were scarcely uttered when he felt a tap on his shoulder, and looking round, perceived a little rosy woman, no bigger than a butterfly, who held her tiny fist clenched in a menacing attitude. She looked scornfully at him, and said: 'Now listen, you churl, you! hence-forward you shall straightway become everything you wish; only mind, you must remain under one form for at least an hour.' Then she gave him a slap in the face, which made his cheek tingle as if a bee had stung him, and disappeared with just so much sound as a dewdrop makes in falling.

Nick rubbed his cheek in a pet,° pulling wry faces and showing his teeth. He was boiling over with vexation, but dared not vent it in words lest some unlucky wish should escape him. Just then the sun seemed to shine brighter than ever, the wind blew spicy from the south; all Giles's roses looked redder and larger than before, while his cherries seemed to multiply, swell, ripen. He could refrain no longer, but, heedless of the fairy-gift he had just received, exclaimed, 'I wish I were sparrows eating——' No sooner said than done: in a moment he found himself a whole flight of hungry birds, pecking, devouring, and bidding fair to devastate the envied cherry-trees. But honest Giles was on the watch hard by; for that very morning it had struck him he must make nets for the protection of his fine fruit. Forthwith he ran home, and speedily returned with a revolver furnished with quite a marvel-lous array of barrels. Pop, bang—pop, bang! he made short work of the sparrows, and soon reduced the enemy to one crestfallen biped with broken leg and wing, who limped to hide himself under a holly-bush. But though the fun was over, the hour was not; so Nick must needs sit out his allotted time. Next a pelting shower came down, which soaked him through his torn, ruffled feathers; and then, exactly as the last drops fell and the sun came out with a beautiful rainbow, a tabby cat pounced upon him. Giving himself up for lost, he chirped in desperation, 'O, I wish I were a dog to worry you!' Instantly—for the hour was just passed—in the grip of his horrified adversary, he turned at bay, a savage bull-dog. A shake, a deep bite, and poor puss was out of her pain. Nick, with immense satisfaction, tore her fur to bits, wishing he could in like manner exterminate all her progeny. At last, glutted with vengeance, he lay down beside his victim, relaxed his ears and tail, and fell asleep.

Now that tabby-cat was the property and special pet of no less a personage than the doctor's lady; so when dinner-time came, and not the cat, a general consternation pervaded the household. The kitchens were searched, the cellars, the attics; every apartment was ransacked; even the watch-dog's kennel was visited. Next the stable was rummaged, then the hay-loft; lastly, the bereaved lady wandered disconsolately through her own private garden into the shrubbery, calling 'Puss, puss,' and looking so intently up the trees as not to perceive what lay close before her feet. Thus it was that, unawares, she stumbled over Nick, and trod upon his tail.

Up jumped our hero, snarling, biting, and rushing at her with such blind fury as to miss his aim. She ran, he ran. Gathering up his strength, he took a flying-leap after his victim; her foot caught in the spreading root of an oak-tree, she fell, and he went over her head, clear over, into a bed of stinging-nettles. Then she found breath to raise that fatal cry, 'Mad dog!' Nick's blood curdled in his veins; he would have slunk away if he could; but already a stout labouring-man, to whom he had done many an ill turn in the time of his humanity, had spied him, and, bludgeon in hand, was preparing to give chase. However, Nick had the start of him, and used it too; while the lady, far behind, went on vociferating, 'Mad dog, mad dog!' inciting doctor, servants, and vagabonds to the pursuit. Finally, the whole village came pouring out to swell the hue and cry.

The dog kept ahead gallantly, distancing more and more the asthmatic doctor, fat Giles, and, in fact, all his pursuers except the bludgeon-bearing labourer, who was just near enough to persecute his tail. Nick knew the magic hour must be almost over, and so kept forming wish after wish as he ran,—that he were a viper only to get trodden on, a thorn to run into some one's foot, a man-trap in the path, even the detested bludgeon to miss its aim and break. This wish crossed his mind at the propitious moment; the bull-dog vanished, and the labourer, overreaching himself, fell flat on his face, while his weapon struck deep into the earth, and snapped.

A strict search was instituted after the missing dog, but without success. During two whole days the village children were exhorted to keep indoors and beware of dogs; on the third an inoffensive bull pup was hanged, and the panic subsided.

Meanwhile the labourer, with his shattered stick, walked home in silent wonder, pondering on the mysterious disappearance. But the puzzle was beyond his solution; so he only made up his mind not to tell his wife the whole story till after tea. He found her preparing for that meal, the bread and cheese set out, and the kettle singing softly on the fire. 'Here's something to make the kettle boil, mother,' said he, thrusting our hero between the bars and seating himself; 'for I'm mortal tired and thirsty.'

Nick crackled and blazed away cheerfully, throwing out bright sparks, and lighting up every corner of the little room. He toasted the cheese to a nicety, made the kettle boil without spilling a drop, set the cat purring with comfort, and illuminated the pots and pans into splendour. It was provocation enough to be burned; but to contribute by his misfortune to the well-being of his tormentors was still more aggravating. He heard, too, all their remarks and wonderment about the supposed mad-dog, and saw the doctor's lady's own maid bring the labourer five shillings as a reward for his exertions. Then followed a discussion as to what should be purchased with the gift, till at last it was resolved to have their best window glazed with real glass. The prospect of their grandeur put the finishing-stroke to Nick's indignation. Sending up a sudden flare, he wished with all his might that he were fire to burn the cottage.

Forthwith the flame leaped higher than ever flame leaped before. It played for a moment about a ham, and smoked it to a nicety; then, fastening on the woodwork above the chimney-corner, flashed full into a blaze. The labourer ran for help, while his wife, a timid woman, with three small children, overturned two pails of water on the floor, and set the beer-tap running. This done, she hurried, wringing her hands, to the door, and threw it wide open. The sudden draught of air did more mischief than all Nick's malice, and fanned him into quite a conflagration, He danced upon the rafters, melted a pewter-pot and a pat of butter, licked up the beer, and was just making his way towards the bedroom, when through the thatch and down the chimney came a rush of water. This arrested his progress for the moment; and before

he could recover himself, a second and a third discharge from the
enemy completed his discomfiture. Reduced ere long to one blue
flame, and entirely surrounded by a wall of wet ashes, Nick sat and
smouldered; while the good-natured neighbours did their best to
remedy the mishap,—saved a small remnant of beer, assured the
labourer that his landlord was certain to do the repairs, and observed
that the ham would eat 'beautiful.'

Our hero now had leisure for reflection. His situation precluded
all hope of doing further mischief; and the disagreeable conviction
kept forcing itself upon his mind that, after all, he had caused more
injury to himself than to any of his neighbours. Remembering, too,
how contemptuously the fairy woman had looked and spoken, he
began to wonder how he could ever have expected to enjoy her gift.
Then it occurred to him, that if he merely studied his own advantage
without trying to annoy other people, perhaps his persecutor might be
propitiated; so he fell to thinking over all his acquaintances, their for-
tunes and misfortunes; and, having weighed well their several claims
on his preference, ended by wishing himself the rich old man who
lived in a handsome house just beyond the turnpike.° In this wish he
burned out.

The last glimmer had scarcely died away, when Nick found himself
in a bed hung round with faded curtains, and occupying the centre
of a large room. A night-lamp, burning on the chimney-piece, just
enabled him to discern a few shabby old articles of furniture, a scanty
carpet, and some writing materials on a table. These objects looked
somewhat dreary; but for his comfort he felt an inward consciousness
of a goodly money-chest stowed away under his bed, and of sundry
precious documents hidden in a secret cupboard in the wall.

So he lay very cosily, and listened to the clock ticking, the mice
squeaking, and the house-dog barking down below. This was, however,
but a drowsy occupation; and he soon bore witness to its somniferous
influence by sinking into a fantastic dream about his money-chest.
First, it was broken open, then shipwrecked, then burned; lastly, some
men in masks, whom he knew instinctively to be his own servants,
began dragging it away. Nick started up, clutched hold of something
in the dark, found his last dream true, and the next moment was
stretched on the floor—lifeless, yet not insensible—by a heavy blow
from a crowbar.

The men now proceeded to secure their booty, leaving our hero
where he fell. They carried off the chest, broke open and ransacked
the secret closet, overturned the furniture, to make sure that no

hiding-place of treasure escaped them, and at length, whispering together, left the room. Nick felt quite discouraged by his ill success, and now entertained only one wish—that he were himself again. Yet even this wish gave him some anxiety; for he feared that if the servants returned and found him in his original shape they might take him for a spy, and murder him in downright earnest. While he lay thus cogitating two of the men reappeared, bearing a shutter and some tools. They lifted him up, laid him on the shutter, and carried him out of the room, down the back-stairs, through a long vaulted passage, into the open air. No word was spoken; but Nick knew they were going to bury him.

An utter horror seized him, while, at the same time, he felt a strange consciousness that his hair would not stand on end because he was dead. The men set him down, and began in silence to dig his grave. It was soon ready to receive him; they threw the body roughly in, and cast upon it the first shovelful of earth.

But the moment of deliverance had arrived. His wish suddenly found vent in a prolonged unearthly yell. Damp with night dew, pale as death, and shivering from head to foot, he sat bolt upright, with starting, staring eyes and chattering teeth. The murderers, in mortal fear, cast down their tools, plunged deep into a wood hard by, and were never heard of more.

Under cover of night Nick made the best of his way home, silent and pondering. Next morning he gave Giles Hodge a rare tulip-root, with full directions for rearing it; he sent the doctor's wife a Persian cat twice the size of her lost pet; the labourer's cottage was repaired, his window glazed, and his beer-barrel replaced by unknown agency; and when a vague rumour reached the village that the miser was dead, that his ghost had been heard bemoaning itself, and that all his treasures had been carried off, our hero was one of the few persons who did not say, 'And served him right, too.'

Finally, Nick was never again heard to utter a wish.

The Lost Titian

A lie with a circumstance.

WALTER SCOTT°

The last touch was laid on. The great painter stood opposite the masterpiece of the period; the masterpiece of his life.

Nothing remained to be added. The orange drapery was perfect in its fruit-like intensity of hue; each vine-leaf was curved, each tendril twisted, as if fanned by the soft south wind; the sunshine brooded drowsily upon every dell and swelling upland: but a tenfold drowsiness slept in the cedar shadows. Look a moment, and those cymbals must clash, that panther bound forward; draw nearer, and the songs of those ripe, winy lips° must become audible.

The achievement of his life glowed upon the easel, and Titian was satisfied.

Beside him, witnesses of his triumph, stood his two friends—Gianni the successful, and Giannuccione the universal disappointment.

Gianni ranked second in Venice; second in most things, but in nothing first. His *colorito°* paled only before that of his illustrious rival, whose supremacy, however, he ostentatiously asserted. So in other matters. Only the renowned Messer Cecchino was a more sonorous singer; only fire-eating Prince Barbuto a better swordsman; only Arrigo il Biondo a finer dancer or more sculpturesque beauty; even Caterina Suprema, in that contest of gallantry which has been celebrated by so many pens and pencils, though she awarded the rose of honour to Matteo Grande, the wit, yet plucked off a leaf for the all but victor Gianni.

A step behind him lounged Giannuccione, who had promised everything and fulfilled nothing. At the appearance of his first picture—'Venus whipping Cupid with feathers plucked from his own wing'—Venice rang with his praises, and Titian foreboded a rival: but when, year after year, his works appeared still lazily imperfect, though always all but perfect, Venice subsided into apathetic silence, and Titian felt that no successor to his throne had as yet achieved the purple.

So these two stood with the great master in the hour of his triumph: Gianni loud, and Giannuccione hearty, in his applauses.

Only these two stood with him: as yet Venice at large knew not what her favourite had produced. It was, indeed, rumoured, that Titian had long been at work on a painting which he himself accounted his masterpiece, but its subject was a secret; and while some spoke of it as an undoubted *Vintage of red grapes*, others maintained it to be a *Dance of wood-nymphs*; while one old gossip whispered that, whatever else the painting might contain, she knew whose sunset-coloured tresses and white brow would figure in the foreground. But the general ignorance mattered little; for, though words might have named the theme, no words could have described a picture which combined the softness of a dove's breast with the intensity of an October sunset: a picture of which the light almost warmed, and the fruit actually bloomed and tempted.

Titian gazed upon his work, and was satisfied: Giannuccione gazed upon his friend's work, and was satisfied: only Gianni gazed upon his friend and upon his work, and was enviously dissatisfied.

'To-morrow,' said Titian,—'to-morrow Venice shall behold what she has long honoured by her curiosity. To-morrow, with music and festivity, the unknown shall be unveiled; and you, my friends, shall withdraw the curtain.'

The two friends assented.

'To-morrow,' he continued, half amused, half thoughtful, 'I know whose white brows will be knit, and whose red lips will pout. Well, they shall have their turn: but blue eyes are not always in season; hazel eyes, like hazel nuts, have their season also.'

'True,' chimed the chorus.

'But to-night,' he pursued, 'let us devote the hours to sacred friend- ship. Let us with songs and bumpers rehearse to-morrow's festivities, and let your congratulations forestall its triumphs.'

'Yes, *evviva!*° returned the chorus, briskly; and again '*evviva!*'

So, with smiles and embraces, they parted. So they met again at the welcome coming of Argus-eyed night.

The studio was elegant with clusters of flowers, sumptuous with crimson, gold-bordered hangings, and luxurious with cushions and perfumes. From the walls peeped pictured fruit and fruit-like faces, between the curtains and in the corners gleamed moonlight-tinted statues; whilst on the easel reposed the beauty of the evening, over- hung by budding boughs, and illuminated by an alabaster lamp burn- ing scented oil. Strewn about the apartment lay musical instruments and packs of cards. On the table were silver dishes, filled with leaves and choice fruits; wonderful vessels of Venetian glass, containing rare wines and iced waters; and footless goblets, which allowed the guest no choice but to drain his bumper.

That night the bumpers brimmed. Toast after toast was quaffed to the success of to-morrow, the exaltation of the unveiled beauty, the triumph of its author.

At last Giannuccione, flushed and sparkling, rose: 'Let us drink,' he cried, 'to our host's success to-morrow: may it be greater than the past, and less than the future!'

'Not so,' answered Titian, suddenly; 'not so: I feel my star culminate.'

He said it gravely, pushing back his seat, and rising from table. His spirits seemed in a moment to flag, and he looked pale in the moonlight. It was as though the blight of the evil eye had fallen upon him.

Gianni saw his disquiet, and laboured to remove it. He took a lute from the floor, and tuning it, exerted his skill in music. He wrung from the strings cries of passion, desolate sobs, a wail as of one abandoned, plaintive, most tender tones as of the *solitario passero*.° The charm worked: vague uneasiness was melting into delicious melancholy. He redoubled his efforts; he drew out tinkling notes joyful as the feet of dancers; he struck notes like fire, and, uniting his voice to the instrument, sang the glories of Venice and of Titian. His voice, full, mellow, exultant, vibrated through the room; and, when it ceased, the bravos of his friends rang out an enthusiastic chorus.

Then, more stirring than the snap of castanets on dexterous fingers; more fascinating, more ominous, than a snake's rattle, sounded the music of the dice-box.

The stakes were high, waxing higher, and higher; the tide of fortune set steadily towards Titian. Giannuccione laughed and played, played and laughed with reckless good-nature, doubling and redoubling his bets apparently quite at random. At length, however, he paused, yawned, laid down the dice, observing that it would cost him a good six months' toil to pay off his losses—a remark which elicited a peculiar smile of intelligence from his companions—and, lounging back upon the cushions, fell fast asleep.

Gianni also had been a loser: Gianni the imperturbable, who won and lost alike with steady hand and unvarying colour. Rumour stated that one evening he lost, won back, lost once more, and finally regained his whole property unmoved: at last only relinquishing the game, which fascinated, but could not excite him, for lack of an adversary.

In like manner he now threw his possessions, as coolly as if they [had] been another's, piecemeal into the gulph. First his money went, then his collection of choice sketches; his gondola followed, his plate, his jewelry. These gone, for the first time he laughed.

'Come,' he said, '*amico mio*, let us throw the crowning cast. I stake thereon myself; if you win, you may sell me to the Moor to-morrow, with the remnant of my patrimony; to wit, one house, containing various articles of furniture and apparel; yea, if aught else remains to me, that also do I stake: against these set you your newborn beauty, and let us throw for the last time; lest it be said cogged dice° are used in Venice, and I be taunted with the true proverb,—"*Save me from my friends, and I will take care of my enemies.*"'

'So be it,' mused Titian, 'even so. If I gain, my friend shall not suffer; if I lose, I can but buy back my treasure with this night's winnings. His whole fortune will stand Gianni in more stead than my picture; moreover, luck favours me. Besides, it can only be that my friend jests, and would try my confidence.'

So argued Titian, heated by success, by wine and play. But for these, he would freely have restored his adversary's fortune, though it had been multiplied tenfold, and again tenfold, rather than have risked his life's labour on the hazard of the dice.

They threw.

Luck had turned, and Gianni was successful.

Titian, nothing doubting, laughed as he looked up from the table into his companion's face; but no shadow of jesting lingered there. Their eyes met, and read each other's heart at a glance.

One, discerned the gnawing envy of a life satiated: a thousand mortifications, a thousand inferiorities, compensated in a moment.

The other, read an indignation that even yet scarcely realised the treachery which kindled it; a noble indignation, that more upbraided the false friend than the destroyer of a life's hope.

It was a nine-days' wonder in Venice what had become of Titian's masterpiece; who had spirited it away,—why, when, and where. Some explained the mystery by hinting that Clementina Beneplacida, having gained secret access to the great master's studio, had there, by dint of scissors, avenged her slighted beauty, and in effigy defaced her nut-brown rival. Others said that Giannuccione, paying tipsy homage to his friend's performance, had marred its yet moist surface. Others again averred, that in a moment of impatience, Titian's own sponge flung against the canvas, had irremediably blurred the principal figure. None knew, none guessed the truth. Wonder fulfilled its little day, and then, subsiding, was forgotten: having, it may be, after all, as truly amused Venice the volatile as any work of art could have done, though it had robbed sunset of its glow, its glory, and its fire.

But why was the infamy of that night kept secret?

By Titian, because in blazoning abroad his companion's treachery, he would subject himself to the pity of those from whom he scarcely accepted homage; and, in branding Gianni as a traitor, he would expose himself as a dupe.

By Gianni, because had the truth got wind, his iniquitous prize might have been wrested from him, and his malice frustrated in the moment of triumph; not to mention that vengeance had a subtler relish when it kept back a successful rival from the pinnacle of fame, than when it merely exposed a friend to humiliation. As artists, they might possibly have been accounted rivals; as astute men of the world, never.

Giannuccione had not witnessed all the transactions of that night. Thanks to his drunken sleep, he knew little; and what he guessed, Titian's urgency° induced him to suppress. It was, indeed, noticed how, from that time forward, two of the three inseparables appeared in a measure, estranged from the third; yet all outward observances of courtesy were continued, and, if embraces had ceased, bows and doffings never failed.

For weeks, even for months, Gianni restrained his love for play, and, painting diligently, laboured to rebuild his shattered fortune. All prospered in his hands. His sketches sold with unprecedented readiness, his epigrams charmed the noblest dinner-givers, his verses and piquant little airs won him admission into the most exclusive circles. Withal, he seemed to be steadying. His name no more pointed° stories of drunken frolics in the purlieus of the city, of mad wagers in the meanest company, of reckless duels with nameless adversaries. If now he committed follies, they were committed in the best society; if he sinned, it was, at any rate, in a patrician *casa*;° and, though his morals might not yet be flawless, his taste was unimpeachable. His boon companions grumbled, yet could not afford to dispense with him; his warmest friends revived hopes which long ago had died away into despair. It was the heyday of his life: fortune and Venice alike courted him; he had but to sun himself in their smiles, and accept their favours.

So, nothing loth, he did, and for a while prospered. But, as the extraordinary stimulus flagged, the extraordinary energy flagged with it. Leisure returned, and with leisure the allurements of old pursuits. In proportion as his expenditure increased, his gains lessened; and, just when all his property, in fact, belonged to his creditors, he put the finishing stroke to his obvious ruin, by staking and losing at the gambling-table what was no longer his own.

That night beheld Gianni grave, dignified, imperturbable, and a beggar. Next day, his creditors, princely and plebeian, would be upon him: everything must go; not a scrap, not a fragment, could be held back. Even Titian's masterpiece would be claimed; that prize for which he had played away his soul, by which, it may be, he had hoped to acquire a worldwide fame, when its mighty author should be silenced for ever in the dust.

Yet to-morrow, not to-night, would be the day of reckoning; to-night, therefore, was his own. With a cool head he conceived, with a steady hand he executed, his purpose. Taking coarse pigments, such as, when he pleased, might easily be removed, he daubed over those figures which seemed to live, and that wonderful background, which not Titian himself could reproduce; then, on the blank surface, he painted a dragon, flaming, clawed, preposterous. One day he would recover his dragon, recover his Titian under the dragon, and the world should see.

Next morning the crisis came.

After all, Gianni's effects were worth more than had been supposed. They included Giannuccione's *Venus whipping Cupid*—how obtained, who knows?—a curiously wrought cup, by a Florentine goldsmith, just then rising into notice; within the hollow of the foot was engraved *Benvenuto Cellini*, surmounted by an outstretched hand, symbolic of welcome, and quaintly allusive to the name;° a dab by Giorgione, a scribble of the brush by Titian, and two feet square of genuine Tintoret. The creditors brightened; there was not enough for honesty, but there was ample for the production of a most decorous bankrupt.

His wardrobe was a study of colour; his trinkets, few but choice, were of priceless good taste. Moreover, his demeanour was unimpeachable and his delinquencies came to light with the best grace imaginable. Some called him a defaulter, but all admitted he was a thorough gentleman.

Foremost in the hostile ranks stood Titian; Titian, who now, for the first time since that fatal evening, crossed his rival's threshold. His eye searched eagerly among the heap of nameless canvasses for one unforgotten beauty, who had occasioned him such sore heartache; but he sought in vain; only in the forefront sprawled a dragon, flaming, clawed, preposterous; grinned, twinkled, erected his tail, and flouted him.

'Yes,' said Gianni, answering his looks, not words, yet seeming to address the whole circle, '*Signori miei*, these compose all my gallery. An immortal sketch, by Messer Tiziano'—here a complimentary bow—'a veritable Giorgione; your own work, Messer Robusti, which needs no comment of mine to fix its value. A few productions by feebler hands, yet not devoid of merit. These are all. The most precious part of my collection was destroyed (I need not state, accidentally), three days ago by fire. That dragon, yet moist, was designed for mine host, Bevilacqua Mangiaruva; but this morning, I hear, with deep concern, of his sudden demise.'

Here Lupo Vorace of the *Orco decapitato*° stepped forward. He, as he explained at length, was a man of few words (this, doubtless, in theory); but to make a long story short, so charmed was he by the scaly monster that he would change his sign, accept the ownerless dragon, and thereby wipe out a voluminous score which stood against his debtor. Gianni, with courteous thanks, explained that the dragon, still moist, was unfit for immediate transport; that it should remain in the studio for a short time longer; and that, as soon as its safety permitted, he would himself convey it to the inn of his liberal creditor. But on this point Lupo was inflexible. In diffuse but unvarying terms he claimed instant possession of Gianni's masterstroke. He seized it, reared it face upwards on to his head, and by his exit broke up the conclave of creditors.

What remains can be briefly told.

Titian, his last hope in this direction wrecked, returned to achieve, indeed, fresh greatnesses: but not the less returned to the tedium of straining after an ideal once achieved, but now lost for ever. Giannuccione, half amused, half mortified, at the slighting mention made of his performances, revenged himself in an epigram, of which the following is a free translation: —

> 'Gianni my friend and I both strove to excel,
> But, missing better, settled down in well.
> Both fail, indeed; but not alike we fail—
> My forte being Venus' face, and his a dragon's tail.'

Gianni, in his ruin, took refuge with a former friend; and there, treated almost on the footing of a friend, employed his superabundant leisure in concocting a dragon superior in all points to its predecessor; but, when this was almost completed, this which was to ransom his unsuspected treasure from the clutches of Lupo, the more relentless clutches of death fastened upon himself.

His secret died with him.

An oral tradition of a somewhere extant lost Titian having survived all historical accuracy, and so descended to another age, misled the learned Dr. Landau into purchasing a spurious work for the Gallery of Lunenberg; and even more recently induced Dr. Dreieck to expend a large sum on a nominal Titian, which he afterwards bequeathed to the National Museum of Saxe Eulenstein. The subject of this latter painting is a *Vintage of red grapes*, full of life and vigour, exhibiting marked talent, but clearly assignable to the commencement of a later century.

There remains, however, a hope that some happy accident may yet restore to the world the masterpiece of one of her most brilliant sons.

Reader, should you chance to discern over wayside inn or metro-politan hotel a dragon pendent, or should you find such an effigy amid the lumber of a broker's shop, whether it be red, green, or piebald, demand it importunately, pay for it liberally, and in the privacy of home scrub it. It *may* be that from behind the dragon will emerge a fair one, fairer than Andromeda,° and that to you will appertain the honour of yet further exalting Titian's greatness in the eyes of a world.

A Safe Investment

It was a pitchy dark night. Not the oldest inhabitant remembered so black a night, so moonless, so utterly starless; and whispering one to another, men said with a shiver that longer still, not for a hundred years back—ay, or for a thousand years—ay, or even since the world was—had such gross darkness covered the land. Yet those who counted the time protested that morning must now be at hand, ready to break, even while East and West were massed in one common indistinguishable blot of blackness; and those who discerned the signs of the times, those who waited for the morning, looked often towards one house° which could not be hid, for it was set upon a hill, nor over-turned, for it was founded upon a rock, and from which a light streamed pure and steady, shaming the flickering gas-lamps of the town, the dim glare of shops and private dwellings, and the flaring, smoking torches of such wayfarers as thought, by compassing themselves about with sparks, to find safety in their transit to and fro.

On this cheerless night a solitary traveller entered the town by the eastern gate. He rode a white horse:° about both the beast and his rider there was something foreign, or if not foreign, at any rate unusual. The man was keen and military of aspect, and had the air of one bound on some mission of importance. The horse seemed to know his road without guidance, to turn hither or thither by instinct, not to loiter, yet not to make haste. They passed through the eastern gate, which was opened wide before them: without let or hindrance they entered in, and the horse's hoofs° struck once on the paved road.

In an instant, at the western outskirts of the city a flare of red light shot up. Out came houses into view from the night darkness; to right and left they flashed out for a moment: for a moment you could spy through the windows people sitting at table, reading, working, dancing, as the case might be: you could note a bird's cage hanging here or there, a cat or two creeping along the gutter, a few foot-passengers arrested by the unexpected glare looking round them in all directions for its source, a single carriage threading its way cautiously along the dangerous streets: for a moment—then a cry went up, then there came the crash and crush of a tremendous explosion, and then darkness settled once more over its own dominion; whilst through the darkness those who could not see each other's faces heard each other's groans, cries for help, shrieks of terror or of agonizing pain. All the gas-lamps of the city had gone out as though at a single whiff, for it was an explosion of the great central gasworks which had taken place. And the darkness deepened.

To the south of the city lay the sea. Day and night its surges were never still nor silent; day and night ships heaved on its bosom, passing in or out of harbour, laden with passengers, with gold, silks, provisions, merchandise of all sorts.° On this night, if any one had had owl's eyes to peer with, he might have discerned that the deep boiled like a pot of ointment; he would have seen in a score, yea, in a hundred vessels, the sailors at their wits' end reeling to and fro, and staggering like drunken men; whilst the strong masts snapped like straws, and the tough, hollow ship-sides stove in as though they had been of paper— till captains, crews, and passengers, were fain to cast overboard freights and treasures, rarities from the ends of the earth, corn, and wine, and oil—to cast these overboard, and at length, abandoning the ship, to flee for their lives in boats, on planks, on pieces of the vessel, too happy if with bare life they escaped to land, beggared but alive. Meanwhile those on the quays could guess, though they could not see, the ruin, as wretch after poor wretch struggled to shore; but for one who came, a score at least were seen no more for ever.

In a central quarter of the town stood the old-established county bank, concerning which the townspeople had long boasted that not the national bank itself was safer. In panic years it had remained unaffected by the surrounding pressure; it had stood firm, and stand it would whilst the town was a town: so said its directors, its shareholders, the public voice in unison. But on this certain night of all nights in the year, when ship after ship went down with entire costly cargoes, and scores and hundreds of hands on board; when the gasworks exploded, to the obvious utter ruin of the shareholders; when a report spread that the treasurer of the chief railway company had absconded with all the funds in his hands, a report confirmed as night wore, and soon established as a fact; on this night of all nights, the dismayed citizens turned in thought to their bank. Every man beheld an enemy in his neighbour, an enemy who would forestall others and save himself at all costs; and in the panic of accumulated losses man after man bent his steps towards the bank. The doors were besieged; with loud cries the men—and the women too, for many of these had flocked thither impelled by the instinct of self-preservation—men and women beset the doors, demanding instant admittance, and clamouring for their money deposits to be restored to them then and there. The pressure waxed irresistible; the doors yielded; a terrified clerk or two strove vainly with plausible words to appease the foremost applicants; then desperately discharged claim after claim in notes, sovereigns, silver, till the last sixpence—down to the last penny—was disbursed. When it became known that the old-established secure bank had stopped payment before it had met a tithe of its liabilities, it was as much as the clerks could do to escape with whole skins from the infuriated, disappointed populace.

But more troubles were to come. At the railway station a telegram had been received early in the evening intimating that a branch bank in an adjacent town had been constrained by sudden pressure to stop payment, though, as it was hoped, only momentarily. This disastrous news had been studiously confined to one or two parties, who hoped to profit by being in advance of their neighbours; but soon a second telegram of like import came in from another quarter; then a third; and it became impossible any longer to suppress the facts. A terrible commotion ensued on 'Change; there was scarcely a house in all the town where ruin, or at the least reverse, had not entered.

But what, after all, were these partial local failures? Before the night was over another telegram arrived, and it transpired that the main national bank itself had broken.°

Then a cry went up through the length and breadth of the land.

When our wayfarer reached the Exchange it was crowded by persons of all ranks and ages, brought together by the bond of a common disaster. He dismounted, tethered his white horse to the railings outside, and entering joined the concourse within, apparently with no further object than to observe and listen, passing from group to group, pausing sometimes a longer, sometimes a shorter period, here or there as the case might demand. Most of the persons present—of those at least who were not simply paralysed and struck dumb by their misfortunes—stood disputing in loud, excited tones, as to the causes and details of the present public calamities;—whose carelessness it was which had occasioned the gas explosion; how many vessels and lives, and what value of cargo, had perished in the storm, some rating the probable loss at millions and some at tens of millions; what hope there might still be of a dividend from the local bank; whether any of the reported failures had been without fraud; what head the country could make against the vast smash of the national bank. But here and there some one man or woman seemed, in the hubbub of rage and dismay, to be wrapped in private, personal grief, alien from the general cares.

One such, a half-frantic elderly woman, huddled in a corner, was tearing her hair and crying out in broken, half-articulate speech. The strange traveller approached her, and in a voice of great sympathy inquired into the source of her passionate sorrow. Then, weeping and gnashing her teeth, she shrieked her answer: 'My son, my son, he has been cashiered to-day from his regiment! His commission was all we had in the world, and he was all I loved in the world.' An old sullen man, accosted by the traveller, replied shortly that his strong-box had been broken open and rifled by thieves, and that as he was removing a small remnant of money left to him from his own house to a place of security, the few precious coins had slipped through a hole in the bag and been lost. Another man, being questioned, seemed to find some relief in complaint, and answered readily that he had embarked enormous capital in constructing a reservoir for water, on a scale amply sufficient for the supply of the whole town, but that, at the very moment when he hoped to realise cent per cent upon his original out-lay, a flaw had been discovered in the main aqueduct, and it was then perceived, too late, that all the cisterns were broken and could hold no water. Every tale was diverse, yet, in fact, every one was the same. Each speaker had sunk all that he had in some plausible investment, the investment had burst like a bubble, and now one and all in desperate sorrow could but bewail their ruin as without remedy. They had no eyes, no thought, no sympathy, save each man for himself; none stretched a helping hand to his neighbour, or spoke a word of comfort, or cared who sank or who swam in this desolation which had come like a flood.

From such as these it was vain to demand hospitality. The traveller went out from amongst them, remounted his horse, and pursued his way along the darkened, deserted streets, between rows of tall houses, in which the voice of mirth and music seemed silenced for ever. Now at one door, now at another, he knocked to ask for refreshment, but always without success. Sometimes no answer was vouchsafed to his summons; sometimes he was turned away with churlish indifference, or even with abuse for having ventured to disturb the household in its night of distress.

At last he observed one cottage, which, detached from other residences, stood alone in its trim garden-plot. In this only, amongst all the dwellings he had passed, there shone a light. He dismounted once more, tethered his horse to the wicket-gate, followed the gravel-path, and knocked gently at the house-door. A calm, cheerful-looking woman opened to him, and seeing a stranger at that late hour, conceived at once that he was a wayfarer in quest of repose and refreshment, and bade him enter and be welcome. Then, while he sat down by the fire, she hastened to set before him milk and bread, meat, wine, and butter. This done, she ran out and led the horse under an open shed (she had no stable), and there provided it with clean straw and fodder.

Now when the traveller had eaten and drunk and sat awhile, he began to question her concerning her prosperity and cheerfulness in that night of ruin; and she, as the others had done, answered him all that he would know.

'My money,' said she, 'is not invested as so many in this town have invested theirs. When I was yet young, One told me that riches do certainly make to themselves wings and fly away; and that gold perisheth, though it be purified seven times in the fire. Nevertheless He added that, if I chose, there could with my gold and silver be made ready for me an ever-lasting habitation, to receive me when the present fashion shall have passed away; and that I might lay up for myself treasure where neither moth nor rust doth corrupt, and where thieves do not break through and steal. So, when I was willing, He further informed me by what means I should send my deposits to that secure house whereof the Owner will be no man's debtor. On the first day of the week I was to go up to the branch-house upon the hill—you see it, sir, out to the East yonder; there, where a light shines to lighten every one that goeth into the house; and according as I had been prospered, I was to drop somewhat into the money-chest kept there. All such sums would be placed to my account, and would bear interest. But besides this, I was apprised that the Owner of the house employs many collectors, who may call at any moment, often at the most unlikely moments, for deposits. From these I was to take heed never to turn away my face, but I was to give to them freely, being well assured that they would carry all entrusted to them safely to my account. Thus, sometimes a fatherless child calls on me, sometimes a distressed widow; sometimes a sick case comes before me; sometimes a stranger, sir, as you have done this very night, demands my hospitality. And as I know whom I have trusted, and am persuaded that He will keep that which I commit to Him, I gladly spend and am spent, being a succourer of many, and looking for the recompense of the reward.'°

So when the strange traveller had rested awhile, his horse also having been refreshed, he rose before daybreak, mounted, and rode away. Whence he came and whither he went I know not, but he rode as one that carries back tidings to Him that sent him. Also this I know, that some, being mindful to entertain strangers, have entertained angels unawares.°

DEVOTIONAL PROSE

From SEEK AND FIND: A DOUBLE SERIES OF
SHORT STUDIES OF THE BENEDICITE

Waters Above the Firmament

The heavens declare the glory of God; and the
firmament sheweth his handywork. Ps. xix. 1

Since many of the 'Waters that be above the firmament' are named one
by one further on in the Canticle, let us for the moment dwell on the
firmament itself, 'the sky, which is strong, and as a molten looking
glass' (Job xxxvii. 18).

To our eyes it appears blue, sometimes deepening towards purple,
sometimes passing into pale green; purple, an earthly hue of mourning,°
and green our tint of hope. One colour seems to prophesy of that day
when the sign of the Son of Man shall appear in heaven, and all the
tribes of the earth shall mourn (St. Matt. xxiv. 30): one, to symbolize
that veil of separation beyond which faith and love discern our ascended
Lord, and whereinto hope as an anchor of the soul sure and stedfast
entereth (Heb. vi. 19, 20). Remote from either extreme stretches the
prevalent blue, pure and absolute: thus the sky and its azure become
so at one in our associations, that all fair blue objects within our reach,
stone or flower, sapphire or harebell, act as terrene° mirrors, conveying
to us an image of that which is above themselves, as 'earthly pictures
with heavenly meanings.' And although the atmosphere is in reality
full of currents and commotions, yet to our senses the sky appears to
stand aloof as the very type of stability; overarching and embosoming
not earth and sea only, but clouds and meteors, planets and stars.
Beneath it and within it all moves, waxes, wanes, while itself changes
not: setting before us as by a parable the little-loftiness of
the loftiest things of time; 'there be higher than they' (see Eccles. v. 8).
Yet has the unchanging sky no final stability, but at its appointed
hour it shall be rolled up as a scroll and shall pass away (Is. xxxiv. 4;
Rev. vi. 14).

Thus while all the good creatures of God teach us some lesson concerning the unapproached perfections of their Creator, that which they display is a glimpse, that which they cannot display is infinite. 'They shall perish, but Thou shalt endure' (Ps. cii. 26).

Sun and Moon

> God made two great lights; the greater light to rule the
> day, and the lesser light to rule the night. GEN. i. 16

Both lights great: one exceeding the other: both good. Such a graduation of greater and less, both being acceptable to Him Who made them, pervades much if not the whole of the world in which we live: sun and moon, man and woman; or to ascend to the supreme instance, Christ and His Church. I, being a woman, will copy St. Paul's example and 'magnify mine office' (Rom. xi. 13). Probably there were in his day persons who rated the Apostle of the Gentiles, as such, far below the Apostle of the Jews (1 Cor. ix. 1–6; Gal. ii. 8), and one aspect of truth may have been honoured by such an estimate: yet was not the estimate exhaustive, for it was not one which embraced the entire field of God's Love towards His human family. What said God Himself when hundreds of years before He spake of Christ? 'It is a light thing that Thou shouldest be My Servant to raise up the tribes of Jacob, and to restore the preserved of Israel: I will also give Thee for a Light to the Gentiles, that Thou mayest be My Salvation unto the end of the earth' (Is. xlix. 6).

In many points the feminine lot copies very closely the voluntarily assumed position of our Lord and Pattern. Woman must obey: and Christ 'learned obedience' (Gen. iii. 16; Heb. v. 8). She must be fruitful, but in sorrow: and He, symbolised by a corn of wheat, had not brought forth much fruit except He had died (Gen. iii. 16; St. John xii. 24). She by natural constitution is adapted not to assert herself, but to be subordinate: and He came not to be ministered unto but to minister; He was among His own 'as he that serveth' (1 St. Peter iii. 7; 1 Tim. ii. 11, 12; St. Mark x. 45; St. Luke xxii. 27). Her office is to be man's helpmeet: and concerning Christ God saith, 'I have laid help upon One that is mighty' (Gen. ii. 18, 21, 22; Ps. lxxxix. 19). And well may she glory, inasmuch as one of the tenderest of divine promises takes (so to say) the feminine form: 'As one whom his mother comforteth, so will I comfort you' (Is. lxvi. 13).

In the case of the twofold Law of Love, we are taught to call one Commandment 'first and great,' yet to esteem the second as 'like unto it' (St. Matt. xxii. 37–39). The man is the head of the woman, the woman the glory of the man (1 Cor. xi. 3, 7). 'There is one glory of the sun, and another glory of the moon' (xv. 41). It used to be popularly supposed that 'the moon walking in brightness' (Job xxxi. 26) is no more than a mirror reflecting the sun's radiance: now careful observation leads towards the hypothesis that she also may exhibit inherent luminosity.° But if our proud waves will after all not be stayed, or at any rate not be allayed (for stayed they must be) by the limit of God's ordinance concerning our sex, one final consolation yet remains to careful and troubled hearts: in Christ there is neither male nor female, for we are all one (Gal. iii. 28).

In the Old Testament history two miracles are recorded as having suspended planetary law: one having been wrought during the Jewish conquest of the land of promise (Josh. x. 12–14); the other long afterwards, when Israel had ceased to be a kingdom and Judah was dwindling towards a penal captivity (2 Kings xx. 8–11). The first miracle concerned divers nations, the second an individual trembling saint; one asserted the Divine supremacy, the other exemplified the Divine compassion. If we learn from all such portents that the nations are before God as a drop of a bucket and as the small dust of the balance (Is. xl. 15), that He will by no means clear the guilty (Ex. xxxiv. 7), that He doth not willingly afflict the children of men (Lam. iii. 33), and, not least, that He far better than ourselves knows whether lengthened or shortened life be our best blessing, for on this point Hezekiah's subsequent fall through pride makes a sad suggestion (2 Chron. xxxii. 24–26), we shall have learned enough; even if we never fathom the physical conditions of miracles. A miracle is a Divine suspension or reversal of natural law: and surely our conception of a natural law and of a miracle will be adequate when we come to realise them as Job (xl. 19) was instructed to estimate behemoth: 'He that made him can make His sword to approach unto him.'

If we be docile disciples of that Master Who judgeth not according to the sight of the eyes (Is. xi. 3), then by the defects as well as by the aptitude of our natural faculties He will instruct us. It is merely to our sight that the sun obliterates the stars, the sun being in truth of inconsiderable bulk when compared with many of them: yet by reason of its nearness to our eyes it fairly puts them all out, until only an act of recollection can during the daylight hours summon before our consciousness the ever-present, ever-luminous multitudinous lights of the sky. When the glare of this world dazzles the eyes of our soul, such an act of recollection is what we need; bringing home to our conscious love the presence of Him Who is ever present, and Who is pledged to be our very present help in trouble (Ps. xlvi. 1). Moses 'endured, as seeing Him Who is invisible' (Heb. xi. 27): yet the Law, his portion, was not glorious, as compared with the excelling glory of the Gospel which we have inherited (2 Cor. iii. 6–11). Shall we who possess more aim at less?

Faith accepts, love contemplates and is nourished by, every word, act, type, of God. The Sun, to our unaided senses the summit of His visible creation, is pre-eminently the symbol of God Himself: of God the giver, cherisher, cheerer of life; the luminary of all perceptive beings; the attractive centre of our system. The Sun, worshipped under many names and by divers nations, is truly no more than our fellow-creature in the worship and praise of our common Creator; yet as His symbol it none the less conveys to us a great assurance of hope. At the voice of one man it stood still, in the strait of another it retrograded: thus we see illustrated the prevalence of prayer, and the strong grasp of man's sore need upon the succouring strength of Him Who made him. Elias, at whose word rain was withheld or granted, stands not alone as our encouraging example (1 Kings xvii. 1; St. James v. 17, 18). Abraham's entreaty prescribed the limit of Sodom's doom (Gen. xviii. 23–32). One said to Jacob, 'Let Me go:' but Jacob denied Him except He blessed him, and prevailed (Gen. xxxii. 24–30). The Lord said to Moses, 'Let me alone:' yet Moses let Him not alone, and Israel was saved (Exod. xxxii. 7–14).

'The Lord God is a sun and shield: the Lord will give grace and glory: no good thing will He withhold from them that walk uprightly. O Lord of hosts, blessed is the man that trusteth in Thee' (Ps. lxxxiv. 11, 12).

Seas and Floods

> When that which is perfect is come, then that which
> is in part shall be done away.   1 COR. xiii. 10

These words in which St. Paul treats of partial knowledge, incomplete revelation, imperfect sight, childhood (1 Cor. xiii. 9–12), though each of those is good and not evil in its allotted sphere and during its assigned period,—seem in some sort applicable to the sea also, according to St. John's vision of the final consummation of all things: 'I saw a new heaven and a new earth: for the first heaven and the first earth were passed away; and there was no more sea' (Rev. xxi. 1). Equally, the sun and moon appear then to be, if not obliterated, at the least superseded: 'The city had no need of the sun, neither of the moon, to shine in it: for the glory of God did lighten it, and the Lamb is the light thereof' (v. 23).

At first reading 'there was no more sea,' our heart sinks at foresight of the familiar sea expunged from earth and heaven; that sea to us so long and so inexhaustibly a field of wonder and delight. 'Was Thy wrath against the sea . . . ? The overflowing of the water passed by: the deep uttered his voice, and lifted up his hands on high' (Hab. iii. 8, 10).

Whatever mystery may attach to this subject, various plain points are, I think, open to our consideration. The Inspired Volume seems written rather for our instruction as regards ourselves, and consequently as regards the visible creation in reference to ourselves, than from a more general purpose of enlarging our knowledge touching matters wholly extraneous; and many a subject too wide or too deep for our grasp may yet teach us an unmistakable lesson.

'No more sea' does not exclude from the presence of the Throne 'a sea of glass like unto crystal' (Rev. iv. 6); or, be it the same sea or not, 'as it were a sea of glass mingled with fire' whereon the victorious redeemed take their stand (xv. 2). Thus we shall not lose the translucent purity of ocean, nor yet a glory as of its myriad waves tipped by sunshine; no, nor even the volume of its voice, when all God's servants up-lift their praises 'as the voice of many waters' (xix. 5, 6). What shall we lose? Not our friends, for the sea shall give up its dead (xx. 13), when earth also shall no more hide her blood or cover her slain (Is. xxvi. 21). What shall we lose? A barrier of separation: for the exultant children of the resurrection find firm footing and stand together upon their heavenly sea,—bitterness and barrenness: for the pure River of Water of Life flows between banks crowned with fertility, and even now its refreshment is for whoso thirsteth and whosoever will drink (Rev. xxii. 1, 2, 17). Troubled restless waters we shall lose with all their defilement (Is. lvii. 20), and with waves that toss and break themselves against a boundary they cannot overpass (Jer. v. 22), and with the moan of a still-recurrent ebb, 'The sea is not full' (Eccles. i. 7). We feel at once that the sea as we know it, a very embodiment of unrest, of spurning at limits, of advance only to recede, that such a sea teaches us nothing concerning that rest which remaineth to the people of God (Heb. iv. 9); who having pressed toward the mark and obtained the prize (Phil. iii. 14) enjoy their final felicity in a heaven which can be no heaven at all except to persons whose wills and whose affections are at one with the will and love of God. 'There was war in heaven' (Rev. xii. 7) would be repeated to all eternity, could we conceive it otherwise.

Floods, whether defined as rain-born or snow-born torrents, noisy and destructive in their day but dwindling to nothing as time goes on, or as any river or other body of running water especially in its moments of turbulence or of overflow (as we read how 'Jordan overfloweth all his banks all the time of harvest,' Josh. iii. 15: see also the imagery of Is. viii. 6, 8; Jer. xlvi. 7, 8; xlvii. 2), in either case some of the associations which invest the sea attach equally to floods.

'He bindeth the floods from overflowing; and the thing that is hid bringeth He forth to light. Hast thou entered into the springs of the sea? or hast thou walked in the search of the depth?' (Job xxviii. 11; xxxviii. 16).

Whales and All That Move in the Waters

> Ask now the beasts, and they shall teach thee; and the
> fowls of the air, and they shall tell thee: or speak to the
> earth, and it shall teach thee: and the fishes of the sea
> shall declare unto thee.   JOB xii. 7, 8

We may, even without travelling inland or skywards, meet with speci-mens of all these our instructors (the earth, of course, only excepted) on the surface or under the surface of the waters. For, to instance merely a few readily remembered animals, icy seas abound in 'sea monsters' that 'draw out the breast' (Lam. iv. 3), whales, walruses, seals; aquatic birds, such as swans and gulls, are at the least as truly at home on or immediately above the water, as in the higher regions of air or on land; fishes, even so-called flying fishes and those exceptional individuals which we are certified traverse fields and mount trees, have still their head-quarters in the liquid element; while a myriad of inferior ani-mated creatures wriggle in wet mud, burrow in wet sand, or take up their station between high and low water-mark. I think however we may hold it as true for the most part that such breathing beings as inhabit two or even three elements show at their best rather in the water than on the land: seals, for instance, are awkward on land, at ease in the water; so in a degree are swans, ducks, geese; but when from earth we turn to air we notice that seagulls, if not all the aquatic fowl, are magnificent flyers as well as good swimmers. As to a crocodile,

I will not pretend to decide in which habitat he shows to most advantage.

What then is the lesson which these creatures of many aspects and many grades are to teach us? Perhaps a study of that whole twelfth chapter of Job from which my initial-text is taken may lead us to answer not incorrectly: they protest that God Almighty is, in the ultimate tracking backwards and upwards of all secondary causes, the One only Maker and Doer. When once we recognise this truth, not as a prison wall to be kicked against, but as an immovable foundation to be built upon, foes may continue to harass us from without, but the battle of life within is already half won, the rebel within being subdued, and the traitor within silenced; for not that which cometh from without defileth a man, but that which proceedeth from within. (See St. Mark vii. 14–23.)

The Old Testament has its one prominent historic fish, the 'great fish' of Jonah (i. 17; ii. 10; St. Matt. xii. 40). In those Books which our Church, adhering exclusively to the Hebrew Canon, segregates under the designation of Apocrypha, there appears a second noteworthy fish, and this like the former overruled to effect purposes of mercy, the medicinal fish of Tobias (Tobit vi. 1–8, 16, 17; viii. 1–3; xi. 7–13). We read that the fish of the Nile perished in the first plague of Egypt (Ex. vii. 19–21). How popular amongst the Jews were fish as food we may infer from certain murmurs of emancipated Israel in the wilderness, and perhaps from a consequent speech of Moses (Num. xi. 4, 5, 22: see also Song of Solomon vii. 4): long afterwards we notice fish among the goods brought on the Sabbath Day to the Jerusalem market by men of Tyre, and prohibited by Nehemiah (xiii. 16–21). The Nile and some if not all of its live tenants having been idolised in Egypt, we discern a special appropriateness in that clause of the Second Commandment which forbids to the chosen nation all images of aquatic creatures (Ex. xx. 4; Deut. iv. 15–18): nor did Israel at the Exodus leave behind all temptation to fish-worship; in the Holy Land they encountered it once more on their own borders, the Philistine idol Dagon, on which in the days of the Judges a summary divine vengeance fell, bearing the semblance of a fish-man (1 Sam. v. 1–4).

Fishes proper are, I think, as a class and to human instinct among the least sympathetic of living creatures. Their surface is comparatively cold and hard; their eye corresponds. Which of us, even supposing such a chance to occur,—which of us would feel drawn to fondle a scaly slippery person? Beholding fishes so cold, so clean, so compact, one might fancy them destitute not of souls only but of hearts also. Yet have they an abundance of good gifts whereby to honour God and cheer man. Gold or silver or a humming-bird does not surpass the vivid lustre and delicacy of their changeable tints; their motions are replete with strength and grace; their swiftness is a sort of beauty; their outlines present unnumbered curves and angles of harmony or quaintness; their bulks varying between the vast and the minute are all alike fashioned according to individual capabilities and requirements. If, descending below fishes, we contemplate certain minor marine organisms, the opulence of beauty and defect of sympathy strikes us anew. Sea anemones are perfect sensitive-flowers to the eye, but clammy and uncomfortable to the touch: shells may on the surface rival rose-leaves and rainbows, but many times they ensconce only an uncomely tenant without features, without intelligible expression. If on the contrary we make fish our starting-point along the upward instead of the downward scale, immediately much becomes different: and among the sea mammals we recognise an ugliness more beautiful than insipid beauty; clumsy contours ennobled by an expression which seeming to proceed straight from their hearts certainly comes straight to ours.

Little do we know of the scope or the future of our brute fellow-creatures: nay, what do we know so as to fathom it even of their actual present? Familiarity with what they are and what they do proves to us that they exert memory, intelligence, affection: but we do not ourselves possess faculties whereby to define the limits of all they are and all they are not. One thing however is absolutely clear: they are entrusted to man's sovereignty for use, not for abuse. If land may cry out and furrows complain against a tyrannical owner (Job xxxi. 38, 39), if the Holy Land emptied of inhabitants enjoyed a compensation for those Sabbaths whereof lawlessness had deprived her (Lev. xxvi. 34, 35; 2 Chron. xxxvi. 20, 21), much more may not life wantonly destroyed and nerves without pity agonised enter a prevalent appeal against men who do such things or take pleasure in them? (See Rom. i. 28–32: 'inventors of evil things, . . . unmerciful.') God weighed the claims of the 'much cattle' of Nineveh, as well as of the human infants (Jonah iv. xi.): if we honestly weigh the claims of all our sentient fellow-creatures, I think we shall forbear to adopt some pretty fashions in dress, and to follow up some scientific problems. Ours is indeed the law of liberty, nevertheless a law it is and we shall be judged thereby (St. James ii. 12): it is at our own peril that we make it an occasion to the flesh (Gal. v. 13), or a cloak of maliciousness (1 St. Pet. ii. 16). At first sight actions may appear transient, done and done with; but accumulating experience bears a contrary witness. We have seen that a fiery destruction perpetuated instead of obliterating many details of Pompeian social life; and we are now assured that sounds can not only be registered, but also stored up and reproduced.° Alas for us, if when the fashion of this world passes away (1 Cor. vii. 31) and partial knowledge is done away (xiii. 9, 10), the groans of a harmless race sacrificed to our vanity or our curiosity should rise up in the judgment° with us and condemn us.

'O Lord, Thou preservest man and beast' (Ps. xxxvi. 6).

Spirits and Souls of the Righteous

> Have the gates of death been opened unto thee? or hast thou
> seen the doors of the shadow of death?   JOB xxxviii. 17

To us Christians the land of the shadow of death is no longer the dominion of the king of terrors, but rather a tiring-closet for the bride of the King of kings. There having put off the corruptible and the mortal she prepares to put on incorruption and immortality (1 Cor. xv. 52, 53), meanwhile making melody in her heart to the Lord. We seem to hear her singing a psalm of thanksgiving, the very psalm of her risen Saviour: 'The lines are fallen unto me in pleasant places. My heart is glad, and my glory rejoiceth: my flesh also shall rest in hope. For Thou wilt not leave my soul in hell. Thou wilt shew me the path of life' (Ps. xvi. 6, 9–11; Acts ii. 22–28).

We may still reverently ask, 'I have put off my coat; how shall I put it on?' (Song of Sol. v. 3); but it must be with the enquiring mind of faith, not with the cavilling mind of doubt. We may search what or what manner of time the Spirit of Christ testifies beforehand touching the Resurrection, but it must be with the joyful confidence of Abraham, when he also heard of life as it were from the dead: alike in laughter, he and Sarah were unlike in the motive of their laughter (Gen. xvii. 17; xviii. 12–15; Rom. iv. 18–21).

Mankind, though still no further advanced than to see through a glass darkly (1 Cor. xiii. 12), may, on comparing its later with its earlier generations, say, thankfully, 'Whereas I was blind, now I see' (see St. John ix. 25). Perhaps the tone of the Old Testament is nowhere more startling at first sight, than in a few passages on the subject of death: for that here and there a text does baffle interpretation and challenge faith, cannot be denied: though love even then never fails to find a clue by its own intuition of the love of God, resting and rejoicing now in what it shall know hereafter. Thus does deep respond to deep at the noise of the waterspouts, for 'many waters cannot quench love, neither can the floods drown it' (Ps. xlii. 7; Song of Sol. viii. 7). If an ordinary believer trembling on the brink of the grave were now to lament as saintly Hezekiah of old lamented (Is. xxxviii. 10–20) it would at the least surprise us.

But we (thank God) can never be called upon to realize what it was to precede, not to follow, Christ into the valley of the shadow of death. Once for all our Good Shepherd has gone before His own sheep: whenever now He puts them forth it is only to go home to Him along the very path which He has already trodden (see St. John x. 4). Of old it was far otherwise. Think what it may have been for Abel to pass (as it seems) first of the whole human family into the veiled world; and after him went forth each soul in individual loneliness, much as Abraham who knew not whither he went (Heb. xi. 8): it needed a David, and him under inspiration, in such a transit to 'fear no evil' (Ps. xxiii. 4). True it is that Moses showed at the bush that the dead rise (St. Luke xx. 37, 38): but if some in Israel were slow of heart to interpret that text, what are the mass of ourselves in comprehending many another? To be alone was never indeed at any period the lot of a faithful soul; but to feel alone has been, and is, one besetting trial of man: how keen is this trial and in a sense how unsuited to our constitution we may deduce both from a Divine sentence true of Adam even in his original innocence (Gen. ii. 18), and also from a Messianic psalm (lxxxviii. 8, 18), from a Messianic prophetic vision (Is. lxiii. 3–5), and from words uttered by our Lord Himself in foresight (St. John xvi. 32) and in the crisis (St. Mark xv. 34) of His atoning passion.

Of actual glimpses into the realm of departed souls the Old Testament affords us very few. Once and once only do we behold a saint reappear from his grave: 'An old man cometh up; and he is covered with a mantle. And Saul perceived that it was Samuel. . . . And Samuel said to Saul, Why hast thou disquieted me, to bring me up?' (1 Sam. xxviii. 14, 15). From these words we gather, yet at most by implication, that the elect soul was dwelling in a quiet abode and cared not to be disquieted. Thus Job (iii. 17–22) also spoke when he thought to rejoice exceedingly and be glad if only he could find a grave: 'There the wicked cease from troubling; and there the weary be at rest.' A second utterance of disembodied Samuel shows him, as in the days of his mortality, so then once again moved by the spirit of prophecy (1 Sam. xxviii. 19). The dead, however, are as a rule they who characteristically 'go down into silence' (Ps. cxv. 17): not any of themselves, but Isaiah xiv. 9–11) and Ezekiel (xxxii. 21) only, acquaint us with that mighty stir in the underworld which greeted the fallen king of Babylon, and that voice out of the midst of Hades which spake to overthrown Egypt.

But when from the intermediate state we turn faithful eyes towards the final beatitude, all becomes flooded no longer with mist but with radiance: that which baffles our vision is not darkness but light,—light not dubious though partly undefined. Thus has it been with the Church of God from Abel downwards (Heb. xi. 4–14, &c.): thus will it be to the end of time (1 Cor. xv. 51–54). Full quotations become impossible by reason of abundance: but over and over again we recognise the one glorious hope of immortality persisting in patriarchs, singing in psalmists, rejoicing in prophets (e.g. Job xix. 25–27; Ps. xlix. 15; Is. xxvi. 19; Hos. xiii. 14). We know that this mortal life is the sufficient period of our probation, we know that the life immortal is the sufficing period—if we may call eternity a period—of our reward: let us not fret our hearts by a too anxious curiosity as to that intermediate state which hides for the moment so many whom we love and whom we hope to rejoin, for even now we know that 'the souls of the righteous are in the hand of God, and there shall no torment touch them' (Wisdom iii. 1).

Powers

> The devil, taking Him up into an high mountain, shewed unto Him all the kingdoms of the world in a moment of time. And the devil said unto Him, All this power will I give Thee, and the glory of them: for that is delivered unto me.   St. Luke iv. 5, 6

Around the Almighty Creator we behold the universe come into existence in obedience, harmony, perfection (Gen. i.; Neh. ix. 6; Rev. iv. 11). Around the Almighty Redeemer earth and its inhabiters though weak (Ps. lxxv. 4, Prayer-Book version) rage in impotent rebellion (Ps. ii. 1; xlvi. 1–3, 6). One stronger than they holds them as slaves, plies them as tools, wields them as weapons against their Maker and Master: all the foundations of the earth are out of course (lxxxii. 5); and not man alone, but the blind forces of nature also seem to surge and swell against Him to Whom the nations are as a drop of a bucket, and Who taketh up the isles as a very little thing (Is. xl. 15).

As God saw fit to curse the passive ground for Adam's sake (Gen. iii. 17), so it pleased our Divine Saviour to suffer many things not from sinners only, but from inanimate or irrational nature also: though ever and anon He vanquished her opposition or enriched her niggardliness, 'Hitherto shalt thou come, but no further' (see Job xxxviii. 11).

Christ, we are taught, was born in the winter, a season impoverished of leaves, flowers, fruit, sunshine, when the voice of birds is silent (see Song of Sol. ii. 11–13). The inn which housed other Israelites housed not Him (St. Luke ii. 7). Desert places which for His precursor brought forth locusts and wild honey, spread no table for Him (St. Matt. iii. 1–4; iv. 1, 2). The water of Jacob's well remained, at least for a while, inaccessible to Him: and He, whose first miracle supplied wine to His friends, Himself sat patiently athirst (St. John ii. 1–11; iv. 6–11). A village where Samaritans dwelt at home shut its doors against Him: and He who of old had avenged His insulted prophet by fire, Himself journeyed meekly elsewhere in search of hospitality (St. Luke ix. 51–56; 2 Kings i. 9–12). Earth which furnished holes and nests for foxes and birds, provided no resting-place for Him (St. Luke ix. 58). The barren fig-tree mocked His hunger with leaves only (St. Matt. xxi. 18, 19). On all these occasions irresponsible nature, involved in the curse of man's guilt and sometimes directed by his will, hid as it were her face from her Maker: while in one instance alone° did He pronounce upon her a sentence of immediate punishment. But other occasions there were when contrariwise He vouchsafed to assert His absolute dominion over His creatures; 'Thou hast scattered Thine enemies with Thy strong arm. The heavens are Thine, the earth also is Thine' (Ps. lxxxix. 10, 11). Thus He stilled the tempest (St. Mark iv. 35–39), He raised the dead (St. Luke vii. 11–15; viii. 49–55; St. John xi. 38–44), by His word He cast out devils and assigned to them their habitation (St. Mark v. 2–15).

'God hath spoken once; twice have I heard this; that power belongeth unto God' (Ps. lxii. 11). Great, unfathomable is the mystery of powers set in array against God. 'Shall the ax boast itself against him that heweth therewith? or shall the saw magnify itself against him that shaketh it? as if the rod should shake itself against them that lift it up, or as if the staff should lift up itself, as if it were no wood' (Is. x. 15). St. Paul tells us of principalities, powers, rulers of darkness, spiritual wickedness, which wrestle with God's elect (Eph. vi. 12) whom whoso toucheth, toucheth as it were the apple of the eye (Zech. ii. 8; see Deut. xxxii. 10). Yet more awful are our Lord's own words at the moment of His arrest: 'This is your hour, and the power of darkness' (St. Luke xxii. 53).

'He that is not with Me is against me:' 'He that is not against us is on our part' (St. Matt xii. 30; St. Mark ix. 40). Neutrality is impossible; and were it possible, woe to that man who there took up his position: 'I would,' says Christ to lukewarm Laodicea,—'I would thou wert cold or hot' (Rev. iii. 15); neutral Meroz brought upon itself a curse and not a blessing (Judges v. 23). All created powers great or small, visible or invisible,—every man's powers,—my own,—must run their course, must attain the end towards which in very truth they are directed, must consciously or unconsciously effect the purposes of God (see 2 Cor. vi. 1; Acts iv. 27, 28). Free will, that one power which God Himself refuses to coerce, free will it is that renders possible our self-destruction; and that on the other hand furnishes us with the one solitary thing which as a king we can give unto our all-giving beloved King (see 2 Sam. xxiv. 23, 24). Creatures devoid of free-will abide safe and blessed within the will of God; but they cannot withhold, and therefore they cannot genuinely give. Would we, if we could, choose by once for all foregoing choice to offer for ever after unto the Lord our God of that which doth cost us nothing? This were to love mistrustfully, if to love at all: Christ help us to trust entirely because we love much.

Jesus said: 'All power is given unto Me in heaven and in earth' (St. Matt, xxviii. 18).

'Now unto Him that is able to keep you from falling, and to present you faultless before the presence of His glory with exceeding joy, to the only wise God our Saviour, be glory and majesty, dominion and power, both now and ever. Amen' (St. Jude 24, 25).

From LETTER AND SPIRIT:
NOTES ON THE COMMANDMENTS

The First Great Commandment, including that Second which is its like, necessarily includes the entire Decalogue: while of the Decalogue the first four Commandments, being traceable to the First but not to the Second, become characteristically *the* substance of that First Commandment.

And being four in number, these commandments naturally range themselves (though not in exactly corresponding order) under those four powers of man (heart, soul, mind, strength), which are summoned to fulfil the Great Commandment. God claims our whole selves, all we are, all we have, all we may become; and doubtless the all-important feature of the Great Commandment is that we must keep back nothing: still, it may in fact help us to keep back nothing if, so to say, we sift and sort our resources; and offer not simply *all* as a whole, but *each* one by one.

Yet before we descend to classification, it is necessary to make sure that we do without evasion or abatement offer all and keep back nothing. A Jew, quoting the letter of the Decalogue, might plead that the point of his First Commandment was to 'have none other gods but' the One true God. Not so a Christian, nourished 'by every word that proceedeth out of the mouth of God.'° To him—to us, the point of our First Commandment is that all we are, and all we have, must be not merely withheld from false gods, but devoted to the true God.

Of this, as of all its dependent excellences, we find but one perfect example, our Lord Jesus Christ. Of its contrary we find specimens on every hand and in endless variety.

Adam and Eve illustrate two sorts of defection (1 Tim. ii. 14). Eve made a mistake, 'being *deceived*' she was in the transgression: Adam made no mistake: his was an error of will, hers partly of judgment; nevertheless both proved fatal. Eve, equally with Adam, was created sinless: each had a specially vulnerable point, but this apparently not the same point. It is in no degree at variance with the Sacred Record to picture to ourselves Eve, that first and typical woman, as indulging quite innocently sundry refined tastes and aspirations, a castle-building spirit (if so it may be called), a feminine boldness and directness of aim combined with a no less feminine guessiness as to means. Her very virtues may have opened the door to temptation. By birthright gracious and accessible, she lends an ear to all petitions from all petitioners. She desires to instruct ignorance, to rectify misapprehension: 'unto the pure all things are pure,'° and she never suspects even the serpent. Possibly a trace of blameless infirmity transpires in the wording of her answer, '*lest* ye die,' for God had said to the man '. . . in the day that thou eatest thereof thou *shalt surely* die:' but such tenderness of spirit seems even lovely in the great first mother of mankind; or it may be that Adam had modified the form, if it devolved on him to declare the tremendous fact to his second self. Adam and Eve reached their goal, the Fall, by different routes. With Eve the serpent discussed a question of conduct, and talked her over to his own side: with Adam, so far as appears, he might have argued the point for ever and gained no vantage; but already he had secured an ally weightier than a score of arguments. Eve may not have argued at all: she offered Adam a share of her own good fortune, and having hold of her husband's heart, turned it in her hand as the rivers of water. Eve preferred various prospects to God's Will: Adam seems to have preferred one person to God: Eve diverted her 'mind' and Adam his 'heart' from God Almighty. Both courses led to one common result, that is, to one common ruin (Gen. iii.).

Whatever else may be deduced from the opening chapters of Genesis, their injunction of obedience is plainly written; of unqualified obedience, of obedience on pain of death.

To do anything whatsoever, even to serve God, 'with all the strength,' brings us into continual collision with that modern civilized standard of good breeding and good taste which bids us avoid extremes. Such modern standard may be regarded as having by ancient anticipation brought King Saul into collision with the Prophet Samuel in the matter of Amalek and especially of Agag (1 Sam. xv. 1–33). Saul stood far in advance of many a conqueror when he abhorred destruction for the mere sake of destruction; he seemed to enlist both piety and prudence on his own side by proposing to utilize the condemned cattle. It may have evinced a mind suavely cosmopolitan, possibly even some far-sighted appreciation of the balance of power, when he spared Agag. On the other hand, the letter of the standing law (Ex. xvii. 14–16) and the word of the immediate commandment were explicitly in favour of extermination; and Samuel, God's mouthpiece, saw no room for two opinions as to whether the Lord meant what He had plainly said. 'Behold, to obey is better than sacrifice;' summed up his simple view of the crisis: 'Because thou hast rejected the word of the Lord. He hath also rejected thee from being king.' (*See also* 1 Kings xx. 28–42 for a somewhat similar incident in the career of Ahab.) Saul, alas! choice and goodly as he was, does in this perilous matter of slack service act as a warning beacon at more than one turning point of his course. Towards the commencement of his reign, and under the first prolonged strain of danger, his courage held out during seven days, but failing at the last moment undermined his throne (1 Sam. xiii. 8–14). His zeal somewhile extirpated witches and wizards, till at length at a desperate pass he himself had recourse to one woman with a familiar spirit, and heard his own and his sons' death-doom pronounced (1 Sam. xxviii. 3–20). He fought in person his last battle against the enemies of Israel, yet after all died as a fool dieth (1 Sam. xxxi. 1–6).

If we may accept Adam, Eve, Saul, as illustrating defective heart, mind, strength, in loyalty to Almighty God, we seem still in search of a representative of defective 'soul.' But here reaching (so to say) the very throne of man's free-will service, the noblest element of his noble nature, we observe how soul-defection being the root of every defection, and in itself including all defection, expresses itself in each breach of any commandment, be that breach one of commission or of omission, yet is not itself to be expressed in any separate form: it prompts, it pervades, it incurs the guilt of every transgression; nevertheless to us creatures of sense it becomes perceptible not otherwise than through effects wrought by means of agents,—as indeed, as regards our own faculties, is the case with all causes, even with our God Himself.

*   *   *

It is well and best to be ruled by the highest motive, yet is it not necessarily evil to be influenced by lower considerations. St. Paul speaks of one who 'doeth well,' even when naming another who 'doeth better.' In the same context he tells us: 'The unmarried woman careth for the things of the Lord, that she may be holy both in body and in spirit: but she that is married careth for the things of the world, how she may please her husband' (1 Cor. vii. 34, 38). These two contrasted figures (the married woman and the virgin) may, I think, be studied as illustrative of the First and Second Commandments.

She whose heart is virginal abides aloft and aloof in spirit. In spirit she oftentimes kneels rather than sits, or prostrates herself more readily than she kneels, associated by love with Seraphim, and echoing and swelling the 'Holy, Holy, Holy,'° of their perpetual adoration. Her spiritual eyes behold the King in His beauty; wherefore she forgets, by comparison, her own people and her father's house. Her Maker is her Husband, endowing her with a name better than of sons and of daughters. His Presence and His right hand are more to her than that fulness of joy and those pleasures which flow from them. For His sake rather than for its own she longs for Paradise; she craves the gold of that land less because it is good than because it is His promised gift to her. She loves Him with all her heart and soul and mind and strength; she is jealous that she cannot love Him more; her desire to love Him outruns her possibility, yet by outrunning enlarges it. She contemplates Him, and abhors herself in dust and ashes. She contemplates Him, and forgets herself in Him. If she rejoices, it is on spiritual heights, with Blessed Mary° magnifying the Lord; if she laments, it is still on spiritual mountain-tops, making with Jephthah's daughter° a pure oblation of unflinching self-sacrifice. The air she breathes is too rare and keen for grosser persons; they mark the clouds which involve her feet, but discern not those early and late sunbeams which turn her mists to rainbows and kindle her veiled head to a golden glory. Her heart talks of God; 'Seek ye My Face—Thy Face, Lord, will I seek;'° until truly her danger in the Day of Judgment would rather seem that she should not have recognised Christ's brethren to whom she ministered, than that she should have overlooked Him in them.

The Wife's case, not in unison with that other, yet makes a gracious harmony with it. She sees not face to face, but as it were in a glass darkly. Every thing, and more than all every person, and most of all the one best beloved person, becomes her mirror wherein she beholds Christ and her shrine wherein she serves Him. Her vocation is composed of indulgences and privileges as well as duties; yet being her vocation, she religiously fulfils it 'as to the Lord, and not unto men.'° Her earthly love and obedience express to her a mystery; she takes heed to reverence her husband, as seeing Him Who is invisible; her children are the children whom God has given her, the children whom she nurses for God. She sits down in the lowest place, and is thankful there. She is faithful over the few things, and not impatient to rule over the many things; she is faithful in that which is another man's, and can wait patiently for that which is her own. As the Cloudy Pillar deigned indifferently to head the Exodus or to bring up the rear of the children of Israel, so she leads or follows; and is made all things to all her own, if by any means she may save some; while like that sacred Symbol she also veils her perfections from alien eyes, reserving the luminous fire of her gifts and graces to him most of all whose due they are, and in him to the Maker of them both (see Ex. xiv. 19, 20).

And we may trace no less clearly the correspondence (if I may call it so) of these two 'holy estates' with the First and Second Commandments, by weighing and sifting the characteristic temptation of each vocation: the Virgin tends to become narrow, self-centred; the Wife to worship and serve the creature more than the Creator.

* * *

Under the Levitical law blasphemy ranked as a capital offence (Lev. xxiv. 15, 16); false oaths were forbidden (xix. 12); religious vows became binding (Num. xxx. 2). In harmony with which is the Preacher's exhortation, 'Be not rash with thy mouth, and let not thine heart be hasty to utter any thing before God: for God is in heaven, and thou upon earth: therefore let thy words be few. . . . When thou vowest a vow unto God, defer not to pay it; for He hath no pleasure in fools: pay that which thou hast vowed. Better is it that

thou shouldest not vow, than that thou shouldest vow and not pay'
(Eccles. v. 2, 4, 5).

Our Lord, in His Sermon on the Mount, enforces and enlarges our
obligations: 'Ye have heard that it hath been said by them of old time,
Thou shalt not forswear thyself, but shalt perform unto the Lord thine
oaths: but I say unto you, Swear not at all; neither by heaven; for it is
God's throne: nor by the earth; for it is His footstool: neither by
Jerusalem; for it is the city of the Great King. Neither shalt thou swear
by thy head, because thou canst not make one hair white or black. But
let your communication be, Yea, yea; Nay, nay: for whatsoever is more
than these cometh of evil' (St. Matt. v. 33–37). And on another occasion
He pronounced a Woe on the Scribes and Pharisees for sin in this very
matter: 'Woe unto you, ye blind guides, which say, Whosoever shall
swear by the temple, it is nothing; but whosoever shall swear by the gold
of the temple, he is a debtor! Ye fools and blind: for whether is greater,
the gold, or the temple that sanctifieth the gold? And, Whosoever shall
swear by the altar, it is nothing; but whosoever sweareth by the gift that
is upon it, he is guilty. Ye fools and blind: for whether is greater, the gift,
or the altar that sanctifieth the gift? Whoso therefore shall swear by the
altar, sweareth by it, and by all things thereon. And whoso shall swear
by the temple, sweareth by it, and by Him that dwelleth therein. And he
that shall swear by heaven, sweareth by the Throne of God, and by Him
that sitteth thereon' (St. Matt, xxiii. 16–22).

These passages, besides condemning prevaricating oaths and (at the
very least) oaths on trivial occasions, open our eyes to the dignity of
creation in general, and consequently to the reverence which should
pervade and check our speech. For not only 'heaven' and 'Jerusalem;'
'earth' also and our own 'head' must not be lightly invoked. In every
creature° is latent a memorial of its Creator. Throughout and by
means of creation God challenges each of us, 'Hath not My hand made
all these things?'° Our prevalent tone of mind should resemble that of
the Psalmist when he proclaimed: 'The heavens declare the glory of
God; and the firmament sheweth His handywork;'° saying elsewhere
in the same vein, 'When I consider Thy heavens, the work of Thy
fingers, the moon and the stars, which Thou hast ordained; what is
man . . .?'° Nay, more, we should exercise that far higher privilege
which appertains to Christians, of having 'the mind of Christ;'° and
then the two worlds, visible and invisible, will become familiar to us
even as they were to Him (if reverently we may say so), as double
against each other; and on occasion sparrow and lily will recall God's

Providence, seed His Word, earthly bread the Bread of Heaven, a plough the danger of drawing back; to fill a bason and take a towel will preach a sermon on self-abasement; boat, fishing-net, flock or fold of sheep, each will convey an allusion; wind, water, fire, the sun, a star, a vine, a door, a lamb, will shadow forth mysteries. Versed in such trains of thought the mind becomes reverential, composed, grave; the heart imbued with such associations becomes steadied and ennobled; and out of the abundance of such a heart the mouth impulsively speaks that which is good and edifying; not corrupt communications, or foolish talking and jesting which are not convenient, or idle words whereof an account will have to be given. A Christian is one whose smooth fair outer surface of manner covers and reveals a transparent depth of character, and whose hidden man of the heart is fairer than are any outward features; he puts away childish things, and that foolishness which is bound up in the heart of a child; he keeps his tongue from evil and his lips that they speak no guile, and because he is privileged to name the Name of Christ he departs from iniquity.

* * *

If from Adam downwards every single person ever born still exists maintaining unbroken by death one continuity of individual existence from birth to this moment, from this moment to the Day of Judgment, when we all must stand face to face not with our Judge only but equally with each other, then is it no light offence to traduce the dead, to blacken recklessly their memory, to cultivate no tenderness for them, helpless and inoffensive as they now lie with all their sins of omission or commission on their heads. Party feeling, whether called religious zeal or national antagonism or political creed, becomes simple malice and is simply devilish when it leads us not only to condemn opponents (or it may even be those merely to whom we ourselves are opposed) but to wish that they may really be as unworthy as history or rumour makes them, to court and hug and blaze abroad every tittle of evidence which tells against them, to turn a dull ear and lukewarm heart to everything which tells in their favour. 'Charity . . . rejoiceth not in iniquity, but rejoiceth in the truth.'° It is a solemn thing to write history. I feel it a solemn thing to write conjectural sketches of Scripture characters; filling up outlines as I fancy, but cannot be certain, may possibly have been the case; making one figure stand for this virtue and another for that vice, attributing motives and colouring conduct. Yet I hope my mistakes will be forgiven me, while I do most earnestly desire every one of my personages to be in truth superior to my sketch.

From TIME FLIES: A READING DIARY

January 2

1

A certain masterly translator has remarked that whatever may or may not constitute a good translation, it cannot consist in turning a good poem into a bad one.°

This suggestive remark opens to investigation a world-wide field. Thus, for instance, he (or she) cannot be an efficient Christian who exhibits the religion of love as unlovely.

Christians need a searching self-sifting on this point. They translate God's law into the universal tongue of all mankind: all men of all sorts can read them, and in some sort cannot but read them.

Scrupulous Christians need special self-sifting. They too often resemble translations of the letter in defiance of the spirit: their good poem has become unpoetical.

They run the risk of figuring as truthful offensively, conscientious unkindly, firm feebly, in the right ridiculously. Common sense has forsaken them: and what gift or grace can quite supply the lack of common sense?

Reverently I quote to my neighbour (and to *myself*) the grave reproof of St. James: 'My brethren, these things ought not so to be.'°

Stars, like Christians, utter their silent voice to all lands and their speechless words to the ends of the world. Christians are called to be like stars, luminous, steadfast, majestic, attractive.

January 3

2

Scrupulous persons, — a much tried and much trying sort of people, looked up to and looked down upon by their fellows.

Sometimes paralysed and sometimes fidgeted by conscientiousness, they are often in the way yet often not at hand.

The main pity is that they do not amend themselves. Next to this, it is a pity when they gratuitously attempt what under the circumstances they cannot perform.

Listen to an anecdote or even to a reminiscence from their lips, and you are liable to hear an exercise on possible contingencies: a witticism hangs fire, a heroic example is dwarfed by modifying suggestions. Eloquence stammers in their mouth, the thread even of logic is snapped.

Their aim is to be accurate; a worthy aim: but do they achieve accuracy? Such handling as blunts the pointed and flattens the lofty cannot boast of accuracy.

These remarks have, I avow, a direct bearing on my own case. I am desirous to quote here or there an illustrative story or a personal reminiscence: am I competent so to do? I may have misunderstood, I may never have understood, I may have forgotten, in some instances I cannot recall every detail.

Yet my story would point and clench my little essay.

So here once for all I beg my readers to accept such illustrations as no more than I give them for; true or false, accurate or inaccurate, as the case may be. One perhaps embellished if I have the wit to embellish it, another marred by my clumsiness.

All alike written down in the humble wish to help others by such means as I myself have found helpful.

January 15

'In the beginning God created the heaven and the earth.'
Both perfect, and no mention of hell.
No hell needed, while heaven and earth abode as God made them.
Hell is not a primary necessity, but a contingent necessity.
'Lo, this only have I found, that God hath made man upright; but they have sought out many inventions.'°
Satan's initial work is not on record for us.
Adam's initial work of production (so far as we are told) was sin, death, hell, for himself and his posterity.
Not that he made them in their first beginning: but he, as it were, re-made them for his own behoof.° Never had the flame kindled upon him or the smell of fire passed upon him, but for his own free will, choice, and deed.

January 16

Love understands the mystery, whereof°
We can but spell a surface history:°
Love knows, remembers: let us trust in Love:
Love understands the mystery.

Love weighs the event, the long pre-history,
Measures the depth beneath, the height above,
    The mystery, with the ante-mystery.

To love and to be grieved befits a dove
    Silently telling her bead-history:°
Trust all to Love, be patient and approve: 10
    Love understands the mystery.

February 8

1

A heaven of ceaseless music,—a monotonous heaven, a heaven of
ceaseless endless weariness, say some.

Yet surely this heaven of music (if for argument's sake we may so
define the Christian heaven of the Beatific Vision) is obviously and
characteristically otherwise.

For is music monotonous? On the contrary, a monotone is not music.

No single note however ravishing amounts to music: musical it may
be, but not music.

How is it to become an element of music? By forming part of
a sequence. Change, succession, are of the essence of music.

Therefore, when our Christian heaven is by condescension to man's
limited conceptions represented as a heaven of music, that very figure
stamps it as a heaven, not of monotony, but of variety.

For in music one sound leads unavoidably to a different sound,
one harmony paves the way to a diverse harmony.

A heaven of music seems rather a heaven of endless progression,
of inexhaustible variety, than a heaven of monotony.

February 9

2

If music, because opposed to monotony, typifies celestial ever fresh
delight; vocal music, as the highest form of so high an art, exhibits
special appositeness in illustration of heaven.

For the voice is inseparable from the person to whom it belongs. The
voice which charms one generation is inaccessible to the next. Words

cannot describe it, notes cannot register it; it remains as a tradition, it lingers only as a regret: or, if by marvellous modern appliances stored up and re-uttered, we listen not to any imitative sound, but to a reproduction of the original voice.

In St. John's vision we read of 'the harps of God': but the human voices worthy of such accompanying instruments are the actual voices of the redeemed who sing the new song.°

The song indeed is new: but those singing voices are the selfsame which spake and sang on earth, the same which age enfeebled and death silenced.

'And I look for the Resurrection of the Dead.'°

February 10

Perhaps one reason why music is made so prominent among the revelations vouchsafed us of heaven, is because it imperatively requires living agency for its production.

For I think that from this connection music produced by mere clockwork is fairly excluded: ingenious it may be, but inferior it cannot but be.

Music, then, demands the living voice for its utterance, or, at the least, the living breath or the living finger to awaken a lifeless instrument.

Written notes are not music until they find a voice.

Written words are words even while unuttered, for they convey through the eye an intellectual meaning. But musical notes express sound, and nought beside sound.

A silent note, then, is a silent sound: and what can a silent sound be?

The music of heaven, to become music, must have trumpeters and harpers as well as harps and trumpets, must have singers as well as songs.

'Glorious things are spoken of thee, O city of God. . . . As well the singers as the players on instruments shall be there.'°

February 11

I

I see that all things come to an end.°

No more! while sun and planets fly
    And wind and storm and seasons four,

And while we live and while we die,—
   No more.

Nevertheless old ocean's roar
And wide earth's multitudinous cry
   And echo's pent reverberant store°

Shall hush to silence bye and bye:—
   Ah, rosy world gone cold and hoar!
Man opes no more a mortal eye,   10
   No more.

February 12

2

But Thy commandment is exceeding broad.°

Once again to wake, nor wish to sleep;
   Once again to feel, nor feel a pain!—
Rouse thy soul to watch and pray and weep
   Once again.

Hope afresh, for hope shall not be vain:
Start afresh along the exceeding steep
   Road to glory, long and rough and plain.

Sow and reap: for while these moments creep,
   Time and earth and life are on the wane.
Now, in tears; to-morrow, laugh and reap   10
   Once again.

February 14

Feast of St. Valentine

Various saints of this name are commemorated today. One, a priest, was put to death for the faith under the second Emperor Claudius about the year 270.

With St. Valentine's Day stands popularly associated the interchange of 'Valentines': this custom having its origin, we are informed, in a pagan ceremony wisely exchanged for a Christian observance.

And thus our social habit, even if degenerate, assumes a certain dignity: we connect it not merely with mirth and love, but with sanctity and suffering. The love exhibits a double aspect and accords, or should accord, with heaven as well as with earth.

Never is interchange of affection more appropriate than on a holy day: only let the sentiment be serious, modest, honourable, ready for self-sacrifice. 'Fair maid of February' is a name for the snowdrop, and seems to wed love to innocence. Valentines as pure as snowdrops will not disgrace the Day even of a martyr who has washed his 'robes, and made them white in the Blood of the Lamb'.°

February 15

Doeth well, . . . doeth better.   1 COR. vii. 38°

My love whose heart is tender said to me,
  'A moon lacks light except her sun befriend her.
Let us keep tryst in heaven, dear Friend,' said she,
  My love whose heart is tender.

From such a loftiness no words could bend her;
Yet still she spoke of 'us,' and spoke as 'we,'
  Her hope substantial while my hope grew slender.

Now keeps she tryst beyond earth's utmost sea,
  Wholly at rest tho' storms should toss and rend her;
And still she keeps my heart and keeps its key,   10
  My love whose heart is tender.

February 20

A great many years ago, I do not recall how many, I visited a large waxwork exhibition° brilliant with costumes, complexions, and historical effigies.

And entering that gorgeous assembly I literally felt shy!

The real people present did not abash me: it was the distinguished waxen crowd which put me out of countenance.

Now looking back I laugh at my own absurdity. Why then recount it? Because it seems to furnish a parable of many passages in many lives.

Things seen are as that waxwork, things unseen as those real people. Yet over and over again we are influenced and constrained by the hollow momentary world we behold in presence, while utterly obtuse as regards the substantial eternal world no less present around us though disregarded.

Will we not rise above an awe of waxwork?

February 27

A handy Mole who plied no shovel°
To excavate his vaulted hovel,
While hard at work met in mid-furrow
An Earthworm boring out his burrow.
Our Mole had dined and must grow thinner
Before he gulped a second dinner,
And on no other terms cared he
To meet a worm of low degree.
The Mole turned on his blindest eye
Passing that base mechanic by;   10
The Worm entrenched in actual blindness
Ignored or kindness or unkindness;°
Each wrought his own exclusive tunnel
To reach his own exclusive funnel.

A plough its flawless track pursuing
Involved them in one common ruin.
Where now the mine and countermine,°
The dined-on and the one to dine?
The impartial ploughshare of extinction
Annulled them all without distinction.   20

February 28

The difference between heaven and human attempts at describing
heaven may, I think, be illustrated by the difference between pure
colour and pigments or dyes.

Such colour as is cast by a prism is absolutely pure, intangible,
incapable (it would appear) of analysis. It is not so much as a film: it is,
so to say, a mode, a condition.

Far otherwise is it with dyes and pigments. These exhibit colour,
while their substance is by no means colour, but is merely that field
upon which light renders visible one or other of its component tints.
Animal, vegetable, or mineral, the substance may be; oily, gummy,
watery, simple, compound; however dense or however translucent,
equally an appreciable body.

Now just as prismatic hues take no hold of aught on which they fall,
but like the pure light which is their parent are shifting, evanescent,
intangible; while dyes seize on what they come in contact with and

affect it permanently: so any literal revelation of heaven would appear to be over spiritual for us; we need something grosser, something more familiar and more within the range of our experience.

The heavenly symbol attracts: what will be the heavenly reality?

It was blessed to know Christ on earth: what will it be to know Him not as mortal eye hath seen, or mortal ear heard, or mortal heart conceived?

March 4

My first vivid experience of death (if so I may term it) occurred in early childhood in the grounds of a cottage.°

This little cottage was my familiar haunt: its grounds were my inexhaustible delight. They then seemed to me spacious, though now I know them to have been narrow and commonplace.

So in these grounds, perhaps in the orchard, I lighted upon a dead mouse. The dead mouse moved my sympathy: I took him up, buried him comfortably in a mossy bed, and bore the spot in mind.

It may have been a day or two afterwards that I returned, removed the moss coverlet, and looked . . . a black insect emerged. I fled in horror, and for long years ensuing I never mentioned this ghastly adventure to anyone.

Now looking back at the incident I see that neither impulse was unreasonable, although the sympathy and the horror were alike childish.

Only now contemplating death from a wider and wiser view-point, I would fain reverse the order of those feelings: dwelling less and less on the mere physical disgust, while more and more on the rest and safety; on the perfect peace of death, please God.

March 5

Where shall I find a white rose blowing?—°
    Out in the garden where all sweets be.—
But out in my garden the snow was snowing
    And never a white rose opened for me.
Nought but snow and a wind were blowing
    And snowing.

Where shall I find a blush rose blushing? —
　　On the garden wall or the garden bed. —
But out in my garden the rain was rushing
　　And never a blush rose raised its head.   10
Nothing glowing, flushing or blushing;
Rain rushing.

Where shall I find a red rose budding? —
　　Out in the garden where all things grow. —
But out in my garden a flood was flooding
　　And never a red rose began to blow.
Out in a flooding what should be budding?
All flooding!

Now is winter and now is sorrow,
　　No roses but only thorns to-day: 20
Thorns will put on roses to-morrow,
　　Winter and sorrow scudding away.
No more winter and no more sorrow
To-morrow.

March 18

FEAST OF ST. EDWARD, King of the West Saxons. Born about the
year 962; murdered, 978 or 979.

We are happy in that the Anglican Calendar does not appear to define
this good young monarch as a martyr, though elsewhere he has been
styled such. By a popular account he fell a victim to the jealousy of his
stepmother Elfrida, who, wishing her own son to mount the throne,
opened a way by causing Edward the elder half-brother to be stabbed.

Great is our privilege as members of the English Church, in that we
are not commanded, or invited, or in any way encouraged to assert
what contradicts history, or to override facts by pious beliefs, or in any
form to hold 'the thing that is not.'

When we reflect on points susceptible of improvement in our
beloved Mother Church, it is well to betake ourselves to prayer; well
also to give thanks for her grace of sincerity, and to sue out,° each one
of us for himself, his own individual share of so fundamental a grace.

If we are not truthful one by one, we shall never add up as a truthful
community.

April 1

A CASTLE-BUILDER'S WORLD

The line of confusion, and the stones
of emptiness. ISAIAH xxxiv.11°

Unripe harvest there hath none to reap it
   From the misty, gusty place;
Unripe vineyard there hath none to keep it
   In unprofitable space.
Living men and women are not found there,
   Only masks in flocks and shoals;
Flesh-and-bloodless hazy masks surround there
   Ever wavering orbs and poles;
Flesh-and-bloodless vapid masks abound there,
   Shades of bodies without souls.   10

April 2

I have an impression (for I will not relate my adventure quite positively) that in my youth, being at that time too ignorant to appreciate such a rarity, in one of my country walks I found what I can only call a four-leafed trefoil.°

Perhaps I plucked and so destroyed it: I certainly left it, for most certainly I have it not.

Not that I thought nothing of it: I thought it curious, pointed it out, I daresay, to my companion, and left it.

Now I would give something to recover that wonder: *then*, when I might have had it for the carrying, I left it.

Once missed, one may peer about in vain all the rest of one's days for a second four-leafed trefoil.

No one expects to find whole fields of such: even one, for once, is an extra allowance.

Life has, so to say, its four-leafed trefoils for a favoured few: and how many of us overlook once and finally our rare chance!

Well, whether literally or figuratively, but one thing then remains for us to do: to walk humbly and thankfully among this world's whole fields of three-leafed trefoil.

April 13

A cold wind stirs the blackthorn°
    To burgeon and to blow,
Besprinkling half-green hedges
    With vegetable snow.°

Through coldness and through keenness,
    Dear hearts, take comfort so:
Somewhere or other doubtless,
    These make the blackthorn blow.

April 20

    Piteous my rhyme is,
What while I muse of love and pain,°
Of love misspent, of love in vain,
Of love that is not loved again:
    And is this all then?
    As long as time is
Love loveth. Time is but a span,
The dalliance space of dying man:
And is this all immortals can?
    The gain were small then.   10

    Love loves for ever,
And finds a sort of joy in pain,
And gives with nought to take again,
And loves too well to end in vain:
    Is the gain small then?
    Love laughs at 'never,'
Outlives our life, exceeds the span
Appointed to mere mortal man:
That which love is and does and can,
    Is all in all then.   20

April 28

I

A friend° once vividly described to me how in a country walk he had remarked cobwebs shaped more or less like funnels or tunnels, one end open to the road, while deep down at the other end lay in wait the spider.

I walked a little about the same country, and failed to observe the spider. Fortunately for me I was not a fly.

The spider was on the alert in his sphere, my friend was on the alert in his higher sphere; I alone, it would seem, was not on the alert in either sphere.

If we turn all this into a parable, and magnify the spider to human or superhuman scale, what must become of the wayfarer who strolls along not on the alert in any sphere?

April 29

2

That funnel web seems to me an apt figure of the world.

It exhibits beauty, ingenuity, intricacy. Imagine it in the early morning jewelled with dewdrops, and each of these at sunny moments a spark of light or a section of rainbow. Woven, too, as no man could weave it, fine and flexible, frail and tenacious.

Yet are its beauties of brilliancy and colour no real part of it. The dew evaporates, the tints and sparkle vanish, the tenacity remains, and at the bottom of all lurks a spider.

Meanwhile a fly has been tempted in through the wide mouth of easy access: a fly who returns no more. What becomes of the fly takes place (happily) out of sight: the less seen of that fly the better.

Or suppose that a pitiful passer by stops and stoops to rescue the fly in mid funnel before the spider clutches it. Out it comes alive indeed, but to what a life!

If its wings are not left behind, they are swathed around it as by a mummy cloth; and if its legs remain, so also are they.

Fine and flexible, frail and tenacious, the web clings to the fly, although the fly clings not willingly to the web.

At the worst, it must lie immovable and starve. At the best, it must live an uncouth, hampered, degraded life, at least for a time.

And this creature that can scarcely, or that cannot crawl, is a creature endowed with wings!

May 16

If love is not worth loving, then life is not worth living,
   Nor aught is worth remembering but well forgot,

For store is not worth storing and gifts are not worth giving,
　　If love is not;

And idly cold is death-cold, and life-heat idly hot,
And vain is any offering and vainer our receiving,
　　And vanity of vanities is all our lot.

Better than life's heaving heart is death's heart unheaving,
　　Better than the opening leaves are the leaves that rot,
For there is nothing left worth achieving or retrieving,　　10
　　If love is not.

May 20

That Song of Songs which is Solomon's,
　　Sinks and rises, and loves and longs,
Through temperate zones and torrid zones,
　　That Song of Songs.

Fair its floating moon with her prongs:
Love is laid for its paving stones:
　　Right it sings without thought of wrongs.

Doves it hath with music of moans,
　　Birds in throngs and damsels in throngs,
High tones and mysterious undertones,　　10
　　That Song of Songs.

May 21

'The half was not told me,' said Sheba's Queen,°
　　Weighing that wealth of wisdom and of gold:
'Thy fame falls short of this that I have seen:
　　The half was not told.

'Happy thy servants who stand to behold,
Stand to drink in thy gracious speech and mien;
　　Happy, thrice happy, the flock of thy fold.

'As the darkened moon, while a shadow between
　　Her face and her kindling sun is rolled,
I depart; but my heart keeps memory green:　　10
　　The half was not told.'

May 28

They lie at rest, our blessed dead:°
The dews drop cool above their head,
They knew not when fleet summer fled.

Together all, yet each alone:
Each laid at rest beneath his own
Smooth turf or white allotted stone.

When shall our slumber sink so deep,
And eyes that wept and eyes that weep
Weep not in the sufficient sleep?

God be with you, our great and small,   10
Our loves, our best-beloved of all,
Our own beyond the salt sea wall.

June 3

I

'The bottomless pit'° mentioned several times in the Apocalypse is
not (I believe) named in any other Book of Holy Scripture. To us
Christians it is revealed 'for our admonition, upon whom the ends of
the world are come.'°

Whatever other idea we may form of the bottomless pit, whatever
other feature we may think to detect within its undefined horror,
two points stand out unmistakably: as a *pit* it is a place into which to
fall; as *bottomless*, it appears to be one within which to fall lower and
lower for ever and ever.

Herein lies one distinct thought for ourselves: an awful thought.
A deep fall, indefinitely deep, so long as any bottom at any depth
underlies the lapser, must at length be arrested and must stop.
However mangled or shattered, and on whatever floor landed, the
wretch cannot cease there to lie: self-destroyed, indeed, yet accessible
to Mercy and Help if these deign to look so low, and lift with recover-
ing hands, and carry home on shoulders rejoicing.

But in the *bottomless* pit I see a symbol of that eternal antagonism
and recession by which created free will seems able to defy and baffle
even the Almighty Will of the Creator. At a standstill anywhere,
though on the extreme boundary of time or space, the sinner might be
overtaken by the pursuing Love of God: but once passing beyond

those limits, eternity sets in; the everlasting attitude appears taken up, the everlasting recoil commenced.

Beyond the grave no promise is held out to us of shipwreck, great fish, dry land, to turn us back towards the Presence of God from our self-chosen Tarshish.°

June 4

2

I have read how matter can be exploded, or at the least can be conceived of as exploded, from the sun, with such tremendous force as to carry it beyond the radius of solar attraction.

That attraction which unifies and sways a whole harmony of dependent planets, recalls not one atom which has passed beyond the pale.

> O Christ my God Who seest the unseen,
>   O Christ my God Who knowest the unknown,
>   Thy mighty Blood was poured forth to atone
> For every sin that can be or hath been.
>
> O Thou Who seest what I cannot see,
>   Thou Who didst love us all so long ago,
>   O Thou Who knowest what I must not know,
> Remember all my hope, remember me.

June 6

> Heartsease I found, where Love-lies-bleeding°
>   Empurpled all the ground:°
> Whatever flowers I missed unheeding,
>   Heartsease I found.
>
>   Yet still my garden mound
> Stood sore in need of watering, weeding,
>   And binding things unbound.°
>
> Ah, when shades fell to light succeeding,
>   I scarcely dared look round:
> 'Love-lies-bleeding' was all my pleading,
>   Heartsease I found.

10

June 7

I

Who could have foreseen that Manna, type of 'the true Bread from heaven,' would have been withheld° on the Sabbath Day, which day prefigures that final rest which remaineth for the people of God?

Nay, rather: for that one day the Manna assumed permanence.

The Israelites no longer gathered, because they possessed it. On other days they measured it; on that holyday of rest they no longer measured, but simply enjoyed it.

Even so throughout the eternal Sabbath there will be no need of Sacraments, those outward and visible signs of inward and spiritual grace given unto us;° because the elect will be once and for ever one with Christ.

Moreover, since each Jewish Sabbath prefigured that supreme Sabbath Day which was truly an high day, and which we Christians observe as Easter Even; therefore it doubly behoved that no Manna should fall thereon, for Christ Himself hath said: 'The days will come, when the Bridegroom shall be taken away from them, and then shall they fast in those days.'°

June 8

2

Nevertheless, although the Manna on six successive days fell within the reach of all, those only who had gathered and stored it on the sixth day of toil, possessed it on the final day of rest.

On that seventh day, any who had it not already laid up could not find it, though they might seek it carefully with tears.

Some who thus sought and found it not, were reproved; and the fault was laid to their own charge.

We Christians in the Sacrament of Christ's Most Blessed Body and Blood, enjoy access to the True Bread from heaven; and to us our loving Lord has said: 'This do in remembrance of Me.'° If in our present day of discipline we neglect thus to lay up Christ in our hearts, and so despise our birthright; on what plea can we lay claim to our blessing, even indissoluble union with Christ, in the day of blessing?

June 9

Roses on a brier,
   Pearls from out the bitter sea,
Such is earth's desire
   However pure it be.

Neither bud nor brier,
   Neither pearl nor brine for me:
Be stilled, my long desire;
   There shall be no more sea.°

Be stilled, my passionate heart;
   Old earth shall end, new earth shall be;   10
Be still, and earn thy part
   Where shall be no more sea.

June 26

If ever I deciphered a 'Parable of Nature' surely I did so one summer night at Meads.°

The gas was alight in my little room with its paperless bare wall.

On that wall appeared a spider,° himself dark and defined, his shadow no less dark and scarcely if at all less defined.

They jerked, zigzagged, advanced, retreated, he and his shadow posturing in ungainly indissoluble harmony. He seemed exasperated, fascinated, desperately endeavouring and utterly helpless.

What could it all mean? One meaning and one only suggested itself. That spider saw without recognising his black double, and was mad to disengage himself from the horrible pursuing inalienable presence.

I stood watching him awhile. (Presumably when I turned off the gas he composed himself.)

To me this self-haunted spider appears a figure of each obstinate impenitent sinner, who having outlived enjoyment remains isolated irretrievably with his own horrible loathsome self.

And if thus in time, how throughout eternity?

July 4

FEAST OF THE TRANSLATION OF ST. MARTIN, BISHOP OF TOURS

As a general proposition, it surely is most pious and most reverential to leave the dead at rest in their graves.

Often, moreover, as in the case of this St. Martin, holy men have loved and observed an ascetic retirement which seems doubly indisposed towards posthumous translation.

Had this well-meant rite been more charily practised, such reticence might at least in some measure have checked that scandalous multiplicity of relics, which has assigned duplicate heads and an overplus of members to the same Saint in the face of abashed Christendom.

Not but what some exhumations for honourable enshrinement may have been praiseworthy: amongst which let us hope this of St. Martin ranks. Indeed, as a case more or less in point and 'written for our learning,' we read in Genesis how 'Joseph took an oath of the children of Israel, saying, God will surely visit you, and ye shall carry up my bones from hence:' which oath being observed, the Patriarch's remains were transported out of Egypt into the Holy Land of Promise. But as bearing on ourselves and on our own practice, surely all Christendom *is* 'holy ground.'

Now if I have betrayed prejudice, I beg my reader's pardon. Meanwhile I well remember how one no longer present with us,° but to whom I cease not to look up, shrank from entering the Mummy Room at the British Museum under a vivid realisation of how the general resurrection might occur even as one stood among those solemn corpses turned into a sight for sightseers.

And at that great and awful day, what will be thought of supposititious heads and members?

July 6

Two frogs I met in early childhood have lingered in my memory: I frightened one frog, and the other frog frightened me.

The frightened frog evinced fear by placing its two hands on its head: at least, I have since understood that a frog assumes this attitude when in danger, and my frog assumed it.

The alarming frog startled me, 'gave me quite a turn,' as people say, by jumping when I did not know it was near me.

My fright was altogether without justifying cause. Not so the first frog's: for presumably my warm finger made the cool creature uncomfortable. Besides, how could it tell what was coming next? although in truth I meant it no harm.

I wish that as regards their intention as much could nowadays be certified for some of the wisest of this world, and that every scared frog were like my scared self, unreasonable.

But seeing that matters are as they are—because frogs and such like cannot in reason frighten us now,—is it quite certain that no day will ever come when even the smallest, weakest, most grotesque, *wronged* creature will not in some fashion rise up in the Judgment with us to condemn us, and so frighten us effectually once for all?°

July 7

Contemptuous of his home beyond°
The village and the village pond,
A large-souled Frog who spurned each byeway,
Hopped along the imperial highway.°

Nor grunting pig nor barking dog
Could disconcert so great a frog.
The morning dew was lingering yet
His sides to cool, his tongue to wet;
The night dew when the night should come
A travelled frog would send him home.   10

Not so, alas! the wayside grass
Sees him no more:—not so, alas!
A broadwheeled waggon unawares
Ran him down, his joys, his cares.
From dying choke one feeble croak
The Frog's perpetual silence broke:
'Ye buoyant Frogs, ye great and small,
Even I am mortal after all.
My road to Fame turns out a wry way:
I perish on this hideous highway,—   20
Oh for my old familiar byeway!'

The choking Frog sobbed and was gone:
The waggoner strode whistling on.

Unconscious of the carnage done,
Whistling that waggoner strode on,
Whistling (it may have happened so)
'A Froggy would a-wooing go:'°
A hypothetic frog trolled he
Obtuse to a reality.

O rich and poor, O great and small,   30
Such oversights beset us all:
The mangled frog abides incog,°
The uninteresting actual frog;
The hypothetic frog alone
Is the one frog we dwell upon.

July 13

I

Let none despair of any grace, however remote from their original lot.

I once looked over a fine collection° of old Venetian glass vessels.

By no means, I suppose, were any two of these precisely similar, not a mould from without but a breath or a blast from within having shaped them.

Some perhaps might be described as quaint, others certainly as elegant, many, if not all, as beautiful.

But the point of beauty which astonished me was that one or more of the specimens had caught, as it were, a momentary grace such as charms us in many flowers. Such a contour, a curve, an attitude if I may so call it, did here or there one of these old glasses exhibit, as a petrified blossom bell might retain, or as flexibility itself or motion might show forth if these could be embodied and arrested.

Inert glass moulded from within caught the semblance of such an alien grace.

Now God's grace moulds us from within.

July 14

2

In the same collection of glass, but not among the Venetian specimens, stood two antique Greek vases, mended, I believe, though to all intents flawless, portly and oxydised.

What words can describe their beauty? Placed as they were aloft in my friend's drawing-room, one might stand for sunrise, the other for moonrise.

Sunrise was brilliant as the most gorgeous pheasant; *moonrise* exquisite as the most harmonious pigeon. But, as I said before, words do not describe them: I cannot exaggerate, I can only misrepresent their appearance.

Well, with these unrivalled vases vivid in my memory, I one day rescued from an English roadside ditch° a broken bottle: and it was also oxydised! So, at least, I conclude: for in a minor key it too displayed a variety of iridescent tints, a sort of dull rainbow.

Now my treasure-trove was nothing to those others: yet could not their excess of beauty annul its private modicum of beauty.

There are, I presume, many more English ditches than Greek Islands, many more modern broken bottles than antique lustrous vases. If it is well for the few to rejoice in sunrise and moonrise, it is no less well for the many to be thankful for dim rainbows.

July 17

I

To this hour I remember a certain wild strawberry growing on a hedgerow bank, watched day by day while it ripened by a little girl° and by my yet younger self.

My elder instructed me not to pluck it prematurely, and I complied.

I do not know which of us was to have had it at last, or whether we were to have halved it. As it was we watched, and as it turned out we watched in vain: for a snail, or some such marauder, must have forestalled us at a happy moment. One fatal day we found it half-eaten, and good for nothing.

Thus then we had watched in vain: or was it altogether in vain? On a very lowly level we had obeyed a counsel of prudence, and had practised self-restraint.

And shall the baulked watches of after-life prove in vain? 'Let patience have her perfect work.'°

July 18

2

'Half-eaten and good for nothing,' said I of the strawberry. I need not have expressed myself with such sweeping contempt.

Some snail may have been glad to finish up that wreck. Some children might not have disdained the final bite.

Yet to confine my reflections to snails and their peers: why should not they have a share in strawberries?

Man is very apt to contemplate himself out of all proportion to his surroundings: true, he is 'much better than they,' yet have they also their assigned province and their guaranteed dues.

Fruits for man, green herb for other living creatures, including creepers on the earth, is the decree in Genesis. Thus for the Garden of Eden: and why not thus, as regards the spirit of the decree, here and now?

But man, alas! finds it convenient here to snap off a right and there to chip away a due. Greed grudges their morsel to hedgerow birds, and idleness robs the provident hare of his winter haystack, and science pares away at the living creature bodily, 'And what will ye do in the end thereof?'°

August 4

When I was in north Italy, a region rich in sunshine, heat, beauty, it struck me that after all our English wild scarlet poppies excelled the Italian poppies in gorgeous colour.

I should have expected the direct contrary; the more sunshine, surely the more glow and redness: yet it appeared otherwise when I came to look.

Perhaps sheer stress of sunshine tended to bleach as well as to dye those poppies.

And if so, they aptly symbolize those 'always rejoicing'° Christians who are, notwithstanding, so sorrowful during the present distress.

For on earth souls need bleaching as well as developing and embellishing. Only in heaven will the sun cease to smite on the just made perfect, and the vehement east wind cease to beat on them.

August 5

Of each sad word, which is more sorrowful,
    'Sorrow' or 'Disappointment?' I have heard
Subtle inflections baffling subtlest rule,
    Of each sad word.

Sorrow can mourn: and lo! a mourning bird
  Sings sweetly to sweet echoes of its dule,°
    While silent disappointment broods unstirred.

Yet both nurse hope, where Penitence keeps school
  Who makes fools wise and saints of them that erred:
Wise men shape stepping-stone, or curb, or tool,   10
    Of each sad word.

October 14

A sensual Christian resembles a sea anemone.

  In the nobler element, air, it exists as a sluggish unbeautiful excrescence.

  In the lower element, water, it grows, blows and thrives.

  The food it assimilates is derived not from the height, but from the depth.

  It possesses neither eyes nor ears, but a multitude of feelers.

  It squats on a tenacious base, gulps all acquisitions into a capacious chasm, and harmonises with the weeds it dwells amongst.

  But what will become of it in a world where there shall be no more sea?

December 17

Earth grown old yet still so green,
  Deep beneath her crust of cold
Nurses fire unfelt, unseen,—
  Earth grown old.

We who live are quickly told:°
Millions more lie hid between
  Inner swathings of her fold.°

When will fire break up her screen?
  When will life burst through her mould?
Earth, earth, earth, thy cold is keen,   10
  Earth grown old.

December 29

Love came down at Christmas,
  Love all lovely, Love Divine,

Love was born at Christmas,
    Star and Angels gave the sign.

Worship we the Godhead,
    Love Incarnate, Love Divine,
Worship we our Jesus,—
    But wherewith for sacred sign?

Love shall be our token,
    Love be yours and love be mine,   10
Love to God and all men,
    Love the universal sign.

Thursday in Holy Week

And the Vine said, ... Should I leave my wine, which cheereth God
and man, and go to be promoted over the trees?   JUDGES ix. 13°

The great Vine left its glory to reign as Forest King:—
'Nay,' quoth the lofty forest trees, 'We will not have this thing;
We will not have this supple one enring us with its ring;
Lo, from immemorial time our might towers shadowing;
Not we were born to curve and droop, not we to climb
    and cling;
We buffet back the buffeting wind, tough to its buffeting.°
We screen great beasts, the wild-fowl build in our heads
    and sing,
Every bird of every feather from off our tops takes wing:
I a king, and thou a king, and what king shall be our king?'

Nevertheless the great Vine stooped to be the Forest King,
While the forest swayed and murmured like seas that are
    tempesting:
Stooped and drooped with thousand tendrils in thirsty
    languishing;
Bowed to earth and lay on earth, for earth's replenishing;
Put off sweetness, tasted bitterness, endured time's
    fashioning;°
Put off life and put on death: and lo! it was all to bring
All its fellows down to a death which hath lost the sting,
All its fellows up to a life in endless triumphing,—
I a king, and thou a king, and this King to be our king.

Rogation Tuesday

On this day we are urged to intercede for foreign missions.

Following the sequence of St. Luke's narrative,° the second phase of our Divine Master's threefold temptation sets before us (I humbly think) one snare which in the very nature of such work must more or less beset missionary enterprises, and which if yielded to may render them even worse than useless.

For if, as the proverb° asserts, we cannot touch pitch and be clean, it must be perilously difficult to set up one's tent amid Satan's own surroundings and continue in no way the worse for that neighbourhood.

The world and the flesh flaunt themselves in very uncompromising forms in the devil's own territory. And all the power and the glory of them set in array before a man whose work forces him to face and sift them day and night, may well make such an one tremble for himself and betake himself to his knees.

And if he for himself, so we for him: not merely of charity, but strictly also of justice.

For he is our proxy, fulfilling that function which being incumbent upon the Church as a body, many of us cannot, and most of us do not even attempt. It was no hardship, but a privilege, for Aaron and Hur° to uphold the champion hands of Moses.

And if he and we with one voice beseech for him and his mission God's grace and benediction, then doubtless we may look for such an answer to prayer, as will enable him in peace and safety to go upon the lion and adder, treading the young lion and the dragon under foot.°

He will stand steadfast upon his watchtower hearkening for God's word to him.

He will be raised up to sit even in heavenly places in Christ Jesus, and from that 'exceeding high mountain'° will estimate and despise the world, and the things of the world.

From THE FACE OF THE DEEP: A DEVOTIONAL
COMMENTARY ON THE APOCALYPSE

Prefatory Note

If thou canst dive,° bring up pearls. If thou canst not dive, collect amber. Though I fail to identify Paradisiacal 'bdellium,' I still may hope to search out beauties of the 'onyx stone'.°

A dear saint°—I speak under correction of the Judgment of the Great Day, yet think not then to have my word corrected—this dear person once pointed out to me Patience as our lesson in the Book of Revelations.

Following the clue thus afforded me, I seek and hope to find Patience in this Book of awful import. Patience, at the least: and along with that grace whatever treasures beside God may vouchsafe me. Bearing meanwhile in mind how 'to him that knoweth to do good, and doeth it not, to him it is sin.'°

Now if any deign to seek Patience in my company, I pray them to remember that One high above me in the Kingdom of Heaven heads our pilgrim caravan.

O, ye who love to-day,
Turn away
From Patience with her silver ray:
For Patience shows a twilight face,
Like a half-lighted moon
When daylight dies apace.

But ye who love to-morrow,
Beg or borrow
To-day some bitterness of sorrow:
For Patience shows a lustrous face
In depth of night her noon;
Then to her sun gives place.

Chapter V

6. **And I beheld, and lo, in the midst of the Throne and of the four beasts, and in the midst of the elders, stood a Lamb as it had been slain, having seven horns and seven eyes, which are the seven Spirits of God sent forth into all the earth.**

If the preceding chapter (IV) unfolds a vision of the Creator surrounded and worshipped by His creation, this present chapter appears more particularly to set before us in vision the Redeemer, always well pleasing to God His Father, and to Whom is given all power in Heaven and in earth.

Doubtless a thread of perfect sequence runs throughout Divine Revelation, binding it into one sacred and flawless whole. But not so do feeble eyes discern it. I can but study piece by piece, word by word, unworthy even to behold the little I seem to observe.

Much of this awful Apocalypse opens to my apprehension rather a series of aspects than any one defined and certified object. It summons me to watch and pray and give thanks; it urges me to climb heavenward. Its thread doubtless consists unbroken: but my clue is at the best woven of broken lights and shadows, here a little and there a little. As when years ago I abode some while within sight of a massive sea rock, I used to see it put on different appearances: it seemed to float baseless in air, its summit vanished in cloud, it displayed upon its surface varied markings, it passed from view altogether in a mist, it fronted me distinct and solid far into the luminous northern summer night, still appearing many and various while all the time I knew it to be one and the same,—so now this Apocalypse I know to be one congruous, harmonious whole, yet can I read it only as it were in disjointed portions, some to myself inexplicable, some not unmistakably defined; all nevertheless, please God, profitable to me for doctrine, for reproof, for correction, for instruction in righteousness.

Chapter VIII

1. **And when He had opened the seventh seal, there was silence in heaven about the space of half an hour.**

There seems to be a sense in which heaven waits on earth; in which (if I dare say so) God waits on man. Thus heaven now keeps silence as a prelude to earthly events, portents, vicissitudes.

Yet need not this celestial silence convey to us (I conjecture) any notion of interruption in the day and night harmony of worship before the Throne, any more than time interrupts eternity. For because we dare not think of God Who 'inhabiteth eternity'° as changing to a habitation of time, we thence perceive that time and eternity co-exist, are simultaneous: if, that is, they be not rather different aspects of one and the same continuity.

If from the songs of heaven we learn to sing and make melody to the Lord with both voice and understanding, equally from the silence of heaven we may learn somewhat.

Whilst heaven kept silence it appears it may have been looking or preparing to look earthwards. And of old David declared: 'I will keep my mouth with a bridle, while the wicked is before me. I was dumb with silence, I held my peace, even from good.'° Thus from Angels above and from a saint below, I may study that meekness of righteous indignation, that discretion of holy zeal, which brings not railing accusations nor risks doing harm even by good words.

Silence seems unnatural, incongruous, in heaven. On this occasion and remotely we may surmise it to be a result of the Fall, for when earth first saw the light in panoply of beauty the morning stars sang together and all the sons of God shouted for joy: sinless earth, for sinless it then seems to have been whether or not inhabited, called forth instead of silencing an outburst of celestial music.

I think one may view this 'silence' as a figure of suspense. Reversing which proposition, I perceive that a Christian's suspense ought to present a figure of that silence.

And if so, suspense should sustain my heart in heavenly peace even whilst fluttering over some spot of earth; and should become my method of worship, when other modes fail me; and should be adopted by my free will, whenever by God's Will it befalls me; and should not hinder heaven from appearing heaven to me, or divorce me from fellowship with angels, or make me speak unadvisedly with my lips. Faithful, hopeful, loving suspense would be rich in evidence of things not seen and not heard; and would neither lag nor hurry, but would contentedly maintain silence during its imposed 'half-hour.' A shorter time? no, on pain of rashness: a longer time? no, on pain of sullenness.

This silence followed and waited upon an act of our Lord: 'when He had opened the seventh seal.'—'Unto Thee lift I up mine eyes, O Thou that dwellest in the heavens. Behold, as the eyes of servants look unto the hand of their masters, and as the eyes of a maiden unto the hand of her mistress; so our eyes wait upon the Lord our God, until that He have mercy upon us.'°

'About the space of half an hour.'—Not finally, not for long. 'Our God shall come, and shall not keep silence. . . . He shall call to the heavens from above, and to the earth, that He may judge His people. . . . . And the heavens shall declare His righteousness.'°

> The half moon shows a face of plaintive sweetness
>   Ready and poised to wax or wane;
> A fire of pale desire in incompleteness,
>   Tending to pleasure or to pain:—
> Lo, while we gaze she rolleth on in fleetness
>   To perfect loss or perfect gain.
>
> Half bitterness we know, we know half sweetness;
>   This world is all on wax, on wane:
> When shall completeness round time's incompleteness
>   Fulfilling joy, fulfilling pain?—

10

Lo, while we ask, life rolleth on in fleetness
To finished loss or finished gain.

Chapter XII

1. And there appeared a great wonder in heaven; a woman
clothed with the sun, and the moon under her feet, and
upon her head a crown of twelve stars:

The Preacher, the son of David, King in Jerusalem, has left on record:
'I know that, whatsoever God doeth, it shall be for ever: nothing can be
put to it, nor anything taken from it; and God doeth it, that men should
fear before Him. That which hath been is now; and that which is to be
hath already been; and God requireth that which is past.'° Thus the
past which we know, presages the future which we know not.

And Greater than that King and Wiser than that Preacher, our Lord
Himself said to His disciples: 'Have ye understood all these things?
They say unto Him, Yea, Lord. Then said He unto them, Therefore
every scribe which is instructed unto the kingdom of heaven is like unto
a man that is an householder, which bringeth forth out of his treasure
things new and old.'° Now as every Christian 'is instructed unto the
kingdom of heaven,' he cannot be destitute of a treasure whence to
bring forth somewhat; new it may be, old it cannot but be.

Of this Apocalypse the occult unfulfilled signification will be new;
the letter is old. Old, not merely because these eighteen hundred years
it has warned us to flee from the wrath to come; but also because each
figure appeals to our experience, even when it stands for some object
unprecedented or surpassing.

A rose might preach beauty and a lily purity to a receptive mind,
although the ear had not yet heard tell of the Rose of Sharon and Lily
of the Valleys.°

'A woman clothed with the sun, and the moon under her feet, and
upon her head a crown of twelve stars.' —Whatever else may here be
hidden, there stands revealed that 'great wonder,' weakness made
strong and shame swallowed up in celestial glory. For thus the figure
is set before our eyes. Through Eve's lapse, weakness and shame
devolved on woman as her characteristics, in a manner special to herself
and unlike the corresponding heritage of man.

And as instinctively we personify the sun and moon as *he* and *she*,
I trust there is no harm in my considering that her sun-clothing

indicates how in that heaven where St. John in vision beheld her, she will be made equal with men and angels; arrayed in all human virtues, and decked with all communicable Divine graces: whilst the moon under her feet portends that her sometime infirmity of purpose and changeableness of mood have, by preventing,° assisting, final grace, become immutable; she has done all and stands; from the lowest place she has gone up higher. As love of his Lord enabled St. Peter to tread the sea, so love of the same Lord sets weak woman immovable on the waves of this troublesome world,° triumphantly erect, despite her own frailty, made not 'like unto a wheel,'° amid all the changes and chances of this mortal life.

Eve's temptation and fall suggest the suitableness and safety of much (though by no means of all) ignorance, and the wholesomeness of studying what is open without prying into what is secret. We have no reason to doubt that the forbidden fruit was genuinely 'pleasant to the eyes':° as such she might innocently have gazed upon it with delight, and for that delight might profitably have returned thanks to the Author and Giver of all good. Not till she became wise in her own conceit, disregarding the plain obvious meaning of words, and theorizing on her own responsibility as to physical and intellectual results, did she bring sin and death into the world. The Tree of the Knowledge of Good and Evil was as it were a standing prophet ever reiterating the contingent sentence, Thou shalt surely die. This sentence, plain and unmistakable, she connived at explaining away, and being deceived, was undone.

Eve exhibits one extreme of feminine character, the Blessed Virgin the opposite extreme. Eve parleyed with a devil: holy Mary 'was troubled'° at the salutation of an Angel. Eve sought knowledge: Mary instruction. Eve aimed at self-indulgence: Mary at self-oblation. Eve, by disbelief and disobedience, brought sin to the birth: Mary, by faith and submission, Righteousness.

And yet, even as at the foot of the Cross, St. Mary Magdalene, out of whom went seven devils, stood beside the 'lily among thorns,'° the Mother of sorrows: so (I humbly hope and trust) amongst all saints of all time will stand before the Throne, Eve the beloved first Mother of us all. Who that has loved and revered her own immediate dear mother, will not echo the hope?

Again and eminently, the heavenly figure under consideration presents an image of the Church: 'the King hath brought me into His chambers.'°

'Who is she that looketh forth as the morning, fair as the moon, clear as the sun, and terrible as an army with banners?'° All glorious she is within by the Indwelling of the Holy Spirit, and effluent glory envelopes her as with the sun for a garment. The moon, set below, may never again eclipse the sun; yet inasmuch as the perfect life had to be developed out of the imperfect, the unchangeable out of the changeable, therefore the moon abides underlying that consummated glory. Twelve stars compose her crown, a twelvefold splendour. I have seen the Twelve Apostles suggested as the interpretation of this symbol; and well may it direct our thoughts to their glorious company, the illumination of their doctrine, the shining light of their example. Perhaps there will be no harm in an additional gloss. The eternal state of the Church Triumphant is expressed by her sun-vesture; the moon beneath her feet memorializes her temporal probation while militant in this world; the twelve stars may—may they not? for earth's day is as night when compared with heaven's day—may remind us of those twelve hours in the day during which she was bound to walk and work in accordance with our Lord's own words and practice. Thus her probation issues in glory, a glory all the more glorious because of that probation. 'Give her of the fruit of her hands; and let her own works praise her in the gates.'° Or if *stars* seem too incongruous an emblem of any *daylight* hours; I call to mind both that there shall be no night there, and that certain benefactors have for their allotted dignity to shine as the stars for ever and ever: whereby stars take rank in the everlasting day.

Or rather, what real connection is there between stars and night more than between stars and day? Earth's shadows approach them not in their high places; nor so far as we can trace, affect them in any way, or do aught in their regard beyond revealing them to mortal ken. Our perception varies, not their lustre.

Chapter XIII

2. **And the beast which I saw was like unto a leopard, and his feet were as the feet of a bear, and his mouth as the mouth of a lion: and the dragon gave him his power, and his seat, and great authority.**

This Apocalyptic beast combines in its one aspect features of three distinct and successive beasts of Daniel's vision: 'Behold, the four winds of the heaven strove upon the great sea. And four great beasts came up from the sea, diverse one from another. The first was like a lion, and had eagle's wings: I beheld till the wings thereof were plucked, and it was lifted up from the earth, and made stand upon the feet as a man, and a man's heart was given to it. And behold another beast, a second, like to a bear, and it raised up itself on one side, and it had three ribs in the mouth of it between the teeth of it: and they said thus unto it, Arise, devour much flesh. After this I beheld, and lo another, like a leopard, which had upon the back of it four wings of a fowl; the beast had also four heads; and dominion was given to it. After this I saw in the night visions, and behold a fourth beast, dreadful and terrible, and strong exceedingly; and it had great iron teeth: it devoured and brake in pieces, and stamped the residue with the feet of it: and it was diverse from all the beasts that were before it; and it had ten horns. I considered the horns, and, behold, there came up among them another little horn, before whom there were three of the first horns plucked up by the roots: and, behold, in this horn were eyes like the eyes of man, and a mouth speaking great things.'°

Daniel's vision has been expounded as concerning the successive empires of Babylon, Persia, Greece; personified respectively as lion, bear, leopard. The fourth yet more mysteriously appalling beast stands over to what was then and may still be the future. St. John's vision may haply already concern ourselves, or at any rate will concern others like us. Its lesson is for all and is for me.

Whatever this Apocalyptic beast may prove in fulness of time, it exhibits some likeness to that world, flesh, devil, which are my daily antagonists; of which I must daily, hourly, momentarily beware.

The world is like a leopard. Beautiful but spotted; soft, graceful, sportive, yet a devourer, a destroyer. 'A leopard shall watch over their cities.'° Nor can the leopard change his spots. 'Love not the world, neither the things that are in the world. If any man love the world, the love of the Father is not in him. For all that is in the world, the lust of the flesh, and the lust of the eyes, and the pride of life, is not of the Father, but is of the world. And the world passeth away, and the lust thereof: but he that doeth the Will of God abideth for ever.'°

The flesh is like a bear. Its hug is deadly. 'How long wilt thou sleep, O sluggard? when wilt thou arise out of thy sleep? Yet a little sleep, a little slumber, a little folding of the hands to sleep: so shall thy poverty come as one that travelleth, and thy want as an armed man.'° The bear treads with his whole foot upon the earth, and his gross aspect is prominently of the earth earthy.°

The devil is like a lion: as a roaring lion he walketh about seeking whom he may devour. He is as a lion's whelp lurking in secret places. 'Rescue my soul from their destructions, my darling from the lions.'°

World, flesh, devil, comprise all sources and varieties of my temptations. Repelling these three wherever found, I shall not fail to repel them even if in my own mortal day they appear concentrated into one ghastly head, one obscene monster.

On the other hand: if I succumb to them separately, how shall I cope with them should they rise up against me as one?

But that word *the world* is frequently used to denote a great portion of the human race. How little must I love the world? How much may I love it?—Love it to the fulness of thy heart's desire, so thou love it with self-sacrifice; for thus to love it is after the Mind of God, the Pattern of Christ: 'God so loved the world, that He gave His Only Begotten Son, that whosoever believeth in Him should not perish, but have everlasting life. For God sent not His Son into the world to condemn the world; but that the world through Him might be saved.'°

> Love is alone the worthy law of love:
>> All other laws have pre-supposed a taint:
>> Love is the law from kindled saint to saint,
> From lamb to lamb, from tender dove to dove.
> Love is the motive of all things that move
>> Harmonious by free will without constraint:
>> Love learns and teaches: love shall man acquaint
> With all he lacks, which all his lack is love.
> Because Love is the fountain, I discern
>> The stream as love: for what but love should flow   10
>>> From fountain Love? not bitter from the sweet!
>> I ignorant, have I laid claim to know?
>>> Oh teach me, Love, such knowledge as is meet
> For one to know who is fain to love and learn.

This world is not my orchard for fruit or my garden for flowers. It is however my only field whence to raise a harvest.

What is the world? Wherein resides its harmfulness, snare, pollution? Left to itself it is neither harmful, ensnaring, nor polluting. It becomes all this as the passive agent, passive vehicle if I may so call it, of the devil, man's outside tempter, and of the flesh, man's inside tempter. There is no inherent evil in cedar and vermilion, horses and chariots, purple and fine linen; nay, nor in sumptuous fare, in down, silk, apes, ivory, or peacocks. St. Peter himself objects not to hair, gold, apparel,° but to women's misuse of them. An alabaster box° of precious ointment becomes good or bad simply according to the use it is put to. Through envy of the devil death came into the world, and man hath sought out many inventions;° but the heavens and the earth, and all the host of them when made and finished were beheld to be 'very good.'°

Lord Jesus, everywhere and always inspire us to refuse the evil and to choose the good; and I beseech Thee, give us grace never to judge our neighbour rashly, whilst one by one we ourselves endeavour to learn and perform Thy Will.

Christ exchanged heaven for earth to enable man to exchange earth for heaven. Hast Thou done that for me, and will I not do this for Thee?

'The dragon gave him his power, and his seat, and great authority'—constituting him, so to say, diabolical viceroy. The flesh is even now such a viceroy, having the world for a throne, while the devil keeps out of sight ruling by deputy.—Or the world is a stage, the flesh an actor, the devil prompter and scene-shifter.

Chapter XVII

3. So he carried me away in the spirit into the wilderness: and I saw a woman sit upon a scarlet-coloured beast, full of names of blasphemy, having seven heads and ten horns.

He who exhibits is an angel, and he who inspects is a saint: yet does this exalted pair betake themselves into 'the wilderness,' there and not elsewhere to set themselves face to face with an impersonation of abominable wickedness. So likewise did their and our Divine Master do when He deigned to confront Satan. And if the Standard Bearer among ten thousand, and if the flower of His armies did thus, it leaves us an example that we should tread in their steps.

Some innocent souls there are who from cradle to grave remain as it were veiled and cloistered from knowledge of evil. As pearls in their native deep, as flower-buds under Alpine snow, they abide unsullied: the lot has fallen unto them in a fair ground. But for most persons contact with evil and consequent knowledge of evil being unavoidable, is clearly so far ordained: they must achieve a more difficult sanctity, touching pitch yet continuing clean, enduring evil communications yet without corruption of good manners.

To each such imperilled soul, Angel and Apostle here set a pattern. If we too would gaze unscathed and undefiled on wickedness, let us not seek for enchantments, but set our face toward the wilderness. Strip sin bare from voluptuousness of music, fascination of gesture, entrancement of the stage, rapture of poetry, glamour of eloquence, seduction of imaginative emotion; strip it of every adornment, let it stand out bald as in the Ten stern Commandments. Study sin, when study it we must, not as a relishing pastime, but as an embittering deterrent. Lavish sympathy on the sinner, never on the sin. Say, if we will and if we mean it, Would God I had died for thee:° nevertheless let us flee at the cry of such, lest the earth swallow us up also.

Wherever the serpent is tolerated there is sure to be dust for his pasture: he finds or he makes a desolate wilderness of what was as the Garden of Eden. Only an illusion, a mirage, can cause a barren desert to appear in our eyes as a city of palaces, an orchard of fruits.

This woman Babylon sits upon a scarlet beast, it appears not whether as upon a throne or as upon a chariot: if a throne, steadfast in evil; if a chariot, swift unto perdition. Moreover, in a former verse we read of her as sitting 'upon many waters':° a point to be noted further on.

The woman and the beast by a foul congruity seem to make up a sort of oneness, after the fashion of a snail and its shell. If she removes he is the motor; she is lifted aloft to the extent of his height; her stability depends on his. In semblance he is her slave, in reality her master.

4. **And the woman was arrayed in purple and scarlet colour, and decked with gold and precious stones and pearls, having a golden cup in her hand full of abominations and filthiness of her fornication:**

5. **And upon her forehead was a name written, Mystery, Babylon the Great, The Mother of Harlots and Abominations of the Earth.**

The beast is scarlet, and the woman wears scarlet. He is full of names of blasphemy, and her names are of the same sort.

He is scarlet as sin. She is both scarlet and particoloured, decked with such gauds as St. Paul warns us women against.° As it seemed possible to study the sun-clothed exalted Woman (ch. xii.) as a figure of the all-glorious destiny awaiting the Virtuous Woman, so now I think this obscene woman may (on the surface) be studied as illustrating the particular foulness, degradation, loathsomeness, to which a perverse rebellious woman because feminine not masculine is liable.

Execrable, for aught we know, as any devil, beast, man, of them all, the resources and so to say the tactics of Babylon differ from theirs: she and they proceed to a common goal by distinct paths. They have (such as it is) counsel and strength for war: she less astute in counsel, less hardy in war, makes of her own self a trap, a bait, a ruinous prize.

She seduces, not coerces. She tyrannizes by influence, not by might. Filthy she is, but she proffers filthiness in a golden cup. No heart of husband safely trusts in her, no children arise up and call her blessed: vile mother is she of vile daughters, all alike bedizened, perfumed, debased to hell; all alike blood-suckers, as we read: 'The horseleach hath two daughters, crying, Give, give.'°

Some have opined that a woman's wickedness even exceeds that of a man; as Jezebel stirred up Ahab, and Herodias outstripped Herod on feet swift to shed blood. But this point must stand over for decision to the Judgment of that Only Judge to whom each and all of us will one day stand or fall. Solomon meanwhile by warning man against woman has virtually warned woman against herself: 'When wisdom entereth into thine heart, and knowledge is pleasant unto thy soul; discretion shall preserve thee, understanding shall keep thee. . . . To deliver thee from the strange woman, even from the stranger which flattereth with her words; which forsaketh the guide of her youth, and forgetteth the covenant of her God. For her house inclineth unto death, and her paths unto the dead. None that go unto her return again, neither take they hold of the paths of life':—'The lips of a strange woman drop as an honeycomb, and her mouth is smoother than oil: but her end is bitter as wormwood, sharp as a two-edged sword. Her feet go down to death; her steps take hold on hell. Lest thou shouldest ponder the path of life, her ways are moveable, that thou canst not know them':— 'A foolish woman is clamourous: she is simple, and knoweth nothing. For she sitteth at the door of her house, on a seat in the high places of the city, to call passengers who go right on their ways: Whoso is simple, let him turn in hither. . . . But he knoweth not that the dead are there; and that her guests are in the depths of hell.'°

> Our Mothers, lovely women pitiful;
>   Our Sisters, gracious in their life and death;
>   To us each unforgotten memory saith:
> 'Learn as we learned in life's sufficient school,
> Work as we worked in patience of our rule,
>   Walk as we walked much less by sight than faith,
>   Hope as we hoped despite our slips and scathe,°
> Fearful in joy and confident in dule.'°
> I know not if they see us or can see:
>   But if they see us in our painful day,   10
>   How looking back to earth from Paradise
>   Do tears not gather in those loving eyes?—
>   Ah, happy eyes! whose tears are wiped away
> Whether or not you bear to look on me.

'Upon her forehead was a name written, Mystery . . .'—The mystery is announced to all; but is not explained to all, if to any.

Intelligence may be required of some: faith is required of all.

Is it disappointing to be restricted to faith? Faith, the grace, is a higher endowment than intelligence, the gift.

A revealed unexplained mystery is (as it were) my Tree of Knowledge accessible whilst forbidden; a theme for prayer, not a bait for curiosity. Ignorance by virtue of good will takes rank as a part of obedience.

To be of one mind with God is universal knowledge in embryo.

9. And here is the mind which hath wisdom. The seven heads are seven mountains, on which the woman sitteth.

So teach us to number our days that we may apply our hearts unto wisdom; that we may receive the instruction of wisdom, justice and judgment and equity. O Lord, Who givest wisdom, Who layest up sound wisdom for the righteous; teach us in the way of wisdom, lead us in right paths. Furnish our lips with wisdom: let us not die for want of wisdom. Grant us wisdom with the just, the lowly, the well advised; that with the prudent we may understand our way, and ceasing from our own wisdom may learn of Thee, Lord Jesus Christ our Wisdom. Amen.

The Virtuous Woman whose price is far above rubies 'openeth her mouth with wisdom; and in her tongue is the law of kindness.'° Wisdom, then, associates with kindness: to cultivate kindness is to frequent the society of wisdom. A clue especially vouchsafed to us women.

I observe that while to Moses celestial patterns were displayed and on him was poured the radiance of direct revelation; and that whereas 'Bezaleel and Aholiab, and every wise-hearted man, in whom the Lord put wisdom and understanding to know how to work all manner of work for the service of the sanctuary,'° so wrought: 'all the women that were wise-hearted did spin with their hands, and brought that which they had spun, both of blue, and of purple, and of scarlet, and of fine linen. And all the women whose heart stirred them up in wisdom spun goats' hair.'° Thus coverings, curtains, veils, were assigned to the women: to the men those sacred things enshrined beneath and within.

So long as he or she who 'standeth without'° can hear the Bridegroom's Voice, surely it is joy fulfilled.

'The seven heads are seven mountains, on which the woman sitteth.'—The interpretation lies above and beyond my range: the symbol conveys a lesson.

Mortal life is, so to say, a tissue of sevens; and each seven must be guarded against the fascination of that World whereof 'the woman' (be she ultimately what she may) exhibits characteristics.

Guard, so far as in thee lieth, innocence in infancy, reverence in childhood, holiness in youth, aspiration in maturity, patience on the decline, perseverance in age, hope in death. Is it too late for thyself? Then guard them in others: and as to thyself, at least redeem the remaining time from waste and snatch thy grave from desecration. Guard others and thyself against that world which defiles innocence by contact, substitutes foolhardiness and false shame for reverence, violates holiness, paralyzes aspiration; which breeds selfishness instead of patience, frivolity instead of perseverance; which is too corrupt, too dead, too twice dead for hope in death. And whilst the seven stages of life compose thus a sort of week, each stage is itself composed of weeks of days, seven within seven, seven after seven, each and all needing the Gift of Sevenfold Grace to consecrate labours and hallow rest.

Yet as St. Paul exhorts not his converts to go out of the world, but to act rightly in it; and much more as our Divine Master offering up His High Priestly Prayer spake, saying: 'I pray not that Thou shouldest take them out of the world, but that Thou shouldest keep them from the evil,'—let us not be afraid of her terror, but sanctify the Lord God in our hearts. We cannot prevent the World's besetting, haunting, overshadowing us: only let us not suffer her to *sit down*.

Dante in the Divina Commedia (*see* my sister's *A Shadow of Dante*) tells us how he 'dreamed of a woman stammering, squinting, lame of foot, maimed of hands, and ashy pale. He gazed on her, and lo! under his gaze her form straightened, her face flushed, her tongue loosed to the Siren's song.'°

> Foul is she and ill-favoured, set askew:
>   Gaze not upon her till thou dream her fair,
>   Lest she should mesh thee in her wanton hair,
> Adept in arts grown old yet ever new.
> Her heart lusts not for love, but thro' and thro'
>   For blood, as spotted panther lusts in lair;
>   No wine is in her cup, but filth is there
> Unutterable, with plagues hid out of view.
> Gaze not upon her; for her dancing whirl
>   Turns giddy the fixed gazer presently:
>   Gaze not upon her, lest thou be as she
>   When at the far end of her long desire

10

Her scarlet vest and gold and gem and pearl
And she amid her pomp are set on fire.

'Seven heads . . . seven mountains'—seven deadly sins: these sustain the World, and the World fosters these. High crested Pride, volcanic Anger, smooth sloped Lust, overhanging Envy, undermined Avarice, swine pasturing Gluttony, landslip Sloth. A dark continent of spiritual geography.

10. **And there are seven kings: five are fallen, and one is, and the other is not yet come; and when he cometh, he must continue a short space.**

From evil rulers and pernicious laws, from obeying man by disobeying God, from misusing our short space, for short is our space,
Good Lord, save us:
Lest we become as a plant that buds not, as a bud that blows not, as a flower that fruits not, in our short space until the harvest, our only space.

11. **And the beast that was, and is not, even he is the eighth, and is of the seven, and goeth into perdition.**

From comradeship with devils and disciples of devils, from persisting in sin and passing away into perdition,
Good Lord, save us:
Lest it had been better for us never to have been born, never to have known the way of life, never to have heard of Thee by the hearing of the ear, never to have beheld the Kingdom of Heaven set open to all believers.

12. **And the ten horns which thou sawest are ten kings, which have received no kingdom as yet; but receive power as kings one hour with the beast.**

From selling our birthright for a mess of pottage, from bartering eternity for one hour,
Good Lord, save us:
Lest we receive our good things in this life, and after that be tormented.

13. **These have one mind, and shall give their power and strength unto the beast.**

From the counsel and deed of them,
Good Lord, save us:

Lest we spend money for that which is not bread, and our labour for
that which satisfieth not.

14. **These shall make war with the Lamb, and the Lamb
shall overcome them: for He is Lord of lords, and King of
kings: and they that are with Him are called, and chosen,
and faithful.**

From choosing the evil and refusing the good, from setting ourselves
in no good way, from the tactics of Balak and the end of Balaam,
Good Lord, save us:
Lest we who are dust set ourselves in the balance against Thee: and
lo! we are dust in the balance.

15. **And he saith unto me, The waters which thou sawest, where
the whore sitteth, are peoples, and multitudes, and
nations, and tongues.**

From following a multitude to do evil, from sinful compliances, from
saving our life but not with Thy salvation,
Good Lord, save us:
Lest amid multitudinous glory and pomp and rejoicing we be put to
open shame and perish together.

16. **And the ten horns which thou sawest upon the beast, these
shall hate the whore, and shall make her desolate and
naked, and shall eat her flesh, and burn her with fire.**

From such hatred of sin as is not love of righteousness, from hating
not sin but sinners, from casting the stone of condemnation whereby
we condemn ourselves,
Good Lord, save us:
Lest out of our own mouth we be condemned where there is no
respect of persons.

17. **For God hath put in their hearts to fulfil His will, and to
agree, and give their kingdom unto the beast, until the
words of God shall be fulfilled.**

From fulfilling a Divine behest in the spirit of rebellious Absalom,
apostate Jeroboam, bloodthirsty Edom, Caiaphas harder than flint,
Good Lord, save us:
Lest in us be fulfilled that other word also: 'Depart from Me, ye
cursed, into everlasting fire, prepared for the devil and his angels.'

18. And the woman which thou sawest is that great city, which reigneth over the kings of the earth.

From the lust of the flesh and the lust of the eyes and the pride of life, from foreheads of brass and hearts of stone,
> Good Lord, save us:

Lest in the end we be past renewing unto salvation, and there be none to save us.
> Yea, Good Lord, save us. Amen.

'And there are seven kings.'—The Revised Version preserves this reading marginally, whilst the text gives: 'And they [*i. e.* the "mountains" mentioned in the previous verse] are seven kings.' Suggesting a many-sided significance in at least one of the images employed: if in one, perhaps in others. For here the original figure is 'seven heads': *mountains* and *kings* alike belong to the angelic interpretation.

'And the beast . . . even he is the eighth, and is of the seven':—in the Revised Version: '. . . is himself also an eighth, . . .'—As moral goodness or depravity finds expression in the face, whilst the seat of life is the heart; so a seven-headed monster may infuse into every head his own hideous vitality, whilst each head acts independently of its fellows as mouthpiece and intelligent agent to the abominable animating principle. Perhaps the beast's being 'also an eighth' may inspire a dread that in the final death-struggle of Satan against Christ, wickedness superhuman or subhuman (whichever it should be termed) will take the field openly and visibly; and will act in person, as well as through the instrumentality of its miserable mortal allies.

The seven heads have not only the beast for a basis, but have moreover the seated woman for a superincumbent load: the one detaches them from earth, the goodness of nature; the other blocks them out from the sky, the goodness of grace.

I think not as interpretation but as meditation such thoughts may spring from the text.

Have we sought great things for ourselves? Seek them not. Ten kings receive authority, but it is with the beast, and for one hour. 'Yea, even like as a dream when one awaketh.'°

'The Lamb shall overcome them: for He is Lord of lords, and King of kings'—Although both the Lion and the Lamb are titles belonging to our Lord, here in the day of battle we read of Him as the Lamb, not as the Lion. Whatever inscrutable reasons there may be for this choice of a designation, one or two obvious ones suggest themselves. Thus is accomplished one of the Beatitudes: 'Blessed are the meek: for they shall inherit the earth.' Thus Christ in His own adorable Person heads the army of those who 'out of weakness were made strong, waxed valiant in fight, turned to flight the armies of the aliens.'° Thus, 'the weakness of God' stands forth as 'stronger than men.' 'Not by might, nor by power, but by My Spirit, saith the Lord of hosts.'° And thus also by a condescension of grace, Jael, a certain woman (*see* Judges ix. 53), Esther, Judith, become figures illustrative of like truth.

Weakness, however, is not *as* weakness this more than conqueror. Our Redeemer's weakness was rather the triumph of His strength, because to become weak and work mightily through weakness He laid aside His strength and kept it in abeyance. Our weakness, if it is to win a victory, must include a voluntary element; at the least so far as to will in concert with the Divine Will, and never to have recourse to illicit weapons.

And I think that in these days of women's self-assertion and avowed rivalry with men, I do well to bear in mind that in a contest no stronger proof of superiority can be given on either side than the *not* bringing into action all available force. As yet, I suppose, we women claim no more than equality with our brethren in head and heart: whilst as to physical force, we scout it as unworthy to arbitrate between the opposed camps. Men on their side do not scout physical force, but let it be.

Does either man or woman doubt where superiority resides, when at chess one player discards a pawn in favour of the other?

Society may be personified as a human figure whose right hand is man, whose left woman; in one sense equal, in another sense unequal. The right hand is labourer, acquirer, achiever: the left hand helps, but has little independence, and is more apt at carrying than at executing. The right hand runs the risks, fights the battles: the left hand abides in comparative quiet and safety; except (a material exception) that in the *mutual* relations of the twain it is in some ways far more liable to undergo than to inflict hurt, to be cut (for instance) than to cut.

Rules admit of and are proved by exceptions. There are left-handed people, and there may arise a left-handed society!

> Content to come, content to go,
> Content to wrestle or to race,

Content to know or not to know,
　　Each in his place;

Lord, grant us grace to love Thee so
　　That glad of heart and glad of face
At last we may sit high or low
　　Each in his place:

Where pleasures flow as rivers flow,
　　And loss has left no barren trace,　　　　10
And all that are, are perfect so
　　Each in his place.

'And they that are with Him are called, and chosen, and faithful':—
or according to the Revised Version: 'And they also shall overcome
that are with Him, called and chosen and faithful':—thus, towards the
end, sending thought back to the beginning, to the ever-recurring
'overcometh' of the Messages to the Seven Churches, that 'over-
cometh' on which depends each consummating benediction.

God of His free Love calls and chooses: man's faithfulness certifies
the call, until by overcoming he crowns all by final perseverance.

Lord Jesus, give us hearing ears, responsive wills, some fear, much
faith, much hope, most love.

'The waters . . . where the whore sitteth, are peoples, and multitudes,
and nations, and tongues.'—'Raging waves of the sea, foaming out
their own shame.'°

'The ten horns which thou sawest upon the beast, these shall hate
the whore.'—The Revised Version supplies a noticeable variation:
'The ten horns . . . and the beast, these shall hate . . .,' thus uniting all
in one close confederacy, as in ver. 13 *ante*: 'These have one mind, and
shall give their power and strength unto the beast.'

Whatever further the wise may elicit from this passage and its
sequel, even the foolish may deduce somewhat. The kingdom of the
beast is essentially unalterably a kingdom of hatred, hatred underlying
any and every appearance of its spurious love: sift such love, and the
residuum will be hatred. In the day of her foul attractiveness the lost
woman was idol, mistress, plaything: in the day of her decay she
becomes a prey, and there is none to help her. The drunken with blood
must herself be devoured.

Evil may subserve evil, yet be overruled for good. Thus the horns
spring from the beast, and in their turn give their kingdom unto the beast:
wherefore? because 'God hath put in their hearts to fulfil His Will.'

'The woman . . . is that great city, which reigneth over the kings of the earth.'—'Without controversy'° who then, what then, is she?

She seems to include or invite all which tempts man at his earthly proudest and mightiest: ambition shedding blood as water, with garments rolled in blood scarlet as her array; enervating luxury, as she herself sits inert on her scarlet beast; sensual excess foul as her cup; licence that is not liberty, but is chains and fetters like her bravery of gold and pearls and precious stones. Woe to her dupes! 'Lo, this is the man that made not God his strength; but trusted in the abundance of his riches, and strengthened himself in his wickedness.'°

Such as this, then, is she. From all this and from whatsoever besides she may be, may we every one of us great or small be delivered. Amen.

Chapter XVIII

11. **And the merchants of the earth shall weep and mourn over her; for no man buyeth their merchandise any more.**

Those *kings* did at least bewail Babylon for herself: these *merchants* bewail her because of their own impoverishment. They all alike are 'of the earth,' yet is there a finer and a coarser clay.

Only I must beware of reckoning that sympathy with evil *in itself* is nobler than sympathy with evil *in its effects*. Neither is nobler: one may be baser. From both, O Lord, deliver us.

12. **The merchandise of gold, and silver, and precious stones, and of pearls, and fine linen, and purple, and silk, and scarlet, and all thyine wood, and all manner vessels of ivory, and all manner vessels of most precious wood, and of brass, and iron, and marble,**

13. **And cinnamon, and odours, and ointments, and frankincense, and wine, and oil, and fine flour, and wheat, and beasts, and sheep, and horses, and chariots, and slaves, and souls of men.**

'A man's life consisteth not in the abundance of the things which he possesseth.'° We know that it is so now: we shall see that it is so then. If either, his death rather than his life consisteth in such.

'Brethren, the time is short: it remaineth,' that they that buy be 'as though they possessed not; and they that use this world, as not abusing it: for the fashion of this world passeth away.'°

Yet on the same principle that we are bidden redeem the time because the days are evil, Christians find ways to redeem these other creatures despite their evil tendency. Gold and silver they lend unto the Lord: He will pay them again. Precious stones and pearls they dedicate to the service of His Altar. With fine linen, purple, silk, scarlet, they invest His Sanctuary; and fragrant 'thyine' wood they carve delicately for its further adornment. Vessels of ivory, of most precious wood, of brass, iron, marble, are refined to serve as lavers, ennobled to become alms coffers or alms dishes. They burn cinnamon, odours (the Revised Version for 'odours' gives 'spice and incense'), frankincense, for a sweet savour in the Divine Presence. Wine, fine flour, wheat, constitute their most pure Oblation. With ointments and oil they comfort Christ in His beloved sick members. With beasts and sheep they spread a feast for His poor. On horses and in chariots they carry His Gospel afar. And ministering rather than being ministered unto, they tend bodies and travail for souls. (For 'slaves' the margin gives as literal 'bodies.')

'The glory of the Lord shall endure for ever: the Lord shall rejoice in His works.'°

Whoso has the spirit of Elijah, though his horse and chariot have come up out of Egypt, yet shall they receive virtue as 'of fire'° to forward him on his heavenward course. And this despite a horse being but a vain thing to save a man.

14. **And the fruits that thy soul lusted after are departed from thee, and all things which were dainty and goodly are departed from thee, and thou shalt find them no more at all.**

Or according to the Revised Version: 'And the fruits which thy soul lusted after are gone from thee, and all things that were dainty and sumptuous are perished from thee, and men shall find them no more at all': — reminding us of St. Paul's words to the Colossians: '. . . The rudiments of the world . . . (Touch not; taste not; handle not; which all are to perish with the using).'°

As regards the second clause of the doom (*in this verse*), the two Versions suggest each its own sense. The Authorized, as if those objects of desire may have been not destroyed but withdrawn whilst the craving remains insatiable. According to both texts the loss appears absolute, final, irreparable; but (collating the two) that which *departs* instead of *perishing* leaves behind it in addition to the agony of loss the hankering, corroding misery of absence.

15. The merchants of these things, which were made rich by her, shall stand afar off for the fear of her torment, weeping and wailing,
16. And saying, Alas, alas, that great city, that was clothed in fine linen, and purple, and scarlet, and decked with gold, and precious stones, and pearls!
17. For in one hour so great riches is come to nought. And every shipmaster, and all the company in ships, and sailors, and as many as trade by sea, stood afar off,

This desolation which we have not yet seen must one day be seen. Meanwhile we have known preludes, rehearsals, foretastes of such as this: so that looking back through the centuries we may take up our lamentation and say:—

Alas Sodom once full of bread! From empty fulness, Good Lord, deliver us.

Alas Tyre whose merchants were princes! From riches but not toward God, Good Lord, deliver us.

Alas the man whose barns sufficed not! From heart and hands shut close, Good Lord, deliver us.

Alas Dives clothed in purple and fine linen! From remediless destitution, Good Lord, deliver us.

And looking forward we may say:—

Alas any whom the unknown day and hour find unprepared! From the folly of the foolish virgins, Good Lord, deliver us.

And looking around us trembling we needs must say:—

Alas England full of luxuries and thronged by stinted poor, whose merchants are princes and whose dealings crooked, whose packed storehouses stand amid bare homes, whose gorgeous array has rags for neighbours! From a canker in our gold and silver, from a moth in our garments, from blasted crops, from dwindling substance, from righteous retribution abasing us among the nations, Good Lord, deliver us. Amen.

Chapter XX

10. **And the devil that deceived them was cast into the lake of fire and brimstone, where the beast and the false prophet are, and shall be tormented day and night for ever and ever.**

'The getting of treasures by a lying tongue is a vanity tossed to and fro of them that seek death.'°

Did Satan then seek death? Yes, even if he named not death that which he sought. He sought not life: and thereupon seeking somewhat he sought death. A fearful parallel holds good: as he, so we, if we seek not life seek death.

O Christ our only Life, our Life immortal, Who of old hast declared, 'I am found of them that sought Me not'; say to us also 'Behold Me, behold Me,'° and with the word give the grace. So shall we not die but live and declare Thy works, O Lord: so with all living shall we praise Thee as I do this day. Amen.

Satan is 'that old serpent';° and in the serpent tribe we observe ghastly, loathly, emblematic likenesses of Satan. Constrictors some of them, some vessels of venom; flat heads, unemotional eyes, forked darting tongues are amongst them: silent, insinuating, gliding, they are upon us before we know that they are near. Yet of all living creatures which my memory records no one in Satanic suggestion approaches, to my own thinking, the octopus.

One single small octopus in an aquarium is all I have seen. It had a fascination for me. Inert as it often appeared, it bred and tickled a perpetual suspense: will it do something? will it emerge from the background of its water den? I have seen it swallow its live prey in an eyewink, change from a stony colour to an appalling lividness, elongate unequal feelers and set them flickering like a flame, sit still with an air of immemorial old age amongst the lifeless refuse of its once living meals. I had to remind myself that this vivid figure of wickedness was not in truth itself wickedness.'

'Where the beast and the false prophet are.'—'Art thou also become weak as we: art thou become like unto us?'°

Recognition appears no less essential to the rancorous horror of hell than to the felicity of heaven. Recognition points and clenches hatred as well as love. If so be they are immured eternally together, what other soul could be to Caiaphas as Judas, or to Judas as Caiaphas? or to the Pharisee as his own twofold more child of hell, or to that child as that Pharisee?

Alas for seducer and seduced who once called their bond love, and behold it is loathing! 'Day and night for ever and ever.'

12. **And I saw the dead, small and great, stand before God; and the books were opened: and another book was opened, which is the book of life: and the dead were judged out of those things which were written in the books, according to their works.**

On the dead for whom once Thou diedst, Lord Jesus, have mercy.

On the living for whom Thou ever livest, have mercy.

Thou Who wast arraigned before a corrupt judge, O Incorruptible Judge, have mercy.

Thou Who knowest what is in man, O Son of Man, have mercy.

Thou Whose works were all good, have mercy.

Thou Whose life, in the sight of the unwise, once hung in suspense before Pilate, have mercy.

Thou Who Thyself ever knowest what Thou wilt do, have mercy.

On the small, mercy.

On the great, mercy.

Thou Who art unlike us in Thy sinlessness, on us sinners have mercy.

Thou Who art like us in Thy Humanity, on us Thy brethren and Thy sisters, have mercy.

Blot out our evil works from Thy Book of Works, and have mercy.

Write our names in Thy Book of Life, and have mercy.

Blot not out our names, but have mercy.

Give us tears from the Fountain of Thy Mercy.

Store our tears in Thy bottle, with Thine own tears shed for us in pure mercy.

And whatever we lack let us not lack Thy mercy. Amen.

'Stand before God'—past kneeling, past praying; not to be converted, but sentenced. *Now*, not *then*, is the day of salvation: not *then* except for the already saved.

My page in the Book of Works is to me awful: the contents are my own, the record is not my own. It is my life's record without oversights, without false entries or suppressions: any good set down accurately as good; all evil, unless erased by Divine Compassion, set down accurately as evil. Nothing whatever is there except what I have genuinely endeavoured, compassed, done, been: I meant it all, though I meant not to meet it again face to face. It is as if all along one had walked in a world of invisible photographic cameras charged with instantaneous plates.

The Book of Life may seem yet more awful, kept secret as it has been from the foundation of the world in the knowledge of God Omniscient.

Yet is it really so? It is in fact no independent statement, but appears to be essentially an index or summary of the other. I who composed although I compiled not my Book of Works, I myself virtually entered or entered not my name in the corresponding Book of Life: to dread this beyond the other, is to dread a sum total rather than those very items which produce the total.

For whilst we read that 'the dead were judged out of those things which were written in the Books,' it was none the less 'according to their works.'

To William Michael Rossetti, 19 September 1853

[. . .] This morning I commenced a remarkable doggrel on the P.R.B. &c.; but perhaps if I give you a sample of it you may not pant for its completion.

> The two Rossettis (brothers they)
> And Holman Hunt and John Millais,
> With Stephens chivalrous and bland,
> And Woolner in a distant land,
> In these six men I awestruck see
> Embodied the great P.R.B.
> D. G. Rossetti offered two
> Good pictures to the public view:°
> Unnumbered ones great John Millais,
> And Holman more than I can say
> +   +   +   +   +   +   +
> William Rossetti calm and solemn
> Cuts up his brethren by the column.°
> +   +   +   +   *   *   *

You may guess that at this point of my letter I came to a stand, from the extra finish bestowed on the three last asterisks. [. . .]

To Amelia Barnard Heimann, 3 April 1862

At length I have the satisfaction of begging your acceptance of my little book: pray receive it as a small expression of my very true love for you and yours, and let it serve as a remembrancer between us of unfailing kindness on your part and affection on mine.

In the volume is one piece° (p. 148) of which perhaps you might expect me to make no mention to you: yet this is the very one of which I will ask your permission to speak. I cannot bear to be for ever silent on the all-important topic of Christianity: indeed, how could I love you and yours as I do, have received so many favours at your hands, and felt so often your good example, without longing and praying for faith to be added to your works? Dear old friend, do not be offended with me;

but believe that the love of Christ and of you all constrains° me. If aught I have said offends you, be sure the offence lies in the words, not in the heart from which they come warm.

After Easter I look forward to calling on you: till then Lent and our mourning° keep me at home. [. . .]

To Adolph Heimann, [?April 1862]

On the subject of my little book I have not received kinder or dearer letters than the two which you and your wife have sent me. But some of my verses have grieved you: I recall titles and subjects, and suspect *At Home*, and *Shut Out*, of being amongst these offenders. If *sad and melancholy*, I suggest that few people reach the age of 31 without sad and melancholy experiences: if *despondent*, I take shame and blame to myself, as they show that I have been unmindful of the daily love and mercy lavished upon me. But remember, please, that these and the rest have been written during a period of some 14 years, and under many varying influences of circumstances, health and spirits; that they are moreover not mainly the fruit of effort, but the record of sensation, fancy, what not, much as these came and went. My next volume—should a next volume ever come to pass—may, I hope, show an improved tone of mind and feeling: but for the present, you must even accept the actual volume with all its shortcomings. [. . .]

To Alexander Macmillan, [1 December 1863]

I enclose my receipt and many thanks for the cheque—and many more thanks for the kind words of encouragement you give me. Miss Proctor I am not afraid of: but Miss Ingelow° (judging by extracts; I have not yet seen her actual volume)—would be a formidable rival to most men, and to any woman. Indeed I have been bewailing that she did not publish with you.

Few things within the range of probability would give me greater pleasure than to see in print my second volume: but I am sadly convinced that I have not by me materials, equal both in quantity and quality, to what are already before the public. And, if one conviction can go beyond another, I am yet more firmly convinced that my system of not writing against the grain is the right one, at any rate as concerns myself. Had a second edition of *Goblin Market* been called for, one considerably augmented would have been at once feasible: but a second volume must I fear stand over to the indefinite future.

To Dante Gabriel Rossetti, 7 May 1864

Don't think me a perfect weathercock. But why rush before the public with an immature vol.? I really think of not communicating at all with Mac at present: but waiting the requisite number of months (or years, as the case may be) until I have a sufficiency of quality as well as quantity. Is not this after all my best plan? If meanwhile my things become *remains*,° that need be no bugbear to scare me into premature publicity. Not that the brotherly trouble you have already taken need be lost, as your work will of course avail when (and if) the day of publication comes. [. . .]

To Dante Gabriel Rossetti, 23 December 1864

[. . .] True, O Brother; my Alchemist° still shivers in the blank of mere possibility: but I have so far overcome my feelings and disregarded my nerves° as to unloose the Prince, so that wrapping-paper may no longer bar his progress. Also I have computed pages of the altogether-unexceptionable, and find that they exceed 120: this cheers though not inebriates. Amongst your ousted I recognize sundry of my own favourites, which perhaps I may adroitly re-insert *when* publishing day comes round: especially am I inclined to show fight for at least one *terza-rima*° in honour of our Italian element. Meanwhile I have sent 3 (I hope) pot-boilers to Mac's Mag.

Think, if you all are so kind as to wish me amongst you on Monday, whether I shall not be sharing your wish: if unbeknown I could look in upon you sucking pulp of (metaphorical) plums and peaches I should not fear the fate of my own Bogie.° But common sense rules that here I must remain° and nurse my peccant chest; which, after making great apparent progress, has this morning entered a protest against being considered well. So a potion or two must form part of my Christmas fare. If ever you should look in upon us, you know you will be a boon: but I can't wish you or any other of my consanguines to come shivering down in this weather to the detriment of their bodily well-being or mental peace.

Your notes on the Davenport *séance*° are most interesting. To me the whole subject is awful and mysterious; though, in spite of my hopeless inability to conceive a clue to the source of sundry manifestations, I still hope simple imposture may be the missing key:—I hope it, at least, so far as the hope is not uncharitable; at any rate, I hope without any qualification that you and William escaped bumping bangs to the maiming of your outer men.°

As to news, it has become to me a creature of the past: look elsewhere for news, but not to me. I lugged down with me a 6 vol. Plato, and this promises me a prolonged mental feast: Jean Ingelow's 8th edition is also here, to impart to my complexion a becoming green tinge. [. . .]

To Dante Gabriel Rossetti, 30 [January 1865]

Here at last is an Alchemist reeking from the crucible. He dovetails properly in to his niche. Please read him if you have the energy; then when you return him to me I must give a thorough look over to the annotated Prince; lastly I do hope vol. 2.° will be possible. One motive for haste with me is a fear lest by indefinite delay I should miss the pleasure of thus giving pleasure to our Mother, to whom of course I shall dedicate: suppose—but I won't suppose anything so dreadful: only, knowing her intense enjoyment of our performances, I am keenly desirous to give her the pleasure *when possible*. He's not precisely the Alchemist I prefigured, but thus he came and thus he must stay: you know my system of work.

I am much better indeed, yet beyond a certain point I don't get: however, obviously I cannot remain here quite indefinitely.

Of course I know that to make vol. 2. we must have recourse to some not skimmed by you as cream, but I have a predilection for some of these; and I have by me one or two new little things which *may* help:—at this moment I feel sanguine.

Your affect. bore
C. G. R.

P.S. I don't think I shall announce my Alchemist at home till I hear from you. Of course you may remark that the 1st verse is an old one.

To Dante Gabriel Rossetti, 10 [February 1865]

I am indulging in a holiday from all attempt at *Progress* whilst Mamma is with me: she gone (alas!) I hope to set to with a will. Thanks for annotations,° to be attended to. Do you know, I don't think it would have done to write the *Alchemist* without the metric jolt, however unfortunate the original selection of such rythm may have been: but we will file and polish. How shall I express my sentiments about the terrible tournament? Not a phrase to be relied on, not a correct knowledge on the subject, not the faintest impulse of inspiration, incites me to the tilt: and looming before me in horrible bugbeardom stand 2 tournaments in Tennyson's *Idylls*.° Moreover the Alchemist according to original convention took the place of the lists: remember this in my favour, please. You see, were you next to propose my writing a classic epic in quantitative hexameters or in the hendecasyllables which might almost trip up Tennyson, what could I do? Only what I feel inclined to do in the present instance, plead good will but inability. Also (but this you may scorn as the blind partiality of a parent) my actual *Prince* seems to me invested with a certain artistic congruity of construction not lightly to be despised: 1st a prelude and outset; 2nd an alluring milkmaid; 3rd a trial of barren boredom; 4th the social element again; 5th barren boredom in a more uncompromising form; 6th a wind up and conclusion. See how the subtle elements balance each other and fuse into a noble conglom.! Thanks for the 2 valued prospective cuts;° (qu. have you a design of a tournament by you?!) and for the work on *Goblin Market* block.

Lizzie's poems were posted to you before your last reached my hands: so I trust that days ago you received them safe and sound, and so I shall conclude unless I hear to the contrary. I think with you that, between your volume and mine, their due post of honour is in yours.° But do you not think that (at any rate except in your volume) beautiful as they are they are almost too hopelessly sad for publication *en masse*? Perhaps this is merely my overstrained fancy, but their tone is to me even painfully despondent: talk of my bogieism, is it not by comparison jovial? However, if on careful re-reading the tone, &c., subsides to my excited imagination, it will give me sincerest pleasure if you will grace my volume by their presence. Meanwhile how odd it seems that just III my admiration is rejected by you as ineligible: about VI° I am rather inclined to agree in your verdict sweet and pathetic as it is. [. . .]

To Dante Gabriel Rossetti, 3 [March 1865]

This morning as the 'post' is no longer running after me (like the coffin after a man in a very nightmarish story I once read), I can go into details.

1. *Prince's Progress.* I think the plot now is obvious to mean capacities without further development or addition.—*Aftermath*° is left for various reasons: the most patent I need scarcely give; but also I think it gives a subtle hint (by symbol) that any more delays may swamp the Prince's last chance. In the same way, the obnoxious *pipe* having been immolated on the altar of sisterly deference, *Now the moon's at full*° seems to me happily suggestive of the Prince's character. Of course I don't expect the general public to catch these refined clues; but there they are for such minds as mine.

2. *Material.* I have a puerile fancy for making *vol. 2.* the same number of p.p. as *vol. 1.*: also I independently think that some of the squad are not unworthy of a place amongst their fellows. Unless memory plays me false, Mrs Browning's *My Heart and I* does not clash with my *Tomorrow*:° if it does, I could easily turn my own *heart* into *wish*, and save the little piece for which I have a kindness. Again, I am much inclined to put in one *terza rima*; though whether my *Judgment* or *Captive Jew*° I am not resolved; the *Judgment* is already published in one of Mr Shipley's books: and *Martyrs' Song* (in the same volume) was so honourably mentioned in a review we saw, that that seems to constitute some claim on reprint. I will try not to spoil my volume or deal a deathblow to my reputation, however.

3. *Transmission to Mac.* Might I, instead of sending direct, send them through your brotherly hands? When I have put them in order I should be so glad if you would put the finishing touch to their arrangement. That is one reason for wishing to send them through you; and another is that then I foresee you will charitably do the business details, my wish being for same terms° as *Goblin Market.* One single piece in vol. 2. belongs neither to Mac nor to myself; to wit, *L.E.L*; but I have Miss Emily Faithfull's permission to make use of it: perhaps however considering this it would be well to print at the Victoria Press, as *G.M.* was printed by Bradbury and Evans for a similar reason:—but of course this question belongs to the publisher to decide. May I hope that you will again look at my proofs as they go through the press? if so, you had better have them before they come to me: and then I think I shall send them home for lynx-eyed research after errors, before letting them go to press:—but perhaps I may be snug at home again before my first proof hatches. [. . .]

To Dante Gabriel Rossetti, 6 [March 1865]

You confer favours as if you were receiving them, and I am proportionately thankful: but what says the Poet?

Feelings there are, &c, — °

So I need not aim at self-expression. I hope the peccant 'word or two'
may yet be tackled between us: meanwhile I readily grant that my
Prince lacks the special felicity (!) of my *Goblins*; yet I am glad to
believe you consider with me that it is not unworthy of publication.
What a most delightful pair of woodcuts; thank you with all my heart.
Do you think that two small points° in the frontispiece might advisably
be conformed to the text? to wit, the Prince's 'curly black beard' and
the Bride's 'veiled' face: all else seems of minor moment. Surely the
severe female who arrests the Prince somewhat resembles my phiz. Of
course you shall have back the charming sketches; only *via* home
instead of direct from me, as I know the pleasure their sight will give
our Mother to whom I take the liberty of lending them, but I will ask
her not to delay returning them to you.

If I don't get back the last miscellaneous batch I sent you in the
course of a few posts, I will send you the rest of the vol. without wait-
ing for it, and trust to your kindly placing them judiciously amongst
their fellows. Of course the *Prince* himself it is quite useless to send me
back. In vol. 2 you will find a longish thing (not only finished, but
altogether written just now; and indeed finished since last I wrote to
you) which no one has yet seen. I don't know whether you will deem
it available; if not, please let me have it again and I will fill deficit from
the squad; if on the other hand it passes muster it will I believe stop
the gap single-handed: *Under the Rose* it is called, in default of a better
name. But please tell me whether you don't think it will after all be
well to put in *Martyrs' Song* and the *terza rima* from *L. Mystica*? They
have won a word of praise from Mr Cayley, and a review (I forget
which) has been enthusiastic about me in *L. M.*; so perhaps they might
take: and using these, I will soothe your feelings by suppressing my
Captive Jew without a murmur. There's a bait!

To be tooked and well shooked is what I eminently need socially, so
Jean Ingelow will be quite appropriate treatment should she transpire:
she has not yet done so. [. . .]

To Dante Gabriel Rossetti, [11 March 1865]

'Mine truthfully' is a critic begging the loan of *Goblin Market* for
purpose of reviewing it along with Jean Ingelow and Mrs Ed. Thomas.
I mean to be propitious and lend it: fortunately I have a copy down here.

My merits are to be discussed in the *Rose, Shamrock & Thistle*;° a fearful periodical I cannot but fear, but do not know: do you know it?

Thanks emphatic and copious on all points. I think—especially if the *Royal Princess* is retained, which I leave to your decision—we can well spare one of the 4 pieces you name from Vol. 2., as far as bulk goes. My preference would be for *Shilling Mag.* to get *Amor Mundi*: but 'tin' is too luminously alluring to be rejected, whichever Mr. Sandys may select. It is rather triumphant, too, Mr Lucas wanting me the Pariah of *Once-a-Week*.° Of course I needn't say how much I should prefer you as my illustrator to the world in general; but can well believe that you have not time for Mr Shipley, any more than for the May *Shilling Mag.* I should have said before that of course the two *Eves*° may go together, as you think.

'Bessie Parkes' is comparatively flattering: call me 'Eliza Cook'° at once and be happy. Please make your emendations, and I can call them over the coals in the proofs:—only don't make vast changes as 'I am I'. *Hairy* I cannot feel inclined to forego, as it portrays the bud in question but please cut out *their* (in same line, about poppies, in *Prince's P.*), and also kindly substitute *heat* for *frost*,° which certainly seems right, and was I fancy at some period my meaning. I will try my hand again over *For me, shyness had grown*,° when it reaches me in print. *Songs in a Cornfield* is one of my own favorites, so I am specially gratified by your and Mr Swinburne's praise.

You would be a dear turning up in these parts: but I *do* hope to be at home again at very latest today 4 weeks.

Meanwhile, is not Vol. 2. at last ripe for transmission to Mac? I feel a pardonable impatience. *Of course* I am setting to work chewing the cud you serve to me: but we won't keep back Vol. 2. for the unapproached result. Do you know, I do seriously question whether I possess the working power with which you credit me; and whether all the painstaking at my command would result in work better than—in fact half so good as—what I have actually done on the other system. It is vain comparing my powers (!) with yours: (a remark I have never been called upon to make to any one but yourself). However, if the latent epic should 'by huge upthrust'° come to the surface some day, or if by laborious delving I can unearth it, or if by unflagging prodment you can cultivate the sensitive plant in question, all the better for me: only please remember that 'things which are impossible rarely happen'°— and don't be too severe on me if in my case the 'impossible' does not come to pass. Sometimes I could almost fear that my tendency is rather towards softening of the brain (say), than towards further development of mind. There's a croak! [. . .]

To Dante Gabriel Rossetti, 13 [March 1865]

You are a kind old thing, thanks many: — now for orderly answers.

1. The *Prince* shall keep your modification of stanza 2, as regards the main point: though 'I am I' is so strong within me that I again may modify details. Please look at my M. S. and if (as I suspect) I have written (same stanza) 'How long shall I wait come *heat* come rime' — oblige me by substituting *frost* for *heat*,° as under your charming sketch. Never mind the Prince's beard, if you please, though I won't record his waste of time in shaving: only please don't mulct me of the Bride's essential veil.

2. *Lowest Room* pray eject if you really think such a course advantageous, though I can't agree with you: still it won't dismay me that you should do so; I am not stung into obstinacy even by the Isa and Adelaide° taunt in which I acknowledge an element of truth.

3. Don't you think we might advantageously eject *Royal Princess* also, which is rather a spite of mine?

4. Of course proposals 2, 3, go on the supposition that *Under the Rose* is preferred by you: otherwise such a diminution of bulk is abhorrent. *U. the R.* herewith (book-post) I meekly return to you, pruned and re-written to order. As regards the unpleasant-sided subject I freely admit it: and if you think the performance coarse or what-not pray eject it, retaining *Lowest Room* and *Royal Princess*; though I thought *U. the R.* might read its own lesson, but very likely I misjudge. But do you know, even if we throw *U. the R.* overboard, and whilst I endorse your opinion of the unavoidable and indeed much-to-be-desired unreality of women's work on many social matters, I yet incline to include within female range such an attempt as this: where the certainly possible circumstances are merely indicated as it were in skeleton, where the subordinate characters perform (and no more) their accessory parts, where the field is occupied by a single female figure whose internal portrait is set forth in her own words. Moreover the sketch only gives the girl's own deductions, feelings, semi resolutions; granted such premises as hers, and right or wrong it seems to me she might easily arrive at such conclusions: and whilst it may truly be urged that unless white could be black and Heaven Hell my experience (thank God) precludes me from hers, I yet don't see why 'the Poet mind'

should be less able to construct her from its own inner consciousness than a hundred other unknown quantities. Practical result: if you retain *U. the R.*, I think it would be well placed last in the secular section.°

5. Squad finally rejected for vol. 2., though I keep my commercial eye upon it for Magazine pot-boilers.

6. In the *Prince* I entertain a dreadful certainty that I wrote *dye*° and a dreadful conviction that the singular of *dice* is *die*. It is in a stanza which occurs shortly before his start up the mountain, at the end of his stay with the friendly ferry-boat family; stanza begins

'Slip past, slip fast:'—

will you rectify, and spare me contempt? Spelling, alas, never was my forte.

7. You will oblige me if you will kindly remove *Bird and Beast* and *Portraits* from among the *Devotional*: I too thought that *B. and B.* would be appropriately followed by *Eve*. Of course too (if you retain it) *Lowest Room* must shift its quarters. Do you know I was originally staggered by

'It's up the second pair'—,°

but re-reading and laziness reconcile one to many things; and had it not a certain Patmorean flavour? At this stage of humiliation dare I further avow that I did hope *U. the R.* possessed a not un-Crabbed aspect?° Alas for author's vanity.

[. . .] Still no Jean Ingelow;—I hope, by the by, that *Under the Rose* is less dismal than the *Star's Monument* and *4 Bridges* of oppressive memory: the deduction of *Lowest Room* and *Royal Princess* will still leave vol. 2 of adequate length.

Your affectionately grateful sister
Christina G. Rossetti

P.S. Please don't throw away what pieces you turn out of vol. 2., but kindly preserve them for me: I don't know whether I possess otherwhere such correct copies.

To Dante Gabriel Rossetti, *31 March [1865]*

After 6 well defined and several paroxysms of stamping, foaming, hair-uprooting, it seems time to assume a treacherous calm: and in this (comparatively) lucid interval I regain speech.

1. *U. the R.* Yes, suppress that 'screech'.°

2. *Jessie Cameron.* Stanza 2 I cannot consent to sacrifice; to my conception of the plot and characters it really is essential: concede me that Stanza 2 with a good grace.

3. *Bird or Beast.* The last 4 lines of the first stanza are (I confess) stupid; but the last 4 of the second I like. What would you say to omitting those first 4 altogether, but retaining the other 4 by arranging the whole piece in quatrains? If, however, this proposal distresses you let the 8 go.

4. *Ghost's Petition.*° Please cut it short as you suggest.

5. I admit the less simple character of the second *Song in a Cornfield*, and admit it as a blemish: a yet graver one however it would seem to me to make one of a party of reapers who are resting under the 'burden of full noonday heat' suddenly burst forth with 'Gone were but the Winter'.° This therefore we will, please, set aside. But would you prefer to fill the gap with one of the two songs which I enclose? If so, your kindness will I am sure not shirk pasting it over the defaulter: unless you think said defaulter worth cutting out and erecting into an independent existence, when it might figure under the cheerful title *If so*, or any other you like.

6. How is it possible that not only you recognize no. 1 of *Spring Fancies* but resuscitate defunct lines from memory? The great original stands as *The Spring Quiet* in a little book dated 1847;° a little book so primitive that for aught I know you did not drag its depths for G.M. vol.: whence pray do not deduce that it contains other treasures, for I am not aware that it does. I will send you an exact copy of its primeval form: then will you most kindly set it right from the printed copy? but suppressing 5th lines and keeping extra stanzas as you judge best—or on second thoughts I will retain certain alterations which I know are in the printed copy, and which were the result of mature reflection, and will make the sea-stanza come last as you put it; but I must still trust to your kindness to compare and alter it by the printed copy in case I get a word here or there wrong. Only of course I will not trouble you to do any of this unless you think the piece worth adding to *vol. 2.*

7. After all which I shall hope the M.S. *will* go to Mr Macmillan; but if that enterprizing publisher has been prodding you it is *di proprio moto*,° not instigated in word by me. Your woodcuts are so essential to my contentment that I will wait a year for them if need is—though (in a whisper) 6 months would better please me: but perhaps it might be as well to commence *printing* as soon as may be, in case that Fata Morgana of delight, my sight of Italy with William,° should by any

manner of means come to pass; of course *if* the proofs could be got through before our start in May it would be charming.

I am delighted to find that *The Shilling Mag.* has got *Amor Mundi*, and to foresee Mr Sandys as my illustrator. But won't the *Shilling Mag.* pay me whatever it may owe me of its own accord and on its own scale? without, that is, any claim on my part. Did you see a prettyish little ballad by Alice Macdonald° in a recent *Once-a-Week*? this is an independent sentiment all by itself, not connected with aught that goes before or with aught that follows.

To return to my perpetual *Vol.* 2. May I remind you (without being too great a bore) of the one piece which belongs neither to Mac nor to me, to wit *L.E.L.*, the property of the Victoria Press? I mention it in case it should be expedient to give Miss Faithfull the printing of Vol. 2.; essential it is not, as I have her permission to reprint. [. . .]

To Dante Gabriel Rossetti, [?April 1865]

Thanks many. On almost all points I succumb with serenity: now for remarks.

Meggan and *Margaret* are, I suppose, the same name: but this does not disturb me. Do you think it need? *Meggan* was suggested by Scotus° once to me, and comes out of a Welsh song-book. *May, Meggan, Margaret*, sound pretty and pleasant.

Last Night: metre slightly doctored.

Royal Princess.° *Some to work on roads*, &c, is by so much one of the best stanzas that I am loath to sacrifice it. Is it so very like Keats? I doubt if I ever read the lines in question, never having read the *Isabella* through. I do not fight for the *R.P.*'s heroism; though it seems to me that the royal soldiers might yet have succeeded in averting *roasting*. A *yell* is one thing, and a *fait accompli* quite another.

L.E.L.° Adopted, your enormous improvement. I am glad you retain my pet name.

One Day. The changes you notice do not exist, either in *v.* 2 or elsewhere. It is copied word for word from the print in Mac, to the best of my remembrance.

Margery: has lost her 3 stanzas, and gained thereby.

By the Sea has superseded *A Yawn*;° for which however I retain a sneaking kindness.

3 Nuns:° *stet* be it.

Bird's Eye View: I have made 3 alterations. Was not aware of the inconvenient resemblances.

Ghost's Petition: I have cut out *night thro'—moonlight thro'*.°

Following your advice I have copied from Grandpapa's vol. *Vanity of Vanities*, *Gone for ever*, and the *Lady Isabella* sonnet. Don't you think this last would do very well as sequence to the one called *A Portrait*? But please re-arrange as seems well to you. For the moment I will place it as I think.

All these make up the bulk of *Goblin Market* within a few pages. Now for meek divergence from your programme.

I incline to reinstate *The Bourne*, partly because Mac likes it & it is already in print, partly because I like it, partly because it has been set to music very prettily by Alice Macdonald.

I have found & introduced 1 more Sonnet; which indeed was merely accidentally omitted in copying. Here it is: [. . .] = This I dub *In Progress*.°

Last of all, could you re-consider your verdict on *Come & See*?° It is, to own the truth, a special favourite of mine; and seems to me unlike any other in the volume, or indeed in *G.M.* I have moreover altered what you call the *queer rhyme*. In short I should like particularly to put this piece in, and it has already been printed by Mr Shipley. If however after all you cannot bear it, would you rather see *Easter Even*° put back? This is no particular liking of my own; but Mrs Scott told me that Scotus was struck by it quite remarkably, in Mr Shipley's volume where it is. Either of these 2 would make up the deficit, if my very careful calculation is as exact as I hope.

I don't think we need this time resort to the *Dead City*. As to *Amore e Dovere* it would surely require evisceration to the extent of *v. 2*. I think I could hunt up *1*, or possibly even *2*, Italian trifles to go with it: yet these would leave the Italian element in such an infinitesimal minority as scarcely to justify its introduction.

If none of all my expedients will pass muster with you, I have but to launch forth into the rag and bone store; thence, by main force, something must emerge.

I hope after this vol. (if this vol. becomes a vol.) people will respect my nerves and not hint for a long long while at any possibility of vol. 3. I am sure my poor brain must lie fallow and take its ease, if I am to keep up to my own mark.

I do not send you the *groans* herewith, because if you will kindly answer (what very little needs an answer) I will *page*° said groans before consigning them to your brotherly hands.

To Dante Gabriel Rossetti, [?spring 1870]

[. . .] it becomes scarcely optional when one is a person of one idea. It is impossible to go on singing outloud to one's one-stringed lyre. It is not in me, and therefore it will never come out of me, to turn to politics or philanthropy with Mrs Browning: such many-sidedness I leave to a greater than I, and having said my say may well sit silent. 'Give me the withered leaves I chose'° may include the dog-eared leaves of one's first last and only book.° If ever the fire rekindles availably tanto meglio per me°:—at the worst I suppose a few posthumous groans may be found amongst my remains. Here is a great discovery: 'Women are not Men'—and you must not expect me to possess a tithe of your capacities, though I humbly—or proudly—lay claim to family likeness. All this is for you, not for Mr Stillman, for whom however are all our cordial regards. [. . .]

To Dante Gabriel Rossetti, 14 [December 1875]

[. . .] Now for a little bit about my new ed..° It gratifies me much to receive your sympathetic praise, & find you care to accept the copy I store for you. The whole subject of youthful poems grows anxious in middle-age, or may at some moments appear so: one is so different, & yet so vividly the same. I am truly sorry if I have judged amiss in including the 'Lowest Room',—which, however, I remind you had already seen light in Mac.'s Mag.. To my thinking it is by no means one of the most morbid or most personal of the group: but I am no good judge in my own cause. As to 'John', as no such person existed or exists I hope my indiscretion may be accounted the less: & 'Flora' (if that is the 'next' you allude to) surely cannot give deep umbrage. The latter I hardly think as open to comment as 'My Secret', but this last is such a favorite with me that please don't retort 'Nor do I—'. Further remarks,° if any, when we meet.

To Augusta Webster, [?later 1878]

You express yourself with such cordial openness that I feel encouraged to endeavour also after self-expression—no easy matter sometimes. I write as I am thinking and feeling, but I premise that I have not even to my own apprehension gone deep into the question; at least, not in the sense in which many who *have* studied it would require depth of me. In one sense I feel as if I had gone deep, for my objection seems to myself a fundamental one underlying the whole structure of female claims.

Does it not appear as if the Bible was based upon an understood unalterable distinction between men and women, their position, duties, privileges? Not arrogating to myself but most earnestly desiring to attain to the character of a humble orthodox Xtian, so it does appear to me; not merely under the Old but also under the New Dispensation. The fact of the Priesthood being exclusively man's, leaves me in no doubt that the highest functions are not in this world open to both sexes: and if not all, then a selection must be made and a line drawn somewhere.—On the other hand if female rights are sure to be overborne for lack of female voting influence, then I confess I feel disposed to shoot ahead of my instructresses, and to assert that female *M.P.'s* are only right and reasonable. Also I take exceptions at the exclusion of married women from the suffrage,—for who so apt as Mothers—all previous arguments allowed for the moment—to protect the interests of themselves and of their offspring? I do think if anything ever does sweep away the barrier of sex, and make the female not a giantess or a heroine but at once and full grown a hero and giant, it is that mighty maternal love which makes little birds and little beasts as well as little women matches for very big adversaries. [. . .]

Nor do I think it quite inadmissible that men should continue the exclusive national legislators, so long as they do continue the exclusive soldier-representatives of the nation, and engross the whole payment in life and limb for national quarrels. I do not know whether any lady is prepared to adopt the Platonic theory of female regiments;° if so, she sets aside this objection: but I am not, so to me it stands.

To Augusta Webster, [?later 1878]

Many who have thought more and done much more than myself share your views,—and yet they are not mine. I do not think the present social movements tend on the whole to uphold Xtianity, or that the influence of some of our most prominent and gifted women is exerted in that direction: and thus thinking I cannot aim at 'women's rights.'

Influence and responsibility are such solemn matters that I will not excuse myself to you for abiding by my convictions: yet in contradicting you I am contradicting one I admire.

To an Unnamed Correspondent, 23 [?] 1888

Pray allow me gratefully to acknowledge the high compliment implied by your enquiry. If I could, I would help your young people to surpass me!

But it happens that my 'style' resulted not from purposed training so much as from what I may call hereditary literary bias and from constant association with my clever and well read Parents. Neither nursery nor schoolroom secluded their children from them,—indeed, our household was too small for any such separate system: and tho' my sister and my two brothers studied more or less, of myself it may be said (to my disgrace) that I picked up more than I learned. I do not recollect that I was ever exercised in English composition as a task, tho' to all of us it early became more or less of a delight.

Perhaps the nearest approach to a 'method' I can lay claim to was a distinct aim at conciseness: after a while I received a hint from my sister that my love of conciseness tended to make my writing obscure, and I then endeavoured to avoid obscurity as well as diffuseness. In poetics my elder brother was my acute and most helpful critic, and both prose and verse I used to read aloud to my dearest Mother and my sister: but of my nearest and dearest my second brother alone now remains to me. [. . .]

NOTES

1847   *Verses: Dedicated to Her Mother* (London, 1847)
1862   *Goblin Market and Other Poems* (London, 1862)
1866   *The Prince's Progress and Other Poems* (London, 1866)
1870   *Commonplace, and Other Short Stories* (London, 1870)
1875   *Goblin Market, The Prince's Progress and Other Poems*
            (London, 1875)
1881   *A Pageant and Other Poems* (London, 1881)
1890   *Poems* (London, 1890)
1893   *Verses* (London, 1893)
1896   *New Poems by Christina Rossetti*, ed. William Michael
            Rossetti (London, 1896)
1904   *The Poetical Works of Christina Georgina Rossetti*, ed. William
            Michael Rossetti (London, 1904)
Arseneau et al. Mary Arseneau et al. (eds.), *The Culture of Christina Rossetti:
            Female Poetics and Victorian Contexts* (Athens, Ohio, 1999)
BCP   *The Book of Common Prayer*
Bell   Mackenzie Bell, *Christina Rossetti: A Biographical and Critical
            Study* (London, 1898)
BL   British Library
CGR   Christina Georgina Rossetti
Crump   *The Complete Poems of Christina Rossetti*, ed. R. W. Crump,
            3 vols. (Baton Rouge, 1979–90)
D   'Devotional Pieces' section of *1862* or *1866*
D'Amico   Diane D'Amico, *Christina Rossetti: Faith, Gender and Time*
            (Baton Rouge, 1999)
DGR   Dante Gabriel Rossetti
DGRL (DW) *Letters of Dante Gabriel Rossetti*, ed. Oswald Doughty and
            John Robert Wahl, 4 vols. (Oxford, 1965–7)
DGRL (F) *The Correspondence of Dante Gabriel Rossetti*, ed. William E.
            Fredeman et al. (Cambridge, 2002–)
DGRW   *The Works of Dante Gabriel Rossetti*, ed. William Michael
            Rossetti, 2 vols. (London, 1911)
FD   *The Face of the Deep: a Devotional Commentary on the
            Apocalypse* (London, 1892)
FL   *The Family Letters of Christina Georgina Rossetti*, ed. William
            Michael Rossetti (London, 1908)
FQ   *Spenser's Faerie Queene*, ed. J. C. Smith, 2 vols. (Oxford,
            1909)
Hassett   Constance W. Hassett, *Christina Rossetti: The Patience of
            Style* (Charlottesville, 2005)
Hatton   Gwynneth Hatton, 'An Edition of the Unpublished
            Poems of Christina Rossetti, with a Critical Introduction

	and Interpretative Notes to All the Posthumous Poems', unpublished thesis, St Hilda's College, Oxford (1955)
Kent	David A. Kent (ed.), *The Achievement of Christina Rossetti* (Ithaca, NY, 1987)
Kooistra	Lorraine Janzen Kooistra, *Christina Rossetti and Illustration: A Publishing History* (Athens, Ohio, 2002)
L	*The Letters of Christina Rossetti*, ed. Antony H. Harrison, 4 vols. (Charlottesville, 1997–2004)
LS	*Letter and Spirit: Notes on the Commandments* (London, 1883)
Marsh	Christina Rossetti, *Poems and Prose*, ed. Jan Marsh (London, 1994)
N&Q	*Notes and Queries*
OED	*The Oxford English Dictionary* (Oxford, 1884–1928; repr. 1933)
P	Portfolio Society
PL	John Milton, *Paradise Lost*, ed. Alastair Fowler (London, 1968)
PP	John Bunyan, *The Pilgrim's Progress*, ed. Roger Sharrock (Harmondsworth, 1965)
RES	*Review of English Studies*
RP	*Rossetti Papers 1862 to 1870*, ed. William Michael Rossetti (London, 1903)
SF	*Seek and Find: A Double Series of Short Studies of the Benedicite* (London, 1879)
SP	*Selected Prose of Christina Rossetti*, ed. David A. Kent and P. G. Stanwood (Basingstoke, 1998)
SPCK	Society for Promoting Christian Knowledge
TF	*Time Flies: A Reading Diary* (London, 1885)
VP	*Victorian Poetry*
WMR	William Michael Rossetti

References to Shakespeare are to Peter Alexander (ed.), *William Shakespeare: The Complete Works* (London, 1951).

POEMS

3 SAPPHO. *Date*. 11 September 1846. *Publication*. Included in the privately printed volume *1847*. *Text*. Bodleian MS. Don. e. 1/1. The manuscript is in the hand of Maria Francesca Rossetti.

Title. A Greek woman poet of the late seventh century BC, and an important figure of the 'poetess' in the nineteenth century: for CGR's exploitation of the tradition of Sappho poems, see Introduction, pp. xxx–xxxi.

ll. 13–14. *Living . . . alone*. In Felicia Hemans's 'The Last Song of Sappho', she is 'unsought, unwatch'd-for' (l. 36), and her ceaseless cry is 'Alone, alone!' (l. 4).

THE DEAD CITY. *Date*. 9 April 1847. *Publication*. The first poem in the privately printed volume *1847*. *Text*. *1847*, which incorporates some substantive revisions of the notebook manuscript.

Title. In the notebook manuscript (in Maria Francesca Rossetti's hand) the title is 'The City of Statues' (Bodleian MS. Don. e. 1/2). 'The reader will, no doubt, perceive that it bears a certain relation to a story in *The Arabian Nights*, which was one of the comparatively few books which my sister, from a very early age, read frequently and with delight' (WMR in *1904*, 466). This is 'The Story of the First of the Three Ladies of Baghda'd' [or 'The Story of Zobeide'] (*Hatton*, 187), in which a lady voyages by sea to a land where everyone except a prince, a Muslim, has been 'converted into black stones' in punishment for worshipping fire and not God (*The Thousand and One Nights*, tr. Edward William Lane (London, 1839), 1. 195, 197–8; for CGR's 'partiality for Lane's Arabian Nights', see *L* 2. 156). In the poem petrification seems to be punishment decreed by God, to whom the speaker prays in the last line (l. 275), but punishment for 'luxury and pride' (ll. 100, 163–4) rather than for worshipping false gods. The banquet in ll. 166–265 was perhaps suggested by the banquet in Tennyson's sleeping palace in 'The Day-Dream', to which the poem also bears a certain relation (*Marsh*, 73), even though these banqueters are dead, not sleeping. The speaker's vision of the dead city is a divine disclosure (ll. 273–5); and the whole narrative is probably to be taken as a dream vision which then contains the further vision of the city (cf. ll. 77–8, and note to l. 275; and also the explicit uncertainty in 'An Old-World Thicket', ll. 1–2: 'Awake or sleeping (for I know not which) | I was or was not mazed within a wood').

l. 2. *hardihood*. Boldness. The word invokes the heroism of the knights of quest romance (e.g. *FQ* 1. 4. 38, 'fiers hardy-hed').

l. 3. *tangled way*. In that there is no straight way through these 'mazes' (l. 32), the opening of the poem recalls the dark wood in which the fearful Dante finds himself in *Inferno*, 1. 1–3; but this wood is not yet dark (l. 7; cf. l. 66), and the speaker is not yet fearful (l. 2; cf. 69).

4 l. 25. *master*. 'This has been remarked upon [*Bell*, 194] as a palpable make-rhyme, on the assumption that (if either of the two) the word ought to be "mistress". But there is no clear reason why the "I" of the narrative should be a woman; a phrase a little further on strongly suggests the contrary—"Before me the birds had never Seen a *man*"' (WMR in *1904*, 466). But that is not a strong suggestion to the contrary, and *Hatton* describes CGR's illustration of the poem in a copy of *1847*: 'a girl with long golden hair and dressed in a long, rose-coloured dress, walking with head raised between strange trees bearing mauve and yellow flowers' (p. 187). That the protagonist is a woman would also accord with the poem's model in *The Thousand and One Nights*.

ll. 38–40. *Where . . . test*. A prelapsarian state: death and woe have not been brought into this world.

7 l. 123. *chrysoprase*. A golden-green stone.

8 l. 171. *cate*. Delicacy.

8 l. 176. *All the vessels were of gold*. Cf. *The Thousand and One Nights*, 1. 195: 'entering the King's palace, I found all the vessels of gold and silver remaining in their places, and the King himself seated in the midst of his chamberlains and viceroys and wezeers, and clad in apparel of astonishing richness'.

10 l. 235. *unweeting*. Unwitting, unaware. CGR may have taken the word from Elizabeth Barrett Browning's 'Catarina to Camoëns', l. 45, in *Poems* by Elizabeth Barrett Barrett (London, 1844). (In a footnote to the first part of 'Three Nuns', dated 10 May 1850, in the manuscript of 'Maude', CGR notes an echo of the refrain of Barrett Browning's poem.) In the manuscript, this line reads 'With a look no longer flitting'; there is an aborted attempt at revision, in pencil, below the line. The revision is one of the few substantive revisions of the notebook manuscript made when the poem was printed in *1847*.

l. 239. *she blushed*. Cf. Tennyson, 'The Day-Dream': 'The Sleeping Palace', l. 32.

11 l. 274. *So . . . mystery?*. A revision of the manuscript's 'So much woe and luxury?'.

l. 275. *And . . . prayed*. Cf. the end of 'Repining', ll. 247–52.

SPRING QUIET. *Date*. 1847. *Publication*. A four-stanza version was published in *Macmillan's Magazine*, 11 (April 1865), 460, as the first of three 'Spring Fancies' (in *Crump*, 3. 36). This six-stanza version was published in *1866*. For the revision of the poem for publication in *1866*, see letter to DGR of 31 March [1865] (p. 395, above). In the notebook manuscript (Bodleian MS. Don. e. 1/3), the letter P is pencilled beside the title, indicating that this was a poem of which a copy was submitted to the Portfolio Society (on which, see Introduction, p. xxi, above). The Portfolio copy was submitted with the title ' "Solitude" ' (CGR Collection (C0222), Princeton University Library). *Text*. *1866*.

l. 3. *covert*. Thicket which protects and conceals game. To the speaker, it would also be a place of safety for her (cf. ll. 16–17).

l. 4. *Where the birds sing*. In the 1865 periodical version, they sing '| Ding-ding, ding-a-ding' (a similar fifth line to the stanza was pencilled, by CGR, in the notebook manuscript which is in Maria Francesca Rossetti's hand). Cf. the pages' song, 'It was a lover and his lass', in *As You Like It*, 5. 3. 14–31, where the lovers walk out 'In spring time . . . | When birds do sing, hey ding a ding, ding. | Sweet lovers love the spring'.

12 REPINING. *Date*. December 1847. *Publication*. *The Germ*, 3 (March 1850), 111–17. 'It is, of all the poems by Christina Rossetti which appeared in that short-lived magazine, the only one which she did not afterwards reprint' (WMR in *1904*, 460). It is listed in the table of contents as the work of 'Ellen Alleyn'. 'My impression is that [CGR] placed her poems at the disposal of [DGR], to be used (whether with or without real name) much as [DGR] chose. He invented and inserted the name "Ellen Alleyn", and only after he had done this did [CGR] know anything

about it' (WMR, in *Bell*, 203–4); 'this was my brother's concoction, as Christina did not care to figure under her own name' (WMR, introduction to the facsimile reprint of *The Germ* (London, 1901), 21). The version published in *The Germ* is about half the length of that in the manuscript. *Text. The Germ.*

Title. 'An Argument' in the manuscript in the notebook Bodleian MS. Don. e. 1/4. 'The reader will readily perceive that this poem is to some extent modelled upon [Thomas] Parnell's *[The] Hermit*. The moral, however, is different. Parnell aims to show that the dispensations of Providence, though often mysterious, are just. Christina's thesis might be summarized thus: Solitude is dreary, yet the life of man among his fellows may easily be drearier; therefore let not the solitary rebel' (WMR in *1904*, 460). In Parnell's poem, the hermit, who has begun to doubt divine providence, is accompanied on a journey by a youth who is later revealed as an angel; and, at the poem's end, the hermit prays and returns to his cave in peace.

l. 1. *alway thro'*. All through.

l. 2. *Spinning . . . away*. She is indeed spinning, but it is also the thread (i.e. the course) of her life that she spins away, the metaphor being emphasized by the transferred epithet *weary*.

13 l. 31. *rise up . . . afraid*. The visitor's command is Christlike (cf. Christ's command to the disciples in Matthew 17: 7: 'Arise, and be not afraid'), as is his command 'follow me' at l. 49 (cf. Matthew 4: 19). That he comes at night, when the woman is in bed, is probably an indication that the remainder of the poem is a series of visions that occur within a sleeping dream.

l. 37. *seemed*. Which is not to say that he *is* what he seems. The young man in a white robe in Mark 16: 5 is usually taken to be an angel; and this visitor is at least that (thus the nimbus that illuminates the room, ll. 40–2), if not more than that. His major analogue in CGR's poetry is the 'one like an angel' who, for a time, accompanies the speaker of 'From House to Home' (l. 45, and see note, p. 435). Cf. WMR's comparison with Parnell's 'The Hermit' (see headnote above).

l. 38. *charities*. Feelings of affection.

l. 51. *friend*. A revision of the notebook manuscript's 'Love' (the same revision being made in l. 104). With the woman's desire to stay where she is, in the company of her friend, compare 'From House to Home', ll. 65–70.

ll. 60–1. *Forth . . . over*. An incidental reprise of the divinely ordained passages of the Red Sea (Exodus 14: 22) and the Jordan (Joshua 3: 17).

14 l. 86. *succous*. Sappy.

15 l. 124. *And swelled . . . swell*. In the manuscript, deleted lines follow which tell of a mother and her dying son on the ship's deck. The son dies, and the mother then prays for her own death: '[She prayed for death; and ere the day | She with her son was far away]'.

15 l. 134. *manifold*. Many.

17 l. 176. '*Lord . . . peace*'. Cf. Simeon's words in Luke 2: 29.   *part* Depart.

18 l. 218. *armament*. Gathering of military forces.

19 A PAUSE OF THOUGHT. *Date*. 14 February 1848. The second digit of the month day has been overwritten as 4 in the notebook Bodleian MS. Don. e. 1/4. *Publication*. First published in *The Germ*, 2 (February 1850), 57, listed in the table of contents as the work of 'Ellen Alleyn'. It is entered in two Bodleian notebooks: in MS. Don. e. 1/4 it is a complete poem; in MS. Don. e. 1/9 it is the first section of a three-part poem, dated 25 July 1854, with the title 'Three Stages' (in *Crump*, 3. 232–4). *Text. 1862*.

Title. In Bodleian MS. Don. e. 1/4, the title is 'Lines | In memory of Schiller's "Der Pilgrim"'. In Schiller's poem, a young pilgrim sets out in search of a goal, placing his hope in the 'Dim and holy words of Faith, | "Wander forth—the way is open, | Ever on the upward path— | Till thou gain the Golden Portal, | Till its gates unclose to thee"'; but yet he finds that his goal is ever more distant, that 'Earth will never meet the Heaven, | Never can the THERE be HERE!' (*The Poems and Ballads of Schiller*, trans. Edward Bulwer Lytton, 2 vols. (Edinburgh, 1844), 1. 27–8).

l. 2. *hope deferred made my heart sick*. Cf. Proverbs 13: 12.

WHAT SAPPHO WOULD HAVE SAID HAD HER LEAP CURED INSTEAD OF KILLING HER. *Date*. 7 December 1848. *Text*. ll. 1–56, Bodleian MS. Don. e. 1/5; ll. 57–66, Pierpont Morgan MA 1879. The Pierpont Morgan manuscript is a leaf removed from the Bodleian notebook by WMR, on the other side of which is written 'Song' ('When I am dead, my dearest'). WMR gave the leaf to Mackenzie Bell, and replaced it in the notebook with an inserted leaf on which he copied ll. 57–66 and, on the other side, 'Song'.

Title. See Introduction, p. xxx–xxxi.

20 l. 28. *under*. Subdued.

21 l. 39. *prunes*. Preens.

l. 52. *Meet*. Not only 'fitting' but, in relation to the *narrow* bed, 'close-fitting' (*OED*, 1).

SONG ('WHEN I AM DEAD, MY DEAREST'). *Date*. 12 December 1848. *Publication. 1862. Text. 1862*.

22 l. 6. *With showers and dewdrops wet*. That is, not wet with tears.

ll. 15, 16. *haply*. Perhaps. The continuing consciousness of the soul after death is a topic of speculation (cf. 'Remember', ll. 11–12): 'You see Christina does not say there will not be recognition after the Resurrection, for then she was quite certain there would be recognition. She only expresses uncertainty on the point during the intermediate state after death and before the Resurrection' (WMR, as recalled in *Bell*, 211).

TO LALLA, READING MY VERSES TOPSY-TURVY. *Date*. 24 January 1849. *Text*. Bodleian MS. Don. e. 1/5. In l. 31, 'wisest' has been deleted in pencil, and 'wiser' written alongside. I take this to be WMR's corrective revision, made when preparing the poem for publication in *1896*, and have retained the deleted reading.

Title. Lalla 'was a pet name given to Henrietta Polydore, daughter of our Uncle Henry. The name was her own baby invention, I think. She became consumptive, and died in America in 1874, aged about twenty-eight' (WMR in *1904*, 491).

23 SONG ('OH ROSES FOR THE FLUSH OF YOUTH'). *Date*. 6 February 1849. *Publication*. First published in *The Germ*, 2 (February 1850), 64, listed in the table of contents as the work of 'Ellen Alleyn'. *Text. 1862*.

Title. The title in the notebook manuscript is 'A Song in a Song' (Bodleian MS. Don. e. 1/5). There, these two stanzas are preceded by three stanzas which introduce a speaker who mourns for a woman who has died, and who now sings this song—the song that the dead woman herself used to sing.

l. 2. *laurel*. The *laurel* is a name for the bay *Laurus nobilis*, which is emblematic of poetic distinction; here, however, the two plants appear to be distinguished (cf. l. 6; and 'Old and New Year Ditties. 3', l. 5) and it may therefore be the cherry laurel *Prunus laurocerasus*, a plant which has leaves of a brighter green than the dark-leafed bay.

l. 3. *ivy*. The evergreen plant may be chosen to represent both the hope of eternal life, and also weakness (it needs support; cf. 'An Old-World Thicket', l. 9).

HAVE YOU FORGOTTEN? *Date*. 16 February 1849. *Text*. Bodleian MS. Don. e. 1/5. The manuscript has been revised in pencil, but without corresponding deletions other than the light deletion of 'the', l. 3. The revisions have been incorporated into the text for this edition. WMR has pencilled on the manuscript 'must be Bouts rimés'—that is, a sonnet written to given end-rhymes as a test of poetic skill (see WMR in *1904*, 490). It shares the looseness of the genre; but WMR, evidently, did not know this for certain, and other sonnets written to *bouts rimés* are not given titles in the notebooks. For example, seven sonnets are gathered in MS. Don. e. 1/5 under the heading '[Bouts rimés] Sonnets' (in *Crump*, 3. 162–5), but without titles. (A copy of the first of these sonnets ('Amid the shades of a deserted hall') was made for the Portfolio Society, and it is in this Portfolio copy (CGR Collection (Co222), Princeton University Library) that the sonnet is given the title 'Ruin'; the draft in the Janet Camp Troxell Collection (Co189), Box 1, Folder 22, Princeton University Library, is untitled.) If this sonnet was indeed written to *bouts rimés*, it would seem that CGR subsequently thought it, unusually, worthy of a title.

24 l. 12. *a second chime*. A revision of 'another chime'.

AN END. *Date*. 5 March 1849. *Publication*. First published in *The Germ*, 1 (January 1850), 48, without attribution (as were all contributions to that first issue), but retrospectively attributed to 'Ellen Alleyn' in a revised table of contents in the February 1850 issue. *Text. 1862.*

24 l. 1. *Love, strong as Death.* Cf. Song of Solomon 8: 6.

TWO PURSUITS. *Date.* 12 April 1849. *Text.* Bodleian MS. Don. e. 1/5.

25 ll. 1, 11. *'Follow, follow'.* Cf. Christ's command 'Follow me' (Matthew 4: 19).

DREAM LAND. *Date.* April 1849. *Publication.* First published in *The Germ*, 1 (January 1850), 20, without attribution, but then attributed to 'Ellen Alleyn' in a revised table of contents in the February 1850 issue. *Text. 1862.*

Illustration. 'Christina made three coloured designs to this lyric. In the first we see the "She" of the poem journeying to her bourne. She is a rather sepulchral-looking, white-clad figure, holding a cross; the "single star" and the "water-springs" are apparent, also a steep slope of purplish hill which she is leaving behind. The second design gives the nightingale singing on a thorny rose-bough. In the third, "She" is rising and ascending winged; her pinions are golden, of butterfly-form' (WMR in *1904*, 478).

l. 1. *sunless rivers.* Recollecting Coleridge's 'Kubla Khan', where 'the sacred river, ran . . . Down to a sunless sea', ll. 3–5.

l. 8. *lot.* That which was ordained for her by God; and also—in the local sense of 'a piece of land'—an indirect reference to the grave (cf. 'Ash Wednesday' ['Jesus, do I love Thee?'], ll. 15–17, in *Crump*, 3. 35; 'Dead Hope', ll. 11–14, in *Crump*, 1. 208).

l. 11. *lorn.* Forlorn, desolate.

l. 20. *The purple land.* Probably the world of mortality that must be left behind: *purple* is 'an earthly hue of mourning' (*SF*, and p. 317, above).

ll. 21–2. *grain | Ripening.* An eschatological detail, anticipating the harvest in which the souls of the righteous will be gathered into heaven (see Revelation 14: 14–16; *FD*, 363–7).

26 AFTER DEATH. *Date.* 28 April 1849. *Publication. 1862. Text. 1862.*

l. 2. *strewn with rushes.* The setting is influenced by Pre-Raphaelite medievalism. In this context, *rosemary* and *may* both have Marian connotations: May, when the hawthorn (may) blooms, is Mary's month (Catherine Maxwell, 'The Poetic Context of Christina Rossetti's "After Death"', *English Studies*, 76 (1995), 149).

REST. *Date.* 15 May 1849. *Publication. 1862. Text. 1862.*

l. 1. *lie heavily upon her eyes.* Contradicting the commonplace wish that the earth lie lightly upon the dead (e.g. in the Latin grave inscription *sit tibi terra levis*).

l. 6. *curtained.* The implied image is of sleeping in a curtained bed.

l. 7. *irked.* Troubled, wearied.

27 l. 8. *almost Paradise.* But not quite: the implication is that, here, *Paradise* is synonymous with 'heaven', and not a name for the intermediate state

of rest between death and resurrection (which may, however, in comparison with the troubling world, come close to the peace that will be found in heaven).

LIFE HIDDEN. *Date*. 23 July 1849. *Text*. Bodleian MS. Don. e. 1/6.

REMEMBER. *Date*. 25 July 1849. *Publication*. *1862*. *Text*. *1862*. The octave of this sonnet contradicts the ostensible thrust of Shakespeare's Sonnet 71, 'No longer mourn for me when I am dead'; the sestet does then turn towards self-denial, but that is far from Shakespeare's self-asserting self-denial ('for I love you so, | That I in your sweet thoughts would be forgot, | If thinking on me then should make you woe', ll. 6–8). But whether these interesting dis/similarities mean that CGR's sonnet is 'modelled' on Shakespeare's (as John Kerrigan (ed.), *The Sonnets and A Lover's Complaint* (1986), 44) is questionable. On 3 December 1864, CGR responded to W. H. Budden's observation that one of her sonnets—one which 'cannot have been written less than 15 years ago'—showed a 'singular coincidence' with lines of Shakespeare's (*L* 1. 204). Neither her sonnet, nor what was presumably a sonnet of Shakespeare's, is identified in the letter; but, among the small number of her sonnets written not less than fifteen years before—and in print by—1864, this would seem that most likely to have drawn Budden's observation. But CGR commented that she had no recollection of ever reading the lines of Shakespeare that Budden had in mind, and was perhaps even less likely to have read them when she composed her sonnet.

ll. 7–8. *Only . . . pray*. The insistent tone of *you understand* is possibly to be understood in the context of controversy over the revival, by Tractarian clerics, of praying for the dead—a practice that, to their opponents, could imply a revival of the 'Romish' doctrine of purgatory (explicitly rejected in Article XXII, *BCP*). Here, the dead can be remembered only.

28 ll. 11–12. *For . . . had*. Probably referring to uncertainty over the continuing consciousness of the soul in the intermediate state between death and resurrection. The sense is: '*if*, following the decomposition (*corruption*) of my body, my soul is left one thought that I had when living, that thought will be "*Better by far* . . ."' (ll. 13–14)'. It is less likely, but not impossible, that the *vestige* of those thoughts is to be left not to the speaker, but to the 'you' of the sonnet: '*if* one thought can survive my death, the thought I would leave you—by means of this utterance/poem—would be "*Better by far* . . ."'. But where Shakespeare's sonnet makes ironic use of the topos of the speaker being remembered through his verse ('if you read this line, remember not | The hand that writ it', ll. 6–7), the speaker of this sonnet is not explicitly a poet (her hand is what she is held by, not what she writes with, l. 3), and the 'you' is not explicitly a reader.

('SO I GREW HALF DELIRIOUS AND QUITE SICK'). *Date*. 24 September 1849. *Text*. A typescript of CGR's letter to WMR of 24 September 1849, Janet Camp Troxell Collection (C0189), Box 2, Folder 25, Princeton

University Library. In l. 13 of this typescript, the typist's *slept* has been deleted, and *wept* written in by WMR in correction.

28 A *bouts rimés* sonnet, written to end-rhymes given by WMR (*L* 1. 27).

A DIRGE. *Date*. 18 January 1851. *Text*. Bodleian MS. Don. e. 1/7.

l. 8. *silently*. An adverbial qualification of *lies* (l. 6).

l. 11. *dawn*. In the manuscript this has been revised, in pencil, to ', lying lorn;'. In the present edition, this is taken to be WMR's revision, made when preparing the poem for publication in *1896* (as *Hatton*, 223; against *Crump*, 3. 436), correcting the imperfect rhyme. The revision makes *quickening* a noun; in its other occurrences in CGR's poetry, it is a participle.

29 l. 16. *passionless for*. Insusceptible to.   *joy and woe*. A totalizing phrase: nothing at all moves her (even though *As* — 'as (the sand)' — does encourage an individuating reading: 'as unaffected by joy as by woe').

l. 18. *yet*. In time, even though she is not at present fair.

l. 19. *Branch of the Living Vine*. Cf. the parable of the True Vine, John 15: 1–10.

l. 21. *Sun*. The capitalization draws attention to the play on 'Son' (as in George Herbert, 'The Sonne'). Cf. 'An Old-World Thicket', l. 148: 'The sun had stooped to earth though once so high'.

'A FAIR WORLD THO' A FALLEN.' ——. *Date*. 30 August 1851. *Text*. Bodleian MS. Don. e. 1/7.

Title. The title cites an argument which has been presented to the speaker. The theological problem which is explicit in this sonnet—that of the status of the postlapsarian world: whether man only was corrupted by the Fall, or whether the world itself was corrupted—is usually only implicit in CGR's poetry.

l. 10. *Bind up the wounded*. Cf. the story of the Good Samaritan (Luke 10: 34).

'A BRUISED REED SHALL HE NOT BREAK'. *Date*. 13 June 1852. *Publication*. *1862 (D)*. *Text*. *1862*.

Title. From Isaiah 42: 3, referring to God's 'servant'—a text read by CGR as referring to Christ. When used as a title for this poem— a dialogue between Christ and the individual soul—the text is to be understood as a promise that Christ's work will not be destructive, breaking what is already bruised: i.e. fallen man who inherits original sin.

l. 1. *I will accept thy will to do and be*. In order that fallen man may come into a right relationship with God (that is, be justified). Acceptance is not on the basis of what man does and is (i.e. his works), but on the basis of his will (e.g. to love Christ, ll. 3–4). Cf. Article 11, 'Of the Justification of Man', *BCP*: 'We are accounted righteous before God, only for the merit of our Lord and Saviour Jesus Christ by Faith, and not for our own works or deservings'.

l. 2. *hatred*. For the necessity of hating evil, see Augustine, *De civitate Dei*, 14. 6.

l. 5. *fruitful*. Cf. Article 12, 'Of Good Works', *BCP*: 'Albeit that Good Works, which are the fruits of Faith, and follow after Justification, cannot put away our sins, and endure the severity of God's Judgment; yet are they pleasing and acceptable to God in Christ, and do spring out necessarily of a true and lively Faith; insomuch that by them a lively Faith may be as evidently known as a tree discerned by the fruit'.

l. 6. *germs*. Seeds.

30 l. 7. *the better part*. The phrase is derived ultimately from Luke 10: 42: 'Mary hath chosen that good part' of hearing Christ's word.

l. 8. *I cannot will*. Sinful man is utterly dependent upon the divine grace that predisposes him to faith (prevenient grace) (cf. l. 23). See Article 10, 'Of Free-Will', *BCP*: 'The condition of Man after the fall of Adam is such, that he cannot turn and prepare himself, by his own natural strength and good works, to faith, and calling upon God: Wherefore we have no power to do good works pleasant and acceptable to God, without the grace of God by Christ preventing [i.e. going before] us, that we may have a good will, and working with us, when we have that good will'.

l. 18. *constrain*. Compel.

l. 21. *hate*. To be understood in the light of l. 2.

l. 23. *infuse*. Pour in: a theological term for the work of divine grace upon man. The 'Protestant' position on justification is that, while man is not righteous, God declares him righteous by imputing Christ's righteousness to him; the 'Catholic' position is that man is not only declared righteous, but is made righteous through the infusion of divine grace with which man cooperates. In the Protestant view, sanctification, enabled by grace, follows from justification; in the Catholic view, sanctification is needed for justification. The Protestant position is set against any suggestion that man is justified by his own merit: man is justified by faith only, not by his works. The Catholic position is set against any assumption that God's declaration of man as righteous removes the need for man to become righteous. Yet these extreme positions are difficult to hold apart entirely: e.g., the faith by which man is alone justified is itself dependent upon the working of grace upon man (see note to l. 8). This poem evidences the influence of Tractarianism in bringing justification into closer contact with sanctification than it might be in Evangelical formulations of justification by faith alone; but it is careful to avoid any implication that acceptance is on the basis of man's good works (see notes to ll. 1 and 5).

l. 24. *deprecate*. Pray against (especially, against an evil). The individual soul, which cannot will and cannot even wish to love Christ, can at least not wish against the working of divine grace: that is the extent of the cooperation of which sinful man is capable.

30 MOONSHINE. *Date*. 16 June 1852. *Text*. Bodleian MS. Don. e. 1/7. In
the manuscript, 'To' is pencilled beneath the undeleted 'For' in l. 64.
(Two other revisions are made to the poem, with corresponding dele-
tions.) In this edition 'To' is taken as a revision contemplated, but not
decided, by CGR, and the undeleted reading is retained.

Title. Both 'moonlight', and perhaps also moonlight 'taken as the type of:
an appearance without substance; something unsubstantial or unreal'
(*OED*, 2). Interpretation of the title will depend on whether the lover is
taken to be malign or not: his invitation in the second stanza resembles
those given by the angelic (or Christlike) figures in 'Repining' (l. 49) and
'From House to Home' (ll. 73-6), but his freezing smile in l. 44 is not
angelic. The poem's closest analogue may be the ballad 'The Dæmon
Lover' (cf. headnote to 'Amor Mundi'), which CGR almost certainly
knew in the version in Walter Scott's collection of ballads, *The Minstrelsy
of the Scottish Border*. There, a married woman's former lover lures her
away to sea, but she soon notices that something is wrong—his ship is
no ordinary ship, 'dismal grew his countenance', and he has a cloven
foot—as he sails her to hell. The poem's title may have been suggested
by Thomas Lovell Beddoes, 'The Ghosts' Moonshine', in *Poems* (1851).

32 l. 10. *Truly*. Firmly, and also faithfully.

'TO WHAT PURPOSE IS THIS WASTE?'. *Date*. 22 January 1853. *Publication*.
ll. 78-89 were revised for publication in *TF* (entry for July 5). *Text*.
Bodleian MS. Don. e. 1/7.

Title. From Matthew 26: 7-8, where a woman pours precious ointment
from an alabaster box on Christ's head: 'But when his disciples saw it,
they had indignation, saying, To what purpose is this waste?' The title's
question is answered through a vision of all creation praising God—
a biblical topos of which Psalm 96: 11-12 is perhaps the statement
closest to this poem: 'Let the heavens rejoice, and let the earth be glad;
let the sea roar, and the fulness thereof. Let the field be joyful, and all
that is therein: then shall all the trees of the wood rejoice' (cf. ll. 49-64).
But the context for this, in both psalm and poem, is ultimately eschato-
logical: creation is called upon to rejoice 'Before the Lord: for he cometh,
for he cometh to judge the earth: he shall judge the world with righteous-
ness, and the people with his truth' (Psalm 96: 13) (cf. ll. 125-33).

l. 1. *windy*. Blown through by the wind: cf. l. 58.

l. 2. *A lily budding in a desert place*. For the thought (and that of ll.
18-19, and of this opening verse paragragh generally) see Thomas
Gray, 'Elegy Written in a Country Churchyard', ll. 53-6: 'Full many a
gem of purest ray serene | The dark unfathomed caves of ocean bear: |
Full many a flower is born to blush unseen, | And waste its sweetness
on the desert air'.

33 l. 43. *Mine eyes were opened*. This is nothing other than revelation
through vision granted by God: thus the passive.

l. 52. *One wind*. The Holy Spirit.

34 l. 72. *Is type of her, the Undefiled*. The white lily prefigures the soul which has been cleansed by Christ's blood (for *arrayed in white* (l. 73), see Revelation 7: 13). The feminine personification derives from Song of Solomon 5: 2: 'Open to me, my sister, my love, my dove, my undefiled'— which, on a Christianizing reading, is taken as Christ the lover's words to the individual or to the Church as a whole.

l. 89. *As any King*. This line, and l. 124, are the last lines on notebook pages, and it is not therefore wholly certain that CGR assumes (as this edition does) that a paragraph break follows them.

35 l. 93. *leafed out of sight*. Hidden by leaves.

l. 103. *Who hath weighed the waters [?]*. God has (Job 28: 25).

l. 121. *Who witnessed that His work was good*. Cf. Genesis 1.

36 FROM THE ANTIQUE | ONE SEA-SIDE GRAVE. The three-stanza poem 'From the Antique' is dated 6 February 1853 in the notebook manuscript (Bodleian MS. Don. e. 1/7). A two-stanza poem, composed of the second and third stanzas of the unpublished poem—with the former stanza largely rewritten—was first published in the *Century Illustrated Monthly Magazine*, 28 (May 1884), 134, as 'One Sea-side Grave'. So radical is this revision of the poem, it is best understood as a reconception which produces two distinct works rather than two versions of the same work. Both the unpublished and the published poems are presented here. The text of the published poem is that of *1890*.

FROM THE ANTIQUE. *Title*. The title presents the poem as a translation of, or an imitation of, a classical poem (though the classical model is doubtless purely notional), indicating that the speaker is pagan. It is a thoroughly conventional device of the period, although CGR's use of it is not necessarily so conventional (see Introduction, pp. xxx–xxxi). CGR wrote two other poems entitled 'From the Antique': ('The wind shall lull us yet'), dated 10 December 1852, in *Crump*, 3. 207; and ('It's a weary life, it is'), dated 28 June 1854, included in this edition (p. 45).

l. 10. *So . . . morn*. See Introduction (p. xxxi).

37 WHITSUN EVE. *Date*. 18 May 1853. *Text*. Bodleian MS. Don. e. 1/7.

Title. Whitsun Eve is the day before Whit Sunday (i.e. Pentecost) on which the descent of the Holy Spirit (Acts 2) is commemorated. The name ('white Sunday') is understood to derive from the white baptismal robes worn at this time (cf. note to l. 11).

l. 1. *dove*. In the context of a poem for Whitsuntide, the dove is— however inexplicitly—a symbol of the Holy Spirit. Cf. *TF* (Whitsun Eve), 271: 'as a Dove, He cometh to dove-like souls'—dove-like, because souls which are filled with the Spirit may be offered to God (as, in the Old Testament, doves are offered in sacrifice): 'By Thine Indwelling make us doves'.

l. 11. *Our . . . shed*. That is, by means of the sacrament of baptism in which man's sin is washed away. Whether the sacrament of infant baptism did so regenerate (which was the High Church and Tractarian position, and one seemingly supported by the baptism liturgy of *BCP*), or whether the sacrament was a sign of necessary subsequent regeneration (the Evangelical position), was a debate which intensified in the late 1840s, with the Church of England's tolerance of the Evangelical position eventually leading some to convert to Roman Catholicism—William Dodsworth, CGR's parish priest at Christ Church, Albany Street, being one of them.

37 l. 14. *Thou . . . snow*. The poem is to be seen as a sonnet, but is a series of couplets—a deceptive form perhaps chosen in light of the poem's monolithic whiteness.

WHAT?. *Date*. May 1853. *Text*. Bodleian MS. Don. e. 1/8.

l. 1. *Strengthening as secret manna*. Manna sustained the Israelites in the wilderness (Exodus 16); and it is a type (i.e. prefiguration) of the Eucharist (cf. *TF*, June 7–8 (p. 351, above)), of which the benefit is the 'strengthening and refreshing of our souls' (Catechism, *BCP*).

l. 5. *banner*. Cf. Song of Solomon 2: 4: 'He brought me to the banqueting house, and his banner over me was love'.

38 A PAUSE. *Date*. 10 June 1853. *Text*. Bodleian MS. Don. e. 1/8.

l. 3. *love-bound*. The sense is torn between 'bound by (human) love' and 'bound for (divine) love'.

ll. 12–13. *the tardy . . . golden*. Cf. Tennyson, 'Locksley Hall', ll. 31–2, *Poems* (1842): 'Love took up the glass of Time, and turn'd it in his glowing hands; | Every moment, lightly shaken, ran itself in golden sands'.

l. 14. *glory*. A ring of light around the head (e.g. as in depictions of Christ or of saints).

SONG ('TWO DOVES UPON THE SELFSAME BRANCH'). *Date*. One of a group of poems headed 'Odds and Ends' which were copied into the notebook Bodleian MS. Don. e. 1/8 in September 1853. *Publication*. *1862*. *Text*. *1862*.

l. 1. *Two . . . branch*. Doves are a common symbol of constant love.

39 SLEEP AT SEA. *Date*. 17 October 1853. *Publication*. *1862 (D)*. *Text*. *1862*.

Title. The title in the notebook Bodleian MS. Don. e. 1/8 is 'Something like Truth'. 'Maria showed me the other day two poems of yours which are among the best you have written for some time only the title of one "Something like Truth" seems very like a whale. What does it mean? The latter verses of this are most excellent, but some which I remember vaguely, about "dreaming of a lifelong ill" (&c. &c. ad libitum) smack rather of the old shop. I wish you would try any rendering either of narrative or sentiment from real abundant Nature, which presents much more variety even in any one of its phases than all such "dreamings"' (DGR to CGR [8 November 1853], *DGRL (F)* 1. 293). DGR remembers vaguely ll. 55–6.

l. 1. *Sound*. i.e. measure the depth of water using a line weighted with a lead *plummet* (l. 3).

l. 21. *types*. Symbols.

40 l. 41. *spirits*. Cf. the 'troop of spirits blest' in Coleridge, 'The Rime of the Ancient Mariner' (1817), l. 349 (identified, in the prose gloss, as angelic spirits) (Jerome J. McGann, *The Beauty of Inflections* (Oxford, 1985), 249 n. 24).

41 l. 74 *amain* At full speed.

'CONSIDER THE LILIES OF THE FIELD'. *Date*. 21 October 1853. *Publication*. *1862 (D)*, in which it precedes 'The World', in which flowers do nothing but deceive.

Title. From Matthew 6: 28.

l. 7. *scarlet*. Probably with whorish connotations (see Revelation 17: 3–5) which then inform the *scorn* (l. 8) in which it is held when it contaminates the wheat crop (cf. 'scarlet sinners', *TF*, August 11).

l. 9. *virtue*. Medicinal power.

l. 11. *lilies*. Symbolic of purity.

42 l. 17. *humble*. Because these lessons are read by a low-growing flower (*OED*, 2c), and because they are lessons of the beauty of humility (of which the violet is a symbol).

A STUDY (A SOUL). *Date*. 7 February 1854. *Text*. CGR Collection (C0222), Princeton University Library, a copy submitted to the Portfolio Society.

Title. 'A Soul', in the Bodleian notebook MS. Don. e. 1/8. 'A Study' is almost certainly the subject set by the Portfolio Society (cf. Jean Ingelow's Portfolio submission 'A Study', Harry Ransom Center, University of Texas at Austin).

l. 1. *Parian*. Of the white marble of Paros. In the light of ll. 2–4, the comparison may be prompted by Cleopatra's words when the Clown enters with the 'aspic' in *Anthony and Cleopatra*, 5. 2. 236–8: 'My resolution's plac'd, and I have nothing | Of woman in me. Now from head to foot | I am marble-constant'.

42 THE BOURNE. *Date*. 17 February 1854. *Publication*. First published in *Macmillan's Magazine*, 7 (March 1863), 382. The two stanzas were excised from a twelve-stanza unpublished poem, '"There remaineth therefore a rest"' (in *Crump*, 3. 226–8). The manuscript in the notebook Bodleian MS. Don. e. 1/8 shows DGR's pencilled direction 'Take 2 stanzas', with these two stanzas being numbered 1 and 2. *Text. 1866*.

Title. Cf. *Hamlet*, 3. 1. 79–80, 'The undiscover'd country, from whose bourn | No traveller returns'.   *Bourne*. Either 'boundary' or 'destination of a journey'.

43 ll. 6–10. *Youth . . . contain*. Cf. *1 Henry IV*, 5.4. 88–92. In the unpublished poem '"There remaineth therefore a rest"', this stanza is in the context

of stanzas in which death's levelling of social and economic hierarchy is explicit: in the grave, the proud 'must mingle with the crowd'; 'In the wrappings of a shroud | Jewels would be out of place'; 'High and low and rich and poor, | All will fare alike at last'. The last five stanzas then turn to the hope of heaven.

43 PARADISE. *Date.* 28 February 1854. *Publication.* First published in Orby Shipley (ed.), *Lyra Messianica*, 2nd edn. (London, 1869), 365–6 (*Crump*, 3. 530). *Text. 1875.*

Title. In the notebook Bodleian MS. Don. e. 1/8 the title is 'Easter Even'. *Lyra Messianica* included another poem of CGR's entitled 'Easter Even' (in *Crump*, 3. 33–4), and there the poem was retitled 'Paradise: in a Dream' (in distinction from 'Paradise: in a Symbol', which was also included).

l. 17. *the fourfold River.* Cf. Genesis 2: 10: Paradise restores elements of the lost paradise of Genesis (first things generating last things).

ll. 25–6. *The Tree . . . fruits.* Cf. Revelation 22: 2.

44 l. 33. *the gate called Beautiful.* The name of one of the gates of the Jerusalem temple (Acts 3: 2); CGR gives it to a gate of the heavenly Jerusalem of Revelation 21.

l. 35. *golden streets.* Cf. Revelation 21: 21.

l. 36. *glassy pool.* Cf. Revelation 4: 6: 'And before the throne there was a sea of glass like unto crystal'.

ll. 39–40. *Eye . . . conceived.* Cf. 1 Corinthians 2: 9.

l. 46. *narrow way.* Cf. Matthew 7: 14.

THE WORLD. *Date.* 27 June 1854. *Publication. 1862 (D). Text. 1862.* 'The primary sense (of course subsidiary to some spiritual meaning) appears to be that the world—like other devils, spectres, and hobgoblins—appears *in propria persona* in the night-hours only; it is then that she is recognized for the fiend she actually is' (WMR in *1904*, 182). In personifying the duplicitous world as a woman, the sonnet draws on Proverbs 5: 3–5 (see note to l. 14). A literary model for this duplicitous being is Spenser's double being, Duessa ('I that do seeme not I, Duessa am', *FQ* 1. 5. 26), the fair embodiment of falsehood. It is when Duessa is disrobed that her true foulness is revealed (*FQ* 1. 8. 46–9). The world's nightly exposure of her true identity has some resemblance to Geraldine's unrobing in Coleridge's 'Christabel' (ll. 245–54), which discloses to Christabel a sight so disturbing that it must not be described. Yet, in CGR's poetry, the world's foulness is not always disclosed as plainly as it is in this sonnet, nor is its foulness always so unquestionable: in *1862*, the sonnet, with its sweet deceiving flowers, is placed immediately after ' "Consider the Lilies of the Field" ' in which flowers point beyond themselves.

ll. 3–4. *Loathsome . . . hair.* Compare the monster Error who lurks within the delights of the Wandering Wood in *FQ* 1. 1. 14: 'Halfe like a serpent horribly displaide, | But th'other halfe did womans shape retaine, | Most lothsom, filthie, foule, and full of vile disdaine'.

l. 6. *full satiety*. The overemphatic tautology ought to excite suspicion. Cf. 'Books in the Running Brooks' (in *Crump*, 3. 57–9).

l. 10. *the naked horror of the truth*. Cf. the naked truth of Duessa, *FQ* 1. 8. 46–9.

l. 14. *take hold on hell?*. See Proverbs 5: 3–5: 'For the lips of a strange woman drop as an honeycomb, and her mouth is smoother than oil: But her end is bitter as wormwood, sharp as a twoedged sword. Her feet go down to death; her steps take hold on hell'. In *PP*, Faithful recalls this text when Wanton promises him 'all carnal and fleshly content', 103–4.

45 GUESSES. *Date*. 27 June 1854. *Text*. Bodleian MS. Don. e. 1/8.

l. 17. *a hill*. The topography is symbolic: the pathway of l. 14 will not be downhill (cf. 'Amor Mundi').

FROM THE ANTIQUE. *Date*. 28 June 1854. *Text*. Bodleian MS. Don. e. 1/8.

Title. See note on the title of 'From the Antique' ('I wish that I were dying') (p. 413), and Introduction, p. xxxi.

l. 1. *It's a weary life, it is; she said*. Cf. the refrain of Tennyson's 'Mariana', *Poems* (1842): 'She said "I am aweary, aweary; | I would that I were dead!"'.

46 l. 9. *wag on*. Take its course (*OED*, 7c).

TWO CHOICES. *Date*. October 1854. *Text*. Bodleian MS. Don. e. 1/9. In the manuscript, the title is deleted along with a total of twenty lines of verse. A line is pencilled beneath l. 14, with the word 'Stop', which is to be taken as DGR's intervention. Two four-line stanzas (which had followed l. 4 and l. 10) have been deleted by both CGR and WMR; twelve concluding lines have been deleted by WMR only—effecting DGR's instruction, which CGR had not herself carried out. WMR's deletions take the form of a discontinuous Z pencilled through stanzas (cf. his known deletions in 'Look on This Picture and on This' and in 'Sir Winter', BL Ashley MS. 1364 (1)). The deletion of the concluding twelve lines rendered the poem's title unintelligible, and it is therefore to be presumed that it was WMR who deleted the title. The pencilled title 'Listening' is in WMR's hand (as *Hatton*, 233; against *Crump*, 3. 452). In this edition, the concluding twelve lines, and CGR's title, have been restored.

l. 1. *cushat dove*. Wood pigeon.

47 ECHO. *Date*. 18 December 1854. *Publication*. *1862*. *Text*. *1862*.

THE FIRST SPRING DAY. *Date*. 1 March 1855. *Publication*. *1862*. *Text*. *1862*.

48 MY DREAM. *Date*. 9 March 1855. *Published*. *1862*. *Text*. *1862*.

WMR remarked that 'nothing seems as if it could account for so eccentric a train of notions, except that [CGR] in fact dreamed them'—only to note that CGR in fact did not (see note to ll. 1–2). Criticism has most often accounted for the dream by concentrating on the supposedly phallic growth of the crocodile; but the assumption that this is a sex dream becomes less persuasive once the poem's primary generic affiliation is understood. The poem demonstrates CGR's assimilation of the mode of biblical apocalyptic, in which beasts represent kingdoms that rise and fall—even though the poem transposes the genre of apocalyptic beast vision into a less portentous, distinctly playful, mode (see Simon Humphries, 'Christina Rossetti's "My Dream" and Apocalypse', *N&Q* 55/1 (March 2008), 54–7). The poem conflates the topos of beasts emerging from the sea (Daniel 7: 3; Revelation 13: 1) with that of the location of the visionary beside a river (Daniel 8: 2; 10: 4). The exact location of this vision, on the Euphrates, is significant: there lies Babylon, symbol of worldly power—indeed, of bestial, devouring power (cf. Jeremiah 51: 34, 44)—which will, in time, face divine judgement (note to ll. 3–4). And the wingèd vessel that approaches the kingly crocodile appears intent on vengeance (l. 41; note to l. 38). The poem probably also draws upon literary mediations of biblical apocalyptic. The third of Spenser's *Visions of the Worlds Vanitie*, a series of moralizing sonnets within a dream structure, uses the crocodile 'cram'd with guiltles blood' (l. 32) as a figure of tyrannical power. And the eighth sonnet of *The Visions of Bellay* uses the seven-headed beast from the sea of Revelation 13 and 17 to present a vision of the destruction of Rome: a vision of an overflowing river from which the beast emerges to devour indiscriminately, only then for 'the wrathfull winde' to make it vanish— a vision which may be the immediate literary model for CGR's poem. Once the poem's primary generic model is understood, the suggestion that it might have some topical reference to the Crimean War (Lionel Stevenson, *The Pre-Raphaelite Poets* (1972), 95) begins to seem by no means eccentric. (CGR can hardly not have had a particular interest in the war: in 1854 she had applied to follow an aunt's example of serving as a nurse in Florence Nightingale's mission, but was turned down as being too young; WMR in *1904*, p. lvi.) Yet CGR's application of apocalyptic is always generalizing: Babylon is every worldly power, in every time. Which suggests that the beast in this poem is, ultimately, more than a figure of Russian expansionism, and that the wingèd vessel is a more potent force than even the British fleet.

Illustration. 'I possess a little bit of paper, containing three illustrations of her own to *The Dream*, and bearing the date 16 March '55. There is (1) the dreamer slumbering under a tree, from which the monarch crocodile dangles; (2) the crocodile sleeping with "unstrung claw", as the "winged vessel" approaches; and (3) the crocodile as he reared up in front of the vessel, and "wrung his hands"' (WMR in *1904*, 479).

ll. 1–2. *Hear . . . truth.* 'In a copy of her collected edition of 1875, I find that [CGR] has marked the piece "not a real dream"' (WMR in *1904*, 479).

ll. 3–4. *Euphrates*. That this location is significant is underlined by the departure from literary tradition (and fact) that it necessitates: a crocodile ought to be on the river with which it would rhyme—the Nile (compare Spenser, *Visions of the Worlds Vanitie*, 29; *FQ* 1. 5. 18). *Jordan*: in Joshua 3: 15–16 'Jordan overfloweth all his banks all the time of harvest', yet its waters are divided so that the Israelites can cross (with which event, compare the wingèd vessel's taming of the waters in ll. 42–5).

ll. 13–14. *Each . . . grew*. Compare Thomas Lovell Beddoes, 'A Crocodile', in *Poems* (1851), ll. 3–4: 'The brown habergeon of his limbs enamelled | With sanguine almandines and rainy pearl'.

49 l. 26. *battened*. Fed gluttonously. The use of the word may be influenced by Tennyson's 'The Kraken', in *Poems, Chiefly Lyrical* (1830)—a poem with its own relation to biblical apocalyptic—in which the monster 'will lie | Battening upon huge seaworms in his sleep'. DGR copied out Tennyson's poem in his letter to CGR of [8 November 1853], *DGRL (F)* 1. 295. For a biblical text which connects such bestial devouring with kingly power, see Jeremiah 51: 34: 'Nebuchadrezzar the king of Babylon hath devoured me [i.e. Israel], he hath crushed me, he hath made me an empty vessel, he hath swallowed me up like a dragon, he hath filled his belly with my delicates, he hath cast me out'. Cf. Spenser, *The Visions of Bellay*, ll. 105–6.

l. 27. *He knew no law, he feared no binding law*. The emphasis on the beast's lawlessness suggests the influence of William Dodsworth's diagnosis of the turbulence of 1848 in his Advent sermons of that year. Dodsworth—then CGR's parish priest at Christ Church, Albany Street—takes the rising of the beast from the sea in Revelation 13 to figure the rise of the Antichrist, 'the lawless one', *The Signs of the Times* (London, 1849), 78–9, 83–4.

l. 34. *unstrung*. Relaxed.

l. 37. *empire*. Probably 'the insignia of his imperial power' (cf. ll. 17, 19).

l. 38. *wingèd vessel*. An eschatological arrival: in Revelation 19: 11–21 Christ comes on a white horse to judge and to make war, followed by armies on white horses, and the beast of Babylon is destroyed.

l. 48. *appropriate tears*. The duplicitous crocodile, who uses his tears to trap travellers who pity him, is proverbial: e.g. in *FQ*, the weeping Duessa—the double being who is not what she seems—is likened to 'a cruell craftie Crocodile, | Which in false griefe hyding his harmefull guile, | Doth weepe full sore, and sheddeth tender teares' (1. 5. 18). (For Duessa's presence in CGR's poetry, see headnote to 'The World' (p. 416).)

COBWEBS. *Date*. October 1855. *Text*. Bodleian MS. Don. e. 1/9. In l. 7 'are' is pencilled above the undeleted 'is', as if an alternative that was considered but not decided; in this edition the undeleted reading is retained. In l. 11 a colon follows 'the loveless land', and before revision

l. 12 read 'No future hope; no trace of days before,'; in this edition the colon is removed from the end of l. 11 in the belief that it was oversight on CGR's part not to delete it when revising l. 12. The primary source of CGR's conception of a lifeless land is probably Poe's 'The City in the Sea' (see note to l. 9)—a city, presided over by Death, which will in time be received into Hell.

49   l. 1. *It is a land with neither night nor day.* Cf. 'A Coast-Nightmare', l. 8: 'For there comes neither night nor day'—a poem which (together with the shorter poem derived from it, which forms the entry for 1 April in *TF* (p. 345, above) is the closest analogue to this sonnet in CGR's poetry.

50   l. 9. *No ripple on the sea.* Cf. Poe, 'The City in the Sea', in *The Raven and Other Poems* (London, 1846): 'Around, by lifting winds forgot, | . . . The melancholy waters lie' (ll. 9–11), 'For no ripples curl, alas! | Along that wilderness of glass—' (ll. 36–7).

MAY. *Date.* 20 November 1855. *Publication. 1862. Text. 1862.*

AN AFTERTHOUGHT. *Date.* 18 December 1855. *Text.* Bodleian MS. Don. e. 1/9. At l. 36, which is the last line of a notebook page, a stanza break is assumed in this edition.

51   ll. 27–8. *Yet . . . love.* i.e. Adam's.

l. 33. *Willing with the perfect Will.* Euphemizing the Psalmist's declaration of hatred for God's enemies: 'I hate them with perfect hatred' (Psalm 139: 22). Augustine, in a chapter on the relation between the will and the emotions in *De civitate Dei* (14. 6), alludes to this text: man must have perfect hatred of the evil, but must not hate the evildoer (cf. '"A Bruised Reed Shall He Not Break"', l. 2).

l. 34. *flaming sword.* Cf. Genesis 3: 24.

ll. 37–42. *What . . . skies?.* For an explicit statement of the question of whether nature itself was corrupted by man's transgression, see '"A Fair World Tho' a Fallen"'.

l. 43. *rapt on high.* Taken and carried up into heaven. In Christian theology, the term 'paradise' can designate both the earthly paradise (Eden) and a heavenly paradise—whether heaven itself, or whether (as here, l. 44) the intermediate state in which souls wait for the resurrection into heaven. The principle of last things resembling first things invites an identification of the earthly with the heavenly. (This tidies up the problem of the redundant earthly paradise once man has been driven out: in Genesis 2: 7–9, God had planted the garden in Eden expressly for man to live there.) Here the earthly paradise becomes the heavenly paradise (i.e. the intermediate state) through rapture. This may be no more than a figurative statement of the Christian spiritualization of the concept of paradise: CGR is not necessarily suggesting that the earthly paradise was translocated. If so, the questions of ll. 37–42 are superseded rather than answered. But CGR may indeed be suggesting that Eden was taken up. There is no explicit basis for such a suggestion in the canonical scriptures; but the lack of scriptural information may license speculation. Yet there is Paul's account of being 'caught up to the third heaven . . . caught up into paradise' (2 Corinthians 12: 2, 4), although it is not clear from that if paradise is in the 'third heaven' or if the third heaven is being described figuratively as 'paradise' (as Augustine observes, *De Genesi ad litteram*, 12. 34). CGR's reasoning may be that if Paul was caught up into paradise, then paradise itself—if identified with Eden—must itself previously have been caught up into the heavens.

l. 44. *It lies before the gate of Heaven.* In the *Commedia*, the earthly paradise is at the top of Mount Purgatory (and, it would appear, has always been there) (*Purgatorio*, 28); and it is from there that Dante ascends to the first heaven (*Paradiso*, 1).

l. 46. *Rachel comforted.* Cf. Jeremiah 31: 15 // Matthew 2: 18. The abrupt specification of Rachel as among the blessed dead (why Rachel?) may be prompted by the reference to her in Dante's dream immediately before he reaches the earthly paradise (*Purgatorio*, 27. 104–8). There, she is a figure of the contemplative life—paired with Leah, a figure of the active life—which may be why CGR chooses her to represent the slumbering, waiting company (the active | contemplative states becoming analogous to life | death, cf. 'The Convent Threshold', note to l. 140 (p. 432)).

52 l. 57. *the blessed door made fast.* An inclusive reversal of the exclusion of Genesis 3: 24.

MAY —. *Date.* 31 December 1855. *Text.* Bodleian MS. Don. e. 1/9.

Title. In the notebook manuscript, the title 'A colloquy' is deleted.

l. 1. *Life.* A revision, in the manuscript, of 'love'. (The same revision is made in l. 11.)

l. 7. *say me nay.* Refuse me, deny me.

l. 10. *He wanders forth with me.* Cf. the companionable 'one like an angel' of 'From House to Home', l. 45.

53 l. 24. *rank.* Vigorous in growth.

l. 29. *heartsease.* The wild pansy *Viola tricolor*: cf. *TF*, June 6.

l. 31. *And blossoms where I tread.* In the manuscript, a further (deleted) stanza follows:

> [Oh loth to comprehend,
>   Deep rooted in a lie!
> Your heart is dead, my friend;
>   Not love, he cannot die.
> Your eye is dim, your ear
> Is dull and slow to hear:
>   Love's fountain runs not dry,
>   Love's bloom shall not pass by,

He nor begins nor hath an end
    But fills eternity.]

53 SHUT OUT. *Date*. 21 January 1856. *Publication*. *1862*. *Text*. *1862*.

Title. In the notebook Bodleian MS. Don. e. 1/9, the title is 'What happened to me'.

54 ll. 27–8. *And . . . dear*. Cf. 'An Afterthought', ll. 1–5. In the manuscript notebook there is a further deleted stanza after l. 28:

[Oh thought of solace gone before,
    Faint thought of love no love could save,
    By pathway of the narrow grave
At least shall I reach home once more.]

BY THE WATER. *Date*. 7 February 1856. *Text*. Bodleian MS. Don. e. 1/9. A copy was submitted to the Portfolio Society (CGR Collection (C0222), Princeton University Library) with the title 'River Thames (?)'. The Bodleian version is chosen for this edition on evaluative grounds: this is one instance in which the shortening of a notebook version of a poem is not obviously an improvement.

A CHILLY NIGHT. *Date*. 11 February 1856. *Text*. Bodleian MS. Don. e. 1/9.

55 ll. 15–17. *O my mother dear . . . Make a lonely bed for me*. A ballad formula: cf. 'Barbara Allen's Cruelty', in [Thomas Percy (ed.)], *Reliques of Ancient English Poetry* (1765), ll. 51–2: 'O mother, mother, make my bed, | For I shall dye to morrowe'; and the repeated 'mother, make my bed soon' throughout 'Lord Randal', in Walter Scott (ed.), *The Minstrelsy of the Scottish Border*.

56 l. 43. *subtle*. Lacking density.

AMEN. *Date*. 20 April 1856. *Publication*. *1862 (D)*: the last poem in the volume. *Text*. *1862*.

ll. 16–17. *And the latter . . . spices*. Cf. Song of Solomon 4: 16: 'Awake, O north wind; and come, thou south; blow upon my garden, that the spices thereof may flow out. Let my beloved come into his garden, and eat his pleasant fruits'—with the beloved identifiable, in Christian interpretation, as Christ. Here, *latter wind* continues the eschatological imagery of the preceding stanzas: both 'the last of the wind' and 'the wind of the last days'.

A BED OF FORGET-ME-NOTS. *Date*. 17 June 1856. *Text*. BL Ashley MS. 1364 (1).

57 l. 8. *flags*. Wild irises.

l. 16. *a fixèd star*. Cf. Shakespeare, Sonnet 116, a definition of love perhaps echoed in the phrasing of ll. 10–11, and in which love is 'an ever-fixèd mark . . . the star to every wand'ring bark', ll. 5–7.

ll. 19–20. *This . . . breath*. In Romans 8: 18–22, the fallen world waits to be delivered from its corruption: 'For we know that the whole creation groaneth and travaileth in pain together until now' (8: 22).

'LOOK ON THIS PICTURE AND ON THIS'. *Date.* 12 July 1856. *Text.* BL Ashley MS. 1364 (1). The manuscript has a pencilled inversion in l. 3, and pencilled inverted commas in ll. 28, 30: in this edition, these are taken to be WMR's markings made when preparing a shortened text for publication in *1896*, and are disregarded. In the manuscript, l. 12 has no terminal stop.

Title. From *Hamlet*, 3. 4. 53.

l. 3. *Eva.* 'Were it not for the name "Eva", I should be embarrassed to guess what could have directed my sister's pen to so singular a subject and treatment; but that name satisfies me that she was here recurring to a favourite romancist of her girlhood, Maturin . . . In Maturin's novel entitled *Women* there is a personage Eva, and a situation which must certainly have prompted the present poem' (WMR in *1904*, 480). In Charles Maturin's *Women; or Pour et Contre* (1818), the 'situation' is that Charles De Courcy is torn between Eva, a young woman in the care of a puritanical family, and the opera-singer Zaira. He deserts Eva; then, when he hears that Eva is dying, he renounces Zaira; then Eva dies, and he dies, and it turns out that Eva was Zaira's daughter.

58 l. 16. *redundant.* Abundant (e.g. in beauty).

60 l. 87. *the devil's special taint.* Pride (as in 'The Lowest Room', l. 172): cf. *PL* 1. 36–41; the main biblical basis is Isaiah 14: 12–15. In l. 86, *the old bent* is probably fallen man's inclination towards sin.

61 l. 120. *Heaping coals of fire.* Cf. Romans 12: 20.

l. 128. *that day.* The Day of Judgement. (The phrase is biblical.)

THE LOWEST ROOM. *Date.* 30 September 1856. *Publication.* First published in *Macmillan's Magazine*, 9 (March 1864), 436–9. CGR acquiesced in DGR's view—which was not her own—that the poem was not worth inclusion in *1866* (letter to DGR, 13 [March 1865]; p. 393)); DGR later regretted its inclusion in *1875* (see Introduction, p. xxxv). *Text. 1875.*

Title. 'A fight over the body of Homer' in the notebook BL Ashley MS. 1364 (1); published in 1864 as 'Sit Down in the Lowest Room'. The title is taken from Luke 14: 10: Jesus's instruction that the guests at a wedding should choose the lowest place, for 'he that humbleth himself shall be exalted' (14: 11): cf. the poem's last line.

62 ll. 21–3. *the acts . . . Aeacides.* The *Iliad* opens with the wrath of the Greek hero Achilles (i.e. Aeacides, a patronymic derived from his grandfather Aeacus); it ends with the funeral of the Trojan hero Hector, killed by Achilles.

l. 31. *Ajax.* A Greek hero fighting against the Trojans (as is Diomedes, l. 124).

l. 32. *Juno's eyes.* Juno is the Roman name of the Greek goddess Hera, wife of Zeus; 'ox-eyed' is a formulaic epithet for her in the *Iliad* (e.g. 4. 50).

63 l. 46. *shivered.* Splintered.

63 l. 48. *effacing*. Obliterating.

l. 77. *Dian*. Diana is the Roman goddess associated with the moon.

64 l. 88. *To fondle with my hand*. ll. 88–111 are not in the notebook manu-
script, a leaf having been torn out. It is possible (but not knowable) that
the removal of the leaf is to be related to the metonymic fondling
imagined in this line, which is enough to make the industrious sister's
needle err. In the notebook, the extent of the missing passage would
have totalled thirty-two lines of verse, compared with the twenty-four
lines from l. 88 to l. 111 in the published version: the passage has been
shortened by the extent of two stanzas. Elsewhere in the manuscript,
deletions are made by pencilled diagonal lines.

ll. 111–12. *Shall . . . dross?*. Cf. the vision of God's throne in Revelation
4: 5: 'And out of the throne proceeded lightnings and thunderings and
voices; and there were seven lamps of fire burning before the throne,
which are the seven Spirits of God'. In *FD*, CGR takes these to be a
sevenfold form of the Holy Spirit (154). In biblical numerology, seven
signifies completeness. The biblical image of God's refining fire is
common in CGR: Malachi 3: 2–3 is an important biblical source.

65 l. 132. *Ilion*. Troy.

l. 133. *vengeance*. For the death of his friend Patroclus.

66 l. 176. *"Vanity of vanities"*. From Ecclesiastes 1: 2, a book taken (on the
basis of its opening verse) to be the work of Solomon, whose wisdom is
proverbial.

67 l. 200. *Greater than Solomon*. From Matthew 12: 42.

69 l. 249. *God's blessed husbandry*. Cf. 1. Corinthians 3: 9. The image of
husbandry (i.e. the produce of cultivated land) is developed in ll. 250–2.

ll. 269–70. *So . . . soul*. Cf. Luke 21: 19.

l. 280. *And many last be first*. Cf. Matthew 19: 30.

70 A TRIAD. *Date*. 18 December 1856. *Publication*. *1862*. Omitted in *1875*:
'I presume that my sister, with overstrained scrupulosity, considered
its moral tone to be somewhat open to exception' (WMR in *1904*, 480)
(cf. headnote to 'Sister Maude' (p. 440)). *Text*. *1862*.

LOVE FROM THE NORTH. *Date*. 19 December 1856. *Publication*. *1862*.
Text. *1862*.

Title. The title in the notebook BL Ashley MS. 1364 (2) is 'In the days of
the Sea Kings'.

71 l. 29. *with book and bell*. Perhaps 'with religious ceremony' (cf. *Crump*, 2.
322).

IN AN ARTIST'S STUDIO. *Date*. 24 December 1856. *Text*. BL Ashley
MS. 1364 (2).

Title. 'The reference is apparently to our brother's studio, and to his
constantly-repeated heads of the lady whom he afterwards married,
Miss Siddal' (WMR in *1904*, 480).

A BETTER RESURRECTION. *Date.* 30 June 1857. *Publication. 1862 (D). Text. 1862.*

Title. From Hebrews 11: 35, on those who suffered in the hope 'that they might obtain a better resurrection' than the resurrections recorded in the Old Testament: i.e. a resurrection to eternal life. In the poem, the speaker does not pray for a mere renewal of her earthly life (l. 8).

l. 1. *wit.* Quickness of thought.

72 ll. 5–6. *I . . . see.* Cf. Psalm 121: 1: 'I will lift up mine eyes unto the hills, from whence cometh my help'.

l. 7. *My life is in the falling leaf.* That is, in its autumn. Cf. *Macbeth*, 5. 3: 'My way of life | Is fall'n into the sear, the yellow leaf'.

l. 17. *broken bowl.* Cf. Ecclesiastes 12: 6, where a broken golden bowl is an image for the decline of old age to death.

l. 20. *cordial.* Restorative drink. Following on from 'for my soul' (l. 19), the Latin etymology of *cordial* is to be understood: such a drink would work upon the deadened heart of l. 2.

'THE HEART KNOWETH ITS OWN BITTERNESS'. *Date.* 27 August 1857. *Text.* BL Ashley MS. 1364 (2).

Title. Cf. Proverbs 14: 10.

l. 2. *Is finished once.* i.e. finished finally (*once* = once and for all).

l. 12. *still.* Continually.

73 l. 28. *king with king.* Cf. Revelation 1: 6; and *TF*, entry for Thursday in Holy Week, ll. 9, 18 (p. 359, above).

l. 36. *quick.* Living.

l. 41. *too strait.* Not large enough; too narrow.

l. 44. *A fountain sealed.* From Song of Solomon 4: 12: 'A garden inclosed is my sister, my spouse; a spring shut up, a fountain sealed'. The text is taken as addressed by Christ the bridegroom to the individual believer or to the Church as a whole. The metaphor of marriage between Christ and the individual becomes explicit in l. 55 (see note below).

74 ll. 51–2. *Eye . . . conceived.* Cf. 1 Corinthians 2: 9.

l. 55. *There . . . part.* Cf. Jesus on the indissolubility of marriage, Matthew 19: 6: 'What therefore God hath joined together, let not man put asunder'.

IN THE ROUND TOWER AT JHANSI, JUNE 8, 1857. *Date.* Between 2 September and 8 September 1857. The poem was copied into the notebook BL Ashley MS. 1364 (2), but the leaf on which it was written has been removed. (It is listed in the manuscript table of contents at the end of the notebook.) The next poem in the notebook, 'Day Dreams' (i.e. ' "Reflection" ' in this edition), is dated 8 September 1857; the first report of the death of Captain Skene seems to have been that in *The Times* of 2 September. *Publication.* First published in *Once a Week*, 1 (13 August 1859), 140, without ll. 9–12, under the name 'Caroline G.

Rossetti' (Jan Marsh, 'The Indian Mutiny and Christina Rossetti's First Appearance in *Once a Week*', *Journal of Pre-Raphaelite Studies*, NS I (Spring 1992), 16–19). In *1862*, it is the second poem in the volume; in *1875* it is placed before the two poems of 'The German-French Campaign 1870–1871'. *Text. 1862.* The Indian uprising of 1857–8—known, in Britain, as the Indian Mutiny—began in May, the immediate cause being the religious offence given by the use of cow and pig fat in rifle cartridge grease. The mutiny of the regiment of native infantry at Jhansi, in June 1857, began to be reported in the British press at the end of July (*The Times*, 31 July, p. 9, col. f). On 2 September, *The Times* printed an extract from a letter giving details of the deaths of Captain Skene, Superintendent of the Jhansi District, and of his wife. They were among those who 'managed to get into a small round tower when the disturbance began', with Skene and the Assistant Superintendent firing upon the rebels, and 'Mrs. Skene loading for them'; but, when the rebels were taking the tower, 'Skene then saw it was of no use going on any more, so he kissed his wife, shot her, and then himself' (6, col. b). But, on 11 September, *The Times* printed a letter recording that Skene and the others in the fort had in fact surrendered, and had then been taken to a garden where they were killed by the sword (7, col. b). It appears that CGR only became aware of any inaccuracy in the report on which her poem was based after its publication in *1862*, and in *1875* she added a note: 'I retain this little poem, not as historically accurate, but as written and published before I heard the supposed facts of its first verse contradicted'. Yet it is by no means evident from this note—given its reference only to the 'first verse'—that CGR was ever aware that the whole account of the death of Skene and his wife given in the further four verses was, apparently, untrue.

Illustration. 'In that copy of the *Goblin Market* volume in which Christina drew a few coloured designs, she has put a head- and tail-piece to the Jhansi poem. The former is a flag displayed—pink field, with a device of two caressing doves. The latter is the same flag, drooping from its broken staff, and seen on the reverse side, besmeared with blood' (WMR in *1904*, 480).

74 l. 3. *swarming*. The word is taken from the letter printed in *The Times*, 2 September 1857 (p. 6, col. b): 'The rebels, after butchering all in the fort, brought ladders against the tower, and commenced swarming up'.

'REFLECTION'. *Date.* 8 September 1857. *Text.* CGR Collection (Co222), Princeton University Library. In the notebook BL Ashley MS. 1364 (2), the poem is titled 'Day Dreams'; the present title is that of a copy submitted to the Portfolio Society, and is likely to be the subject set by the Society (thus the inverted commas). Jean Ingelow's 'Reflections: Written for The Portfolio Society, July 1862', in *Poems*, 7th edn. (London, 1864), probably provides the date for CGR's submission. The figure of a gazing woman is likely indebted to Letitia Elizabeth Landon's 'Expectation' (included in the posthumous volume *The Zenana and Minor Poems of L.E.L.* (1839)): 'She looked from out the window | With long and asking gaze' from morning to evening, 'Still the girl kept gazing on' (ll. 1–2, 6); but her story teaches a universal lesson—'Human heart this history | Is thy fated lot, | Even such thy watching | For what cometh not' (ll. 25–8), 'Death and night are closing round, | All that thou hast sought unfound' (ll. 35–6).

76 A COAST-NIGHTMARE. *Date.* 12 September 1857. *Publication.* A revised version of ll. 9–18 was published as the entry for 1 April in *TF* (p. 345, above). *Text.* CGR Collection (Co222), Princeton University Library, a copy submitted to the Portfolio Society (see H. B. de Groot, 'Christina Rossetti's "A Nightmare": A Fragment Completed', *RES* 25 (1973), 48–52). The Princeton manuscript is the only complete manuscript copy of the poem, the BL notebook Ashley 1364 (2) containing only ll. 1–4 and 37–40—a leaf having been torn out. WMR noted that the leaf had been removed, but nevertheless published what was left (*1904*, 480). It is to be presumed that the leaf was removed by CGR, but it should not be supposed that this must necessarily be evidence of her later unease with the poem (no attempt has been made to delete or erase ll. 1–4, 37–40). The revision of ll. 9–18 for publication in *TF* may have been the reason for the removal.

Title. The title in BL Ashley 1364 (2) is 'A Nightmare', to which WMR has added in pencil '—Fragment'. The Princeton title is almost certainly an accommodation to the subject set by the Portfolio Society (cf. Jean Ingelow's Portfolio submission 'A coast-scene', Harry Ransom Center, University of Texas at Austin).

l. 1. *friend.* In the BL notebook this is CGR's revision of the deleted 'love' (cf. 'Repining', note to l. 51 (p. 405)).

l. 7. *unripened.* In CGR, imagery of ripening usually invites eschatological contextualization, pointing towards the harvest in which the souls of the righteous will be gathered into heaven (see Revelation 14: 14–16, and commentary in *FD*, 363–7). The emphasis on unripeness in this poem (continued in ll. 9–12) is an indication that this ghostland, where the lost drink of death's waters (l. 28), demands theological contextualization (cf. the darkened world of the octave of the sonnet 'A moon impoverished amid stars curtailed' which was inserted in the commentary on Revelation 8: 12 in *FD*, 255 (in *Crump*, 2. 252): 'No ripening more for olive, grape, or corn', l. 7). CGR did herself indicate explicitly a theological context—uncertain though it is—by revising and publishing ll. 9–18 as a ten-line poem ('A Castle-Builder's World') which forms the entry for 1 April in *TF* (p. 345, above): the Isaian epigraph to that ten-line poem is a strong indication that its ghosts are the damned.

77 l. 28. *death's tideless waters.* An indication that this 'ghostland' (l. 1), like the lifeless land of the sonnet 'Cobwebs', is probably influenced by Poe's 'The City in the Sea': see 'Cobwebs', note to l. 9 (p. 420).

l. 37. *hunts.* In the BL notebook this is CGR's revision of the deleted 'rides' which is the conventional verb used for the way a nightmare—

a feminine monster—sets upon someone in the night (*OED*, *ride* 17a); but, in this context, in that it is a 'lover' (l. 27) who so oppresses the speaker, CGR may have been wary of the sexual suggestiveness of the verb (cf. *OED*, 16). The revisions we see in ll. 1 and 37 were likely made 'to prepare the poem for the semi-public conditions' of the Portfolio Society (de Groot, '*Rossetti*'s "*A Nightmare*"', 50).

77 ANOTHER SPRING. *Date.* 15 September 1857. *Publication. 1862. Text. 1862.*

Title. In the manuscript in notebook BL Ashley MS. 1364 (2), the title 'When Harvest failed' has been deleted, and WMR has pencilled the published title above.

l. 4. *My leafless pink mezereons.* The flowers of *Daphne mezereum* are produced on bare stems in late winter.

78 'FOR ONE SAKE'. *Date.* 25 October 1857. *Text.* BL Ashley MS. 1364 (2).

The poem draws on Tennyson's 'St. Agnes' (Barbara Fass, 'Christina Rossetti and St. Agnes' Eve', *VP* 14 (1976), 45). There, the speaker, a nun, longs to become a bride of Christ: 'far, | Thro' all yon starlight keen, | Draw me, thy bride, a glittering star', *Poems* (1842), ll. 21–3. Tennyson's poem is influenced by his reading of parts of Keats's 'The Eve of St. Agnes', and assumes the reader's knowledge of the legend that, on 20 January, a virgin who fasts may be granted a vision of the one she will love. This legend would seem to inform the sestet of CGR's sonnet; yet the conception of the sonnet is caught between having the speaker dream (as in Tennyson's poem) of herself becoming the bride of Christ, and having her dream (as is apparently the case) of another soul becoming that.

Title. One = One's. The title suggests thanksgiving for the entry of one soul (l. 1) into heaven. The speaker does, however, have hope for her own sake.

ll. 1–2. *One . . . stars.* 'It would seem that some woman known to the authoress (I cannot at all say who it was) had died, and was regarded by her as now a saint in heaven, the "imperishable bride" of Christ. Or possibly the "imperishable bride" is the Christian Church in the abstract' (WMR in *1904*, 480–1).

l. 3. *Wars and rumours of your wars.* In Matthew 24: 6, Jesus talks of the time of trouble that will precede the *parousia* and the end of the world: 'And ye shall hear of wars and rumours of wars: see that ye be not troubled: for all these things must come to pass, but the end is not yet'. WMR suggests, not implausibly, a topical reference to the Indian Mutiny (*1904*, 481); but, if there is topical reference to that event, the event is nevertheless understood in terms of the eschatological scheme.

ll. 6–7. *bars.* Enclosing bulwarks (the immediate source of information on heavenly construction is likely to be DGR's 'The Blessed Damozel' (1850), l. 2). *cars.* Chariots. These lines are indebted to Tennyson's 'St. Agnes': 'Break up the heavens, O Lord! . . . All heaven bursts her starry floors, | And strows her lights below', ll. 21, 27–8. In the light of Tennyson's lines, CGR's heavenly *fountains* are to be understood as fountains of light (cf. 'wells of light' in DGR, 'The Blessed Damozel', l. 70; and in CGR's 'Christian and Jew', l. 3). The biblical basis of the bursting of heaven is Revelation 20: 11, where heaven and earth flee away before the appearance of the new heaven and new earth at 21: 1.

l. 8. *fire to test and purify*. The individual soul's purification by fire is a common topos in CGR (e.g. 'Twice', l. 37 and note (p. 444)); but here the mode is apocalyptic, and the fire is as much the destructive fire that descends from heaven in the final battle with the Devil's forces in Revelation 20: 9.

A BIRTHDAY. *Date*. 18 November 1857. *Publication*. First published in *Macmillan's Magazine*, 3 (April 1861), 498. *Text*. *1862*. The Song of Solomon is one of the poem's intertexts, even though the biblical text's presence is never explicit: 'The voice of my beloved! behold, he cometh leaping upon the mountains, skipping upon the hills . . . My beloved spake, and said unto me, Rise up, my love, my fair one, and come away. For, lo, the winter is past, the rain is over and gone; The flowers appear on the earth; the time of the singing of birds is come, and the voice of the turtle is heard in our land; The fig tree putteth forth her green figs, and the vines with the tender grape give a good smell. Arise, my love, my fair one, and come away' (2: 8–13). It is likely that the poem's first stanza is influenced by the prominence of bold simile in the Song. CGR inherits the tradition of spiritualizing interpretation of the Song in which the 'bride' is taken to be the individual believer or the Church as a whole, and the 'Bridegroom' is Christ—which is not to say that, in this poem, the lover who comes to the speaker can only be taken to be Christ.

l. 6. *halcyon*. Calm.

79 l. 10. *vair*. A squirrel fur.

AN APPLE GATHERING. *Date*. 23 November 1857. *Publication*. First published in *Macmillan's Magazine*, 4 (August 1861), 329. *Text*. *1862*.

l. 9. *Lilian and Lilias*. The sisters' impractically similar names proclaim their lily-like purity.

80 l. 27. *loitered*. Perhaps with meretricious implication: the speaker is now a woman of the night (cf. Laura's loitering in 'Goblin Market', ll. 145, 162, 226).

MY SECRET. *Date*. 23 November 1857. *Publication*. *1862*. *Text*. *1862*.

Title. The title in the notebook BL Ashley MS. 1362 (2) is 'Nonsense'. The *1862* title was changed to 'Winter: My Secret' in *1875*, where the poem is preceded by three other poems with seasonal titles: 'Spring', 'Summer' (in *Crump*, 1. 142–3), and 'Autumn'.

81 AUTUMN. *Date*. 14 April 1858. *Publication*. *1866*. *Text*. *1866*.

The speaker's solitude, the location beside a river, the season, all indicate her relation to Tennyson's 'The Lady of Shalott'; but, where Tennyson's Lady sings, this solitary woman can only moan (l. 17); and where the Lady weaves her 'web'—a figure of art—here we see only a spider's web (ll. 33–40).

Title. The title in the notebook BL Ashley MS. 1364 (2) is 'Ding Dong Bell', probably alluding to the dirge for Ferdinand's father, 'Full fathom five thy father lies', in *The Tempest* (1. 2. 396–404) which is sung by Ariel in the guise of 'a nymph o'th'sea' (1. 2. 301): 'Sea-nymphs hourly ring his knell: | Ding-dong. | Hark! now I hear them—ding-dong bell' (cf. 'Sing me a song—', ll. 9–12, in *Crump*, 2. 36: 'Two mournful sisters, | And a tolling knell, | Tolling ding and tolling dong, | Ding dong bell'; and also 'A Peal of Bells', ll. 16–19, in *Crump*, 1. 49). CGR may associate these sea-nymphs with the singing boat maidens of her poem. The dirge is sung immediately before Miranda sets eyes on Ferdinand.

l. 27. *in dreamless sleep locked fast*. That the speaker is thinking no longer of the swallow but of herself—and that the poem is not positing an intermediate state of sleep for dead birds—is confirmed by the repetition of these words in ('Sleeping at last, the trouble & tumult over'), l. 7: 'Sleeping at last in a dreamless sleep locked fast'. And cf. 'death's dreamless sleep' in 'Sappho', l. 7—a poem recollected in the present poem, its last line ('Unwept, untended and alone') influencing l. 24.

82 l. 36. *it*. i.e. the web.

ADVENT. *Date*. 2 May 1858. *Publication*. *1862 (D)*. *Text*. *1862*. In the Church calendar, Advent is the penitential season of preparation for the coming of Christ—both his first coming which is commemorated at Christmas, and also his awaited second coming. The poem conflates two main biblical intertexts: the parable of the virgins who 'went forth to meet the bridegroom' in Matthew 25: 1–13—a lesson on the importance of being watchful and prepared for Christ's second coming—and the Song of Solomon where the bridegroom is (in Christianizing interpretation) identified as Christ (ll. 53–6 drawing on 2: 10–13). 'In the annotated copy of her Poems Christina wrote against this one: "Liked, I believe, at East Grinstead"' (WMR in *1904*, 473). The Society of St Margaret, an Anglican sisterhood at East Grinstead, was founded by John Mason Neale in 1855.

83 l. 5. *'Watchman, what of the night?'*. From Isaiah 21: 11.

   l. 9. *The Porter watches at the gate*. Cf. Mark 13: 34–6.

84 l. 45. *we hold Him fast*. Cf. the injunctions to hold fast in Revelation 3: 3, 11 (and see *FD* 89).

AT HOME. *Date*. 29 June 1858 (Huntington Library, San Marino, California, HM 6066, which is a leaf, on which the poem's last ten lines are written, taken from the notebook BL Ashley MS. 1364 (2)). *Publication*. *1862*. *Text*. *1862*.

Illustration. 'She illustrated *At Home* with two coloured designs . . . No. 1 shows the blanched form of the ghost in a sky lit with cresset flames. On one side the sky is bright blue, the flames golden; on the other side, dark twilight grey, and the flames red. No. 2 is the globe of the earth, rudely lined for latitude and longitude. The equator divides it into a green northern and a grey-purple southern hemisphere. Over the former flare sunbeams in a blue sky; below the latter the firmament is dimly dark, and the pallid moon grey towards extinction' (WMR in *1904*, 482).

Title. The notebook manuscript title 'After the Pic-nic' is deleted in pencil. The present title was suggested by DGR (letter to CGR, [28 January 1861], *DGRL (F)* 2. 346).

ll. 15–16. '*To-morrow . . . sweet*'. Compare 'From House to Home', ll. 69–70, and its eschatological context: the 'house of lies' (l. 202), the place of pleasure, is not the true heavenly 'home' (l. 73) and is destroyed.

85 ll. 31–2. *Like . . . day.* From Wisdom 5: 14 (*Hassett*, 34), where the simile describes the transience of 'the hope of the ungodly': an ominous text to invoke here (compare *hope*, l. 17; and *the pleasant way*, l. 18, which in CGR's symbolic topography is likely to be the way to destruction).

UP-HILL. *Date.* 29 June 1858 (Huntington Library, San Marino, California, HM 6666, which is a leaf taken from BL Ashley MS. 1364 (2)). *Publication.* First published in *Macmillan's Magazine*, 3 (February 1861), 325. *Text. 1862.*

l. 1. *Does . . . way.* For the pilgrim's uphill path, see *PP*, 266. Herbert's 'The Pilgrimage', with its uphill path that ends in death, may be a poetic model (McGann, *Beauty of Inflections*, 241).

l. 5. *for the night a resting-place.* The intermediate state between the world and heaven (cf. 'Rest', with its period of darkness before 'the morning of Eternity', l. 12).

l. 14. *sum.* The ultimate end or goal (*OED*, 13).

THE CONVENT THRESHOLD. *Date.* 9 July 1858. *Publication. 1862. Text. 1862.* For WMR, the poem seems to combine 'something of the idea of an Héloïse and Abélard with something of the idea of a Juliet and Romeo. The opening lines . . . clearly point to a family feud, as of the Capulets and Montagues; but it is difficult to believe that the passage beginning "A spirit with transfigured face" would have been introduced unless the writer had had in her mind some personage, such as Abélard, of exceptionally subtle and searching intellect' (*1904*, 482). DGR's 'The Blessed Damozel' (first published in *The Germ*, February 1850) is another presence in the poem (cf. the speaker's imagining, in ll. 69–77, of a separation similar to that of the damozel and her lover). In 1890, CGR remarked on the beauty of DGR's poem, while finding that 'it falls short of expressing the highest view, which yet (I hope) it does not contradict' (*L* 4. 209).

Title. 'From the Convent Threshold' in BL Ashley MS. 1364 (3).

86 l. 3. *bar.* Where, in DGR's 'The Blessed Damozel' (1850), the 'bar of Heaven' (l. 2) marks the separation of the damozel from her worldly lover, here the bar is the barrier between two lovers is within the world.

l. 6. *sea of glass.* In Revelation 4: 6 there is a sea of glass before God's throne; in 15: 2 it is 'mingled with fire' (cf. l. 13).

l. 27. *offscouring.* Filth, refuse: from 1 Corinthians 4: 13.

l. 42. *Flee to the mountain.* Cf. Matthew 24: 16 and its context of warning of the eschatological tribulation.

87 l. 44. *secret.* Secluded and secluding (cf. DGR, 'The Blessed Damozel', ll. 80–2: 'That living mystic tree | Within whose secret growth the Dove | Sometimes is felt to be').

l. 48. *knock.* Both physically—'to strike upon the breast' (*OED*, 1b) in a gesture of penitence—and also spiritually (cf. the words of Isabella, who is about to enter a convent, to Angelo, in *Measure for Measure*, 2. 2. 136–8: 'Go to your bosom, | Knock there, and ask your heart what it doth know | That's like my brother's fault').

l. 67. *Lent.* The penitential period extending from Ash Wednesday to Easter Even; here, referring to the speaker's life of penitence.

88 ll. 82–4. *No . . . repents.* Cf. Job 38: 7; Luke 15: 7.

l. 87. *clomb.* Climbed.

l. 88. *clang.* The golden and silver wings of the birds of paradise, tinkling and ringing, seem to make a 'clang' in 'Paradise: in a Symbol', ll. 13–16. An unusual conception: usually birds *clang* in making a loud harsh cry (cf. Milton, *PL* 7. 422).

l. 91. *cars.* Chariots. In classical mythology, the personifications of heavenly bodies drive their chariots across the sky.

l. 118. *tester.* A canopy over a bed. It is *leaden* not only because of the weight of earth, but in reference to a lead coffin: cf. 'The Poor Ghost', ll. 29–31: 'I go home alone to my bed, | Dug deep at the foot and deep at the head, | Roofed in with a load of lead' (in *Crump*, 1. 121).

89 l. 125. *And reeled but were not drunk with wine.* Alludes to the Isaian image of those who have drunk the cup of God's wrath (Isaiah 51: 17, 21).

l. 130. *I cannot write the words I said.* WMR notes that, 'as with the letters of Héloïse to Abélard . . . this seems to be intended for a written outpouring, not a spoken one' (*1904*, 482): the one indication that this is an epistolary dramatic monologue. WMR may have in mind Pope's 'Eloisa to Abelard'.

l. 140. *veiled in paradise.* Veiled by the shadows of the intermediate state, to be unveiled only in heaven (paradise, here, is not heaven). Here, *veiled* may play upon the sense of 'having taken the veil: i.e. entered the convent' (see Michael Wheeler, *Heaven, Hell, and the Victorians* (Cambridge,

1994), 161), a possibility reinforced if CGR connects the enclosure of a paradisal garden (cf. 'Shut Out') with the enclosure of the convent (cf. Charles Allston Collins's 1851 painting *Convent Thoughts*, where the *hortus conclusus* symbolizes the nun's withdrawal from the world and her purity).

CHRISTIAN AND JEW. *Date*. 9 July 1858. *Publication*. *1862 (D)*. CGR sent a copy of *1862* to her Jewish friend Amelia Heimann, drawing this poem to her attention (see letter of 3 April 1862 (p. 385, above)). While 'the Jew' is a conventional topic for a Christian woman poet in the period, this friendship provides an important private context for the poem: the anticipation of what it would be for a Jewish friend to read the poem may account for its being (in comparison with most contemporary treatments of the topic) carefully tactful. *Text*. 1862.

l. 3. *wells of light*. Cf. DGR, 'The Blessed Damozel' (1850), ll. 69–70: 'I'll take his hand, and go with him | To the deep wells of light'—these being the heavenly equivalents of earthly *wells*: i.e. natural pools formed by water springs (not excavated water pits). Both this poem and 'The Convent Threshold'—apparently contemporaneous works—are involved with DGR's poem of longing for union in heaven.

l. 4. *I have not eyes*. The Jew's blindness is an image of unbelief. Cf. John 12: 40 (// Mark 4.12 // Isaiah 6: 10): 'He hath blinded their eyes, and hardened their heart; that they should not see with their eyes, nor understand with their heart, and be converted, and I should heal them', where the Isaian text is taken as prophetic of the Jews' unbelief, which is understood as ordained by God.

90   l. 8. *glory*. Nimbus: i.e. the circle of light surrounding the figure in depictions of saints.

l. 10. *Here shadows are*. Cf. *SF*, 229, where, through the Jews' rejection of Christ, 'the light within the once holy nation had become darkness': 'And though God's mercy afterwards moved many individuals to repentance and conversion, yet as a nation the Jews have ever since their one awful national choice changed place with the Gentiles and seated themselves in darkness' (and see Simon Humphries, 'Who is the Alchemist in Christina Rossetti's "The Prince's Progress"?', *RES* 58 (2007), 688–90).

ll. 17–20. *cry . . . King*. From the vision of the seraphim over the Lord's throne in Isaiah 6: 3: 'And one cried unto another, and said, Holy, holy, holy, is the Lord of hosts: the whole earth is full of his glory'. Their hymn is the Sanctus which ends the preface to the central part of the Communion service in the Order of Holy Communion in *BCP*.

l. 33. *Living Vine*. Cf. the parable of the True Vine in John 15: 1–11.

91   ll. 50–1. *her harpstrings . . . land*. Cf. Psalm 137: 2, 4.

l. 53. *O drunken not with wine*. Cf. Isaiah 51: 21–3, where Israel is told that it will no longer have to drink the cup of God's fury. (Isaiah 51: 23 has already been alluded to in ll. 48–50.)

91 ll. 58–9. *Can these bones live?*—*God knows*. God's question to Ezekiel, and the prophet's answer, at Ezekiel 37: 3, introducing the vision of the resurrection of dry bones (37: 1–14).

A YAWN / BY THE SEA. The six-stanza poem 'A Yawn' is dated 11 November 1858 in the notebook BL Ashley MS. 1364 (3). Three stanzas were excised to form 'By the Sea', first published in *A Round of Days* (London, 1866), 68 (*Crump*, 1. 297). This revision is best understood as producing two distinct works, rather than two versions of the same work. In 'A Yawn', there is simple envy of the existence of the sea creatures; but the published poem 'pauses at the boundary shore of its new-found paradox, viz., that painlessness is a greater deprivation than pain' (*Hassett*, 113). Both the unpublished and the published poems are therefore presented here. The text of 'By the Sea' is that of *1875*.

92 A YAWN. ll. 14–15. *All . . . sea.* Cf. Ecclesiastes 1: 7: 'All the rivers run into the sea; yet the sea is not full; unto the place from whence the rivers come, thither they return again'. In *SF* this passage is read in the eschatological context of the statement in Revelation 21: 1 that, when the new heaven and the new earth come, there will be no more sea: 'What shall we lose? . . . Troubled restless waters we shall lose with all their defilement (Is. lvii. 20), and with waves that toss and break themselves against a boundary they cannot overpass (Jer. v. 22), and with the moan of a still-recurrent ebb, "The sea is not full" (Eccles. i. 7).' (*SF*, 108–9 (p. 321, above)).

l. 22. *argus-eyed*. From classical mythology, in which Argus is a hundred-eyed giant.

93 FROM HOUSE TO HOME. *Date.* 19 November 1858. *Publication. 1862 (D).* *Text. 1862.* In the notebook manuscript BL Ashley 1364 (3), DGR has pencilled 'This is so good it cannot be omitted, but could not something be done to make it less like *Palace of Art*'.

Title. The title's distinction is between the 'house of lies' (l. 202) of the earthly paradise, and the heavenly 'home' (l. 75). The title in the notebook manuscript is 'Sorrow not as those who have no hope' (from 1 Thessalonians 4: 13).

l. 6. *It was a pleasure-place within my soul.* Cf. Tennyson, 'The Palace of Art', ll. 1–2: 'I built my soul a lordly pleasure-house, | Wherein at ease for aye to dwell' (*Poems*, 1842); itself indebted to the 'stately pleasure-dome' of Coleridge's 'Kubla Khan', l. 2.

l. 12. *But to be dashed again?.* In the manuscript a dividing dash is inserted between this line and the next in order to clarify the poem's structure (see note to l. 200).

l. 13. *castle.* In the manuscript CGR wrote 'palace', which DGR—mindful of the poem's debt to Tennyson's 'The Palace of Art'—deleted, then pencilling in 'mansion'.

ll. 15–16. *But . . . fire.* Cf. the windows of Tennyson's palace that, at sunset or sunrise, 'Would seem slow-flaming crimson fires . . . And tipt with frost-like spires', 'The Palace of Art', ll. 49–52.

l. 17. *pleasaunce.* A pleasure-ground belonging to a great house.

94 l. 45. *one like an angel.* The likeness may be deceptive—this may not be, exactly, an angel—but it is no dangerous deception (e.g. an earthly lover mistaken for an angel). The closest analogue to this figure is the apparently angelic visitor of 'Repining'. Another analogue is the figure of Love who walks with the speaker, both of them in sad exile from their home, in '"They Desire a Better Country"' (see ll. 23–8, and note (p. 455)): the angelic figure in this poem is also sad (l. 64). The description in l. 46 draws on apocalyptic. His 'eyes like flames of fire' are like those of Christ—'one like unto the Son of man'—in Revelation 1: 13–14 ('his eyes were as a flame of fire', 1: 14; cf. 2: 18, 19: 12); and these eyes are 'spirit-discerning', as Christ's eyes in Revelation 2: 18 and 23 are searching (in *FD*, 74, CGR takes the 'Eyes like unto a flame of fire' of Revelation 2: 18 to signify 'Omniscience from which nothing is concealed'). In this apocalyptic context, the phrase *one like an angel* would appear to be modelled on the visionary formula of Daniel 7: 13 ('one like the Son of man') and of Revelation 1: 13. And when this angel calls the speaker to 'Come to the distant land' (l. 76)—to which he himself will flee and (as an angel would) fly (l. 73)—he is like Christ the Bridegroom in a Christian interpretation of the Song of Solomon, calling his beloved to 'come away' (2: 10–13).

95 l. 75. *banishment.* The manuscript reads 'punishment'.

l. 77. *avalanche.* Cf. 'Repining', ll. 87–102.

96 ll. 127–8. *While . . . hours.* Cf. *PL* 6. 3: 'the circling hours'.

97 l. 134. *strung up.* Braced, made tense.

l. 141. *the Rock.* Christ (cf. 1 Corinthians 10: 4).

l. 161. *Then . . . scroll.* Cf. Revelation 6: 14: 'And the heaven departed as a scroll when it is rolled together'.

98 l. 169. *a new song.* From Revelation 5: 9.

l. 173. *Tier beyond tier.* Cf. the 'more than a thousand tiers' of the heavenly court in Dante, *Paradiso*, 30. 113.

ll. 175–6. *no . . . names.* Cf. Revelation 2: 17.

99 l. 200. *New-lit with love and praise.* In the manuscript a dividing dash is inserted between this line and the next (see note to l. 12).

ll. 205–6. *Therefore . . . face.* Cf. Luke 21: 19; Isaiah 50: 7.

l. 207. *To pluck down.* This is markedly different from the ambivalent acceptance of the inadequacy of art in 'The Palace of Art', l. 293: 'Yet pull not down my palace towers'.

l. 211. *My . . . Jerusalem.* Cf. Luke 9: 51.

ll. 217–18. *Beauty . . . heaviness.* Cf. Isaiah 61: 3.

99 l. 228. *stay upon*. Trust in, depend upon (cf. Isaiah 50: 10).

100 WINTER RAIN. *Date*. 31 January 1859. *Publication. 1862. Text. 1862*.

101 L.E.L. *Date*. 15 February 1859. *Publication*. First published in *Victoria Magazine* (published by Emily Faithfull), 1 (May 1863), 40–1. The poem was revised by DGR for *1866*. In the notebook manuscript (as in *Victoria Magazine*) lines 1 and 3 of each stanza do not rhyme, and CGR has pencilled the note: 'Gabriel fitted the double rhymes as printed, with a brotherly request I would use them'. *Text. 1866*.

Title. The manuscript title is 'Spring', with the footnote 'L.E.L. by E.B.B.' (BL Ashley MS. 1364 (3)); it became 'L.E.L.' when published in *Victoria Magazine*. The prolific poet Letitia Elizabeth Landon (1802–38) published under the initials 'L.E.L.'. She accompanied her husband to Africa in 1838 and there, two months after her arrival, died. It was rumoured (despite the finding of the inquest) that she had killed herself, her own life becoming inseparable from the doomed women of her poetry.

Epigraph. Cf. Elizabeth Barrett Browning, 'L.E.L.'s Last Question', l. 39: 'One thirsty for a little love?' (*1904*, 482), in *Poems* by Elizabeth Barrett Barrett (1844).

l. 3. *I . . . wall*. Those, on their deathbed, who resign themselves to their death, are said to have turned their face to the wall. The phrase is of biblical origin (2 Kings 20: 2).

102 l. 36. *scathe*. Hurt. The word is DGR's revision of the manuscript 'hurt', but it is a word used elsewhere by CGR (e.g. in the first of the 'Old and New Year Ditties', l. 9, in *Crump*, 1. 89): 'Gabriel's new rhymes are not . . . imports from his own lexicon; . . . he finds the terms in Christina's own poems' (*Hassett*, 84). Similarly, in l. 31 *full of ruth* is DGR's revision of the manuscript 'piteously', and is a phrase taken from 'A Portrait', l. 5, in *Crump*, 1. 122 (*Hassett*, 84).

105 GOBLIN MARKET. *Date*. 27 April 1859. *Publication. 1862*. DGR designed the frontispiece and title page for *1862*: the frontispiece illustrates the text 'Buy from us with a golden curl' (l. 125), the title page the text 'Golden head by golden head' (l. 184) (pp. 103–4). *Text. 1862*. In 1893 CGR told Edmund Gosse that 'in my own intention Goblin Market was no allegory at all, so it does not surprise me that it is inexplicable in detail; neither was the Prince's Progress an allegory' (*L* 4. 325). Yet it is undeniably a tale of temptation, transgression, and redemption—one which demands such theological terminology—and its theological scheme becomes explicit when unmistakably Eucharistic language is deployed in order to draw attention to Lizzie's Christlike actions (ll. 467–74). There is little doubt that the goblin fruits are symbolic of destructive worldly pleasure (cf. 'The World', l. 6). This symbolism is informed by the forbidden fruit of Genesis 3; but the immediate biblical source is Revelation 18, where merchants bring 'the fruits that thy soul lusted after' to Babylon market (18: 11–16) (McGann, *Beauty of*

Inflections, 221–2), even though the context for the fruits in the poem is not, and cannot be, explicitly eschatological. Yet the status of the fruits in the poem—whether they are evil in themselves, or whether they are only open to evil uses—is uncertain: the poem is structured upon contradictory views of the status of 'the world', both sacramental and renunciatory (Simon Humphries, 'The Uncertainty of "Goblin Market"', *VP* 45/4 (Winter 2007, 391–413). The most important literary source for the poem's theological structure is in Bunyan's *The Pilgrim's Progress*, where the deadly effect of eating the fruit of the Orchard of Beelzebub is countered by a Eucharistic purge (*PP*, 240–1, 279–82; see Introduction, pp. xxxi–xxxii). An important model for the theologically significant detailing of this tale of temptation and transgression is *PL*. Among the major sources of the poem's fairy-tale detailing is *A Midsummer Night's Dream* (Ifor B. Evans, 'The Sources of Christina Rossetti's "Goblin Market"', *Modern Language Review*, 28 (1933), 156–65).

Title. In a copy of the 1893 illustrated *Goblin Market*, CGR wrote: '"Goblin Market" first published in 1862 was written (subject of course to subsequent revision) as long ago as April 27. 1859, and in M.S. was inscribed to my dear only sister Maria Francesca Rossetti herself long afterwards the author of "A Shadow of Dante". In the first instance I named it "A Peep at the Goblins" in imitation of my cousin Mrs. [Anna Eliza] Bray's "A Peep at the Pixies" [1854], but my brother Dante Gabriel Rossetti substituted the greatly improved title as it now stands. And here I like to acknowledge the general indebtedness of my first and second volumes to his suggestive wit and revising hand' (quoted in *Crump*, 1. 234).

l. 30. *sound to eye*. The model for this catalogue of fruits (as for the catalogue of trees which opens 'An Old-World Thicket') is the catalogue of the trees of the Wandering Wood in *FQ* which ends with 'the Maple seeldom inward sound' (1. 1. 9), a tree which is not as sound as it looks.

106 l. 66. *gifts*. Lizzie also refers to the goblins' 'gifts' at l. 149. This ought to be the wrong word for what merchants offer, but it may indicate that Lizzie suspects—or knows—that the goblins are not in business to make money. At l. 107 they offer their fruit even though Laura has shown them no money; at l. 439 they throw Lizzie's coin back at her. This malign generosity puts in doubt that critical tradition which takes 'Goblin Market' to be concerned with economics. But Laura talks of buying, not of taking gifts (l. 43).

ll. 67–8. *She . . . ran*. Cf. Bunyan's pilgrim who, when running from the City of Destruction, puts his fingers in his ears in order not to hear his wife and children calling, and does not look back: *PP*, 41. But Lizzie's flight is no knowing desertion of her sister. When, in the frontispiece to *1862* [p. 104], DGR shows Lizzie looking back at Laura as she snips a lock of her hair for the goblins, he misrepresents CGR's conception of Lizzie's flight.

107 ll. 112–13. *One . . . Polly.* 'The authoress does not appear to represent her goblins as having the actual configuration of brute animals; it was Dante Rossetti who did that in his illustration to the poem (he allows human hands, however). I possess a copy of the *Goblin Market* volume, 1862, with marginal water-colour sketches by Christina . . . She draws several of the goblins,—all very slim agile figures in a close-fitting garb of blue; their faces, hands, and feet are sometimes human, sometimes brute-like, but of a scarcely definable type. The only exception is the "parrot-voiced" goblin who cried "Pretty goblin". He is a true parrot (such as Christina could draw one)' (WMR in *1904*, 460).

l. 120. *furze.* Gorse.

108 l. 129. *honey from the rock.* The Israelites 'suck honey out of the rock' in the promised land (Deuteronomy 32: 13).

l. 147. *Jeanie.* 'Pronounced to rhyme with "many" and thus homonymically linked to the fallen woman in DGR's "Jenny"' (*Marsh*, 443).

111 l. 258. *succous pasture.* Juicy food. For this rare sense of *pasture* (*OED*, 2), see Malbecco's 'pasture poysonous' in *FQ* 3. 10. 59. CGR may associate Laura with Malbecco at this point: Malbecco's fate is to waste away with grief and jealousy (see, further, Simon Humphries, 'Christina Rossetti's "Goblin Market" and Spenser's Malbecco', *N&Q* 55/1 (March 2008), 51–4).

l. 260. *tree of life.* See Proverbs 13: 12: 'Hope deferred maketh the heart sick: but when the desire cometh, it is a tree of life'.

112 ll. 314–15. *But . . . died.* The sense may be (1) 'but who, instead of [having] joys brides hope to have, fell sick and died': cf. this sense of *for* at 'Paradise', l. 46. Yet this must assume an ellipsis in l. 314. The sense (2) 'but who fell sick with desire for joys brides hope to have, then died' would be perfectly Rossettian (the state of being sick with desire is encapsulated in Proverbs 13: 12: see note to l. 260); but this sense is difficult to square with what has been said of Jeanie at ll. 153–6, where she is sick with obsessive desire for the joys provided by the goblins—only that. The sense is often taken to be (3) 'but who, because she had had the joys brides hope to have, fell sick and died'. This rests on the identification of these bridal joys with the transitory, and ultimately deadly, joys offered by goblins; yet there is nothing in the poem to suggest that brides hope to eat goblin fruit or to take gifts from goblin men—gifts which Lizzie knows to be 'evil' (1. 66). (The ending of the poem, at ll. 543–51, gives some indication of the joys brides might hope for (see *D'Amico*, 72–3); and, for Laura as a wife and mother, the goblins may now belong to the storied past.) This identification is often prompted by the supposition that *joys* must mean 'sexual intercourse' (surely no more than one of the joys brides hope for), a supposition which literalizes the sexual suggestiveness of the description of the

consumption of fruit in the poem (cf. 'Cousin Kate', ll. 9–10, in *Crump* l. 31: 'He lured me to his palace home— | Woe's me for joy thereof—'). But Jeanie did not have sex with goblins; Jeanie only ate goblin fruit. It is unlikely that CGR would so confuse what is literal with what is not.

113 l. 336. *Mopping and mowing.* Making grimaces.

l. 353. *Russet and dun.* Reddish-brown and dull brown.

l. 354. *Bob.* To try to catch with the mouth.

115 l. 415–16. *Like . . . honey-sweet.* Orange blossom is for brides. Blossom and fruit together on the tree are 'emblematic of bridal purity and marital fecundity, and . . . proleptic of the domestic scene at the conclusion' of the poem (D. M. R. Bentley, in *Kent*, 75).

l. 418. *virgin town.* A town which has never been taken by an enemy force (*OED*, 12f): sets up the sexual innuendo of l. 421.

l. 430. *Lizzie . . . word.* Cf. Christ's silence towards the chief priests before he, like Lizzie at l. 429, is 'mocked' and beaten (Matthew 27: 12–14, 29).

116 l. 465. *Did you miss me?.* Laura, surely, did not: at l. 141, Lizzie is waiting at the gate for Laura; at l. 475, Laura is sitting down indoors.

ll. 467–74. *Never . . . men.* The passage incorporates Eucharistic language to present Lizzie in Christlike terms. See Christ's words in the Prayer of Consecration in the Holy Communion liturgy of *BCP*: 'Take, eat, this is my Body which is given for you . . . Drink ye all of this; for this is my Blood of the New Testament, which is shed for you'. In l. 468, Lizzie talks of *my juices* (rhyming with *my bruises*, l. 467), as if they are from her own body. In l. 470, the distinction between *pulp* and *dew* corresponds to the distinction between the two kinds of Communion, bread and wine. That the fruit which can bring death can, in this sacramental moment, bring life, has a theological basis: see the Exhortations in the Holy Communion liturgy for warnings (for which the biblical basis is 1 Corinthians 11: 27–9) that the sacrament itself has the double power of bringing life to those who receive it worthily, and death to the unworthy.

117 l. 491. *aguish.* Feverish.

l. 494. *wormwood.* A plant proverbial for its bitter taste; figuratively, that which mortifies (cf. Proverbs 5: 4: 'her end is bitter as wormwood').

l. 495. *feast.* Follows on from the Eucharistic language of ll. 467–74: the sacrament is 'a heavenly Feast' in the Communion liturgy of *BCP* (First Exhortation).

l. 498. *lamentable.* Full of, or expressing, sorrow or distress (*OED*, 1). Wringing hands is a traditional gesture of grief or pain (similarly the tearing of clothes and the beating of the breast, ll. 497, 499).

l. 503. *stems the light.* Makes headway against the light (as a bird in flight might 'stem the wind'). Alludes to the belief that eagles, alone among birds, can stare at the sun.

117 l. 509. *lesser flame*. The conception of a greater and a lesser flame (and ll. 507–12 generally) is influenced by Herbert's paired sonnets entitled 'Love'. The first sonnet wonders that man writes only in praise of worldly love, not of divine love. The second sonnet asks that man's love be directed towards God: 'Immortall Heat, O let thy greater flame | Attract the lesser to it: let those fires, | Which shall consume the world, first make it tame; | And kindle in our hearts such true desires, | As may consume our lusts, and make thee way' (ll. 1–5). Laura's self-centred love of pleasure is overborn by her selfless love for her (Christlike) sister.

119 SPRING. *Date*. 17 August 1859. *Published. 1862. Text. 1862.*

Illustration. WMR describes CGR's illustration of the poem in a copy of *1862*: 'it applies to the line "Life nursed in its grave by Death". We see Death, a white and sufficiently "bogyfied" personage, holding on her lap a motionless female form, with yellow hair and pink drapery. A markedly leafless tree rises above the group' (*1904*, 483).

120 l. 22. *cleft*. Divided (i.e. referring to their tails).

SISTER MAUDE. *Date.* Perhaps *c*.1860 (WMR in *1904*, 348). *Publication. 1862*; omitted in *1875. Text. 1862.*

121 NOBLE SISTERS. *Date.* In the notebook manuscript, the leaf on which the poem's last lines and its date were written is missing. The preceding poem, 'Cousin Kate' (in *Crump*, I. 31–2), is dated 18 November 1859; the following poem is 'No Thank You, John', dated 27 March 1860 (Bodleian MS. Film. 933, microfilm of notebook of poems 1859–60). *Publication. 1862. Text. 1862.*

l. 12. *'frayed*. Frightened.

122 l. 46. *Hard . . . door*. In *1875*: 'Who loitered round our door'. The revision may indicate a later sensitivity to sexual suggestiveness, as if the *chamber* door was a door too far (and perhaps as if innuendo might be detected in the line): cf. 'The Prince's Progress', l. 340. But loitering does itself have sexual associations in Rossetti's work (see 'An Apple Gathering', l. 27).

'NO THANK YOU, JOHN'. *Date.* 27 March 1860. *Publication. 1862. Text. 1862.*

Title. CGR told DGR that 'no such person existed or exists' (letter, 14 [December 1875], p. 398, above). WMR records that, in a copy of *1875*, CGR wrote: 'The original John was obnoxious, because he never gave scope for "No, thank you"' (*1904*, 483). WMR took this original John to be the painter John Brett (*FL*, 54).

123 MIRAGE. *Date.* 12 June 1860. *Publication. 1862. Text. 1862.*

ll. 5–6. *I hang . . . lake*. The Psalmist sings of exiled Israel's incapacity to sing: 'By the rivers of Babylon, there we sat down, yea, we wept when we remembered Zion. We hanged our harps upon the willows in the midst thereof' (Psalm 137: 1–2).

124 OLD AND NEW YEAR DITTIES. 3. *Date.* 31 December 1860. *Publication.* In *1862 (D)*, the poem is the last of three end-of-the-year pieces, the others dating from 1856 and 1858, which form the penultimate work in the volume—'Amen' being placed last. (The selection, on evaluative grounds, of only the third of these poems for the present edition is, it should be said, in contravention of CGR's instruction to the editor of an anthology, in 1883, not to select 'an independent poem which forms part of a series or group,—not (for instance) one no. of "Passing Away" or one Sonnet of "Monna Innominata". Such compound work has a connection (very often) which is of interest to the author, and which an editor gains nothing by discarding' (*L* 3. 167).) *Text. 1862.*

l. 3. *in one stay.* In an unchanging state. Cf. Order for the Burial of the Dead, *BCP*: 'Man that is born of a woman hath but a short time to live, and is full of misery. He cometh up, and is cut down, like a flower; he fleeth as it were a shadow, and never continueth in one stay' (Job 14: 1–2).

l. 6. *I shall . . . May.* In having the world claim the power of self-renewal, CGR's poem reconceives its immediate model—Felicia Hemans's 'Passing Away', with its epigraph ' "Passing away" is written on the world, and all the world contains'.

l. 13. *Rust . . . array.* Cf. Matthew 6: 19: 'Lay not up for yourselves treasures upon earth, where moth and rust doth corrupt'.   *array.* Dress. The use of the rhyme word is influenced (as l. 14 confirms) by Hemans's 'Passing Away', ll. 1–4: 'It is written on the rose, | In its glory's full array; | Read what those buds disclose— | "Passing away" '.

ll. 20–2. *Winter . . . May.* Cf. Song of Solomon 2: 11–13. The presence of the Song in the poem has been prepared by l. 16, and is then continued in ll. 23–5.

125 PROMISES LIKE PIECRUST. *Date.* 20 April 1861. *Text.* BL Ashley MS. 1364 (4).

Title. From the proverb 'Promises, like pie-crust, are made to be broken'.

l. 15. *glass.* A mirror or a crystal used for divination.

A ROYAL PRINCESS. *Date.* 22 October 1861. *Published.* First published in *Poems: An Offering to Lancashire* (London, 1863), 2–10 (*L* 1. 169). This volume was produced to raise money for the relief of workers suffering from the depression in the Lancashire cotton industry brought on by the disruption of raw cotton supply during the American Civil War. The publisher was Emily Faithfull, with 'the compositors of the Victoria Press'—women compositors—'volunteering their services' (Isa Craig's preface). The poem was then included in *1866*, even though in CGR's letter to DGR of 13 [March 1865] she suggests omitting it: her letter of [11 March] had left the decision to DGR (see pp. 392, 393, above; cf. *DGRL (DW)* 3. 1380). *Text. 1866.* The manuscript notebook BL Ashley MS. 1364 (4) shows eleven deleted stanzas that were omitted in the 1863 version; a further five stanzas included in the 1863 version were then omitted for *1866*. One effect of these revisions is to give somewhat less prominence to the princess's longing for a lover (see note to l. 36).

126 l. 28. *with equal pen.* Men are accounted exactly as are beasts. (The ordering of the accounts in l. 29 is alphabetical: cattle, then horses, then men.)

l. 36. *though trodden down like mud.* In two of the stanzas in the manuscript notebook that follow at this point, the princess complains that no man then—or ever—declared his love for her (in *Crump*, 1. 284–5). These stanzas are deleted in the manuscript, and their omission in the 1863 text, and then in the *1866* text, gives greater prominence to the princess's developing concern for the people as a whole which is first declared in ll. 34–6.

127 ll. 47–8. *but . . . funeral.* Cf. Orsino in *Twelfth Night*, 1. 1. 4: 'That strain again! It had a dying fall'. Yet, where the object of Orsino's love is an individual, the princess—lacking a 'mate' (l. 27), excluded from 'love's secret lore' (l. 44)—is discovering a generalized love for the people.

128 l. 76. '*After us the deluge*'. The reported words of Louis XV's mistress, Mme de Pompadour, in time of adversity: *Après nous le déluge*. The phrase conveys indifference to whatever turmoil will occur after one's death.

129 l. 104. *I, if I perish, perish.* From Esther 4: 16, where Queen Esther intervenes to protect her people, the Jews: 'and so will I go in unto the king, which is not according to the law: and if I perish, I perish'.

l. 105. *that's the goal I half conceive.* In the manuscript (as in the 1863 version) this is followed by a (penultimate) stanza:

> Once to stand up face to face with heart-pulse loud and hot
> — It may be in this latter day I stand thus in my lot—
> And cry, 'I love you, love you', to those who know me not;

IN PROGRESS. *Date.* 31 March 1862. *Text.* BL Ashley MS. 1364 (4).

GOOD FRIDAY. *Date.* 20 April 1862. *Publication.* First published in Orby Shipley (ed.), *Lyra Messianica* (London, 1864), 236–7; then *1866 (D)*. *Text. 1866.*

l. 2. *That I can stand . . . beneath Thy Cross.* This implies not only an imaginative participation in the witnessing of Christ's passion, but also the ecclesial context of meditation before the cross during Good Friday devotions. Cf. the lines copied into the notebook Bodleian MS. Don. e. 1/8 in September 1853 as '(For under a Crucifix')' (CGR's brackets), in which Christ speaks of his suffering on the cross, and the further suffering inflicted by whoever still rejects him (subsequently revised— removing Christ's statement that he 'Gave up glory, broke My will' for man—and published in *TF* as the entry for Monday in Holy Week, in *Crump*, 2. 225).

130 ll. 15-16. *Greater . . . rock.* In Exodus 17: 6 God tells Moses to smite a rock from which water will then flow.

A DREAM. *Date.* 17 December 1862. *Publication. 1866. Text. 1866.*

Title. In *1875*, the title under which the poem was first published was changed to 'On the Wing'.

l. 3. *pigeons.* A common emblem of constant love.

130 THE QUEEN OF HEARTS. *Date.* 3 January 1863. *Publication.* First published in *Macmillan's Magazine*, 8 (October 1863), 457. *Text. 1866.*

l. 13. *prepense.* Deliberately.

131 A BIRD'S-EYE VIEW. *Date.* 4 March 1863. *Publication.* First published in *Macmillan's Magazine*, 8 (July 1863), 207. *Text. 1866.*

l. 8. *his ominous eye.* The raven is, traditionally, a bird of ill omen (e.g. *Macbeth*, 1. 5. 36-7: 'The raven himself is hoarse | That croaks the fatal entrance of Duncan').

133 A DUMB FRIEND. *Date.* 24 March 1863. *Text.* BL Ashley MS. 1364 (4).

134 l. 25. *rare.* Sparse.

MAIDEN-SONG. *Date.* 6 July 1863. *Publication. 1866. Text. 1866.* WMR notes that the poem was 'something of a favourite' with CGR (*1904*, 462). DGR reports that Gladstone had been heard repeating the poem by heart (letter to Frances Mary Lavinia Rossetti, 2 October 1868, *DGRL (F)* 4. 105).

135 l. 21. *Strawberry leaves.* i.e. strawberry plants.

l. 48. *A fish gasped on the floor.* The hyperbole of ll. 19-20 becomes, here, adynaton.

140 THE LOWEST PLACE. *Date.* 25 July 1863. Publication. *1866 (D)*, the last poem in the volume. *Text. 1866.*

141 SOMEWHERE OR OTHER. *Date.* October 1863. *Publication. 1866. Text. 1866.*

Title. A copy was submitted to the Portfolio Society (CGR Collection (Co222), Princeton University Library) with the title 'A prospective Meeting'.

WHAT WOULD I GIVE?. *Date.* 28 January 1864. *Publication. 1866. Text. 1866.*

ll. 1-2. *What . . . do.* See God's promise of restoration to the remnant of exiled Israel in Ezekiel 11: 19-20: 'And I will give them one heart, and I will put a new spirit within you; and I will take the stony heart out of their flesh, and will give them an heart of flesh: That they may walk in my statutes, and keep mine ordinances, and do them: and they shall be my people, and I will be their God'.

l. 9. *ingrain.* Inherent (originally a term from dyeing: dyed in a fast colour).

WHO SHALL DELIVER ME?. *Date.* 1 March 1864. *Publication.* First published in the *Argosy*, 1 (February 1866), 288. *Text. 1875.*

Title. From Romans 7: 24, on man's captivity to sin: 'O wretched man that I am! who shall deliver me from the body of this death?'

142 l. 11. *self-purged*. (1) 'purged of self'; (2) 'purged by myself'—an impossibility introduced by the question of ll. 8–9, and implicitly repudiated by ll. 22–4.

l. 21. *clog*. Block of wood tied to an animal or a person to prevent escape.

l. 24. *Break . . . free*. In the manuscript in the notebook BL Ashley MS. 1364 (5) there follows a sestet which breaks the stanzaic pattern:

> Lord, I had chosen another lot;
> But then I had not chosen well,
> Only Thy choice for me is good:
>   No different lot in Heaven or Hell
> Had blessed me, rightly understood;
> None other, which Thou orderest not.

(The revision 'diverse' is pencilled above 'different' in the fourth of these lines, but the first reading is not deleted.) The sestet was omitted in both the 1866 periodical publication, and in *1875*.

THE GHOST'S PETITION. *Date*. 7 April 1864. *Publication. 1866*. The last four stanzas of the manuscript version were omitted at DGR's suggestion ('Please cut it short, as you suggest', CGR tells him on 31 March 1865). *Text. 1866*.

Title. 'A Return' in the manuscript in the notebook BL Ashley MS. 1364 (5).

144 l. 75. In the manuscript four more stanzas follow at this point:

> 'Yours I was for sorrow or mirth.
>   My heart is broken: give me a token,
> Give me a token from heaven or earth.' —

> 'Dry your tears, mine own loving wife;
>   The token given came straight from heaven
> That you may bear your most weary life:

> 'Nurse our little baby for God;
>   To sing His praises, when grass and daisies
> Cover us both beneath the sod.

> 'Yet His vineyard its fruit shall yield;
>   Yet our Father will reap and gather
> Sheaf by sheaf all His harvest field.'

145 TWICE. *Date*. June 1864. *Publication. 1866. Text. 1866*.

146 l. 37. *Refine . . . gold*. Cf. *SF*, 50–1: 'God hath deigned to invite each one of us: "My son, give Me thine heart" (Prov. xxiii. 26): the heart offered as a whole burnt-offering to Him becomes fuel not to His consuming

jealousy but to His undying love: "God is love" (1 St. John iv. 8), "He is like a refiner's fire" (Mal. iii. 2)'.

UNDER WILLOWS. *Date*. 27 July 1864. *Text*. BL Ashley MS. 1364 (5).

Title. The willow is associated with forsaken lovers (cf. the 'song of willow' Desdemona sings in *Othello*, 4. 3; 'Willow, willow, willow', in [Thomas Percy (ed.)], *Reliques of Ancient English Poetry* (1765)). But this woman's lover may not have been lost to her by his desertion (there are graves under these willows).

l. 2. *welladay*. An exclamation expressing sorrow. The diction is that of ballads (e.g. Coleridge, 'The Rime of the Ancient Mariner' (1817), l. 139).

147 BIRD OR BEAST?. *Date*. 15 August 1864. *Publication*. *1866*. *Text*. *1866*.

A SKETCH. *Date*. 15 August 1864. *Text*. BL Ashley MS. 1364 (5). WMR, while noting that CGR 'never enlightened me on the subject', took the poem to refer to C. B. Cayley: 'by the date when the verses were written . . . Christina, though the least forward of women, had evinced towards him an amount of graciousness which a man of ordinary alertness would not have overlooked' (WMR in *1904*, 368).

148 SONGS IN A CORNFIELD. *Date*. 26 August 1864. *Publication*. *1866*. *Text*. *1866*.

149 ll. 60–1. *The green . . . thickest*. In *1866* Macmillan printed a full stop after *coil*, and a comma after *thickest*, even though DGR had noticed the error in one of his careful readings of proofs. The present edition punctuates as CGR wished in 1866: 'no stop whatever after *coil* . . . but a colon after *thickest*' (*L* 1. 279). (In the notebook manuscript there is a comma after *thickest*, but the punctuation in the manuscript prepared for the publisher may have differed.) Macmillan corrected some copies of *1866* by hand. (See Lona Mosk Packer, 'Christina Rossetti's "Songs in a Cornfield": A Misprint Uncorrected', *N&Q* 9 (March 1962), 97–100.)

150 ll. 71–85. In the manuscript (BL Ashley MS. 1364 (5)), the second song is not that in *1866*, but the following song:

> We met hand to hand,
> Clasped hands together close and fast,
>   As close as oak and ivy stand:
> But it is past.
> Come day, come night, night comes at last.
>
> We loosed hand from hand,
> We parted face from face,
>   Each went his way to his own land
> At his own pace,
> Each went to fill his separate place.

> If we should meet one day,
> If both by chance should not forget,
>   We should shake hands the accustomed way
> As when we met
> So long ago, as I remember yet.

This song was replaced at the suggestion of DGR on the grounds of its 'less simple character' (see letter to DGR, 31 March [1865] (p. 395, above)). The song was later published in *1875* as the first of two poems under the title 'Twilight Night' (in *Crump*, I. 212).

151 l. 117. In the manuscript notebook, a further twelve lines follow:

> But death will keep her secret,
>   Turf will veil her face,
> She will lie at rest at rest
>   In her resting place.
> No more reaping
>   Wheat thro' the harvest day,
> No more weeping
>   False lover gone away:
> It may be sleeping
>   As dove sleeps in her nest;
> It may be keeping
>   Watch yet at rest.

DESPISED AND REJECTED. *Date*. 10 October 1864. *Publication*. *1866 (D)*. *Text*. *1866*.

Title. From Isaiah 53: 3, read as referring to Christ.

l. 8. *open to Me*. Two of the poem's generative intertexts are invoked: (*a*) Song of Solomon 5: 2, 6: 'I sleep, but my heart waketh: it is the voice of my beloved that knocketh, saying, Open to me, my sister, my love, my dove, my undefiled: for my head is filled with dew, and my locks with the drops of the night . . . I opened to my beloved; but my beloved had withdrawn himself, and was gone . . .'; (*b*) Revelation 3: 20: 'Behold, I stand at the door, and knock: if any man hear my voice, and open the door, I will come in to him, and will sup with him, and he with me'.

152 l. 23. *Then is it nothing to thee?*. Cf. Zion's lament in Lamentations 1: 12.

ll. 57–8. *on my door . . . evermore*. A Passover allusion (from the daubing of a lamb's blood on door posts as a sign to God to spare a household, Exodus 12: 7).

153 JESSIE CAMERON. *Date*. October 1864. *Publication*. *1866*. *Text*. *1866*.

154 l. 59. *unked*. 'Grim, uncanny, dismal' (WMR in *1904*, 485).

156 WEARY IN WELL-DOING. *Date*. 22 October 1864. *Publication*. *1866 (D)*. *Text*. *1866*.

Title. From Galatians 6: 9: 'And let us not be weary in well doing: for in due season we shall reap, if we faint not'.

l. 12. *moil*. Drudge.

PARADISE: IN A SYMBOL. *Date.* 14 November 1864. *Publication.* In Orby Shipley (ed.), *Lyra Messianica*, 2nd edn. (London, 1869), 417–18. *Text. Lyra Messianica* (1869). The typeface used in *Lyra Messianica* is archaic (with a long 's').

Title. 'Birds of Paradise' in the notebook BL Ashley MS. 1364 (6). The published title was chosen to correspond with another CGR poem included in *Lyra Messianica* (1869), 'Paradise: in a Dream' (subsequently retitled 'Paradise').

157 l. 14. *clang.* Not, it seems, in the usual sense when in reference to birds—i.e. a loud, harsh cry—but the noise made by the birds' wings (cf. 'The Convent Threshold, l. 88, and note (p. 432): 'I heard his hundred pinions clang').

ll. 25–6. *Where . . . west.* Cf. Revelation 21: 23.

GROWN AND FLOWN. *Date.* 21 December 1864. *Publication. 1866. Text. 1866.*

Title. 'Alas for me!' in BL Ashley MS. 1364 (6).

158 EVE. *Date.* 20 January 1865. *Publication. 1866. Text. 1866.*

ll. 1–2. *While . . . within.* The location is explained in ll. 36–9. The detail of the door may be generated by the obscure 'sin lieth at the door' in the Cain narrative (Genesis 4: 7).

ll. 13–14. *The Tree . . . twelvefold-fruited.* CGR conflates the tree of life of Genesis 2: 9 with that of Revelation 22: 2 (eschatology generating protology).

159 l. 33. *Cain.* For Cain's murder of his brother Abel—the first death in the world—see Genesis 4.

l. 61. *deprecation.* Prayer for deliverance from distress.

160 THE PRINCE'S PROGRESS. *Date.* ll. 481–540, 11 October 1861; ll. 1–480, January 1865. *Publication.* ll. 481–540 were first published in *Macmillan's Magazine*, 8 (May 1863), 36, as 'The Fairy Prince Who Arrived Too Late'; the extended poem was published in *1866.* 'When Christina Rossetti was looking up, in 1865, the material for a fresh poetical volume, it was, I believe, my brother who suggested to her to turn the dirge ['The Fairy Prince Who Arrived Too Late'] into a narrative poem of some length. She adopted the suggestion—almost the only instance in which she wrote anything so as to meet directly the views of another person' (WMR in *1904*, 461). DGR designed the frontispiece and title page for *1866*: the frontispiece illustrates the text 'You should have wept her yesterday' (l. 531), the title page the text 'The long hours go and come and go' (l. 3). *Text. 1866.* The poem's title is an ironic allusion to *PP*, for this prince is an irresolute pilgrim who will fail in his quest. In a letter of 1863, CGR refers to the poem which was published in *Macmillan's Magazine*, and which became ll. 481–540, as 'my reverse of the *Sleeping Beauty*'. There she is defensive of her departure from fairy-tale tradition: 'except in fairy land such reverses must often occur; yet

I don't think it argues a sound or grateful spirit to dwell on them as predominantly as I have done' (*L* 1. 184). The poem is also a departure from Tennyson's telling of the Sleeping Beauty tale in 'The Day-Dream'. Yet, as the poem's allusive title implies, this poem—like the title poem of *1862*—invites religious interpretation. That is confirmed by an early indication that the princess who is the object of the prince's quest is to be understood as a Christlike figure (see note to ll. 23–4). In this poem, in a deft inversion of Christian spiritualizing interpretation of the Song of Solomon, it is the bride—not the bridegroom—who plays the Christlike part (Joan Rees, 'Christina Rossetti: Poet', *Critical Quarterly*, 26 (1984), 67–8). As in *PP*, the individual quest is mapped onto a plan of history (Mary Arseneau, *Recovering Christina Rossetti* (Basingstoke, 2004), 154). This biblical plan—from the transgression in paradise of Genesis through to the renewal of Revelation—informs the three episodes in which the prince is distracted from his quest. The first, that of the milkmaid with her 'serpent-coils' of hair (l. 94), corresponds to the Fall in Genesis 3. The third, that in which the prince is 'saved' from the river, corresponds to the crossing of the River of Death in *PP* in order to enter the Celestial City (Rees, 'Rossetti: poet', 64). The second, the longest of these episodes, that of the alchemist in a cave in a blighted wasteland, has proved more difficult to insert into this plan. The literary models for this old man include Pope in *PP* (Linda H. Peterson, 'Restoring the Book: The Typological Hermeneutics of Christina Rossetti and the PRB', *VP* 32 (1994), 221–2) and Archimago the magician in *FQ* (Arseneau, *Recovering Rossetti*, 149–50)—both figures of false religion: figures of the Roman Church. This old man may, no less, be a figure of false religion: not of the Roman Church, but of the old dispensation of 'the Jews' or of 'the law' under which fallen man must live, in this plan of history (Simon Humphries, 'Who is the Alchemist in Christina Rossetti's "The Prince's Progress"?', *RES* 58 (2007), 684–97; and see notes to ll. 179, 239). A further literary model for the old man—one which would accord with this interpretation—may be the old Jew, Adonijah, in Charles Maturin's *Melmoth the Wanderer*, ed. D. Grant (Oxford, 1989), 262–72: both figures are confined underground; one is trying to find a way of prolonging life and the other is enduring the consequences of an unnaturally prolonged life; both need a younger man (a prince, a nobleman) to take refuge with them and work for them (see Humphries, 'Who is the Alchemist?', 690–2).

l. 13. *world-end*. Far-away, but probably also with eschatological implication (cf. the threat of destruction that makes Christian flee his city at the beginning of *PP*, 39–41). This is no time for 'ease' (l. 14) (cf. 'Pastime').

ll. 23–4. *Spell-bound . . . sake*. The bride's patience is to be understood as Christlike (cf. what the Christlike Lizzie has suffered for her sister's sake at 'Goblin Market', ll. 473–4). CGR departs from fairy-tale tradition in not putting her Sleeping Beauty into a deep sleep: she watches and waits (cf. ll. 458–62). This is evidence of uneasiness with the connotations of sleep in the context of the poem's religious symbolism: as brides must be watchful for the coming of the bridegroom Christ (Matthew 25: 13), so this bride must watch for the coming of her prince—even if he is no Christlike figure.

161 ll. 40–1. *use . . . fail*. Compare 'From House to Home', ll. 65–70, where the speaker declines to set out for 'the distant land' (l. 76), and in which the eschatological context for the *carpe diem* topos becomes explicit.

162 ll. 89–90. *Ahead . . . edge*. What the prince takes for a reason to delay is, in CGR, likely to be an eschatological warning against delay (cf. 'Pastime').

l. 96. *subtle*. The milkmaid, with her 'shining serpent-coils' of hair, has the subtlety of the serpent in paradise (Genesis 3: 1).

163 l. 100. *mavis and merle*. Song thrush and blackbird.

l. 101. *hodden grey*. Coarse grey woollen cloth.

ll. 121–2. *The grass . . . air*. The description of the wasteland of ll. 121–50 as a whole is indebted to Browning's quest poem, 'Childe Roland to the Dark Tower Came': cf. 'As for the grass, it grew as scant as hair | In leprosy', ll. 73–4. The stanzas from which these comparable passages come share rhyme (rare, air, spare, bare // hair, a-stare, there); and 'astunt' (l. 124)—an eccentric coinage, probably with the sense 'in a stunted state'—may be an attempt at the Browningesque. The abrupt transition to this wasteland is in accord with the episode of the milkmaid being a version of man's transgression in paradise: following the Fall, the very ground is 'cursed' (Genesis 3: 17).

164 l. 153. *outs and ins*. The windings of what, in this pathless landscape, might become paths.

l. 161. *fate*. An indication that the prince's worldview is not Christian (cf. 'doom', l. 19). In classical mythology, one of the personified Fates spins the thread of life, and another cuts it at death (as at l. 236).

l. 169. *cave*. Cf. the cave of Pagan and Pope in *PP*, 99–100.

165 l. 179. *seething-pot*. Taken from one of the visions in the prologue to Jeremiah: 'And I said, I see a seething pot; and the face thereof is toward the north' (1: 13). The vision is obscure, but is interpretable as a vision of disaster inflicted upon Judah in punishment for turning to other gods: 'And I will utter my judgments against them touching all their wickedness, who have forsaken me' (1: 16).

l. 181. *atomy*. Skeleton.

167 l. 239. *stiff-necked*. In the Old Testament, this image conveys Israel's disobedience of God's commands: they are like working beasts which will not obey directions (e.g. Exodus 32: 9). It is then used in Christian writing to designate 'the Jews' who have rejected Christ (cf. Acts 7: 51–2).

167 l. 241. *the old crab was nipped*. A *crab* can be an ill-tempered, intractable person (cf. this old man's likeness to a stubborn mule, l. 239). However, *nipped* implies the cancerous image of the old man's deeds being turned against himself: the nipper nipped. Given the immediate context of death coming to the old man, the implication is that his own work has itself been deadly.

l. 245. *clipped*. Surrounded; encircled.

168 l. 291. *aftermath*. The crop of grass that grows after the first early summer mowing.

169 l. 312. *He must swim for his life*. Cf. the crossing of the River of Death in *PP*, 198–200. The prince may think he is 'saved' (l. 325), but this is 'a parody of Christian salvation' (Rees, 'Rossetti: Poet', 64).

l. 340. *But . . . breast-high*. In *1875*: 'But one propped his head that drooped awry'.

172 l. 422. *fatness*. Fertility (biblical diction: cf. Genesis. 27: 28).

l. 438. *Of her heart to him?*. In *1875*, a stanza is added at this point:

> Above his head a tangle glows
> Of wine-red roses, blushes, snows,
> Closed buds and buds that unclose,
> 　Leaves, and moss, and prickles too;
> His hand shook as he plucked a rose,
> 　And the rose dropped dew.

(Here, 'moss' is not the plant called 'moss', but rather 'the mossy covering of the stalk and calyx of the moss rose' (*OED*, 5a), a group of roses much admired in the mid-nineteenth century.)

174 l. 510. *Kirtle*. Skirt.

175 MEMORY. *Date*. The poem's two parts were conceived as independent poems, the first dated 8 November 1857, the second 17 February 1865. *Publication. 1866. Text. 1866.*

Title. In the notebook manuscripts the first part is entitled 'A Blank' (BL Ashley MS. 1364 (2)), and the second part 'A Memory' (Ashley MS. 1364 (6)). The first part's manuscript title is almost certainly taken from *Twelfth Night*, 2. 4, where Viola, disguised as the page Cesario, tells Orsino of her father's daughter (by which she means herself, but which Orsino will understand to be a sister of Cesario's). This woman loved a man but could not disclose that love (being none other than Viola, loving Orsino). Orsino asks 'And what's her history?'; Viola replies 'A blank, my lord. She never told her love, | But let concealment, like a worm i'th'bud, | Feed on her damask cheek. She pin'd in thought; | And with a green and yellow melancholy | She sat like Patience on a monument, | Smiling at grief' (2. 4. 108–14).

l. 7. *forms*. Perhaps in the sense of 'conventional behaviour'.

l. 15. *idol*. In the light of the manuscript title's allusion to *Twelfth Night*, the imagery of idolatry here may be prompted by Antonio's words about the apparently faithless Sebastian: Antonio had venerated Sebastian's 'image', only to find that appearances have deceived, and that he who had appeared a 'god' is truly no more than an 'idol' (3. 4. 343-9).

l. 16. *Once*. Once and for all.

176 l. 27. *bloodless*. Pale. (The description may be influenced by the lily's symbolization of purity—a state of being free from the sexual stain that originates in the sensual appetite: cf. *OED*, *blood* 6.)

AMOR MUNDI. *Date*. 21 February 1865. *Publication*. First published in the *Shilling Magazine*, 1 (June 1865), 193, illustrated by Frederick Sandys (reproduced in *Kooistra*, 48); in *1875* the poem is placed before 'Up-Hill'. *Text*. *1875*; l. 1, terminal comma removed (there is none in the notebook manuscript, BL Ashley MS. 1364 (6)), and 'O' emended to 'Oh' ('O' probably being a printer's error).

'Mr. Sandys showed a group of two lovers—the man guitar-playing and singing, the woman pleasing herself with a hand-mirror. I do not perceive, however, that such was exactly the authoress's intention. I take it that both her personages are female: one of them a woman, the other the World in feminine shape. The first speaker is the woman, who inquires of the World whither she is going: it is the World who is figured with "love-locks", and as "dear to doat on", and who is afterwards pronounced "false and fleetest". The reader can take or reject this opinion as he likes, for I do not remember ever hearing the point settled by Christina' (WMR in *1904*, 485). WMR then notes: 'I find in one of her editions the following note on the poem: "Gabriel remarked very truly, a reminiscence of *The Demon Lover*"'—a remark that might seem to support Sandys's interpretation, for in that ballad a dead lover returns to claim a woman who has become the wife of another, and then takes her with him to hell (see *Kooistra*, 46-8, who reproduces Sandys's illustration). But, even if the two are man and woman, the roles in the ballad are reversed: the invitation to hell of ll. 3-4 is surely made by the woman of l. 7. It is likely that in this poem, as in the sonnet 'The World', CGR chooses not to determine the gender of the one being tempted.

Title. Latin: 'love of the world'.

l. 1. *Oh, where are you going*. Imitating a ballad opening: cf. 'The Dæmon Lover', in Walter Scott (ed.), *The Minstrelsy of the Scottish Border*, l. 1: 'O where have you been, my long, long, love'.

l. 3. *The downhill path is easy*. Proverbial: e.g. in *PP*, when the pilgrims go up Hill Difficulty, James rightly rejects the proverb '*To go down the hill is easy*', knowing that 'the way to Hell is as down a hill', 266.   *an*. If.

ll. 9-12. *Oh, what . . . hurt*. DGR's remark on the poem's likeness to 'The Dæmon Lover' 'would refer more directly to stanza 3' (WMR in *1904*, 485): 'O what hills are yon, yon pleasant hills [?]' she asks, to be told by

her demon lover that they are 'the hills of heaven'; 'O whaten a moun-
tain is yon [?]' she asks, to be told that it is 'the mountain of hell . . .
Where you and I will go', ll. 57-64.

177 FROM SUNSET TO STAR RISE. *Date*. 23 February 1865. In the manu-
script in notebook BL Ashley MS. 1364 (6), there is a pencilled note
'House of Charity'. WMR, taking this to refer to the Highgate institu-
tion for reclaiming 'fallen' women with which CGR was associated,
wondered if the sonnet might have been written 'as if it were an utter-
ance of one of these women', rather than of the poet herself (*1904*, 485).
But similar pencilled notes in the manuscripts indicate submission to, or
publication in, periodicals or anthologies (e.g. 'Shilling Mag.' is written
beside the title of 'Amor Mundi' in BL Ashley MS. 1364 (6)). The note
is more likely to indicate that the sonnet was given for publication on
behalf of this, or some other, charitable institution. *Publication. 1875.
Text. 1875.*

Title. 'Friends' in the notebook manuscript.

l. 3. *silly*. A conventional literary epithet of sheep (*OED*, 1c):
'poor', 'defenceless', 'deserving of pity'.   *benighted*. Overtaken by
darkness.   *from*. Away from.

l. 7. *wold*. An area of high open land.

l. 9. *hedged*. The image is biblical: God hedges man in, whether to pro-
tect him (Job 1: 10), or to oppress and bewilder him (Job 3: 23;
Lamentations 3: 7). CGR's use of the image, while most obviously
negative, can be taken to have this doubleness.

l. 11. *sedge*. An expanse of rush-like or grass-like plants growing in wet
land.

l. 14. *sometime*. Former; past.

UNDER THE ROSE. *Date*. Written quickly in early March 1865 to fill up
1866 (see letter to DGR, 6 [March 1865]). The poem was not entered
into a notebook. *Publication. 1866. Text. 1866.* WMR records that, in a
copy of *1875*, CGR noted 'This was all fancy, but Mrs. [W. Bell] Scott
afterwards told me of a somewhat similar fact' (*1904*, 462). (WMR him-
self suggested that the fancy may have been prompted by Dickens's
Bleak House.) For CGR's defence of the poem, see the letter to DGR of
13 [March 1865] (pp. 393-4, above).

Title. From Latin *sub rosa*, a phrase meaning 'in secret, in strict con-
fidence'. In *1875*, the epigraph became the poem's title: ' "The Iniquity
of the Fathers Upon the Children" '. The epigraph is from the
Decalogue: 'I the Lord thy God am a jealous God, visiting the iniquity
of the fathers upon the children unto the third and fourth generation of
them that hate me' (Exodus 20: 5).

178 l. 40. *flout and scout*. Mock, deride.

l. 42. *wise*. Manner, way.

l. 46. *one-sided*. On one side of the mile-long track.

l. 53. *old-fashioned boasts*. These boasts of what England (personified as John Bull) would do to invaders belong to the time of the wars at the beginning of the century.

183 l. 211. *mortal*. Long and tedious (*OED*, 8c).

186 l. 357. *Stolen waters are sweet*. From Proverbs 9: 17.

191 l. 533. *pelf*. Money.

EN ROUTE | AN 'IMMURATA' SISTER

EN ROUTE. *Date*. June 1865. *Text*. BL Ashley MS. 1364 (6). Three compositions are entered in the notebook under the heading (or title) 'En Route', separated by short dividing dashes; the first and the third of these were later incorporated (with revisions) into the published poem 'An "Immurata" Sister'. To WMR, these three compositions seemed 'to have little connection one with the other', beside—as he assumed— being all written (as the title and date imply) on CGR's brief journey to Italy (*1904*, 485). Taking these to be three more or less independent compositions gathered under an appropriate heading—rather than a three-section poem with a title—WMR felt able to present, by itself, the second piece, which was not incorporated into 'An "Immurata" Sister', as an unpublished poem in its own right (*1904*, 377). Even though WMR's interpretation of the manuscript evidence may have been influenced by a desire to find justification for publishing lines which he particularly admired—'She never perhaps wrote anything better' (*1904*, 485)—he was probably correct in thinking the three parts of 'En Route' independent compositions. (Compare the gathering of ten pieces, similarly separated by short dividing dashes, under the heading 'Odds and Ends', in Bodleian MS. Don. e. 1/8. Six of these are untitled; four have titles in brackets.) But it is not certain that WMR was correct. He may have overlooked the connection of the first to the third of these pieces by means of the image of life as a river—a connection obscured by revision (see note to ll. 37–8); and CGR's incorporation of these two pieces into a published poem can be seen as confirming that connection. Nor is it impossible that the heading 'En Route' refers to the passage of life to death (even if it does, no less, identify these three pieces as written on CGR's Italian journey)—in which case the three pieces may be more tightly bound together than WMR supposed. It is not impossible that 'En Route' is a three-part poem which was, later, radically reworked as 'An "Immurata" Sister'. Given that uncertainty, this edition presents the complete text of 'En Route' (as WMR did himself in *1896*) alongside that of 'An "Immurata" Sister'.

192 l. 19. *cordial*. Warm and friendly. In the context of this stanza, the word's Latin etymology is to be understood: such friendliness comes from the heart (cf. 'Enrica, 1865', l. 16: 'Warm-hearted and of cordial face').

ll. 37–8. *There's nothing . . . dead*. A revision of 'Yet life runs past though slow to run, | And there is peace among the dead'. The revision thus removed what had been a reprise of the image of life as a river in ll. 1–4.

192 AN 'IMMURATA' SISTER. *Date.* Lines 1–12 and 17–20 were written in June 1865; the manuscript shows that ll. 21–4 were a revision, made at a late stage in the preparation of *1881*, of the corresponding lines in 'En Route' (incomplete bound manuscript of *1881*, Harry Ransom Center, University of Texas, Austin); the date of ll. 13–16 and 25–8 is not known. *Publication. 1881. Text. 1881.*

Title. An immured nun is one belonging to an enclosed order.

193 l. 25. *Sparks fly upward.* From Job 5: 7.

ENRICA, 1865. *Date.* 1 July 1865. *Publication.* First published in *A Round of Days* (London, 1866), 6, under the title 'An English Drawing-Room. | 1865'. *Text. 1875.*

Title. 'E.F.' in the notebook BL Ashley MS. 1364 (6), identified by WMR as Enrica Filopanti, an Italian acquaintance of the Rossettis: 'Signora Filopanti was the lady who, upon Garibaldi's visit to London in 1864, delivered a brief and extemporized harangue to him in public' (*1904*, 486).

194 A DAUGHTER OF EVE. *Date.* 30 September 1865. *Publication. 1875*, where it follows 'Eve'. *Text. 1875.*

Title. 'An Awakening' in the notebook BL Ashley 1364 (6).

l. 1. *A fool I was to sleep at noon.* Cf. the last words spoken by the Fool in *King Lear*, 3. 6. 85: 'And I'll go to bed at noon'.

ll. 4–5. *A fool . . . lily.* Symbolizing premarital sex (the *rose* plucked too soon) and loss of purity (the broken *lily*) (cf. 'An Apple Gathering').

l. 6. *My garden-plot I have not kept.* Informed by Christian iconography in which the *hortus conclusus*—the 'garden inclosed' of Song of Solomon 4: 12—symbolizes purity.

195 A DIRGE. *Date.* 21 November 1865. *Publication.* First published in the *Argosy*, 17 (January 1874), 25. *Text. 1875.*

IN A CERTAIN PLACE. *Date.* 6 March 1866. *Text.* BL Ashley MS. 1364 (6).

Title. In 'From House to Home' (l. 116), the phrase refers to a place revealed in a vision.

196 l. 28. *Oh should I know him then?.* The poem's last line is—together with the personification of 'Love' in its first line—its surest indication that Love may be identified as Christ. In John 20: 14–15, Mary Magdalene, outside the empty sepulchre, 'saw Jesus standing, and knew not that it was Jesus', and then Jesus speaks to her.

'CANNOT SWEETEN'. *Date.* 8 March 1866. *Text.* BL Ashley MS. 1364 (6).

Title. 'Here's the smell of the blood still. All the perfumes of Arabia will not sweeten this little hand' (*Macbeth*, 5. 1. 48–50; Lady Macbeth's words).

197 ll. 25–6. *I ate . . . wine*. Eucharistic language, and an explicit invitation
to identify the speaker's 'love' as Christ, and to understand that the
speaker identifies herself with mankind as a whole which rejected and
killed Christ. This then becomes a prompt to reread the poem in the
light of this: 'I slew my love with a hardened heart' (l. 16) now recalls
both the slaying of the householder's son (i.e. Christ) in the parable of
the Wicked Husbandmen (Matthew 21: 39), and the hardened hearts of
those who rejected Christ (e.g. John 12: 40); 'my feet sought blood in
their goings' (l. 7) recalls Romans 3: 15 on the sinfulness of all mankind,
'Their feet are swift to shed blood'; that 'He loved me because he loved
me' (l. 17), and not for anything the speaker offered him, is—in theo-
logical terms—a statement of God's grace, the divine love that man
does nothing to deserve. Then, in this religious contextualization, the
reader can see the limitations of the speaker's words: the past tense of
ll. 17–20 is inadequate, for the rejected Christ continues to love man.
And the exclamation 'Oh the lost time that comes not back!' (l. 4) can
now be reread in the context of the possibility of 'Redeeming the time'
(Ephesians 5: 16; and compare, in this context, 'folly' (l. 3) and 'fools'
(Ephesians 5: 15)). Yet such religious reading does not exclude the pos-
sibility of a purely secular reading of this as a ballad of rejection and
remorse, one which deploys religious language for secular reference.

AUTUMN VIOLETS. *Publication*. First published in *Macmillan's
Magazine*, 19 (November 1868), 84. *Text. 1875*.

l. 14. *A grateful . . . corn*. See Ruth 2.

'THEY DESIRE A BETTER COUNTRY'. *Publication*. First published in
Macmillan's Magazine, 19 (March 1869), 422–3. *Text. 1875*.

Title. From Hebrews 11: 16.

198 l. 14. *'Follow . . . here'*. Cf. Christ's calls to discipleship (e.g. Matthew
9: 9).

l. 20. *The golden key to ope the golden door*. Cf. the key called Promise in
PP, with which Christian and Hopeful escape from Giant Despair's
prison, Doubting-Castle (156–7). It would be a characteristic surmise,
on CGR's part, that the golden city of Revelation 21 is to be entered by
means of a golden key; but she may, further, be influenced by Milton's
description of the keys of the kingdom of heaven which (in Matthew
16: 19) were given to Peter: '(The Golden opes, the Iron shuts amain)',
'Lycidas', l. 111.

ll. 23–8. *And who . . . sound*. Cf. Dante's *La Vita Nuova*, ch. 9, where
Dante, on a journey, is met by Love in the guise of a traveller: 'And for
the cheer he showed, he seemed to me | As one who hath lost lordship
he had got; | Advancing tow'rds me full of sorrowful thought, | Bowing
his forehead so that none should see' ('Cavalcando l'altr'ier per un
cammino', trans. DGR, *DGRW*, 316).

l. 34. *serried*. Dense.

199 *From* SING-SONG: A NURSERY RHYME BOOK. *Publication*. November 1871, dated 1872; revised edition, 1893. *Text*. 1872 edition; 'I caught a little ladybird', 1893 edition. In the one-stanza rhyme 'Margaret has a milking-pail', a full stop ends l. 4 in both the 1872 and the 1893 editions; but, for this edition, the manuscript colon has been restored in the belief that the full stop is an uncorrected printer's error. *Illustrations*. The book was conceived as being published with illustrations for each rhyme, for which CGR's own illustrations (her 'scratches', she would call them) might serve as a guide (*L* 1. 341–2). In February 1870 the book was offered to Alexander Macmillan (*L* 1. 339, 343)—the publisher of *1862* and *1866*—but CGR, swayed by DGR, did not find his terms satisfactory: 'She has resolved to leave Macmillan after a degree of meanness in his proposals which was really laughable', DGR told Swinburne on 21 February 1870. DGR himself regarded the rhymes as 'admirable things, alternating between the merest babyism and a sort of Blakish wisdom and tenderness. I believe no one could have written anything so absolutely right for babies but herself' (*DGRL (F)* 4. 376). DGR directed CGR to his own publisher, F. S. Ellis, who offered the very attractive terms of a quarter of the published price (*L* 1. 341, 342, 347). DGR further suggested to her that their friend Alice Boyd would be an adequate illustrator, and CGR was pleased with her designs at first (*L* 1. 343–6, 347, 350, 354); but both CGR and DGR were later less satisfied with her work (her beasts and flowers were good, but her people were 'ugly') (*L* 1. 355–8). Ellis, evidently, had lost confidence in Boyd, and by July 1870 there was no immediate likelihood of publication— not least as the sales of *Commonplace, and Other Short Stories*, already published by Ellis, were not encouraging. In early 1871 CGR took up the matter of publication once more. The rhymes had been written not into a notebook but on separate leaves (now bound as BL Ashley MS. 1371), and in March 1871 she noticed that twenty-two of them had not been returned by Ellis (*L* 1. 367–8). By April she had agreed terms that would lead to the book's eventual publication by Routledge (*L* 1. 369). The book was illustrated by Arthur Hughes, at WMR's suggestion (*The Diary of W. M. Rossetti, 1870–1873*, ed. Odette Bornand (Oxford, 1977), 61). His work was found very acceptable (*L* 1. 375, 379–80, 387); it was engraved by the Brothers Dalziel. In 1893 CGR returned to Macmillan for the publication of a revised and enlarged edition (*L* 4. 341–2, 343).

200 'Heartsease in my garden bed'. l. 1. *Heartsease*. The wild pansy *Viola tricolor*.

201 'Twist me a crown of wind-flowers'. l. 1. *wind-flowers*. The poem plays upon the common name for the wood anemone (*Anemone nemorosa*).

202 'I planted a hand'. l. 4. *balm*. In the company of a *palm* (symbolic of triumph) and of a *thorn* (symbolic of suffering), this is chosen for its biblical significance: a plant with healing properties (Jeremiah 8: 22). It would appear, from the absence of an indefinite article, that CGR thinks

of balm as a herb rather than as a tree, and perhaps associates it with the common garden herb *Melissa officinalis*. Her own illustration shows a tall palm and a low-growing thorn; the third plant is slightly lower-growing than the thorn.

203 'Margaret has a milking-pail'. l. 4. *betimes.* Early.

'In the meadow—what in the meadow?'. ll. 6–8. *Jacob's-ladder . . . garden.* The garden plants, contrasted with the meadow's plants—and contrasted with the meadow's rings of darker grass which (a touch of paganism) country people once thought the work of fairies—have names with religious connotations: *Jacob's-ladder* (cf. Genesis 28: 12) is *Polemonium caeruleum*; *Solomon's-seal* is *Polygonatum multiflorum*; in *TF*, 6 June, *Love-lies-bleeding* is the wild pansy *Viola tricolor*, and is probably so here (and not the cultivated *Amaranthus caudatus*).

205 'Who has seen the wind?'. l. 1. *wind.* For the wind as a symbol of the Spirit of God, see John 3: 8: 'The wind (*pneuma*) bloweth where it listeth [i.e. wishes], and thou hearest the sound thereof, but canst not tell whence it cometh, and whither it goeth'—*pneuma* being both 'wind' and 'Spirit'. (See also Introduction, p. xvii.) John Keble, in his poem for Septuagesima Sunday in *The Christian Year* (1827)—the century's best-selling volume of poetry, in a copy of which CGR drew illustrations for each poem—makes this invisible wind/Spirit analogy explicit (and footnotes John 3: 8): 'in the gentler breeze we find | Thy Spirit's viewless way'. Keble's poem provides an explicit statement of the analogical view of the world which underlies CGR's rhyme: 'Two worlds are ours: 'tis only Sin | Forbids us to descry | The mystic heaven and earth within, | Plain as the sea and sky'—where 'mystic' means 'symbolic'. The epigraph to Keble's poem provides the biblical basis: 'The invisible things of Him from the creation of the world are clearly seen, being understood by the things which are made' (Romans 1: 20).

l. 3. *trembling.* For *trembling* in the context of all things in heaven and earth bowing at the name of Jesus, see Philippians 2: 10, 12 (cf. 'Epiphanytide', l. 1: 'Trembling before Thee we fall down to adore Thee', in *Crump*, 2. 218). For an initially less fearful description of creation as inspired to praise its creator, see '"To What Purpose is This Waste?"', ll. 52–64.

'I caught a little ladybird'. For *1893*, CGR added two stanzas to what had been, in *1872*, a one-stanza poem (corresponding to ll. 1–4). The *1893* version, with a third stanza that concentrates on the 'wife', responds to Hughes's illustration in *1872* which, while taking up the indication in CGR's own illustration that the boy's play-wife is a doll and not a girl, had concentrated on the boy and the doll to the exclusion of the ladybird (*Kooistra*, 122–5). But CGR's development of the rhyme sours the contented companionship of Hughes's illustration; the second and third stanzas thus tell of a time subsequent to the boy's initial contentment.

205 l. 3. *caught*. i.e. she is a good 'catch': the language is that of the marriage market (*OED*, catch *n*. 11b).

l. 4. *staid*. Usually descriptive of character or conduct—sober, grave, sedate, free from flightiness (*OED*, 2)—but also used of someone's fixed gaze (*OED*, 1a; cf. l. 10). In the manuscript, *staid* is written above the deleted 'good': at first ll. 3–4 did not conform to CGR's manuscript illustration of the lady wife as only a doll. The revision provides a hinge between rhyme and illustration: *staid* sets up the puzzle of a wife who can, contradictorily, also be 'gay'; the illustration solves the puzzle, for a doll, whatever character is attributed it by a boy, can, materially, never be other than staid.

l. 7. *dolly wife*. Both a dollish wife (cf. *OED* adj.), and a wife who is in fact a mere doll.

l. 11. *wig*. As well as referring to artificial hair, the word is 'jocularly applied to a (natural) head of hair, esp. of a child' (*OED*, 1c): like 'staid' (l. 4), a word that acts as a hinge between play (in which the doll is a child's play-wife) and materiality (a doll's hair—a doll's everything—is artificial).

207 BY WAY OF REMEMBRANCE. *Date*. 1870; a draft of the third sonnet is dated 23 October 1870 (Janet Camp Troxell Collection (Co189), Box 1, Folder 14, Princeton University Library). *Text*. BL Ashley MS. 1369.

l. 11. *Jordan*. The river is a type of death (*a*) as the river of baptism—that sacrament being 'a death unto sin, and a new birth unto righteousness' (Catechism, *BCP*); and (*b*) as the river which Israel crossed to enter the promised land, an event that prefigures entry into heaven (cf. *PP*, 372).   *mystic*. Spiritually symbolic.

208 THE GERMAN-FRENCH CAMPAIGN 1870–1871. *Date*. From the information, in the introductory note, that the poems were 'written during the suspense of a great nation's agony', it is likely that both poems were written between the defeat of France in autumn 1870 and the outbreak of civil war in spring 1871. WMR dates them together as 'Towards January 1871' (*1904*, 387); a fair copy of the first poem—with some substantive variants from the published text, of which the most important is the title (see note below)—is dated 1870 (MSS SC 669, Perry Special Collections, Lee Library, Brigham Young University, Provo). France had declared war on Prussia in July 1870, the immediate occasion being a dispute over the succession to the Spanish throne. The French forces were quickly defeated, but Paris resisted under siege. In March 1871 a revolutionary government, the Commune, was established in Paris; at the end of May it was defeated by the forces of the French government which had been established at Versailles. WMR notes that CGR 'had incomparably more general and native sympathy with the French nationality than with the German' (*1904*, 487) (and see *L* 1. 361). *Publication*. 1875. *Text*. 1875.

Titles. That of part 1 is from Genesis 4: 9–11: 'And the Lord said unto Cain, Where is Abel thy brother? And he said, I know not: Am I my brother's keeper? And he said, What hast thou done? the voice of thy brother's blood crieth unto me from the ground. And now art thou cursed from the earth, which hath opened her mouth to receive thy brother's blood from thy hand'. That of part 2 alludes to the teaching on mourning for the dead in Ecclesiasticus (Sirach) 38, with the obscure verse 22 probably being taken—when paired with the title taken from Genesis—as the words which the dead cry out, reminding the living that they too will die: 'Remember my judgment: for thine also shall be so; yesterday for me, and to day for thee'. The Brigham Young University fair copy of part 1 has the title '"Sirs, ye are Brethren"', from Acts 7: 26.

l. 4. *as one man's hand.* A cloud can be, proverbially, as big as a man's hand; but here there is certainly an allusion to the biblical origin of the phrase, 1 Kings 18: 44, in which appears 'a little cloud out of the sea, like a man's hand'. The allusion implies the divine hand behind this threatening cloud.

ll. 7–10. *Is there . . . field.* The primary source of the eschatological imagery is Revelation 14: 14–20, in which the righteous are harvested, and the blood of the wicked flows from the winepress of the wrath of God.

209 l. 19. *Mother.* i.e. France personified (cf. ll. 1–2).

l. 25. *King.* The King of Prussia. 'If the King of Prussia in his victorious position has the magnanimity to offer generous terms of peace, and if with the road to Paris open before him he has the self restraint not to humiliate his antagonists by setting foot there, surely such forbearance will ennoble him more than a hundred conquests' (letter of September 1870 to Amelia Heimann, *L* 1. 361).

l. 27. *Sheshach.* Babylon, from Jeremiah 25: 26 in which the nations—Babylon last—drink of the cup of God's wrath.

ll. 31–4. *Take . . . hand?.* Based on Psalm 94: 8–9. The Psalmist warns that God 'to whom vengeance belongeth' will punish the wicked (94: 1).

l. 35. *Vengeance is Mine.* From Romans 12: 19.

210 l. 55. *Roll . . . flood.* 'The French have indeed found this strife like the letting out of water. May the flood not drown them' (*L* 1. 361). The image of armies advancing like a flood is biblical (e.g. Jeremiah 46: 7). *whelming* Inundating.

l. 57. *askance.* With disdain.

A CHRISTMAS CAROL. *Publication.* First published in *Scribner's Monthly*, 3 (January 1872), 278. *Text.* 1875.

212 VENUS'S LOOKING-GLASS. *Date.* October 1872 (WMR, in *1904*, 387). *Publication.* First published, with 'Love Lies Bleeding', in the *Argosy*, 15 (January 1873), 31. *Text. 1875.* 'Mr. Cayley sent to my sister a short MS. poem named *The Birth of Venus*, and soon afterwards, 13 October

1872, another shorter poem on the same argument. Upon the latter poem she wrote the following note: "The longer of these two poems was sent me first. Then I wrote one which the second rebuts. At last I wound up by my sonnet *Venus's Looking-glass*". In a copy of her collected *Poems*, 1875, there is also the following note: "Perhaps 'Love-in-Idleness' would be a better title, with an eye to the next one"—i.e. to *Love lies Bleeding*' (WMR in *1904*, 487). As that comment shows, the titles of the two poems are connected not only thematically—this first sonnet concerning worldly love—but by their playing upon the names of wild flowers: Love-in-Idleness and Love-Lies-Bleeding are two names for the wild pansy, *Viola tricolor*; and Venus's Looking-Glass is *Legousia speculum-veneris*. Venus, the Roman goddess of love, is often depicted looking into a mirror; when outdoors, she is often seen in the company of doves (cf. ll. 7–8).

212 LOVE LIES BLEEDING. *Publication.* First published, with 'Venus's Looking-Glass', in the *Argosy*, 15 (January 1873), 31. *Text. 1875.*

l. 7. *afterglow.* The glow in the western sky after sunset.

l. 9. *I mind me.* I remember.

l. 10. *quick.* Living.

A BRIDE SONG. *Publication.* First published in the *Argosy*, 19 (January 1875), 25. *Text. 1875.*

214 l. 41. *The wilderness be as a rose.* Cf. Isaiah 35: 1: 'the desert shall rejoice, and blossom as the rose'.

A ROSE PLANT IN JERICHO. *Publication.* First published in F. G. Lee (ed.), *Lyrics of Light and Life* (London, 1875), 11–12 (*Crump*, 1. 313). *Text. 1875.*

Title. From Ecclesiasticus 24: 14: 'I was exalted like a palm tree in En-gaddi, and as a rose plant in Jericho'. The reference is not to the rose of Jericho (*Anastatica hierochuntica*), which is not a rose.

l. 5. *increase.* Growth.

l. 12. *sweets.* Both 'perfumes' specifically (in this floral context) and 'delights' inclusively. CGR's liking for the word is probably influenced by its use by Herbert (e.g. 'Vertue', l. 10, a poem that CGR thought she had imitated in her 1844 poem 'Charity', in *Crump*, 3. 101; *1904*, 465).

l. 15. *rest upon.* The primary sense is 'rely upon, trust to'.

[DEDICATORY SONNET OF A PAGEANT AND OTHER POEMS (1881)]. *Publication. 1881. Text. 1881.*

l. 7. *dignity.* Honour. The discourse of *service* is that of courtly love poetry.

l. 8. *loadstar.* A star that shows the way.

215 THE KEY-NOTE. *Date.* A torn deleted draft of ll. 1–8 is in the Janet Camp Troxell Collection (C0189), Box 1, Folder 17, Princeton University Library; WMR has pencilled 'c 75' beneath. *Publication.*

1881, where it is placed first in the volume after the contents page (the dedicatory sonnet to CGR's mother precedes the contents page); the verso of the page on which it is printed is blank. The poem introduces the contents of the volume as a poet's late work; and the poem's metaphor of the seasons of a life chimes with the following poem 'The Months: A Pageant'—a work written to be performed by children, and the volume's title poem. The Princeton draft of ll. 1–8 is written beneath the torn draft 'I said "All's over"—& I made my [   ]' (in *Crump*, 3. 336), with which it may have a thematic connection. *Text. 1881.*

Title. The manuscript shows the deleted title 'An Autumn Song' (incomplete bound manuscript of *1881*, Harry Ransom Center, University of Texas, Austin).

l. 1. *Where . . . know*. Cf. Keats, 'To Autumn', ll. 23–4: 'Where are the songs of Spring? Ay, where are they? | Think not of them, thou hast thy music too'.

PASTIME. *Publication. 1881. Text. 1881.*

l. 5. *backing*. Supporting.   *lapping*. Enfolding (cf. 'Dream-Love', l. 4, in *Crump*, 1. 123); with the suggestion of lulling (cf. '"There remaineth therefore a rest for the people of God"', ll. 9–10: 'Come sleep and lap me into perfect calm, | Lap me from all the world and weariness', in *Crump*, 3. 216–17.)

216 'ITALIA, IO TI SALUTO!'. *Date*. CGR returned from her short journey to Italy in June 1865, and WMR dates this poem 'towards July 1865' (*1904*, 379); but that may be no more than an inference from the poem itself, and the poem was not entered in the notebook for this period, BL Ashley MS. 1364 (6). This may be one of CGR's later imaginative returns to that 1865 journey which—with her ill health in the 1870s—she could not expect to repeat (cf. 'Later Life', 21 and 22; *TF*, entries for June 13 and 14). *Publication. 1881. Text. 1881.*

Title. Italian: 'Italy, I salute you!'.

l. 14. *On the old wise*. In the old way.

MIRRORS OF LIFE AND DEATH. *Publication*. Lines 6–135 were first published in the *Athenaeum* (17 March 1877), 350. *Text. 1881.*

l. 3. *Darkly*. Obscurely, dimly.   *glass*. Either a mirror, or a crystal used in magic. Cf. 1 Corinthians 13: 12: 'For now we see through a glass, darkly'. (In l. 1, *mystery* is notably Pauline vocabulary: e.g. 1 Corinthians 2: 7, 'But we speak the wisdom of God in a mystery'.)

ll. 4–5. *Their . . . me*. Life and Death are personified. The primary sense of *shadows*—following on from 'glass', l. 3—is 'reflections' (if the glass is a mirror), or 'insubstantial images' (if the glass is a crystal ball).

l. 6. *As*. Such as. The poem is made up of a series of mirrors in which the title's life–death duality is seen. *As*—which introduces each mirror—is instancing, not likening. It is less likely that the poem is to be taken as a series of epic similes (W. David Shaw, in *Kent*, 40) in which the answering 'so' of the comparison is always absent.

217 l. 16. *Benignantly hot*. DGR queried this, but CGR retained it unchanged: 'Do you know, I like it,—& do not want to be exclusively "dreamily sweet" —, nor fancy that all the rest is so' (*L* 2. 127).

ll. 19–20. *Not . . . Sun*. Sunspots evidence the sun's imperfection.

218 l. 46. *Unwinking*. Alludes to the belief that eagles are able to stare at the sun.

l. 71. *bias*. DGR seems to have been puzzled by this when sent the poem for suggestions for revision before publication in the *Athenaeum*. CGR, writing to him on 10 March 1877, draws his attention to the fact that a mole's fur has 'no right-&-wrong way of the grain (as, for instance a cat's has): it grows like the *biasless* nap of velvet, & as a naturalistic fact this is explained as adapting him to his career of grubbing to & fro'. CGR declined DGR's suggestion to omit the stanzas on the Mouse and the Mole: 'I have however woven in a few fresh "mirrors", & some of these tone down (I hope) any abruptness of the *m. & m.*' (*L* 2. 126).

219 l. 105. *culture*. Cultivation.

220 l. 120. *As . . . deep*. It is proverbial that still waters run deep.

A BALLAD OF BODING. *Published. 1881. Text. 1881*. One literary model for this vision of the destruction of the worldly is Spenser's 'The Visions of Petrarch', six visions of 'this tickle trustles state | Of vaine worlds glorie' (ll. 85–6) (*Marsh*, 445). The conception of three ships—the first two representing worldly love and worldly power, and the third representing renunciation of worldly pleasure for a life of suffering— is probably prompted by the second of Spenser's visions, in which a ship loaded with riches is driven by a storm onto a submerged rock. Coleridge's 'The Rime of the Ancient Mariner' is also a presence (see note to l. 113) (cf. 'Sleep at Sea'). The monster, and its angelic opponent, are figures from apocalyptic; but the poem keeps its independence from any particular passage of biblical apocalyptic.

Title. Boding. Foreboding: a presentiment of what is to happen (especially of evil).

ll. 3–4. *I . . . saw*. Compare Spenser, 'The Visions of Petrarch', ll. 1–3: 'Being one day at my window all alone, | So manie strange things happened me to see, | As much it grieueth me to thinke thereon'.

l. 8. *sackcloth*. Signifies penitence.

l. 9. *two*. A different feast awaits the third crew (see ll. 219–20).

l. 13. *jars*. Discords.

221 l. 18. *onset*. Attack.

l. 21. *Worm*. Serpent. (But 'worm' at l. 180 is a mere worm.)

223 l. 106. *erst*. Former.

l. 113. *a something*. Compare Coleridge, 'The Rime of the Ancient Mariner' (1817), ll. 147–8: 'I beheld | A something in the sky'.

224 l. 138. *beck*. Summoning gesture.

226 YET A LITTLE WHILE. *Publication*. First published in the *University Magazine: A Literary and Philosophic Review* [succeeding the *Dublin University Magazine*], 1 (January 1878), 104. *Text*. *1881*.

Title. Eschatological shorthand, expressing expectation of—and longing for—the end of this world (cf. 'Heaven is not far, though far the sky', in *FD*, 11, entitled 'Yet a Little While' when reprinted in *1893*). Cf. John 16: 16–24.

HE AND SHE. *Publication*. *1881*. *Text*. *1881*.

227 MONNA INNOMINATA. *Published*. *1881*. *Text*. *1881*. CGR's introductory note to this sonnet sequence relates it to the tradition of courtly love poetry, but presents the sequence as a departure from that tradition: in these sonnets, instead of the lady being the object of a male poet's discourse, the lady herself speaks and writes. More precisely, CGR imagines that one of the ladies written by twelfth-century troubadours might have written back. It is likely that CGR's interest in troubadour poetry was excited by the publication of Francis Hueffer's *The Troubadours: A History of Provençal Life and Literature in the Middle Ages* (London, 1878) (*L* 2. 177; Jan Marsh, *Christina Rossetti: A Literary Biography* (London, 1994), 472–3). There, Hueffer explains the modest output of Provençal women poets, in comparison with the production of male poets, as a mark of their not being 'professional or even amateur poets'. For them, 'poetry was not an employment, but an inward necessity. They poured forth their mirth or their grief, and after that relapsed into silence' (Hueffer, *Troubadours*, 282). 'I rather wonder that no one (so far as I know) ever hit on my semi-historical argument before for such treatment,—it seems to me so full of poetic suggestiveness', CGR wrote to DGR in September 1881 (*L* 2. 299). Yet CGR's introductory note does bring into view the immediate literary model for a sonnet sequence in which the lady speaks for herself: Elizabeth Barrett Browning's 'Sonnets from the Portuguese'. Indeed, the explicit medievalism of EBB's third sonnet, in which the speaker is 'A poor, tired, wandering singer' outside of the royal court in which the beloved is 'chief musician', is suggestively contiguous with CGR's imagined historical precedent of a lady troubadour. CGR's reference to EBB's sonnet sequence here has, however, sometimes been taken as a slighting comment, which it is not (see note below). CGR's ambitious appropriation of literary tradition is further indicated by the epigraphs to each sonnet. In taking epigraphs from Dante's *Commedia*, CGR is drawn to passages concerned with poetry (William Whitla in *Kent*, 103): the singing of a hymn by repentant souls (1, 2, and 8); the musician Casella's singing of one of Dante's own early poems (3, 12); the call to Apollo, the god of poetry, for inspiration (4); the poet Statius' expression of his love for Virgil (6); Matilda's suggestion that pagan poets had perhaps seen

something of Eden in their dreams (7); Dante's praise of the scrupulous Virgil (9). This explicit concern with poetry is less evident in the epigraphs taken from Petrarch's *Canzoniere*. The sequence is ambitious also in its form: as 'A Sonnet of Sonnets', the whole sequence of fourteen sonnets has a structure analogous to that of a Petrarchan sonnet, with the sequence's *volta* in sonnet 9 (Whitla, in *Kent*, 117). For WMR, 'It is indisputable that the real veritable speaker in those sonnets is Christina herself, giving expression to her love for Charles Cayley' (*FL*, 97); 'The introductory prose-note . . . [is] a blind interposed to draw off attention from the writer in her proper person' (*1904*, 462). But, while it would be perverse to deny that CGR's relation with Cayley could have informed the work, that relation is not to be taken as the interpretative key to the work. Dramatizing the speaker as a *donna innominata* 'not merely hides the personal reference'—if there is personal reference—'but allows [CGR] to wander at will from the terms of that reference' (Georgina Battiscombe, *Christina Rossetti: A Divided Life* (London, 1981), 132).

Title. Italian: 'unnamed lady'.

227 *Introductory Note. Beatrice*. Dante's *La Vita Nuova* is an account of his love for the earthly Beatrice; his *Commedia* tells of 'how the lost love of earth is found again as one higher, lovelier, and better loved in paradise; and how even this sainted and exalting passion pales at last, and is, as it were, no more accounted of before the supreme revelation of the love of God' (CGR, 'Dante, An English Classic' (1867), in *SP*, 170–1).

'*altissimo poeta*'. 'The highest poet' (as Virgil is addressed in Dante, *Inferno*, 4. 80). *'cotanto amante'*. 'So great a lover': Francesca describes Lancelot thus in *Inferno*, 5. 134. That CGR applies to Dante a phrase associated with erotic (and adulterous) love may indicate ambivalence in her valuation of Dante here (cf. note to the Dante epigraph of sonnet 5, below).

Laura. Petrarch's *Canzoniere* anatomizes his love for Laura. (It should be noted that the extraordinary belief that CGR claimed documentary proof of her own descent from Laura (e.g. in *Arseneau et al.*, 43 n. 36; 99 n. 37) is wholly without foundation; perhaps originating in Marsh, *Rossetti: Biography*, 211–12, or *Marsh*, p. xxiii, misreading a passage in CGR's short biographical essay on Petrarch (*SP*, 167).)

that land and that period. The southern part of France, that of the *langue d'oc*, in the twelfth century.

Albigenses. The term, derived from the town of Albi, designates a dualist twelfth-century heresy of the Languedoc and of northern Italy. 'But it must be remembered that Albigenses . . . is a collective name used by the Catholics almost synonymously with heretics, and without regard to the most important doctrinal and moral variations' (Hueffer, *Troubadours*, 230).

Troubadours. Provençal poets (from Provençal *trobar*, 'to find, to compose poetry'), in whose work the courtly love tradition originates in the twelfth century.

the barrier between them. The lady is usually married to another man. 'But it is nevertheless an undoubted fact . . . that the homage offered by the troubadour and accepted by the lady did not necessarily imply guilty weakness on the part of the latter' (Hueffer, *Troubadours*, 61).

unhappy instead of happy. That is, Elizabeth Barrett Browning's circumstances were not those of a *donna innominata*: she was not divided from her beloved (cf. sonnet 9. 4: 'the happier call', which is most likely that of married life). But, had her circumstances been different—had there been a 'barrier'—she might perhaps have been led to write a sonnet sequence in which such a *donna innominata* would speak for herself. That work—unlike, it is implied, the sonnets which CGR is introducing—would have been the equal of the work of Dante or Petrarch. CGR subsequently found that this sentence could be misunderstood as expressing reservations about EBB's sonnet sequence. T. Hall Caine's review of 1881, in the *Academy*, 20 (27 August 1881), 152, understood her to be suggesting that, in different circumstances, EBB would have produced a more valuable work than the 'Sonnets from the Portuguese'. CGR wrote to DGR in September 1881: 'Surely not only what I meant to say but what I do say is, not that the Lady of those [Portuguese] Sonnets is surpassable, but that a "Donna innominata" by the same hand might well have been unsurpassable. The Lady in question, as she actually stands, I was not regarding as an "innominata" at all,—because the latter type, according to the traditional figures I had in view, is surrounded by unlike circumstances' (*L* 2. 299). For WMR, 'What she says in her letter—that the speaker in her sonnets was not intended for an "innominata at all"—is curious' (*FL*, 97); but WMR, here, misunderstands CGR, who is referring not to her own sonnet sequence but to EBB's.

drawn not from fancy. In contradistinction, it is implied, to 'Monna Innominata'.

1. *Epigraphs.* 'The day that they have said adieu to their sweet friends' (*Purgatorio*, 8. 3). (Translations of epigraphs are those of WMR; editorial emendations are within brackets.) This, and the Dante epigraphs to sonnets 2 and 8, are from a passage in which souls in Purgatory sing the evening hymn *Te lucis ante terminum*. There, evening is the time of day in which travellers think of the friends they have left behind. 'Love, with how great a stress dost thou vanquish me to-day!' (*Canzoniere*, 85. 12).

228 2. *Epigraphs.* 'It was already the hour which turns back the desire' (*Purgatorio*, 8. 1). 'I recur to the time when I first saw thee' (*Canzoniere*, 20. 3).

l. 1. *I wish I could remember.* Pointedly unlike the indelible impression made, at first sight, by Beatrice on Dante, and by Laura on Petrarch.

228 3. *Epigraphs.* 'Oh shades, empty save in semblance!' (*Purgatorio*, 2. 79). From a passage in which Dante tries to embrace one of the souls that arrive in Purgatory—the singer Casella, an old friend—only to realize the impossibility of embracing the insubstantial.   'An imaginary guide conducts [it]' (i.e. his life) (*Canzoniere*, 277. 9). Petrarch feels himself to be on an uncertain path without a trustworthy leader; and yet the dead Laura, in heaven, will now be his guide.

229 l. 14. *there be nothing new beneath the sun.* Cf. Ecclesiastes 1: 9.

4. *Epigraphs.* 'A small spark fosters a great flame' (*Paradiso*, 1. 34). From Dante's invocation to Apollo, asking for the inspiration to accomplish the *Paradiso*.   'Every other thing, every thought, goes off, and love alone remains there with you' (when he sees her eyes) (*Canzoniere*, 72. 44–5).

5. *Epigraphs.* 'Love, who exempts no loved one from loving' (*Inferno*, 5. 103). The words are Francesca da Rimini's, referring to her response to Paolo's love for her. In that their intimacy was unlawful—which is why they are in Hell—it might, at first, be thought odd of CGR to associate the relationship in her sonnets with their story: Francesca's insistence on the power of the god Amor is tantamount to a denial that the lovers had the freedom to resist the temptation. Yet it is probably significant that this is a sonnet which provokes a rebuke which is then countered in sonnet 6 (see note to 6. 1). Moreover, it was not unusual for nineteenth-century readers of Dante to take a less judgemental view of the lovers than may seem to us warranted by what Dante wrote. Cf. Maria Francesca Rossetti's account of how Francesca came to be coupled with Paolo 'in the soul's death no less than in the body's': 'It is said that, deceived by her father, she had given hand and heart to this handsome accomplished youth, and all too late had found that he was but proxy for her real husband, his deformed and repulsive brother Gianciotto. As now, in a lull of the tempest, she told how the sin of an unguarded moment had been avenged by Gianciotto's hand, her words and her lover's tears affected Dante to fainting', *A Shadow of Dante: Being an Essay Towards Studying Himself, His World and His Pilgrimage* (1871), 68.   'Love led me into such joyous hope' (in order to make his life more sorrowful) (*Canzoniere*, 56. 11).

230 l. 3. *leal.* Loyal.

l. 4. *whose noble service setteth free.* Cf. *BCP*, Order for Morning Prayer, Collect for Peace: 'whose service is perfect freedom' (Whitla, in *Kent*, 121).

l. 14. *helpmeet.* Cf. Genesis 2: 18.

6. *Epigraphs.* 'Now canst thou comprehend the quantity of the love which glows in me towards thee' (*Purgatorio*, 21. 133–4). The words are those of the poet Statius when told that Dante's guide is none other than 'that Virgil from whom you took power to sing of men and of gods' (125–6): such love has Statius for Virgil that he tries to embrace Virgil's

feet, forgetting that they are both insubstantial (the epigraph thus connects with the Dante epigraph to sonnet 3).   'I do not choose that Love should release me from such a tie' (i.e. that with which Love has bound him) (*Canzoniere*, 59. 17).

ll. 1–2. *your . . . most*. The beloved's *rebuke* would seem to have been provoked by the sestet of sonnet 5, taken to imply that her love for him would exclude her love for God.

l. 4. *Lot's wife*. Although warned by angels not to, Lot's wife looked back at the destroyed cities of Sodom and Gomorrah, and was turned into a pillar of salt (Genesis 19: 26).

231 7. *Epigraphs*. 'Here always Spring and every fruit' (*Purgatorio*, 28. 143): the Earthly Paradise. The words are Matilda's, speculating that the poets of old who wrote of the Golden Age had perhaps dreamt of Eden—a speculation that pleases Virgil and Statius.   'Conversing with me, and I with him' (*Canzoniere*, 35. 14). Petrarch escapes the company of men, seeking out deserted places where no one will see how he burns with love; and yet nowhere is so wild that he can escape Love, who comes talking with him.

l. 11. *for your art*. Probably 'for your skill [in solving such problems]' rather than (as Whitla, in *Kent*, 124) 'for [your] poetry' (cf. 'Later Life', 16, ll. 3–4).

l. 12. *his Book*. That is, Solomon's (ll. 13–14 are from the Song of Solomon 8: 6).

8. *Epigraphs*. 'As if he were to say to God, "I care for nought else"' (*Purgatorio*, 8. 12).   'I hope to find pity, and not only pardon' (*Canzoniere*, 1. 8). From Petrarch's introductory sonnet which addresses the reader who—in the 'scattered rhymes' which follow—will hear of the poet's troubles 'when I was, in part, another man from that which I am now'. If it should be that the reader knows through experience what love is, the poet hopes to find pity.

l. 1. *'I . . . perish'*. See Esther 4: 16, deciding to plead before her husband, an action that 'is not according to the law'. Esther's dressing in her royal apparel (5: 1–2) is alluded to in ll. 5–6.

l. 8. *Harmless . . . snake*. Cf. Matthew 10: 16.

9. *Epigraphs*. 'O dignified and pure conscience!' (*Purgatorio*, 3. 8): the words refer to Virgil, who has reproached himself for having been distracted from the journey when he and Dante were capivated by Casella's singing of one of Dante's early songs of love in *Purgatorio*, 2 (see epigraphs to 3 and 12).   'Spirit more lit with burning virtues' (*Canzoniere*, 283. 3): the spirit of Laura, who has been taken by Death.

232 l. 8. *turning to the wall*. Resigning herself to her coming death (a common phrase probably derived from 2 Kings 20: 2).

ll. 10–11. *toil . . . morning*. Cf. Luke 5: 5 (Whitla, in *Kent*, 126 n. 44).

232 ll. 11–12. *wrestle . . . day*. Alludes to Jacob's wrestling with the angel, Genesis 32: 24.

l. 14. *to spend and be spent for your sake*. Cf. 2 Corinthians 12: 15.

10. *Epigraphs*. 'With better course and with better star' (*Paradiso*, 1. 40): the reference is to the propitious time of the spring equinox.   'Life flees, and stays not an hour' (*Canzoniere*, 272. 1); 'and Death comes after, in great advances', and Petrarch is caught between what has been and what will be. In this instance, the Petrarch epigraph is in marked contrast with the Dante epigraph: Petrarch feels as if he is to sail into a storm, with no stars to guide him.

233 11. *Epigraphs*. 'Come after me, and leave folk to talk' (*Purgatorio*, 5. 13): Virgil's words to Dante, prompting him when he is momentarily distracted from his pilgrimage.   'Relating the [events] of our life' (*Canzoniere*, 285. 12): Laura, in heaven, directs Petrarch in his worldly journey.

12. *Epigraphs*. 'Love, who speaks within my mind' (*Purgatorio*, 2. 112): the first line of the poem of Dante's which is sung by Casella.   'Love comes in the beautiful face of this lady' (*Canzoniere*, 13. 2) when, sometimes, Petrarch sees Laura in the company of other ladies.

234 13. *Epigraphs*. 'And we will direct our eyes to the Primal Love' (*Paradiso*, 32. 142): words spoken by St Bernard to Dante. So, in CGR's sonnet, the speaker directs her beloved towards God's wholly fulfilling love.   'But I find a burden to which my arms suffice not' (*Canzoniere*, 20. 5). This, and the Petrarch epigraph to sonnet 2, are from a sonnet in which Petrarch tries to write about Laura's beauty, but finds himself inadequate to the task

l. 4. *Nor sparrow fall*. Cf. Matthew 10: 29.

l. 6. *Who . . . weight*. Cf. Job 28: 25.

14. *Epigraphs*. 'And His will is our peace' (*Paradiso*, 3. 85): words spoken by Piccarda, content with the position in Heaven given her by God, wanting no higher.   'Only with these thoughts, with different locks' (i.e. with his hair changed by time) (*Canzoniere*, 30. 32).

235 'LUSCIOUS AND SORROWFUL'. *Publication. 1881. Text. 1881.*

Title. 'These words, "Luscious and sorrowful", are borrowed from a little lyric by [C. B.] Cayley named *Noli me tangere*, which was published in the *Nation* (1866). In that lyric the epithets are applied to the song of the nightingale' (WMR in *1904*, 488). In 1866, CGR had declined a proposal of marriage from Cayley, but their friendship continued until his death in 1883 (*1904*, p. liii). It does not necessarily follow from this that the poem relates to Cayley.

l. 6. *sea*. Cf. Revelation 21: 1: 'And I saw a new heaven and a new earth: for the first heaven and the first earth were passed away; and there was no more sea'.

'HOLLOW-SOUNDING AND MYSTERIOUS'. *Publication. 1881. Text. 1881.*

Title. From Felicia Hemans, 'The Treasures of the Deep', ll. 1–2: 'What hidest thou in thy treasure caves and cells, | Thou hollow-sounding and mysterious main?'.

236 TOUCHING 'NEVER'. *Publication. 1881. Text. 1881.*

A LIFE'S PARALLELS. *Publication. 1881. Text. 1881.*

l. 3. *garner.* Granary.

237 l. 11. *Faint yet pursuing.* From Judges 8: 4: 'And Gideon came to Jordan, and passed over, he, and the three hundred men that were with him, faint, yet pursuing them'. Crossing the Jordan prefigures the crossing of the river of Death (cf. l. 2, and *PP*, 197–200), the entry into the promised land prefiguring the entry of the saints into heaven.

GOLDEN SILENCES. *Publication. 1881. Text. 1881.*

Title. That silence is golden becomes proverbial in the mid-nineteenth century. For the proverb's first recorded occurrence in English, see Book III, chapter 3 ('Symbols') of Thomas Carlyle, *Sartor Resartus* (1833–4), ed. Kerry McSweeney and Peter Sabor (Oxford, 1987), 165–6: 'As the Swiss Inscription says: *Sprechen ist silbern, Schweigen ist golden* (Speech is silvern, Silence is golden); or as I might rather express it: Speech is of Time, Silence is of Eternity'. CGR is likely to have known the chapter; there is evidence of her knowledge of *Sartor Resartus* (see *1904*, 494).

IN THE WILLOW SHADE. *Publication. 1881. Text. 1881.*

l. 7. *heliotrope.* A plant which turns its flowers towards the sun.

238 l. 18. *amain.* With all his strength.

239 l. 59. *The west . . . red.* Eschatological meteorology: cf. 'Pastime'.

l. 63. *The world . . . grieves.* Informed by Romans 8: 22. With ll. 57–64, cf. 'An Old-World Thicket', ll. 61–76, in which the birds stop singing, the wind sighs, the waters seem to weep, and all creation moans.

'ONE FOOT ON SEA, AND ONE ON SHORE'. *Publication. 1881. Text. 1881.*

Title. From *Much Ado About Nothing*, 2. 3. 57–60: 'Sigh no more, ladies, sigh no more, | Men were deceivers ever, | One foot in sea and one on shore, | To one thing constant never'.

240 AN OCTOBER GARDEN. *Publication.* First published in the *Athenaeum* (27 October 1877), 532. *Text. 1881.*

l. 1. *fain.* Inclined.

l. 6. *constraint.* Force (contrasted with the present season's declining power, ll. 4–5). The topic of roses perhaps summons up *All's Well that Ends Well*, 4. 2. 16, 18–20: 'love's own sweet constraint', which leads men to pick women's roses.

241 'SUMMER IS ENDED'. *Publication. 1881. Text. 1881.*

Title. From Jeremiah 8: 20: 'The harvest is past, the summer is ended, and we are not saved'.

241 PASSING AND GLASSING. *Publication. 1881. Text. 1881.*

Title. Either woman is *glassing* (viewing her reflection); or, more likely, the passing things are *glassing* (reflecting) (see *OED*, glass *v*. 4a and 4b).

l. 10. *tiring-glass.* Dressing glass.

ll. 11–16. *The faded . . . Alas!.* With the comfort in these lines, cf. Herbert, 'Life', ll. 13–18.

242 THE THREAD OF LIFE. *Publication. 1881. Text. 1881.*

Title. In classical mythology, one of the Fates spins the thread of life, another cuts it at death (cf. 'The Prince's Progress', l. 236). But CGR has an extended Christian conception of the thread of life (see note to 2, ll. 13–14).

243 2. ll. 13–14. *I am . . . even I.* See also *FD*, 47 (Lona Mosk Packer, *Christina Rossetti* (Berkeley and Los Angeles, 1963), 323): 'Concerning Himself God Almighty proclaimed of old: "I AM THAT I AM", and man's inherent feeling of personality seems in some sort to attest and correspond to this revelation: I who am myself cannot but be myself. I am what God has constituted me: so that however I may have modified myself, yet do I remain that same I; it is I who live, it is I who must die, it is I who must rise again at the last day. I rising again out of my grave must carry on that very life which was mine before I died, and of which death itself could not altogether snap the thread. Who I was I am, who I am I am, who I am I must be for ever and ever. | I the sinner of to-day am the sinner of all the yesterdays of my life. I may loathe myself or be amazed at myself, but I cannot unself myself for ever and ever'.

3. l. 6. *crudeness.* Unripeness.   *sanative.* Healing.

l. 7. *sieve.* Continues the harvest imagery of *winnowing* (l. 4) and *ripeness* (l. 6). This biblical imagery is eschatological, and is completed (if only implicitly) in the resurrection of l. 8. It is clear from l. 12 (see note below) that the immediate source of this imagery is Revelation 14: the first-fruits of 14: 4, then the harvest of 14: 14–16.

l. 9. *as king unto my King.* The conception of the individual as king under the King is derived from Revelation 1: 6 (cf. *TF*, entry for Thursday in Holy Week, ll. 9, 18 (p. 359, above)).

l. 12. *new song.* From Revelation 14: 3.

ll. 13–14. *He . . . victory?.* Cf. 1 Corinthians 15: 55.

AN OLD-WORLD THICKET. *Publication. 1881. Text. 1881.*

Title. In the poem's theological scheme, the sun's descent (see note to ll. 148–50) gives significance to the state of the wood under 'the unseen sun' (l. 27): this, the epigraph's *selva oscura*, is the world under the old dispensation, before the Incarnation. Yet the poem is not only to be read thus—horizontally, as a plan of history—but vertically: true content is to be found not within, but beyond, the wood of the world.

Epigraph. From Dante, *Inferno*, I 2: 'a dark wood'.

l. 2. *mazed*. Both 'stupefied', and also 'bewildered' as if lost in a maze (cf. 'The Dead City', l. 32: 'the mazes of that wood'). Cf. Dante's wood, in which *la diritta via era smarrita*, 'the straight way was lost', *Inferno*, I. 3.

ll. 5–10. *Of . . . be*. The model is the catalogue of the trees of the Wandering Wood in *FQ* I. I. 8–9. There, 'the Maple seeldom inward sound' intimates that the delightful wood as a whole is not what it might seem; here, the *elm that dies in secret from the core* (l. 8) is an ominous intimation that there may be death within this wood (cf. l. 40). The ivy (l. 9) is *weak* because it needs support; but, in this context, the word may take on moral overtones which then infect *free* with the taint of wantonness. No less Spenserian are the vocabulary of seeming in ll. 11–15—which intimates that the contentment offered by this wood may be insubstantial (cf. the Wandering Wood: 'Faire harbour that them seemes', as the Red Cross Knight and Una enter the Wood, *FQ* I. I. 7)—and the 'unseen sun' of l. 27 (cf. the Wandering Wood's trees that 'Did spred so broad, that heauens light did hide', *FQ* I. I. 7).

245 l. 55. *jubilee*. Jubilation.

l. 72. *fain*. Willing.

ll. 74–5. *all . . . fear*. Cf. Romans 8: 22: 'For we know that the whole creation groaneth and travaileth in pain together until now'.

246 ll. 86–7. *deep . . . desire*. Cf. Psalms 42: 7; 130: 1–2.

247 ll. 148–50. *The sun . . . low*. Symbolic of the divine condescension of the Incarnation—of God stooping to the world (cf. *TF*, Thursday in Holy Week, l. 10 (p. 359, above)). There is a play upon *sun*/'Son' (cf. Herbert, 'The Sonne'); and *dying* points to Christ's sacrifice.

248 l. 169. *flock*. Symbolizing the Church.

LATER LIFE: A DOUBLE SONNET OF SONNETS. *Publication. 1881. Text. 1881.*

1. ll. 1–2. *Before . . . God*. Cf. Psalm 90: 2.

249 l. 9. *For . . . Him*. Cf. Job 13: 15.

2. l. 1. *Rend . . . garments*. Cf. Joel 2: 13.

3. l. 5. *unstayed*. Unsupported.

250 4. *Title*. The title 'Today' is deleted in the manuscript, Huntington Library, San Marino, California, HM 6076. Beneath the sonnet is pencilled 'I would tell you more, but I am tired—', a quotation from the first line of Jean Ingelow's 'Songs of the Night Watches: The First Watch: Tired', in *Poems* (London, 1880).

ll. 13–14. *Me . . . me*. Cf. Luke 23: 42–3.

251 6. l. 8. *pack*. An area of floating ice.

252 9. *Title*. The title '"One Star differeth from another Star"' (from I Corinthians 15: 41) is deleted in the manuscript. Above the deleted

title is pencilled '—the stars in Night's pale fillet wrought gleam undividably—'.

252 10. ll. 9–10. *O earth . . . slain*. Cf. Isaiah' 26: 21, read in relation to 26: 19 (a verse understood to refer to the resurrection of the dead).

l. 13. *As . . . windows*. Cf. Isaiah 60: 8.

'*Quali . . . portate*'. 'As doves, called by desire, fly with open steady wings to their sweet nest, carried through the air by their will' (*Inferno*, 5. 82–4, where Francesco and Paolo come thus in answer to Dante's call).

253 13. l. 4. *bruit*. Sound, report.

254 15. l. 1. *Let . . . learn*. Cf. 1 Timothy 2: 11–12.

l. 8. *train*. A line of gunpowder laid to transmit fire to explosives (*OED*, 13).

255 17. *Title*. The title 'Befogged' is deleted in the manuscript. Illegible words are pencilled beneath the sonnet.

l. 4. *one certain beach*. 'I consider that the beach of Hastings and St. Leonard's is here intended' (WMR in *1904*, 463).

18. *Title*. The title 'Late Autumn' has been revised to 'A Heart's Autumn', then deleted, in the manuscript.

l. 7. *bale*. Destruction.

256 l. 12. *gat them hence*. Went from here.

19. *Title*. The title 'Zero' is deleted in the manuscript.

20. l. 2. *solitary bird*. The nightingale.

257 21. ll. 6–7. *each star | Sang*. For singing stars, see Job 38: 7.

22. l. 11. *forget-me-not*. Cf. *TF*, June 14.

258 24. *Title*. The title 'Doubleminded' is deleted in the manuscript.

259 26. *Title*. The title 'Veiled Death' is deleted, and 'Resurgam' pencilled above, in the manuscript.

l. 1. *balk*. Obstruction; disappointment.

27. *Title*. The title 'Memento Mori' is deleted in the manuscript. Above the deleted title is written '"My flesh & my heart faileth"'.

260 'BEHOLD THE MAN!'. *Publication. 1881. Text. 1881.*

Title. Pilate's words when delivering Christ to 'the Jews' to be crucified (John 19: 5).

l. 5. *forsook*. Cf. Matthew 27: 46.

l. 13. *Not . . . came*. Cf. Matthew 10: 34.

l. 14. *night-watches*. Watching for the coming of Christ (cf. e.g. Matthew 24: 42–4).

RESURGAM. *Publication*. First published in the *Athenaeum* (28 January 1882), 124. *Text*. 1890.

Title. 'I will rise again' (Latin). From Matthew 27: 63: 'After three days I will rise again'.

l. 8. *panoply*. A complete armour.

261 l. 13. *wots*. Knows.

A VALENTINE. *Date*. 1882. One of the Valentines written by CGR for her mother each year from 1876 to 1886. 'These *Valentines* had their origin from my dearest Mother's remarking that she had never received one. I, her CGR, ever after supplied one on the day = & so far as I recollect it was a *surprise* every time, she having forgotten all about it in the interim' (BL Ashley MS. 1376). The fair copy was folded, and addressed to 'The Queen of Hearts'. *Text*. BL Ashley MS. 1376.

l. 4. *dove*. The colour, dove-grey, prepares the mythological transition in l. 5: doves are asssociated with the goddess Venus (cf. 'Venus's Looking-Glass', ll. 7–8).

l. 5. *A better sort of Venus*. Venus is the Roman goddess of love (identified with the Greek goddess Aphrodite); she is, especially, the goddess of sexual love. *A better sort* is more than a gently prim glance at the kind of love commonly represented by Venus. It alludes to a distinction made in Plato's *Symposium* (180d) between two kinds of Love: 'If then there were only one Venus, there would have been only one Love. But since there are two, there must be likewise two Loves. And how are there not two, one the elder, and who had no mother, a daughter of Uranus, (Heaven,) whom we name the celestial; the other, younger, a daughter of Jupiter and Dione, whom we call the vulgar. It is necessary then for the Love who works with the latter Venus to be called the vulgar, but the other, the celestial', *The Works of Plato*, tr. Henry Cary, 6 vols. (London, 1848), 3. 491. Vulgar Love is the love of women not less than of boys, and of bodies rather than of minds; celestial Love is that 'not partaking of the female, but only of the male', and of the mind rather than of the body (392–3). CGR read Plato 'over and over again, with ever renewed or augmented zest' (WMR in *1904*, p. lxx). Some of Plato's dialogues—of which we would expect this to be one—discussed difficult subjects: sending Alice Boyd, in 1866, a volume from her six-volume translated edition of Plato, CGR advises 'lest you should take to reading aloud let me warn you not to experiment on the *Phaedrus*; this, if readable at all throughout, is certainly only readable to oneself' (*L* 1. 277–8). That translation was almost certainly Cary's, in Bohn's six-volume set.

l. 7. *Pallas*. Athene, the goddess of wisdom.

BIRCHINGTON CHURCHYARD. *Publication*. First published in the *Athenaeum* (29 April 1882), 538. *Text*. 1890.

Title. DGR was buried at Birchington-on-Sea in April 1882.

262 'A HELPMEET FOR HIM'. *Publication*. First published in *'New and Old': For Seed-Time and Harvest*, 16 (January 1888), 22 (*Crump*, 3. 531). *Text*. *1890*. The form is that of the roundel, as developed by Swinburne in

A Century of Roundels (1883): eleven lines, in three stanzas, on two rhymes, and with the opening word or phrase being used as a refrain in ll. 4 and 11.

262 *Title.* From Genesis 2: 18.

l. 3. *his moon by night.* Cf. *SF* (p. 318, above).

l. 7. *stays.* Supports, sustains.

l. 10. *ruddy and white.* Cf. Song of Solomon 5: 10: 'My beloved is white and ruddy, the chiefest among ten thousand', a text taken by CGR to refer to Christ (see e.g. '"The Chiefest among ten thousand"', in *Crump*, 2. 211). What might, initially, seem to refer only to woman's delighting beauty (cf. l. 1), becomes, when put beside this biblical text, nothing less than a quiet insistence on woman's capacity to imitate Christ.

AN ECHO FROM WILLOWWOOD. *Date.* There seems to be no evidence for WMR's conjecture of *c.*1870, which was based solely on the association of the sonnet with DGR's Willowwood sonnets (*1904*, 487); and that the sonnet was not included in *1875* or *1881*, but was not left unpublished, weighs against that conjecture. *Publication.* Published in *Magazine of Art*, 13 (September 1890), 385, inset in a two-part illustration by Charles Ricketts (reproduced in *Kooistra*, 53) with which CGR was pleased (*L* 4. 212). *Text. Magazine of Art.*

Title. The title alludes to DGR's four Willowwood sonnets which would become sonnets 49–52 of the series 'The House of Life'. In the first sonnet, the lover sits beside a personification of Love, both looking into the water of 'a woodside well'; Love's reflection in the water then becomes that of the lost beloved. 'The sonnet describes a dream or trance of divided love momentarily re-united by the longing fancy' (DGR, 'The Stealthy School of Criticism', *DGRW* 1. 483). CGR's sonnet is thus set back in time from DGR's group, at the point of the division of the lovers. CGR's epigraph is taken from the third sonnet, in which Love sings of those who walk in Willowwood in a state of 'soul-struck widowhood'.

l. 12. *A sudden ripple.* In l. 12 of DGR's first Willowwood sonnet, the 'dark ripples' made in the water by the lover's falling tears, and by Love disturbing the water, produce an image of the beloved, thereby enabling a momentary union.

('THY FAINTING SPOUSE, YET STILL THY SPOUSE'). *Publication.* FD, 248. *Text. 1893.*

ll. 1–2. *Thy fainting spouse . . . Thy dove.* In *FD*, the poem is preceded by prayer to Christ, 'Who hast called the Church Thy sister, love, dove, spouse', 248.

263 'SON, REMEMBER'. *Publication.* First published in *'New and Old': For Seed-Time and Harvest*, 17 (October 1889), 274 (Crump, *Christina Rossetti: The Complete Poems* (Harmondsworth, 2001), 1062); then FD, 480. *Text. 1893.*

Title. From the story of the rich man (Dives) and the beggar Lazarus in Luke 16: 19–31. The beggar, at the rich man's gate, desires the crumbs from the rich man's table (which is not quite to say that he receives them: cf. 'crumbs-solicitous', l. 4). Dives dies and is tormented in the flames of hell, from where he sees the beggar who had once been at his gate now in the company of Abraham. He asks Abraham to be merciful, and to send Lazarus with water to cool his tongue. Abraham replies: 'Son, remember that thou in thy lifetime receivedst thy good things, and likewise Lazarus evil things: but now he is comforted, and thou art tormented'. The sonnet had, in its 1889 periodical publication, the title 'Lazarus Loquitur'; and having Lazarus himself speak—his anticipation, in the sestet, of his and the rich man's state after death being (as we know from the Lukan source) entirely accurate—is CGR's innovative use of the biblical material.

('SLEEPING AT LAST, THE TROUBLE & TUMULT OVER'). *Date.* WMR noted on the back of the manuscript: '13/2/95—I found these verses at Christina's house, in a millboard-case containing some recent memoranda &c—nothing of old date—The verses must I think be the last that C. ever wrote—perhaps late in 1893, or early in 94' (BL Add. MS. 34813). Or, at least, among the last (WMR, in *1904*, 477; Diane D'Amico, 'Christina Rossetti's Last Poem: "Sleeping at Last" or "Heaven Overarches"?', *Victorian Newsletter*, 103 (Spring 2003), 10–16). It should not be supposed, from this information, that the poem must have particular proleptic reference to CGR's own death. *Text.* BL Add. MS. 34813.

STORIES

265 MAUDE. *Date.* The work 'was written out . . . in 1850. I suppose it may have been composed in that year, or a year or two earlier . . . [The poems] were all written without any intention of inserting them in any tale—except only the first two in the trio bouts-rimés sonnets. The MS. of the tale presents a few slight revisions, made at some much later date—perhaps about 1870, or 1875' (WMR (ed.), *Maude: Prose & Verse* (Chicago, 1897), 1–2). The preparation of *Commonplace, and Other Short Stories* (1870) might have been the occasion of such revision, but no version of the story was ever published by CGR. *Text.* Huntington Library, San Marino, California, HM 6065. The tale is thoroughly Tractarian in its concern with worthiness to receive Communion. This is no trivial matter: the Exhortations in the Communion liturgy in *BCP* warn that those who receive the sacrament unworthily receive their own damnation. In promoting frequent reception, the Tractarian movement therefore emphasized correct preparation for receiving the sacrament, and emphasized that the sacrament was itself an aid in the pursuit of worthiness (thus Agnes's warning to Maude that her decision to defer Communion would only deprive her of 'the appointed means of grace'). The tale presents Maude's preoccupation with her own vanity as, itself,

a manifestation of that vanity; but this does not mean that the matter of worthiness to receive is dismissed (Agnes herself once considered deferring Communion). That the tale turns on such technical theological matters has led to it being widely misunderstood. A generic analogue is another Tractarian tale of doubt over worthiness to communicate, Charlotte Yonge's *The Castle-Builders; or, The Deferred Confirmation* (1854) (*SP*, 374 n. 5). The tale also attests the appeal of Anglican sisterhoods, the first of which had been established in CGR's parish of Christ Church, Albany Street.

265 *the following sonnet.* A revision of 'the following careless sonnet'.

267 *round games.* Games (especially card games) in which each plays individually, rather than with a partner.

269 *in quiet colours.* A revision of 'in quiet nun-like colours'.

Proverbs . . . Magic music. Guessing games (see further R. W. Crump (ed.), *Maude: Prose and Verse* (Hamden, Conn., 1976), 85).

Bouts rimés. i.e. a sonnet written to given end-rhymes as a test of ingenuity. 'Our brother Dante Gabriel and myself were, towards 1848, greatly addicted to writing sonnets together to *bouts-rimés* . . . Christina did not do much in the like way; but, being in my company at Brighton in the summer of 1848, she consented to try her chance . . . After the Brighton days she renewed this exercise hardly at all' (WMR in *1904*, 490). But see also the September 1849 sonnet ('So I grew half delirious and quite sick').

270 *This proposal . . . by Agnes.* In the manuscript this has been cancelled (by, it seems, WMR). On the opposite page is noted (by WMR) 'This remains uncancelled'. Three subsequent paragraphs of prose (*Indeed . . . metre*; *There's gratitude . . . sonnet*; *Well, Agnes . . . listen*) have been similarly cancelled, then noted 'not cancelled'.

['I fancy the good fairies dressed in white']. *hack.* Drudge; hired worker (the comparison being to a horse that is let out for hire—the 'miserable hack' of Agnes's sonnet). In the third sonnet, Maude's, a 'hack' is a carriage for hire.

271 ['Some ladies dress in muslin full and white']. *Date.* Summer 1848 (*1904*, 490). WMR has pencilled in the manuscript 'Vanity Fair', the title under which he published the sonnet. This, almost certainly, had been the sonnet's early title. DGR reports, in a letter to WMR of 24 September 1849: 'Mrs. Patmore was greatly pleased with Christina's poems. I do not think the Coventry himself read much of them, but he was delighted with the Sonnet "Vanity Fair"' (*DGRL (F)* 1. 98-9).

l. 3. *dog-cart.* A two-wheeled open cart.

l. 4. *clarence.* A four-wheeled closed carriage.

273 ['She sat and sang alway']. *Date.* 26 November 1848 (Bodleian MS. Don. e. 1/5). *Published.* 1862.

l. 1. *alway.* All the time.

l. 8. *leaves*. Petals (of the hawthorn).

275 *offered me a district*. i.e. a part of the parish in which to do good works.

to vocal perfection. St Andrew's, in Wells Street, consecrated in 1847, was noted for its choral services. In the manuscript, a further deleted sentence follows: 'The language is so against us, so full of cramped vowels and consonants'.

276 ['Sweet sweet sound of distant waters falling']. *Date*. 12 March 1849. In the notebook Bodleian MS. Don. e. 1/5 it has the title 'For Advent'.

ll. 1–2. *Sweet . . . plain*. A distant allusion to the Advent liturgical text *Rorate coeli*, taken from Isaiah 45: 8: 'Drop down, ye heavens, from above, and let the skies pour down righteousness: let the earth open, and let them bring forth salvation'.

277 l. 39. *Let us see our lamps are lighted*. The reference is to the parable of the virgins in Matthew 25: 1–13, a lesson on the importance of being prepared for Christ's second coming (cf. 'Advent').

279 *meditating*. Composing. The use is derived from Virgil, *Eclogue*, 1. 2, by way of Milton, 'Lycidas', l. 66: the inflated diction is immediately punctured by Maude.

280 ['Vanity of vanities, the Preacher saith']. *Date*. 2 June 1849. In the notebook Bodleian MS. Don. e. 1/6 it has the title 'The one Certainty'; there, the title and the first word are in CGR's hand, and the remainder in that of Frances Mary Lavinia Rossetti—an indication, to WMR, of composition during a period of illness (*1904*, 467). Published as 'The One Certainty' in *1862 (D)*.

l. 1. *the Preacher*. See Ecclesiastes 1: 1–2.

281 ['I listen to the holy antheming']. *Date*. 1 June 1848 (entered in the notebook Bodleian MS. Don. e. 1/4 as 'St. Andrew's Church').

282 *proving*. Putting to the test.

We must all die: . . . no more? In the third part of the tale, CGR will contrive a certain theological suspense through the narrative anachrony of recounting Maude's accident, which occurs in the summer, before revealing that she had resumed receiving Communion at Easter.

283 *waits*. Musicians and singers who perform in the streets at Christmas.

['Thank God, thank God, we do believe']. *Date*. 7 March 1849 (Bodleian MS. Don. e. 1/5).

284 l. 28. *Sure-footed*. Unerring. The adjective, commonly applied to beasts (e.g. sheep), prepares for the assertion that the Messenger is, himself, also a sacrificial Offering.

l. 39. *For unto us . . . given*. From Isaiah 9: 6.

285 *seringa*. The name commonly given, at the time, to shrubs of the genus *Philadelphus*.

the world. i.e. those people outside the religious order.

287   *Epithalamium.* A wedding poem.

    profess. Take the vows of a religious order.

288   [Three Nuns 1]. *Date.* 10 May 1850. *Epigraph.* 'This heart sighs, and I know not wherefore' (trans. WMR).

    E non so dir perchè. In the manuscript, *so* has been emended, with a pencil stroke, to *sa.* The emendation seems to be by WMR.

    l. 4. *that.* So that.

    l. 16. *a solitary bird.* Probably not any bird, but the nightingale (thus the comparison to the evening bell, l. 17, and its singing through to matins, l. 39).

    [footnote]. Cf. Barrett Browning's 'Catarina to Camoëns; Dying in His Absence Abroad, and Referring to the Poem in Which He Recorded the Sweetness of Her Eyes', in *Poems* by Elizabeth Barrett Barrett (London, 1844). The somewhat unnecessary note registers Maude's (or the young CGR's) sense of one of her poetic precursors.

289   [Three Nuns 2]. *Date.* 12 February 1849. Composed as an independent poem, and entered in the notebook Bodleian MS. Don. e. 1/5 as 'A Nun'. *Epigraph.* 'It may be sighing for love, but to me it says not so' (trans. WMR).

290   l. 33. *cordial.* i.e. 'comforting the heart'.

    l. 39. *the unknown psalm.* The reference is to the song of the redeemed in Revelation 14: 3: 'And they sung as it were a new song before the throne, and before the four beasts, and the elders: and no man could learn that song but the hundred and forty and four thousand, which were redeemed from the earth'.

    l. 40. *Soon . . . sun.* Cf. the vision of the heavenly Jerusalem at Revelation 21: 23: 'And the city had no need of the sun, neither of the moon, to shine in it: for the glory of God did lighten it, and the Lamb is the light thereof'.

291   l. 58. *After His Likeness.* Cf. Romans 6: 5: 'For if we have been planted together in the likeness of his death, we shall be also in the likeness of his resurrection'.

    ll. 58–60. *Who hath said . . . Therewith.* Cf. Hebrews 10: 23 ('for he is faithful that promised') and Psalm 17: 15 ('I will behold thy face in righteousness: I shall be satisfied, when I awake, with thy likeness') (D'Amico, 56).

    [Three Nuns 3]. *Date.* 10 May 1850. *Epigraph.* 'Answer me, my heart, wherefore sighest thou? It answers: I want God—I sigh for Jesus' (trans. WMR).

    l. 8. *a hidden fount.* Cf. the bridegroom's description of the bride in Song of Solomon 4: 12: 'A garden inclosed is my sister, my spouse; a spring shut up, a fountain sealed'.

l. 9. *clay*. Not only in the sense of clammy earth, but 'earth as the material of the human body (cf. Gen. ii. 7); hence, the human body (living or dead) as distinguished from the soul' (*OED*, 4).

292 ll. 24–5. *Oh for the shadow . . . land*. Cf. Isaiah 32: 2, read as referring to Christ: 'And a man shall be as an hiding place from the wind, and a covert from the tempest; as rivers of water in a dry place, as the shadow of a great rock in a weary land'.

l. 38. *The city builded without hands*. Cf. 2 Corinthians 5: 1.

293 l. 84. *'The Spirit . . . Come'*. From Revelation 22: 17.

the straw spread in front. Its purpose being to diminish the noise of vehicles passing the house of the sick or dying.

294 *something more was required*. Although Agnes can give the correct (Tractarian) guidance, it is only when it is given by a priest that it is effective.

295 ['I watched a rosebud very long']. *Date*. 7 January 1849 (entered in the notebook Bodleian MS. Don. e. 1/5). *Publication*. In *1862 (D)*, with the notebook manuscript title 'Symbols'.

296 ['Sleep, let me sleep, for I am sick of care']. *Date*. 8 June 1849. Copied into the notebook Bodleian MS. Don. e. 1/6 by CGR's mother, Frances Mary Lavinia Rossetti—an indication, to WMR, of composition during a period of illness (*1904*, 467). There, it has the title 'Looking forward'.

297 ['Fade, tender lily']. *Title*. CGR submitted a copy to the Portfolio Society (CGR Collection (Co222), Princeton University Library) with the title 'Autumn'—probably the subject set by the Society rather than CGR's own title.

298 ['What is it Jesus saith unto the soul?—']. *Date*. 2 March 1850. Entered in the notebook Bodleian MS. Don. e. 1/6 under the title (from Matthew 5: 4) '"Blessed are they that mourn for they shall be comforted"'. Lines 1–7 were incorporated, with revisions, in the sonnet for 17 March in *TF*.

l. 10. *strengthening*. In the context of this tale, cf. the Catechism in *BCP*, where the benefit of Communion is 'the strengthening and refreshing of our souls'.

ll. 13–14. *'Winter . . . away'*. Drawing from Song of Solomon 2: 10–13.

NICK. *Date*. In the prefatory note to *1870*, CGR dates the earliest of that volume's stories to 1852. This is likely to be that earliest story (*Bell*, 273); certainly, by the summer of 1853, DGR was trying to get it published, but without success. *Publication*. First published in the *National Magazine*, 2 (October 1857), 375–6 (*Marsh*, 286). *Text. 1870*.

299 *pet*. Fit of irritation.

302 *turnpike*. A toll gate on a main road.

303 THE LOST TITIAN. *Publication.* First published in the *Crayon*, 3 (July 1856), 200–2, signed 'C.G.R.'. *Text. 1870.* The triad of artists in the tale may indicate the influence of Balzac's 'Le Chef-d'œuvre inconnu'. Both tales give conviction to fictional events by incorporating factual details. (In her prefatory note to *1870*, CGR feels it necessary to emphasize that her tale of a lost masterpiece of Titian's—'with whose name I have made free'—is a fiction, not an 'imposture'.) And CGR's tale—although a much lighter piece—is, in its own way, about an unknown masterpiece. In Balzac's tale, as Porbus and Poussin stare in incomprehension at the masterpiece—apparently a chaos of paint—they glimpse, in a corner of the canvas, a trace of the figure of a woman that lies underneath the layers of paint put on by Frenhofer in the deluded belief that he was perfecting, not destroying, his painting.

Epigraph. From *The Antiquary*, ch. 1 (cf. *As You Like It*, 5. 4. 92). In the context of the tale's epigraph, *circumstance* is that particularity of detail which is not only circumlocutory but which gives conviction to a story (or a lie).

304 *cymbals . . . panther . . . winy lips.* The details are drawn from the Bacchic procession in Titian's *Bacchus and Ariadne*.

colorito. Use of colour. Sixteenth-century artistic theory contrasts those painters—in particular, Venetian painters—noted for *colorito* with those noted for *disegno* (drawing). Vasari records that Michelangelo praised the colouring in Titian's work, but regretted its want of design.

305 *evviva!.* Long life!

306 *solitario passero.* Solitary songbird (perhaps not necessarily a sparrow). The reference is more literary than ornithological: the context suggests that Giacomo Leopardi's 'Il passero solitario' may be in CGR's mind (a poem descended from Psalm 102: 7, via Petrarch's 'Passer mai solitario in alcun tetto').

cogged dice. Loaded dice.

308 *urgency.* Insistence.

pointed. Gave an edge to; spiced up.

casa. In this (Venetian) context, more a *palazzo* than a mere 'house'.

309 *to the name.* i.e. Benvenuto ('welcome').

Orco decapitato. The Headless Ogre (the name, if not for much longer, of the inn).

311 *Andromeda.* Offered as a sacrifice to a sea-monster, but saved by Perseus.

A SAFE INVESTMENT. *Publication.* First published in the *Churchman's Shilling Magazine*, 2 (1867), 287–92. *Text. 1870.*

one house. See Matthew 5: 14, 7: 24–5.

a white horse. In Revelation 19: 11–16, Christ comes on a white horse, followed by armies on white horses.

horse's hoofs. In Jeremiah 47: 3, the stamping of horses' hoofs marks the commencement of God's destructive work.

312 *laden . . . merchandise of all sorts.* More particularly, merchandise of the sort traded with Babylon in Revelation 18: 11–13.

313 *the main national bank itself had broken.* A topical detail: the tale draws not only on Revelation 18–19, but on the fears excited by the banking crisis of 1866 caused by the collapse of the Overend Gurney Bank ('the model instance of all evil in business', to Walter Bagehot, *Lombard Street: A Description of the Money Market* (London, 1873), 273).

316 *the recompense of the reward.* See Hebrews 10: 35.

entertained angels unawares. From Hebrews 13: 2.

DEVOTIONAL PROSE

317 *From* SEEK AND FIND: A DOUBLE SERIES OF SHORT STUDIES OF THE BENEDICITE. *Publication.* 1879, by the SPCK. *Title.* The Benedicite is the canticle, to be said or sung, in the Order for Morning Prayer (i.e. Matins) in *BCP*, beginning 'O all ye Works of the Lord, bless ye the Lord: praise him, and magnify him for ever' (*benedicite omnia opera Domini Domino laudate et superexaltate eum in saecula,* Vulgate, Daniel 3: 57). The text is from The Song of the Three Holy Children in the Apocrypha (Vulgate, Daniel 3: 24–90). CGR's book is formed of two series of reflections upon each verse of the Benedicite, the first series headed 'Creation', the second 'Redemption'. (The first five of the six passages included in this edition are taken from the first series.) The title alludes to Matthew 7: 7: 'Ask, and it shall be given you; seek, and ye shall find; knock, and it shall be opened unto you'. The title-page epigraph is from Matthew 13: 44: 'Treasure hid in a field'. *Text.* 1879.

purple, an earthly hue of mourning. In ecclesiastical use, purple is the colour for hangings in Lent. It may be taken to allude to the purple of the kingly robe which is put on Christ when he is mocked as a king (John 9: 2–3), and also to Christ's blood.

terrene. Earthly.

319 *inherent luminosity.* Linda E. Marshall takes this to refer to reports of the 4th Earl of Rosse's research into lunar radiation (in *Arseneau et al.,* 198). If so, CGR has not understood his research, which concluded that the greater part of the moon's heat which reaches the earth is not that which falls from the sun on the moon's surface and is at once reflected, but that which is absorbed and is afterwards radiated ('On the Radiation of Heat from the Moon', *Proceedings of the Royal Society of London,* 17 (1868–9), 436–43).

325 *sounds . . . reproduced.* Thomas Edison produced his first phonograph towards the end of 1877.

the groans . . . should rise up in the judgment. The speculation may be traced to CGR's earliest reading. In a small book 'intended as an innocent exercise for the memory of children', in illustration of the idea of Justice, the child learns (and memorizes) that, although 'the poor injur'd brute' cannot bring a case against 'cruel, oppressive, and base' man in man's courts of law, 'In the high court of heav'n his wrongs are recorded: | There his groans are all heard and his plea is regarded'—the lesson being to respect all creatures lest man be 'repaid', in time, for his treatment of them (J.B., *The Pet Lamb* (London [1824]), 24). A copy of the book was given to Maria Francesca Rossetti by her father on her second birth-day, and later passed to CGR (Harry Ransom Center, University of Texas, Austin). CGR would have a lifelong horror of cruelty to God's creatures. In the last decades of her life, she was active in the anti-vivisectionist cause, circulating pamphlets and petitions, and occasionally attending meetings. Her long-standing relationship with the SPCK was finally soured by its publication of a book condoning vivisection.

328 *one instance alone*. i.e. the barren fig tree to which the previous sentence refers.

329 *From* LETTER AND SPIRIT: NOTES ON THE COMMANDMENTS. *Publication*. 1883, by SPCK. *Title*. In Paul, the distinction between letter and spirit is based upon the concept of a new dispensation: God 'hath made us able ministers of the new testament; not of the letter, but of the spirit: for the letter killeth, but the spirit giveth life' (2 Corinthians 3: 6). The title-page epigraph is from Luke 10: 26, 28: 'What is written in the law? how readest thou? . . . This do, and thou shalt live'. That which is to be done is to follow the two Great Commandments: 'Thou shalt love the Lord thy God with all thy heart, and with all thy soul, and with all thy strength, and with all thy mind; and thy neighbour as thyself' (10: 27). This passage, omitted from the epigraph, is then presented at the beginning of the book, followed immediately by the Decalogue (Exodus 20: 3–17). These are the texts to which CGR offers her 'Notes'—as she describes them in the title, with her usual self-deprecation. Yet, even though the book is structured upon these texts, in its taking the form of a continuous exposition of them this is CGR's most ambitious devotional book: *Bell*, 299 comments that 'In none of her books does she approach more nearly to theological disquisition'.

330 *'by every word . . . God'*. Matthew 4: 4.
     'unto the pure . . . pure'. Titus 1: 15.

332 *'Holy, Holy, Holy'*. Isaiah 6: 3.
     Blessed Mary. Luke 1: 46.
     Jephthah's daughter. Judges 11: 29–40.

333 *'Seek ye . . . seek'*. Psalm 27: 9 (in *BCP*).
     'as to the Lord . . . men'. Colossians 3: 23.

334 *creature*. Created thing.
     'Hath not . . . things?'. Acts 7: 50.
     'The heavens . . . handywork'. Psalm 19: 1.

'When I . . . what is man . . .?'. Psalm 8: 3–4.

'the mind of Christ'. 1 Corinthians 2: 16.

335 'Charity . . . truth'. 1 Corinthians 13: 6.

336 *From* TIME FLIES: A READING DIARY. *Publication.* 1885, by the SPCK. The title-page epigraph is from James Montgomery: '"A day's march nearer home"'. Keble's enormously popular *The Christian Year* (1827), a volume of devotional poems structured upon the ecclesiastical calendar of *BCP*, is a distant generic analogue; but the identification of CGR's book as a 'diary'—'a miscellaneous set of short readings in prose and verse' (*L* 3. 267)—allows the inclusion of more private and idiosyncratic material than is found in Keble's volume. *Text.* 1885.

January 2. turning a good poem into a bad one. DGR, Preface to *The Early Italian Poets* (1861): 'The life-blood of rhythmical translation is this commandment,—that a good poem shall not be turned into a bad one . . . Poetry not being an exact science, literality of rendering is altogether secondary to this chief law. I say *literality*,—not fidelity, which is by no means the same thing' (*DGRW*, 283).

'My brethren . . . be'. From James 3: 10 on man's ungovernable tongue: 'Out of the same mouth proceedeth blessing and cursing. My brethren, these things ought not so to be'.

337 *January 15.* 'Lo . . . inventions'. Ecclesiastes 7: 29.

behoof. Use.

January 16 ('Love understands the mystery, whereof'). The first of the 24 roundels in *TF*. (For the form, see '"A Helpmeet for Him"', head-note (p. 473).) The total number of roundels in the volume may be of numerological significance, according with the twenty-four hours of each day. (That the form of the roundel can itself have chronological significance to CGR is evident in her sense of its rightness as a form for a birthday poem sent to William Bell Scott: 'A roundel seems to fit a round of days', in *Crump*, 3. 339.)

Title. Given the title '"Judge nothing before the time"' (from 1 Corinthians 4: 5) in *1893*.

l. 2. *spell.* Understand.

338 l. 9. *telling her bead-history.* Saying her round of prayers. *Telling* has two senses here: 'counting' (i.e. counting the beads of a rosary in order to count the number of prayers said), and 'relating'.

339 *February 9. new song.* From Revelation 14: 2–3: 'and I heard the voice of harpers harping with their harps: And they sung as it were a new song . . . and no man could learn that song but the hundred and forty and four thousand, which were redeemed from the earth'.

'And I look . . . Dead'. From the end of the Nicene Creed recited in the Communion liturgy of *BCP*: 'And I look for the Resurrection of the dead, And the life of the world to come'.

February 10. 'Glorious things . . . there'. From Psalm 87: 3, 7.

339 *February 11 ('No more! while sun and planets fly')*. *Epigraph*. From Psalm 119: 96 in *BCP*: 'I see that all things come to an end: but thy commandment is exceeding broad'.

340 l. 7. *pent*. To be taken either with *store* in the rare sense of 'having something pent or closely confined within it' (*OED*, 3) or as an epithet transferred from the echoes which are 'shut up, imprisoned' within the store. In this line, *echo* (as *ocean* (l. 5) and *earth* (l. 6)) is personified.

341 *February 14*. *'robes . . . Lamb'*. From Revelation 7: 14.

February 15 ('My love whose heart is tender said to me'). *Epigraph*. From Paul's discussion of marriage, which is considered inferior to celibacy: 'So then he that giveth her in marriage doeth well; but he that giveth her not in marriage doeth better'. Cf. CGR's discussion of the figures of the virgin and the married woman in *LS* (pp. 332–3, above).

February 20. a large waxwork exhibition. Madame Tussaud's (CGR's annotation to a copy of *TF*, Harry Ransom Center, University of Texas, Austin).

342 *February 27 ('A handy Mole who plied no shovel')*. l. 1. *handy*. Clever with the hands.

l. 12. *or . . . or . . .* Either . . . or . . .

l. 17. *countermine*. A defensive underground excavation that intercepts an attacker's excavation (a term from military engineering).

343 *March 4. vivid*. Clearly perceived. The word's etymology (Latin *vivere*, 'to live') is also to be understood: the sentence's parenthesis points to the oddity of saying that those who live have had an experience of death. *cottage*. At Holmer Green in Buckinghamshire, where CGR's grandfather Polidori lived until 1839 (CGR's annotation to a copy of *TF*, Harry Ransom Center, University of Texas, Austin; *1904*, p. xlviii).

March 5 ('Where shall I find a white rose blowing?'). *Publication*. 'This was first printed for a bazaar, held in June 1884, for the Boys' Home at Barnet, founded by Colonel Gillum. It was then named *Roses and Roses*' (*1904*, 469).

344 *March 18. sue out*. Make petition for.

345 *April 1. 'A Castle-Builder's World'*. *Date*. The poem is a revision of ll. 9–18 of the unpublished poem entitled 'A Nightmare' or (in the only complete manuscript) 'A Coast-Nightmare' (p. 76–7, above), which can be dated 12 September 1857.

Title. To have idle dreams is to build castles in the air. The title implies that the poem describes the world which one who has turned from God— who has constructed his or her existence upon a false foundation— will inherit. For a comparable use of the phrase in a religious context, see [Charlotte Yonge], *The Castle Builders; or, The Deferred Confirmation* (1854), a tale of how two sisters—'Wavering unstable Emmeline, unreflecting, easily-led Katherine' (350)—are eventually confirmed in the confidence of the sustaining power of divine grace.

Epigraph. The Isaian epigraph is from the description of the day of God's vengeance upon the lands of the cursed: 'For it is the day of the Lord's vengeance . . . And the streams thereof shall be turned into pitch, and the dust thereof into brimstone, and the land thereof shall become burning pitch. It shall not be quenched night nor day; the smoke thereof shall go up for ever: from generation to generation it shall lie waste; none shall pass through it for ever and ever. But the cormorant and the bittern shall possess it; the owl also and the raven shall dwell in it: and he shall stretch out upon it the line of confusion, and the stones of emptiness' (Isaiah 34: 8–11). When invoked in the Christian context of this poem, the passage becomes interpretable as a warning of that which awaits those who will be damned at the Day of Judgement.

April 2. trefoil. i.e. clover. The incident happened 'At Frome' in Somerset (CGR's annotation to a copy of *TF*, Harry Ransom Center, University of Texas, Austin).

346 *April 13 ('A cold wind stirs the blackthorn'). Title.* The slightly revised version in *1893* is given the title 'Endure hardness' (from 2 Timothy 2: 3).

l. 4. *With vegetable snow.* 'With flakes and sprays of snow' in *1893*.

April 20 ('Piteous my rhyme is'). l. 2. *What while.* While.

April 28. A friend. The painter Frederic Shields, at Birchington (CGR's annotation to a copy of *TF*, Harry Ransom Center, University of Texas, Austin; *L* 3. 257).

348 *May 21 ('"The half was not told me," said Sheba's Queen').* l. 1. *The half was not told me.* From 1 Kings 10: 7.

349 *May 28 ('They lie at rest, our blessed dead'). Date.* The poem was formed by extracting and revising four stanzas from a longer unpublished poem 'A Burthen', dated 16 July 1858, in the notebook BL Ashley MS. 1364 (3) (in *Crump*, 3. 270–2).

June 3. bottomless pit. Revelation 9: 1, 2, 11; 11: 7; 17: 8; 20: 1, 3.

'*for our admonition . . . come*'. From 1 Corinthians 10: 11.

350 *shipwreck . . . Tarshish.* The references are to Jonah 1–2. When called by God to go and denounce Nineveh, Jonah decided to flee to Tarshish. God then sent a storm, and Jonah was thrown into the sea to be swallowed by a great fish which God then ordered to vomit him out onto dry land.

June 6 ('Heartsease I found, where Love-lies-bleeding'). l. 1. *Heartsease . . . Love-lies-bleeding.* Two common names for one plant, the wild pansy *Viola tricolor.* The roundel plays on the names' religious suggestiveness: Heartsease, of comfort; Love-lies-bleeding, of Christ's love and sacrifice (Catherine Musello Cantalupo, in *Kent*, 279).

350 l. 2. *Empurpled*. Purple, in ecclesiastical use, refers to Christ's status — it is the colour of the robe of royalty put on Christ when he is mocked as a king (John 19: 2, 5) — and to his suffering and his blood.

l. 7. *binding*. Primarily 'tying' (of plants), but secondarily 'dressing' (of wounds). For the latter sense, see '"A Fair World Tho' a Fallen." ———', l. 10: 'Bind up the wounded with a tender touch'. (The sense is biblical: e.g. Job 5: 18.) In *1893* the line is revised to: 'And binding growths unbound'.

351 *June 7. 'the true Bread from heaven'*. See John 6: 30–3.   *withheld*. See Exodus 16: 22–6.

those outward . . . us. The definition is that of the Catechism in *BCP*.

'The days . . . days'. From Mark 2: 20.

June 8. 'This do . . . Me'. Cf. Luke 22: 19.

352 *June 9 ('Roses on a brier')*. l. 8. *There shall . . . sea*. See Revelation 21: 1.

June 26. Meads. All Saints Convalescent Hospital at Meads, near Eastbourne (CGR's annotation to a copy of *TF*, Harry Ransom Center, University of Texas, Austin; see *L* 2. 19).

spider. In *PP*, 248, the spider in the Interpreter's House is an emblem of those who are 'full of the venom of sin' but who may yet be saved through faith. CGR, similarly, takes the spider for a figure of the sinner; but, differently, of the impenitent sinner.

353 *July 4. one no longer present with us*. Maria Francesca Rossetti (CGR's annotation to a copy of *TF*, Harry Ransom Center, University of Texas, Austin; and see *L* 2. 181, where CGR declines WMR's offer of an Egyptian mummified body part that had been given him).

July 6. This entry follows thematically from that for July 5, a revised version of ll. 78–89 of '"To What Purpose is This Waste?"'. The incident happened at Holmer Green (CGR's annotation to a copy of *TF*, Harry Ransom Center, University of Texas, Austin).

354 *is it quite certain . . . all?*. Cf. *SF*, where the invention of the phonograph provides an image of this possibility (p. 325, above).

July 7 ('Contemptuous of his home beyond'). l. 4. *imperial*. National, not local.

l. 27. *'A Froggy would a-wooing go'*. For a text of the song, see *The Oxford Dictionary of Nursery Rhymes*, ed. Iona and Peter Opie (1951), 177–81. The song ends with the frog being eaten by a duck.

355 l. 32. *incog*. Incognito: unknown.

July 13. a fine collection. That of the Tebbs family (CGR's annotation to a copy of *TF*, Harry Ransom Center, University of Texas, Austin; *L* 3. 292–3).

356 *July 14. English roadside ditch*. At Cheltenham (CGR's annotation to a copy of *TF*, Harry Ransom Center, University of Texas, Austin).

July 17. a little girl. Maria Francesca Rossetti, at Holmer Green (CGR's annotation to a copy of *TF*, Harry Ransom Center, University of Texas, Austin).

'Let patience . . . work'. From James 1: 4.

357 *July 18. 'And what . . . thereof?'.* From God's condemnation of Jerusalem in Jeremiah 5: 31.

August 4. 'always rejoicing'. From 2 Corinthians 6: 10.

358 *August 5 ('Of each sad word, which is more sorrowful').* l. 6. *dule.* Grief.

December 17 ('Earth grown old yet still so green'). The poem's calendrical reference (cf. ll. 8–9) is made explicit in *1893*, where it is titled 'Advent'.

l. 5. *told.* Counted.

l. 7. *swathings.* Wrappings, i.e. winding-sheets in which bodies are wrapped for burial.   *fold.* Both '(outer) layer, covering' (= 'crust', l. 2), but probably with the secondary sense of '(protective) enclosure' in which the dead rest.

359 *Thursday in Holy Week ('The great Vine left its glory to reign as Forest King'). Epigraph.* From Jotham's parable (Judges 9: 8–15) in which the trees try to choose a king to rule over them. The olive and the fig and the vine decline their offer; only the worthless bramble is interested in the offer. In CGR's counter-parable—informed by the parable of Christ as the true vine in John 15—the vine does condescend to be king over the trees, while the trees resist its rule.

l. 6. *buffet.* A word from Mark's passion narrative (14: 65), read in church on the Monday of Holy Week: Christ's accusers buffet him.

l. 14. *endured time's fashioning.* Became mortal (*time* is to be taken as an antonym of 'eternity' (*OED*, 26)).

360 *Rogation Tuesday. Rogation.* Three days of prayer, called 'rogation' days (from Latin *rogare*, 'to ask') precede Ascension Day in the ecclesiastical calendar.

St Luke's narrative. That of Satan's temptation of Christ in the wilderness in Luke 4: 1–13. In the second temptation (4: 5–8) the devil, 'taking him up into an high mountain, shewed unto him all the kingdoms of the world in a moment of time. And the devil said unto him, All this power will I give thee, and the glory of them: for that is delivered unto me; and to whomsoever I will I give it. If thou therefore wilt worship me, all shall be thine'.

the proverb. Ecclesiasticus 13: 1: 'He that toucheth pitch shall be defiled therewith'.

Aaron and Hur. In Exodus 17: 12, they hold up Moses' heavy hands, an action which influences the outcome of the battle in which the Amalekites are defeated.

to go upon . . . foot. Cf. Psalm 91: 13.

360 *'exceeding high mountain'*. From Matthew's version (4: 8) of what, in Luke, is Christ's second temptation.

FROM THE FACE OF THE DEEP: A DEVOTIONAL COMMENTARY ON THE APOCALYPSE. *Publication*. 1892, published by the SPCK. The title-page epigraph is from Psalm 36: 6: 'Thy judgments are a great deep'. At the end of the commentary is written: '*If I have been overbold in attempting such a work as this, I beg pardon*'.

If thou canst dive. For the imagery of interpretation of scripture as diving into the deep, see also Isaac Williams, *Tracts for the Times*, no. 87, 'On Reserve in Communicating Religious Knowledge', part 4, section 8: scripture contains 'deep and latent meanings', is 'in its secret range thus vast and comprehensive, as the shadow of the heavens in still and deep waters', although 'In attempting too far to dive into it, to illustrate and apprehend its meanings, fallible men may of course greatly err from time to time', 22–3.

'bdellium . . . onyx stone'. See Genesis 2: 12.

361 *A dear saint*. Maria Francesca Rossetti (*Bell*, 63).

'to him . . . sin'. From James 4: 17.

362 *'inhabiteth eternity'*. From Isaiah 57: 15.

'I will keep . . . good'. From Psalm 39: 1–2

363 *'Unto . . . upon us'*. Psalm 123: 1–2.

'Our God . . . righteousness'. From Psalm 50: 3–6.

364 *'I know that . . . past'*. Ecclesiastes 3: 14–15.

'Have ye . . . old'. From Matthew 13: 51–2.

Rose of Sharon . . . Lily of the Valleys. See Song of Solomon 2: 1.

365 *preventing*. i.e. preceding. God's prevenient (or antecedent) grace predisposes fallen mankind to turn towards God prior to any movement on mankind's own part.

the waves of this troublesome world. Cf. the first prayer in the order for Publick Baptism of Infants in *BCP*.

'like unto a wheel'. From Psalm 83: 13 (in *BCP*).

'pleasant to the eyes'. See Genesis 3: 6.

'was troubled'. See Luke 1: 29.

'lily among thorns'. See Song of Solomon 2: 2.

'the King . . . chambers'. See Song of Solomon 1: 4.

'Who is she . . . banners?'. Song of Solomon 6: 10.

366 *'Give . . . gates'*. Proverbs 31: 31.

367 *'Behold . . . great things'*. From Daniel 7: 2–8.

'A leopard . . . cities'. From Jeremiah 5: 6.

'Love not . . . for ever'. 1 John 2: 15–17.

'How long . . . armed man'. Proverbs 6: 9–11.

of the earth earthy. The phrase is from 1 Corinthians 15: 47.

368 *'Rescue . . . lions'.* From Psalm 35: 17.

'God so loved . . . saved'. John 3: 16–17.

hair, gold, apparel. See 1 Peter 3: 3.

alabaster box. See Mark 14: 3–9.

369 *many inventions.* See Ecclesiastes 7: 29.

very good. See Genesis 1: 31.

370 *Would God I had died for thee.* From David's lament for Absalom, 2 Samuel 18: 33.

'upon many waters'. Revelation 17: 1.

St. Paul warns us women against. See 1 Timothy 2: 9.

371 *'The horseleach . . . give'.* From Proverbs 30: 15.

'When wisdom . . . depths of hell'. In Proverbs 2: 10–11, 16–19; 5: 3–6; 9: 13–16, 18.

l. 7. *scathe.* Hurt.

l. 8. *dule.* Grief.

372 *'openeth . . . kindness'.* Proverbs 31: 26.

'Bezaleel . . . sanctuary'. Exodus 36: 1

'all the women . . . hair'. Exodus 35: 25–6.

'standeth without'. See Song of Solomon 2: 9.

373 *'I pray not . . . evil'.* John 17: 15.

'dreamed . . . song'. Dante in *Purgatorio*, 19. The quotation is from Maria Francesca Rossetti, *A Shadow of Dante* (1871), 162.

376 *'Yea . . . awaketh'.* Psalm 73: 19 (in *BCP*).

377 *'out of weakness . . . aliens'.* Hebrews 11: 34.

'Not by might . . . hosts'. Zechariah 4: 6.

378 *'Raging waves . . . shame'.* From Jude 13.

379 *'Without controversy'.* The phrase is from 1 Timothy 3: 16.

'Lo . . . wickedness'. Psalm 52: 7.

'A man's life . . . possesseth'. From Luke 12: 14.

380 *'Brethren . . . away'.* From 1 Corinthians 7: 29–31.

'The glory . . . works'. Psalm 104: 31.

'of fire'. Cf. 2 Kings 2: 11.

The rudiments . . . using. From Colossians 2: 20–2.

382 *'The getting . . . death'.* Proverbs 21: 6.

'I am found . . . behold me'. From Isaiah 65: 1.

'that old serpent'. Revelation 20: 2.

'Art thou also . . . unto us?'. Isaiah 14: 10.

LETTERS

385 TO WILLIAM MICHAEL ROSSETTI, 19 SEPTEMBER 1853. *Text*. Angeli-Dennis Collection, Box 6–1, University of British Columbia.

two Good pictures. CGR had modelled for the figure of Mary in DGR's *The Girlhood of Mary Virgin* (1849) and *Ecce Ancilla Domini!* (1850).

William . . . column. The reference is to WMR's reviews, in the *Spectator*, of the work of other members of the Pre-Raphaelite Brotherhood. To 'cut up' is to review with destructive severity.

TO AMELIA BARNARD HEIMANN, 3 APRIL 1862. *Text*. Mark Samuels Lasner Collection, on loan to the University of Delaware Library.

one piece. 'Christian and Jew', on p. 148 of *1862*.

386 *constrains*. Compels.

our mourning. Lizzie Siddal, DGR's wife, had died of a laudanum overdose in February 1862.

TO ADOLPH HEIMANN, [?APRIL 1862]. *Text*. Mark Samuels Lasner Collection, on loan to the University of Delaware Library.

TO ALEXANDER MACMILLAN, [1 DECEMBER 1863]. *Text*. BL Additions 54975.

Miss Proctor . . . Miss Ingelow. The poets Adelaide Anne Procter (1825–64), and Jean Ingelow (1820–97) whose successful *Poems* was published in 1863.

387 TO DANTE GABRIEL ROSSETTI, 7 MAY 1864. *Text*. Angeli-Dennis Collection, Box 5–11, University of British Columbia.

remains. The unpublished works left by an author, commonly described by this term when published posthumously.

TO DANTE GABRIEL ROSSETTI, 23 DECEMBER 1864. *Text*. Angeli-Dennis Collection, Box 5–11, University of British Columbia.

my Alchemist. The old man of 'The Prince's Progress', ll. 178–246.

my nerves. CGR's expressed sensitivity to DGR's criticisms of her poems should never be taken for mere banter.

at least one terza-rima. One poem in this verse form, 'After This the Judgment', was indeed included in *1866*. Dante's *Commedia* is in *terza rima*, thus giving the form particular significance for a half-Italian poet.

my own Bogie. The spirit of 'At Home'.

here I must remain. CGR is writing from Hastings. She returned to London early in April 1865. A happy consequence of her distance from DGR is this detailed correspondence—exceptional in her surviving letters—over the preparation of her 1866 volume.

the Davenport séance. WMR recalls that, in 1864, the Davenport Brothers 'electrified London by performing, professedly through spiritual agency, various surprising feats, especially that of getting suddenly free from elaborate rope-bindings' (*RP*, 68).

388 *your outer men.* The outer man—his body—is distinguished from the inner (spiritual or psychical) man.

TO DANTE GABRIEL ROSSETTI, 30 [JANUARY 1865]. *Text.* Angeli-Dennis Collection, Box 5–11, University of British Columbia.

vol. 2. That is, *The Prince's Progress and Other Poems* (1866), the follow-up volume to *Goblin Market and Other Poems* (1862).

TO DANTE GABRIEL ROSSETTI, 10 [FEBRUARY 1865]. *Text.* Angeli-Dennis Collection, Box 5–11, University of British Columbia.

389 *annotations.* 'It delights me that you approve of my *Alchemist*; you know I am always nervous in such suspense: thanks for prospective annotations' (letter to DGR, 1 [February 1865]).

Tennyson's Idylls. The two tournaments are in 'Enid' and 'Elaine', *Idylls of the King* (London, 1859), 29–32, 169–73.

prospective cuts. DGR designed the frontispiece and the title page to *1866*. Also, at this time, the *1862* title page was being altered for the second edition of *Goblin Market and Other Poems* (1865).

in yours. DGR had sent Lizzie Siddal's poems. In her letter to DGR of 1 February, CGR had suggested that some of Siddal's work might be included in one of her own volumes (*L* 1. 224).

III . . . VI. WMR identifies III as 'Dead Love', and VI as 'At Last' (*RP*, 76–7).

TO DANTE GABRIEL ROSSETTI, 3 [MARCH 1865]. *Text.* Angeli-Dennis Collection, Box 5–11, University of British Columbia.

390 *Aftermath.* Cf. 'The Prince's Progress', l. 291.

Now the moon's at full. Cf. l. 17.

Tomorrow. Eventually published as the second part of 'Twilight Night' (in Crump, 1. 212). As elsewhere, DGR has been needlessly anxious about CGR's possible debts to other poets.

Judgment or Captive Jew. 'After This the Judgment', first published in *Lyra Mystica* (1865), ed. Orby Shipley, was included in *1866*, and 'By the Waters of Babylon. B. C. 570' was included in *1875*; *Martyrs' Song* was included in *1866*.

same terms. She would receive half of any profits arising from her volumes.

TO DANTE GABRIEL ROSSETTI, 6 [MARCH 1865]. *Text.* Angeli-Dennis Collection, Box 5–11, University of British Columbia.

391 *Feelings there are, &c.* WMR notes: 'this refers to a distich which used to amuse all of us considerably—I don't remember in what "poet" we found it—"Feelings there are that warm the generous breast: | They may be known, but cannot be expressed"' (*RP*, 83).

two small points. In the published frontispiece the prince's right hand covers his face and no beard is visible (cf. l. 64 of the poem), but the dead princess is indeed veiled (cf. ll. 20, 465).

TO DANTE GABRIEL ROSSETTI, [11 MARCH 1865]. *Text.* Angeli-Dennis
Collection, Box 5–11, University of British Columbia.

392 *Rose, Shamrock & Thistle.* Ceased publication with its March 1865
issue.

Shilling Mag. It did indeed get 'Amor Mundi', where it was illustrated by
Frederick Sandys.   *Once-a-Week.* CGR had not been published
in this for some years ('In the Round Tower at Jhansi' had appeared in
1 (13 August 1859), 140, and 'Maude Clare' in 1 (5 November 1859),
381–2), and 'presumably some other poems had been declined' (WMR
in *RP*, 87). The little triumph lies in being rejected by Samuel Lucas
when editor of one magazine, and accepted by him when editor of the
other.

the two Eves. That is, 'Bird or Beast?' and 'Eve', which were placed
together in *1866.*

'Bessie Parkes'. A poet, and activist for women's rights, and also a member
of the Portfolio Society.   *'Eliza Cook'.* An enormously popular
poet; but, for such poets as CGR and DGR, an unsophisticated one.

Hairy...their. Cf. 'The Prince's Progress', l. 33.   *substitute heat for
frost.* Probably in 'The Prince's Progress', l. 7 (in which, confusingly, in
her letter of 13 March, CGR asks DGR to substitute *frost* for *heat*).

For me, shyness had grown. Cf. 'Under the Rose', l. 204.

'by huge upthrust'. From 'The Prince's Progress', l. 149.

'things which are impossible rarely happen'. WMR remembers this to have
occurred in 'an Anglo-German Exercise-book' by their German tutor
Adolph Heimann (*RP*, 87).

393 TO DANTE GABRIEL ROSSETTI, [13 MARCH 1865]. *Text.* Janet Camp
Troxell Collection (Co189), Box 2, Folder 23, Princeton University
Library.

substituting frost for heat. Cf. 'The Prince's Progress', l. 7.

Lowest Room. Excluded from *1866*; included in *1875.*   *Isa and
Adelaide.* The poets Isa Craig and Adelaide Anne Procter.

394 *last in the secular section.* The volume, like *1862*, was divided into a main
unheaded section, and a shorter section headed 'Devotional Pieces'. The
division of these volumes into two distinct sections had been DGR's
suggestion (letter to CGR, [*c.*8 February 1861], *DGRL (F)*, 2. 349).

dye. In 'The Prince's Progress', l. 365.

'It's up the second pair'. Perhaps a line in the draft of 'Under the Rose' that
has been sent to DGR. No draft or fair copy of the poem is known.

a not un-Crabbed aspect. i.e. some resemblance to the work of George
Crabbe.

TO DANTE GABRIEL ROSSETTI, [31 MARCH [1865]. *Text.* Angeli-
Dennis Collection, Box 5–11, University of British Columbia.

395 *that 'screech'.* WMR suggests this may have been 'some subsidiary part' of
'Under the Rose' (*RP*, 93).

Ghost's Petition. For the shortening, see 'The Ghost's Petition', note to l. 75 (p. 444).

Song in a Cornfield. See 'Songs in a Cornfield', notes to ll. 71–85, 117 (pp. 445, 446).   *'Gone were but the Winter'*. DGR had evidently suggested inserting 'Spring Quiet', a poem included in *1866* independently.

a little book dated 1847. The notebook Bodleian MS. Don. e. 1/3.
di proprio moto. Of his own accord.

my sight of Italy with William. In May–June 1865 CGR did indeed travel to Italy with WMR and their mother.

396 *ballad by Alice Macdonald*. Her '"When My Ship Comes Home From Sea"' appeared in *Once-a-Week*, 12 (25 March 1865), 392.

TO DANTE GABRIEL ROSSETTI [?APRIL 1865]. *Text*. Angeli-Dennis Collection, Box 5–11, University of British Columbia.

Meggan and Margaret. In 'Maiden Song'.   *Scotus*. William Bell Scott.

Royal Princess. The stanza, in which DGR had detected a resemblance to Keats, was retained (ll. 31–3). DGR was presumably recalling 'Isabella', ll. 107–10: 'many a weary hand did swelt | In torched mines and noisy factories, | And many once proud-quiver'd loins did melt | In blood from stinging whip'.

L.E.L. For DGR's 'improvement' of the poem, see notes to the poem in this edition (p. 436).

By the Sea . . . . A Yawn. See the texts of both versions in this edition.

3 Nuns. Not published by CGR. (Included in this edition as part of 'Maude'.)

397 *Ghost's Petition . . . thro'*. The leonine rhyme in l. 14, which was indeed cut out.

In Progress. Not published by CGR. (The sonnet is included in this edition (p. 129).)

Come & See. WMR suggests '"I Will Lift Up Mine Eyes Unto the Hills"' (in *Crump*, 1. 224–5): cf. l. 44, 'Saith Jesus: Come and see' (*RP*, 98). The poem had been included in Orby Shipley's *Lyra Eucharistica* (1863). It was omitted in *1866*, but later included in *1875* — suggesting that DGR did not reconsider his verdict on the poem. It is not clear what DGR meant by its queer rhyme, or in what way CGR altered it: there is no major difference between the notebook manuscript (Bodleian MS. Don. e. 1/9) and *1875*. But each of the poem's stanzas does, with some strain, have 'Jesus' as a rhyme word.

Easter Even. Published in Shipley's *Lyra Messianica* (1864); not included in *1866* (in *Crump*, 3. 33–4).

397 *groans.* WMR suggests this was a term given by DGR to those poems he thought 'more peculiarly dismal in tone' (*RP*, 98),   *page.* Paginate.

398 TO DANTE GABRIEL ROSSETTI, [?SPRING 1870]. *Date.* WMR suggests April 1870 (*FL*, 31). William James Stillman had been editor of *The Crayon* at the time of its publication of CGR's story 'The Lost Titian'. In March 1870, DGR went with Stillman for a stay in the countryside which lasted until early May (Oswald Doughty, *A Victorian Romantic: Dante Gabriel Rossetti*, 2nd edn. (London, 1960), 426, 438); on 23 March 1870 DGR wrote to CGR that he and Stillman had been discussing the manuscript of 'Commonplace' (*DGRL (F)* 4. 412). *Text.* Bodleian MSS. Facs. d. 280, photocopy of autograph in Angeli-Dennis Collection, University of British Columbia. 'This letter is imperfect— the first sheet of it has been lost. It would appear that Dante Rossetti had conveyed to his sister a suggestion, made by Mr. Stillman, that she should write some more poems, partaking (in greater or less degree) of "politics or philanthropy". Such would not have been Rossetti's own recommendation: as he was more than commonly opposed to the use of such matter as a subject for poetry' (WMR in *FL*, 31).

'Give me the withered leaves I chose.' From 'Song' ('Oh roses for the flush of youth'), l. 7.

first last and only book. As Harrison suggests, CGR is thinking of *1862* and *1866* as constituting one volume (*L* 1. 349). A combined edition had already been published by Roberts Brothers in Boston in 1866; a combined and enlarged edition was published by Macmillan in 1875.

tanto meglio per me. So much the better for me.

TO DANTE GABRIEL ROSSETTI, 14 [DECEMBER 1875]. *Text.* Angeli-Dennis Collection, Box 5–11, University of British Columbia.

my new ed. That is, *Goblin Market, The Prince's Progress and Other Poems* (1875). DGR had written to CGR on 3 December 1875: 'To-day I have been looking through it with the same intense sympathy which your work always excites in me. Some of the matter newly added is most valuable. *Amor Mundi* is one of your choicest masterpieces; the *Venus* Sonnet and the one following, most exquisite; *Confluents*, lovely, and penetrating in its cadence; and the two poems on the Franco-Prussian War very noble—particularly the second, which is, I dare say, the best thing said in verse on the subject . . . the first of the two poems seems to me just a little echoish of the Barrett-Browning style—fine as the verses and genuine as the motive must be plainly discerned to be. Here, however, it is only in cadence that I seem to notice something of the kind. A real taint, to some extent, of modern vicious style derived from the same source—what might be called a falsetto muscularity—always seemed to me much too prominent in the long piece called *The Lowest Room.* This I think is now included for the first time, and I am sorry for it. I should also have omitted *No thank you, John* (and perhaps the preceding piece ['The Queen of Hearts'] also). The *John* one has the same genesis more or less, and everything in which this tone appears is utterly foreign to your primary impulses. The *Royal Princess* has a good deal of it unluckily, but then that poem is too good to omit. If I were you, I would rigidly keep guard on this matter if you write in the future, and ultimately exclude from your writings everything (or almost everything) so tainted. I am sure you will pardon my speaking so frankly' (*DGRL (DW)* 3. 1380).

Further remarks. On 22 December 1875, CGR writes: 'After impervious density I begin to see light (I think) on your objection to "the Lowest Room"; & I already regret having inserted it, you having scaledipping weight with me. Bulk was a seductive element. However, as to date, it *was* written before my 1st. vol. appeared; so certainly before Miss Jean Ingelow misled me anywhither. I still don't dislike it myself, but can lay no claim to impartiality' (*L* 2. 76).

TO AUGUSTA WEBSTER, [? LATER 1878]. *Text. Bell*, 111–12. *Bell* records that Webster's contributions to the *Examiner* on the subject of women's suffrage were, when reprinted by the National Society for Women's Suffrage, sent to CGR, producing some correspondence. 'Parliamentary Franchise for Women Ratepayers' was reprinted from the *Examiner* of 1 June 1878. Webster argues that it would be no radical measure to give the vote to unmarried women of independent means who pay taxes: their right to vote would follow from their having independent status, which society has already accepted.

399 *the Platonic theory of female regiments.* In *The Republic*, Socrates argues that women should be educated to perform the same duties as men in both peace and war.

400 TO AN UNNAMED CORRESPONDENT, 23 [?] 1888. *Text.* Janet Camp Troxell Collection (C0189), Box 2, Folder 33, Princeton University Library.

FURTHER READING

EDITIONS

R. W. Crump (ed.), *Maude: Prose and Verse* (Hamden, Conn., 1976).

—— (ed.), *The Complete Poems of Christina Rossetti*, 3 vols. (Baton Rouge, 1979–90). A meticulous eclectic edition.

—— (ed.), *Christina Rossetti: The Complete Poems* (Harmondsworth, 2001). Presents Crump's text in one volume; with annotation added by Betty S. Flowers.

Antony H. Harrison (ed.), *The Letters of Christina Rossetti*, 4 vols. (Charlottesville, 1997–2004).

Gwynneth Hatton, 'An Edition of the Unpublished Poems of Christina Rossetti, with a Critical Introduction and Interpretative Notes to All the Posthumous Poems', unpublished thesis, St. Hilda's College, Oxford (1995).

David A. Kent and P. G. Stanwood (eds.), *Selected Prose of Christina Rossetti* (Basingstoke, 1998).

William Michael Rossetti (ed.), *The Poetical Works of Christina Georgina Rossetti* (London, 1904). The memoir and notes are invaluable; the text has been superseded by Crump.

CRITICAL BOOKS

Mary Arseneau, *Recovering Christina Rossetti: Female Community and Incarnational Poetics* (Basingstoke, 2004).

—— et al. (eds.), *The Culture of Christina Rossetti: Female Poetics and Victorian Contexts* (Athens, Ohio, 1999).

Mackenzie Bell, *Christina Rossetti: A Biographical and Critical Study* (London, 1898). The first full-length study, drawing on information from William Michael Rossetti, but less informative than William's short memoir in his 1904 edition.

Kathryn Burlinson, *Christina Rossetti* (Plymouth, 1998).

Raymond Chapman, *Faith and Revolt: Studies in the Literary Influence of the Oxford Movement* (London, 1970).

Diane D'Amico, *Christina Rossetti: Faith, Gender and Time* (Baton Rouge, 1999). The most discerning study of the poetry.

Antony H. Harrison, *Christina Rossetti in Context* (Chapel Hill, 1988).

Constance W. Hassett, *Christina Rossetti: The Patience of Style* (Charlottesville, 2005). The most sensitive and scholarly formalist study.

David A. Kent (ed.), *The Achievement of Christina Rossetti* (Ithaca, NY, 1987).

Lorraine Janzen Kooistra, *Christina Rossetti and Illustration: A Publishing History* (Athens, Ohio, 2002).

Angela Leighton, *Victorian Women Poets: Writing Against the Heart* (London, 1992).

Jan Marsh, *Christina Rossetti: A Literary Biography* (London, 2004). The best researched of recent biographies; sometimes overspeculative (especially in suggesting that Christina was sexually abused by her father—for which there is no evidence).

G. B. Tennyson, *Victorian Devotional Poetry: The Tractarian Mode* (Cambridge, Mass., 1980). Enormously influential study of Tractarian poetics.

CRITICAL ESSAYS

D. M. R. Bentley, 'The Meretricious and the Meritorious in "Goblin Market": A Conjecture and an Analysis', in Kent (ed.), *Achievement of Christina Rossetti*, 57–81.

Catherine Musello Cantalupo, 'Christina Rossetti: The Devotional Poet and the Rejection of Romantic Nature', in Kent (ed.), *Achievement of Christina Rossetti*, 274–300.

Eric Griffiths, 'The Disappointment of Christina G. Rossetti', *Essays in Criticism*, 47 (1997), 107–42.

Simon Humphries, 'Who is the Alchemist in Christina Rossetti's "The Prince's Progress"?', *Review of English Studies*, 58 (2007), 684–97.

—— 'The Uncertainty of "Goblin Market"', *Victorian Poetry*, 45/4, Winter 2007), 391–413.

—— 'Christina Rossetti's "My Dream" and Apocalypse', *Notes and Queries*, 55/1 (March 2008), 54–7.

Jerome J. McGann, 'Christina Rossetti's Poems: New Edition and a Revaluation', in *The Beauty of Inflections: Literary Investigations in Historical Method and Theory* (Oxford, 1985), 207–31.

—— 'Introduction', in Kent (ed.), *Achievement of Christina Rossetti*, 1–19. Emphasizing Rossetti's 'radical alienness'.

Linda E. Marshall, 'What the Dead Are Doing Underground: Hades and Heaven in the Writings of Christina Rossetti', *Victorian Newsletter*, 72 (Fall 1987), 55–60. An essential essay.

Joan Rees, 'Christina Rossetti: Poet', *Critical Quarterly*, 26 (1984), 59–72.

W. David Shaw, 'Poet of Mystery: The Art of Christina Rossetti', in Kent (ed.), *Achievement of Christina Rossetti*, 23–56.

John O. Waller, 'Christ's Second Coming: Christina Rossetti and the Premillennialist William Dodsworth', *Bulletin of the New York Public Library*, 73 (1969), 465–82. An essential essay.

William Whitla, 'Questioning the Convention: Christina Rossetti's Sonnet Sequence "Monna Innominata"', in Kent (ed.), *Achievement of Christina Rossetti*, 82–131.

INDEX OF TITLES

INDEX OF FIRST LINES OF POEMS

	Late Victorian Gothic Tales
JANE AUSTEN	Emma
	Mansfield Park
	Persuasion
	Pride and Prejudice
	Selected Letters
	Sense and Sensibility
MRS BEETON	Book of Household Management
MARY ELIZABETH BRADDON	Lady Audley's Secret
ANNE BRONTË	The Tenant of Wildfell Hall
CHARLOTTE BRONTË	Jane Eyre
	Shirley
	Villette
EMILY BRONTË	Wuthering Heights
ROBERT BROWNING	The Major Works
JOHN CLARE	The Major Works
SAMUEL TAYLOR COLERIDGE	The Major Works
WILKIE COLLINS	The Moonstone
	No Name
	The Woman in White
CHARLES DARWIN	The Origin of Species
THOMAS DE QUINCEY	The Confessions of an English Opium-Eater
	On Murder
CHARLES DICKENS	The Adventures of Oliver Twist
	Barnaby Rudge
	Bleak House
	David Copperfield
	Great Expectations
	Nicholas Nickleby
	The Old Curiosity Shop
	Our Mutual Friend
	The Pickwick Papers

ANTHONY TROLLOPE

The American Senator
An Autobiography
Barchester Towers
Can You Forgive Her?
The Claverings
Cousin Henry
The Duke's Children
The Eustace Diamonds
Framley Parsonage
He Knew He Was Right
Lady Anna
Orley Farm
Phineas Finn
Phineas Redux
The Prime Minister
Rachel Ray
The Small House at Allington
The Warden
The Way We Live Now

	Six French Poets of the Nineteenth Century
HONORÉ DE BALZAC	Cousin Bette Eugénie Grandet Père Goriot
CHARLES BAUDELAIRE	The Flowers of Evil The Prose Poems and Fanfarlo
BENJAMIN CONSTANT	Adolphe
DENIS DIDEROT	Jacques the Fatalist The Nun
ALEXANDRE DUMAS (PÈRE)	The Black Tulip The Count of Monte Cristo Louise de la Vallière The Man in the Iron Mask La Reine Margot The Three Musketeers Twenty Years After The Vicomte de Bragelonne
ALEXANDRE DUMAS (FILS)	La Dame aux Camélias
GUSTAVE FLAUBERT	Madame Bovary A Sentimental Education Three Tales
VICTOR HUGO	The Essential Victor Hugo Notre-Dame de Paris
J.-K. HUYSMANS	Against Nature
PIERRE CHODERLOS DE LACLOS	Les Liaisons dangereuses
MME DE LAFAYETTE	The Princesse de Clèves
GUILLAUME DU LORRIS and JEAN DE MEUN	The Romance of the Rose

GUY DE MAUPASSANT   A Day in the Country and Other Stories
                      A Life
                      Bel-Ami
                      Mademoiselle Fifi and Other Stories
                      Pierre et Jean

PROSPER MÉRIMÉE   Carmen and Other Stories

MOLIÈRE   Don Juan and Other Plays
                      The Misanthrope, Tartuffe, and Other
                        Plays

BLAISE PASCAL   Pensées and Other Writings

ABBÉ PRÉVOST   Manon Lescaut

JEAN RACINE   Britannicus, Phaedra, and Athaliah

ARTHUR RIMBAUD   Collected Poems

EDMOND ROSTAND   Cyrano de Bergerac

MARQUIS DE SADE   The Crimes of Love
                      The Misfortunes of Virtue and Other Early
                        Tales

GEORGE SAND   Indiana

MME DE STAËL   Corinne

STENDHAL   The Red and the Black
                      The Charterhouse of Parma

PAUL VERLAINE   Selected Poems

JULES VERNE   Around the World in Eighty Days
                      Captain Hatteras
                      Journey to the Centre of the Earth
                      Twenty Thousand Leagues under the Seas

VOLTAIRE   Candide and Other Stories
                      Letters concerning the English Nation

ÉMILE ZOLA

L'Assommoir
The Attack on the Mill
La Bête humaine
La Débâcle
Germinal
The Kill
The Ladies' Paradise
The Masterpiece
Nana
Pot Luck
Thérèse Raquin